Innovation in Financial Services: A Dual Ambiguity

Innovation in Financial Services:
A Dual Ambiguity

Edited by

Anne-Laure Mention and Marko Torkkeli

CAMBRIDGE
SCHOLARS

PUBLISHING

Innovation in Financial Services: A Dual Ambiguity,
Edited by Anne-Laure Mention and Marko Torkkeli

This book first published 2014

Cambridge Scholars Publishing

12 Back Chapman Street, Newcastle upon Tyne, NE6 2XX, UK

British Library Cataloguing in Publication Data
A catalogue record for this book is available from the British Library

ISBN (10): 1-4438-6676-8, ISBN (13): 978-1-4438-6676-7

TABLE OF CONTENTS

INTRODUCTION

INNOVATION IN FINANCIAL SERVICES: UNVEILING AMBIGUITY

ANNE-LAURE MENTION
AND MARKO TORKKELI

This book, "Innovation in Financial Services: A Dual Ambiguity" brings together some of the latest thinking in the growing field of innovation in services and more particularly, in financial services. It explores the peculiarities of innovation in financial services firms and surrounding market players, discusses the determinants and success factors of the innovation process and investigates its impact; thus embracing the whole innovation lifecycle. It provides topical insights on the challenges facing the financial industry, such as the convergence with other sectors and the increasing regulatory burden. By combining multidisciplinary approaches and by selecting a number of cutting-edge research models, theories, empirical findings and practitioners' insights, it offers unique and contemporary perspectives on innovation for a sector of paramount importance for the running of our economies.

Financial services represent a considerable economic sector at a global scale. In Europe, for example, financial services represented roughly 6% of gross value added in 2010 (Eurostat). In OECD countries, financial intermediation, real estate, renting and business activities accounted for almost 30% of total value added in 2010, while it represented about 10% in China and 17% in Russia (OECD, online library). Besides its dominant role per se, the financial industry also affects the proper functioning of the entire economy. Despite its central and essential role, this sector has largely been neglected in innovation studies. To some extent, this may be attributed to the fact that innovation is largely hidden, of intangible nature and hard to visualize in financial industries. Additionally, financial firms, rarely have a dedicated Innovation or R&D department and the closest corporate functions in many financial institutions, at least as far as Europe is concerned, is the marketing department, which role may be essential in implementing open innovation, as a form of enhanced collaboration in order to create growth for the company and distinguish itself from its competitors.

Additionally, financial services have long been considered as conservative when it comes to innovation. The natural tendency of financial firms to adopt a risk-adverse attitude, with some notable exceptions, which will be discussed later, combined to the common belief that most financial innovations are mere imitations of existing products, have indeed contributed to this reputation of innovation laggards. After all, can introducing a new savings product, which operates on a D+2/D-2 value dating instead of D+5/D-5, be really considered innovative? The relatively scarce literature stream that, has hitherto focused on innovation in financial services, has mainly unveiled the factors predicting the occurrence of financial innovation and has put strong emphasis on technology-induced and enabled innovations, such as ATMs, mobile banking, e-banking, video banking and the like (e.g. Consoli, 2008; Pennings and Hariento, 1992). The ubiquitous role of information and communication technologies certainly contributes into shaping innovations in financial services, but the human and organizational sides that are intrinsically linked to the adoption of technologies should not be overlooked. Quite surprisingly though, the process of innovating in financial services has been largely disregarded; or has been explored within larger studies embracing all service industries; irrespectively of the distinctive features of the financial sector. Furthermore, the impact that innovation, or the lack of innovation, has had on households, firms and societies, has largely been overlooked too. Nevertheless, it is fairly obvious that financial services have evolved over time, as we describe in more details a bit later and this affects the running of the entire economy. Shifts in banking and accounting practices, increased complexity of procedures and processes have introduced long delays in payments of invoices for procurement services, thus challenging the survival of small and medium-sized firms that do not have the necessary cash flow to absorb these delays. Similarly, the reluctance of banks to grant loans to firms holding few tangible assets, which is typically the case of high technology start ups and potentially high growth firms, is a major hampering factor for economic development, growth and competitiveness. We support that innovation in financial services has a critical role to play so as to sustain the operations of the other economic sectors.

Recently, innovation in financial services has attracted increasing attention and criticism since the beginning of the financial and subsequent economic turmoil. Nobel Laureate Paul Krugman states that it is "hard to think of any major recent financial innovations that actually aided society" (The New York Times, 2009). Critics of financial innovations argue that recent innovations were not aiming at the "enhancement of the ability of the financial sector to perform its social function" (Joseph Stiglitz, cited by The Economist, February 2012), but rather embraced "opaque pricing including billing tricks and traps … that encourages unsafe lending practices" (Pew Charitable Trusts, 2009, cited by Lerner and Tufano, 2011) and had hardly any visible effect on the productivity of the economy according to Volcker, quoted in 2009. Furthermore, Volcker also stated that ATM was the only financial innovation he can think of that has improved society. Overall, this has fuelled a negative perception of novelties developed in this industry. With this book, our intent is to illustrate that innovation should not be feared as such, as it is an acknowledged driver of growth and competitiveness and it should bring benefits for the society as a whole. Nevertheless, we claim that innovation should be properly designed, sustainably managed and correctly implemented. In our view, beneficial financial innovation is the type of innovation that serves the interests of individual customers, households and states, thus positively affecting the functioning of society as a whole. Along these lines, we adopt a broad conception of financial innovation, which encompasses both the process of innovating in financial services and its outcomes, i.e. the introduction of novelties either internally or in the market, irrespectively of their degree of novelty. Accordingly, innovations do not have to be developed internally but can be either jointly developed with partners in the context of strategic alliances, cooperation agreements, joint ventures or can represent mere adoptions of externally developed innovations. More specifically, our definition embraces "changes in the offerings of banks, insurance companies, investment funds and other financial service firms, as well as modifications to internal structures and processes, managerial practices, new ways of interacting with customers and distribution channels" (Mention and Torkkeli, 2012).

Over the last decades, financial industries have gone through significant changes and shifts, which may be attributable to several contextual elements: the changes in the macroeconomic conditions; the accrued automation of processes and the increasing role of information and communication technologies; the concomitant wide scale digitalization and dematerialization; the subsequent waves of regulation, deregulation and re-regulation; the massive trend towards consolidation and constitution of bank-insurance conglomerates, through large mergers and acquisitions; drastic changes in the demand for financial services and in customer preferences; the shift from an intermediation business to fee producing, off-balance sheet activities; stronger requirements regarding capital requirements and capital adequacy; the introduction of new market players offering competitive products and services, such as loans, credit facilities and insurance contracts; the emergence of branchless banks, the progressive disappearance of physical branches especially in remote areas, and the shift towards a "do it yourself" model for basic transactions such as payments; and finally, the globalization and increasing cross-border trade (Flier et al., 2001; Goddard et al., 2007; Mention and Torkkeli, 2012; Rossignoli and Arnaboldi, 2009). All these phenomena, ranging from technological change to regulatory frameworks, have stimulated innovations, in various forms and extents within financial firms. They have also triggered a reshaping of the industry, with increasing linkages among market players, either through cooperation or to a large extent, co-opetition, leading to the emergence of new ecosystems. Another interesting feature, characterizing the evolution of the financial sector, is the growing importance of crowdfunding. Yet, relatively small in terms of volume, with about 735 MEUR recorded in 2012 and the identification of roughly 200 platforms (European Commission), this new means of financing is increasingly attracting interest, showing a 65% increase in volume in 2012. Another recent trend in the financial sector is the emergence of digital currencies, free of central bank supervision and independent from any country, such as the Bitcoin, which is scrutinized in Hilmola's contribution.

Numerous scholars have highlighted the need for further understanding what financial innovation is, how it happens and which are its effects at different levels, including firm-level performance, impact on the functioning of other firms and on societies. By nature, innovation in and for financial services is highly intangible. It does not materialize itself in similar ways than innovation in manufacturing industries, with tangible products as outcomes. Innovation in financial services is multifaceted, with the traditional distinction between product, service and process innovations being largely irrelevant, as it also applies for most service industries (de Jong et al., 2003). The outcome of the innovation process is usually largely relying on a combination of multiple innovation types and frequently resulting in a bundle of new products and services, which are offered through innovative channels to customers. Recent literature and trends have stressed out that challenges for innovation in financial services are multifold and mainly stem from the undeniable role of regulation, the relative lack of formal appropriability mechanisms, the dominant use of new technologies including social media, the shift in behavior and towards accrued customer centricity, the automation of processes and the rebuilding of trust and confidence (Mention and Torkkeli, 2012). These and other topical matters are discussed in this book, which combines pure academic and practitioners' perspective, thus enriching the debate with insights from multiple stakeholders.

Many business leaders and scholars alike have been debating about the proliferation of regulations for financial institutions, highlighting the complexity that those regulations create and the increasing compliance, audit and risk management costs. Scholars have been arguing whether regulation acts as an innovation catalyst or is a hampering factor (Marcus, 1981). Miller (1986) claims that regulation has been one of the main drivers for successful innovations, for decades. On the other hand, Merton (1995, p.471) contends that regulation can hinder the proper functioning of the "engine of innovation" and consequently constrain the achievement of greater efficiencies in the financial system, as a whole. Kane (1997), who coined the term "regulatory dialectic", posits that these subsequent waves of regulation, de-regulation and re-regulation, induce short-term innovations, which do not positively impact the financial system regarding improved efficiency or market effectiveness, in the long run (Anderloni and Bongini, 2009). Another leading scholar in the field of financial innovation, Lerner, further develops that the regulatory burden may deter young and inexperienced firms from engaging into the innovation process, due to resource scarcity and, therefore, provides argumentation that such a regulatory burden may create innovation barriers. From the practitioners' perspective, regulation is also perceived as a means to increase transparency, to reinforce customer protection and, also, to stimulate innovation. The latter can be exemplified by the elaboration of the UCITS (Undertakings for Collective Investment in Transferrable Securities) at EU level. Another example is MIFID (Market in Financial Instruments Directive), which entered into force in 2007 and requires European banks to comply with greater transparency on pricing structures and risk conflicts, to demonstrate best execution practices and to gain a deeper understanding of customer profiles. Basel II and recent developments also drastically affect bank's operations by aligning capital requirements with modern risk management practices (Fasnacht, 2009). The financial crises also led to a regulatory response from the European authorities, among others. In Europe, this regulatory response has targeted two levels: one at the macro level led by the European System Risk Board and another at the micro level led by a number of authorities. New regulatory structures to supervise the financial regime in the EU, at both the macro and micro levels, should provide more security to the regime against breakdowns.

However, the powers of these supervisory bodies may be limited and better cooperation amongst these individual bodies and with other national and international regulatory bodies may be needed. Furthermore, the observation that internationalization of finance is going backwards, as pointed out by Grülms during his Address at the Innovation for Financial Services event in 2013, is highly preoccupying. The financial industry used to rank among the most globalised ones in the years preceding the financial crisis. According to McKinsey Global Institute, between 1990 and 2007, cross-border bank flows increased about tenfold, reaching about five US trillion. The same indicator for 2012 shows that these flows are currently at a third of this amount, with Europe being the most affected region. This financial fragmentation undeniably challenges one of the greatest promises of globalization, which is the access to foreign capital. Recent illustrations from Southern European countries, where businesses face up to 160 basis-point interest rates than their German counterparts, exemplify the ring-fence, nationally-focused strategies adopted by some economies (Grülms, 2013). Effects of financial fragmentation may induce lower competition, as "often pampered domestic banks do not face nimbler foreign rivals" (Grülms, 2013). In an exploration of 11 Latin-American markets, over an eight-year period characterized by large-scale consolidation, restructuring of the market and internationalization of the sector, Yildirim and Philippatos (2007) have highlighted that domestic banks have increased their efficiency, while deteriorating their profitability, due to reduced margins when threatened in their market positioning by new entrants.

Exploring the drivers of innovation in financial services in one of the most innovative economies in booming Asia, Smith highlights that regulation is a double-edged sword as it simultaneously fosters innovation, through the requirements of adopting new systems, technologies, complying with new rules and also hampers it, as innovation may represent a threat in terms of meeting compliance and risk management policies. The role of public policies and public bodies is also mentioned as one possible driver of innovation, as agencies and focused industrial policies can leverage innovation through investment in education, facilitation of management buy-in and shift in practices. Da Silva also explores the various policies, incentives and instruments that have been elaborated and implemented so as to ensure financial inclusion in a large emerging economy in South America.

Another peculiarity of financial services pertains to the challenges innovators face to appropriate and reap the benefits of their novelties. Until recently, most of the innovations from financial services were not considered eligible for patent protection (Kumar and Turnbull, 2006; Lerner, 2006). This appropriability concern applies to different extents across continents due to the lack of international harmonization surrounding the patentability of computerized business methods although financial patents are now commonplace in the US (Hunt et al., 2009; Tufano, 2003). Lerner (2010) provides evidence that financial patents are being litigated at a much higher rate, by several degrees of magnitude, than that of patents in general. His study unveils that larger entities as well as widely cited patents, usually featuring a high number of claims, are disproportionally prone to litigations. Awareness of the competitive advantages that firms may derive from protecting its critical knowledge assets, such as business methods and software solutions, leads financial firms to set up their internal patent department and incentive systems, as exemplified by the Swiss Re case (Bader, 2007). Nevertheless, financial innovations remain easily imitable and their diffusion across competing institutions is fast (Roberts and Amit, 2003). Product innovation has also been evidenced to experience a relatively short lifecycle, as a result of disclosure requirements and lack of formal protection mechanisms (Rossignoli and Arnaboldi, 2009). In contrast, the same authors contend that other forms of innovation, which relate either to organizational structures or operating systems, cannot be easily replicated by competitors and usually mirror significant changes in financial firms. Latest trends regarding patenting in the financial sector and their impact on performance are discussed in Arnaboldi and Claeys' contribution, which focuses on the US market and explores the relationship between patenting and performance, as well as in Kapoor's chapter, who introduces also new measures based on citation categories and looks into the value-creation process and the linkages with other patenting industries connected to the financial sector in the European setting.

The importance of information technology in financial services is incontestable. Technological change has induced innovations and productivity increases across sectors and industries, although measuring their effects remains a challenge for the academic community. Similarly to other industries, technologies have contributed to reshaping financial sector, in terms of new offerings, new ways of operating and new ways of delivering bundles of services. High frequency trading requiring complex and sophisticated hardware and software, mobile banking and electronic payments relying on extensive infrastructure, interoperable standards and devices illustrate the drastic changes in the industry. Mobile banking solutions are deemed to be the rising star in the area of innovations for financial services and this book exemplifies this tendency. Dennehy et al.

adopt a design science approach in order to design and evaluate a collaboration tool in the form of a Partnership Management Canvas that can assist practitioners to approach partnerships issues when forming an m-payment solution. Online banking is also the core topic of Santonen's contribution, who concentrates on which customization approaches are most valued by online bank end-users and what is their willingness to pay for customized online banking experience. This research exemplifies the importance of knowing and understanding customers' needs and behavior, using this as a guiding tool for designing and delivering innovations. The Schumpeterian view on creative destruction, the initiation of radical innovation, is supported by this evolution since the decentralized nature of information and communication technologies in banking will lead it to "disruptive innovation". Technology is a unique tool, which must be used to satisfy customer needs and it needs to be translated into customer values for a holistic implementation. Developing a better understanding of e-finance innovation services, through the design of a dedicated ontology, is the focus of Yablonsky's chapter, taking into consideration the peculiarities of one leading emerging economy. Moving to developing countries, Gómez-Barroso and Marbán-Flores explore the case of M-Pesa in Kenya, identifying the three main factors, namely the need, the knowledge and the context, which have influenced its development into such a successful venture, with wide and fast adoption.

However several factors can inhibit the realization of innovation. These can be e.g. the desire of the shareholders to achieve a quick short-term profit, the migration of the financial sector from being product-centric to being a customer service provider, the heavy use of technology that goes beyond the capacity of the banks (extreme level of high tech) and cultural issues related to risk-taking. It has also been observed that financial services still suffer from persistent manual processes, which may indicate that there is room for process innovation in this industry. As this kind of innovation cannot easily be copied, it may bring competitive advantage for first movers, and considering that it is incremental in nature, it may appear less risky in nature. Focusing on the realization of service innovation, exemplified in the financial industry, Hydle et al. discuss the intertwined relationships between the fields of innovation and strategy.

The open nature of the innovation process in financial services is another topic addressed in this book, from two perspectives. Martovoy discusses the advantages and disadvantages of adopting open innovation practices for new service development in the context of a small, open, leading European service economy where financial services contribute to about 30% of GDP. Delineating open innovation into inbound, outbound and coupled processes, Salampasis posits that trust acts as a cornerstone in the implementation of such practice. Furthermore, according to Salampasis, trust plays a moderating role between the four antecedents of open innovation adoption, namely knowledge sharing attitude, ambidextrous thinking, collaborative culture and diversity management and the implementation of open innovation. Further opening the black box and adopting a pragmatic approach, Vantomme and De Ruyck depict the process of establishing structural collaboration, both with internal and external stakeholders and its impact in terms of fostering breakthrough innovations using a single case study in the leading Belgian insurance company.

Financial innovation emerges from the failure case of the worldwide financial system. It is perceived within the new rules of "a slow-moving, selective and with a heavy dash of nationalism and regionalism" globalization (Bremmer, 2014, p.104). Within such a turbulent, volatile and constantly changing environment the need for adopting non-predictive strategies becomes imperative (Wiltbank et al., 2006). Financial innovation is bound to play an integrative role towards the determination of the kind of capitalism that will drive the globalized economy in the aftermath of the debt and subprime crises. This requires adaptation and the foundation of a solid strategic intent that will "end the plague of short-termism" and realize the shift from "a quarterly capitalism and toward a true long-term mindset" (Barton and Wiseman, 2014, pp.44-45).

We wish the reader an enjoyable journey and hope it will stimulate fruitful thoughts and subsequent reasoned actions in the field of financial innovation.

References

Anderloni, Luisa, and Bongini, Paola Agnese. "Is financial innovation still a relevant issue?", In L. Anderloni, D.T. Llewellyn, R.H. Schmidt (Eds, 2009), *Financial innovation in retail and corporate banking* (pp. 41-62). Cheltenham: Edward Elgar.

Bader, Martin A., "Managing intellectual property in the financial services industry sector: Learning from Swiss Re", *Technovation*, 28.4 (2007):196-207.

Barton, Dominic and Wiseman, Mark, "Focusing capital on the long term", *Harvard Business Review,* 92.1/2 (2014):44-51.

Bremmer, Ian. "The New Rules of Globalization", *Harvard Business Review*, 92.1/2 (2014):103-107.

Consoli, Davide, "Systems of Innovation and Industry Evolution: The Case of Retail Banking in the UK", *Industry and Innovation*, 15.6 (2008):579-600.

De Jong, J. P. J., Bruins,A., Dolfsma, W. , Meijaard, J. (2003). Innovation in service firms explored: What, how and why? Literature review, Strategic Study B200205, Zoetermeer: EIM Business and Policy Research.

Grülms, Fernand. (2013). Address at the Innovation for Financial Services Conference, Singapore, 24th and 25th October 2013. Available under www.innofin.org

Fasnacht, Daniel. Open Innovation in the Financial Services. Berlin: Springer-Verlag, 2009.

Flier, Bert, van den Bosch, Frans A.J., Volderba, Henk W., Carnevale, Carlo A., Tomkin, Neil, Melin, Leif, Quélin, Bertrand V., Kriger, Mark P. "The changing landscape of the European financial services sector", *Long Range Planning*, 34 (2001):179-207.

Goddard, John, Molyneux, Philip, Wilson, John Ogilvie Stephen and Tavakoli, Manouchehr. "European banking: an overview", *Journal of Banking & Finance*, 37.1 (2007):1911-1935.

Kane, Edward J. "Good Intentions and Unintended Evil: The Case Against Selective Credit Allocation", *Journal of Money, Credit, and Banking*, 9.1 (1977): 55-69.

Kumar, Praveen and Turnbull, Stuart M. "Patenting and licensing of financial innovations", Working paper, CT Bauer College of Business, University of Houston, July. (2006)

Pennings, Johannes M. and Harianto, Farid. "The diffusion of technological innovation in the commercial banking industry", *Strategic Management Journal*, 13.1 (1992):29 – 46.

Lerner, Josh (2006) "The new new financial thing: The origins of financial innovations", Journal *of Financial Economics,* 79.2, (2006):223-255.

—. "The litigation of financial innovations", *Journal of Law and Economics*, 53 (2010):807–831.

Lerner, Josh and Tufano Peter. "The consequences of financial innovation: A counterfactual research agenda", *Annual Review of Financial Economics*, 3 (2011):41-85.

Marcus, Alfred A. (1981) "Policy uncertainty and technological innovation", *Academy of Management Review*, 6.3 (1981):443 – 448.

Mention, Anne-Laure, and Torkkeli, Marko. "Drivers, Processes and Consequences of Financial Innovation: A Research Agenda." *International Journal of Entrepreneurship and Innovation Management* 16.1 (2012): 5-29.

Merton, Robert C. “A functional perspective on financial intermediation”, *Financial Management*, 24.2 (1995):23 – 41.

Miller, Merton H. “Financial innovation: the last twenty years and the next”, *Journal of Finance and Quantitative Analysis*, 21.4 (1986):459 – 471.

Rossignoli, Bruno and Arnaboldi, Francesca. “Financial innovation: theoretical issues and empirical evidence in Italy and in the UK”, *International Review of Economics*, 56.3 (2009):275 – 301.

Tufano Peter. “Financial innovation”, In Handbook of the Economics of Finance: Volume 1A: *Corporate Finance*, ed. GM Constantinides, M Harris, R Stulz, pp. 307–36. New York: Elsevier. 1685 pp

Wiltbank, Robert, Dew, Nicholas, Read, Stuart and Sarasvathy D. Saras. “What to do next? The case for non-predictive strategy”, *Strategic Management Journal*, 27.10 (2006):981-998.

CHAPTER ONE

LABILE FIAT CURRENCIES: SKETCH OF FUTURE ALTERNATIVES

OLLI-PEKKA HILMOLA

1. Introduction

Recent history is full of examples of failed currencies. Typically people nominate Weimar Germany as one from the early 1920s (Fergusson, 1975). However, this rapid hyperinflation after World War I was just an attempt within a series of devaluations. Weimar Germany was trying to get manufacturing competitiveness and jobs back, by means of a massive devaluation of its own currency (Richards, 2012). After this, France and the UK followed; but inflation rates were not as high as in Weimar Germany. This series of competitive devaluations was also seen in the USA, where government confiscated all private gold in 1933 with 20.67 USD per ounce and tied US dollar to gold with 35 USD per ounce; just a couple of years later (basically resulting in a 40.9 % devaluation of its currency). The Fort Knox gold warehouse, with tight safety systems, originates from this period of decision-making-nationalized gold needed to be stored somewhere.

Another, but yet much faster moving series of devaluations took place during the late 1990s, when the Asian crisis hit medium-sized Asian economies, after tiger economies had grown too fast and taken too many toxic contracts with banks (complex derivate contracts with currency and/or interest rate swaps; more see Das, 2012). The Thai Baht was devaluated in 1997 by more than 50 % as did the Malaysian Ringgit and the South Korean Won accordingly. Russia followed this chain of dominoes falling, when in 1998 its currency devaluation was roughly 80 % over a period of one-year. Russia subsequently defaulted on its own foreign public debt. After Russia, the Brazilian Real was devaluated by nearly 40% in the late 1998. Therefore, in the late 1990s and early 2000s, all investors were cautious when dealing with these countries. However, looking back to the changes that took place, we may argue that these very sudden devaluations played out well for all these countries. All of them have recorded significant current account surpluses thereafter (except for Brazil, where fluctuations have continued) and consistent GDP growths (even both in USD terms). It did not take that many years before "emerging markets" were again in hot demand and became popular investment targets from all over the world. In the current global monetary system it pays off to admit that economy or economies have made serious mistakes-the only advice is to make this visibly and promptly. Also it pays off, if the devaluation is high. Of course, savers and other money holders are on the losing side of the equation, but typically countries do better and gain in the long-run.

The world is yet confronted with another possible currency devaluation and great market changes; the valuation of major trading currencies. We illustrate in this chapter that possibly the Euro, USD and Yen are all overvalued against the Chinese Yuan (a much discussed issue, e.g. Burdekin, 2008; Turner, 2008). This is supported by foreign trade statistics and container movements between continents. In most recent years, China has moved towards the right direction with its currency, but these changes have been mild and a consistent decade of long appreciation is missing. Best progress is being made with the USD, but again trade accounts and container trade do not show that kind of favorable changes. Actually the situation is moving to the opposite side. It could be that the current fiat monetary system allowed such huge biases that it takes a lot of time for the system to repair itself back for manufacturing export. In the following pages we show that the current biases are so significant that there is hardly any change to revert back on the gold standard-this would mean, for the system to work, that gold prices should soar at least 10-20 times higher compared to the current prices. Basically the world does not have enough physical gold with respect to the current biases of trade and the valuation of gold is low compared to the required monetary transactions. Together with the gold standard and the looming appreciation of the Yuan, it could also be so that a country, independent and without central banks operating Internet currencies like Bitcoin, could take a more important role compared to the market.

2. Are Happy Days Here Again with a Gold Standard?

In the early 20th century, currencies were tied to gold. In a case of massive accumulation of foreign currency, central banks simply called gold shipments from other countries, which show that they were holding them at their disposal. This resulted in massive changes within the ownership of gold and accumulation was typically activated in countries or continents, which were leading, in an industrial sense (significant trade account surpluses). For example, USA accumulated a lot of its current holdings during the rapid industrialization era. Gold was for example in the early 20th century tied to the USD in a way that 20.67 USD was equivalent to one ounce of gold (31.1 grams). Later the US government confiscated all private gold from domestic markets and this ratio was devaluated to 35 USD per one ounce of gold in 1935. Private ownership declined during the Great Recession, within the entire USA (only jewelry ownership was allowed and set free again in 1974, see Sarnoff, 1980), but this exchange rate lasted within international central bank operations until the Bretton Woods Standard was established at the end of the World War II. In this new currency system the USD was the only currency tied to gold with 35 USD per ounce and all the other joined currencies had fixed rates to the USD. If somebody insisted, USA would send gold instead of dollars; this especially benefitted emerging European manufacturing countries after World War II (like Germany, France, Italy, and Netherlands; see Richards, 2012). However, the Bretton Woods System was cancelled by the 1971 Nixon unilateral announcement, mostly due to public economics (general over-spending and wars) and the erosion of industrial performance. Otherwise the USA would have lost a lot of its gold reserves, should the Bretton Woods arrangement had continued.

After 1971, the whole world has been on the fiat currency arrangement, where currencies are just backed by nothing physical, just having goodwill and trust behind them. It is no wonder that many currencies have faced stiff devaluations in case of economic emergencies or panics (following other than normally distributed returns or changes as argued by Vogel, 2010). One of these moments has been the Asian crisis, which started in 1997 and continued in Russia in 1998. In the long run, some currencies have really lost their value, like the Indian Rupee, which has declined 85-90 % from its value as compared to 1973 and the USD. Similar, but more rapid changes have been recorded regarding the Russian Ruble, which has lost more than 95 % of its value within the last two decades against the USD. The value lost on the Mexican Peso is similar to the Ruble, but the time horizon needs to be extended to four decades. Later on in this chapter, readers may note that China has experienced a similar kind of devaluation from the early 1980's (against the USD, approx. -80 % during 1981-1994) and holding paper currency has not benefitted the savers at all. However, it should be mentioned that in the new fiat currency system, no paper currency is safe. This also concerns the US Dollar, the European Euro and the Japanese Yen. Many governments, and particularly these three, have used the monetary stimulus after the 2008-2009 economic crisis and substantial amounts of money have been digitally printed. Currencies have sustained their values relatively well, but still no guarantee exists that this will be the situation in the future. The fiat system is said to be labile.

It is more than four decades since the world's gold standard was abandoned (Bretton Woods contract) and countries have continuously used small money printing, e.g. to keep economy at some inflation (typically 1-3 % per annum; Turner, 2008). Also during the times economic crisis, governments have used amounts of money to protect their institutions and operations-resulting again in a higher supply of notes. Increasing the amount of money in different currencies around the world, in the last four decades, has caused biases in the world trade accounts, biases which may not be repaired or paid back, should actual payment is demanded. Currently many trade account deficit countries just take more loans to keep up with consumption and public sector demands. Many trade deficit countries are also the greatest buyers of their own governmental debt (own central bank acquires country's governmental bonds; this now the situation e.g. in USA).

An attempt to illustrate the current state of biased trade account performance, globally, is presented below in Table 1, where information from central bank gold holdings and current account performance of the most important countries was brought together. From Table 1 it can be noted that with the current price of gold, many advanced countries could tolerate current account deficits for several months or in very rare cases, like France, several years. It is interesting to note that the USA, the largest gold holder in the world, could finance its current account deficits for nine months with a deficit level of the year 2011. If the average from years 2005 to 2011 is taken into consideration, then this safety net is only just above seven months. Interestingly, Spain and Greece are also in a similar kind of vulnerable position as gold reserves could only carry on for a few more months of deficits. Both of these economically problematic countries hold substantial amounts of gold.

Many issues play a role on Table 1. Some countries have sold off much of their gold after abandoning the Bretton Woods system. This is the case for the UK in early 2000 (276.9 tons; Wener, 2005), but similar substantial sales were executed at the same time in Austria, Belgium, the Netherlands and Switzerland. For some governments, gold is not considered as a safety net or a last-resort type of asset; instead it is seen as an unnecessary old asset, which should be sold to fund other activities. However, the timing of earlier described European gold sales could not have been more poorly selected-selling at low prices in the late 1990s and early 2000. However, the opposite point of views also exists, like Russia and China, which have shown significant accumulation of gold reserves in recent years (Richards, 2012). These countries have been willing to pay for gold, prices that were five times higher than what Europeans sold them off just one or two decades earlier.

Table 1. Current account deficits (year 2011 and average of years 2005-2011) and the availability of gold reserves per each respective country to finance this deficit (Assumption: gold price 1,400 USD per ounce/45,000 USD per kg and world gold reserves of central banks, 30,000 tons). Sources (data): World Gold Council (2013), World Bank (2013)

		Year 2011	Years 05-11
Country	Gold reserves	Months of gold reserves	Months of gold reserves
Brazil	67.0	0.69	2.06
Australia	79.9	1.28	0.99
Ukraine	36.4	1.92	4.29
Greece	112.0	2.12	1.78
Poland	102.9	2.22	2.63
Spain	281.6	2.76	1.56
Turkey	445.3	3.20	6.37
South Africa	125.1	4.94	4.85
India	557.7	5.02	10.69
United Kingdom	310.3	5.11	2.94
Belarus	49.4	5.31	6.59
Peru	34.7	5.61	17.07
Romania	103.7	6.71	4.32
Mexico	124.0	6.92	7.71
Egypt	75.6	7.44	29.76
United States	8133.5	9.43	7.28
Portugal	382.5	12.32	8.85
Pakistan	64.4	15.57	5.81
Italy	2451.8	19.72	24.69
France	2435.4	24.16	40.13
Lebanon	286.8	31.83	37.69

Table 2 . Current account surpluses (year 2011 and average of years 2005-2011) and estimated duration that world gold reserves are gathered by each country (Assumption: gold price 1,400 USD per ounce/45,000 USD per kg, and world gold reserves of central banks, 30,000 tons). Sources (data): World Gold Council (2012), World Bank (2013)

		Year 2011	Years 05-11
Country	Gold reserves	Years to gather world's gold reserves	Years to gather world's gold reserves
Germany	3391.3	5.36	5.87
Saudi Arabia	322.9	8.42	14.14
China	1054.1	9.57	5.20
Japan	765.2	11.05	7.82
Russia	996.4	13.42	16.11
Netherlands	612.5	15.63	23.90
Kuwait	79	19.03	29.98
Singapore	127.4	20.58	31.47
Sweden	125.7	35.41	36.42
Switzerland	1040.1	36.30	30.35
Malaysia	36.4	42.44	45.88
South Korea	104.4	51.61	64.54
Venezuela	365.8	54.68	69.10
Algeria	173.6	68.17	63.74
Denmark	66.5	71.32	115.37
Kazakhstan	130.9	95.26	1279.45
Philippines	192.7	192.44	216.79
Thailand	152.4	226.97	186.87
Austria	280	242.34	120.70
Indonesia	75.9	799.13	240.38
Libya	116.6	953.79	73.02
Bolivia	42.3	2509.46	1217.90

Looking from the other side of the coin-the time of surplus countries earning the entire world's known gold through world trade - we get similar and yet surprising results. It is of course known *a priori*, that China would record well in this with its recent years of significant trade account surpluses, but surprisingly, Germany is as strong as China as the current account performance is being used in surplus evaluation. It would take roughly five years for Germany and China to earn the entire world's central bank gold if their current holdings of gold were taken into account. China's performance dropped a bit since 2011 because energy and particularly oil became so expensive that imports were needed. Together with these two, other leading countries are Saudi Arabia, Japan and Russia. However, a word of caution should be stated about Japan, as due to the nuclear disaster that took place in 2011, all the energy is being produced with (mostly) imported oil, not cost-efficient nuclear power. This is already visible in the most recent current account performance. Surpluses have disappeared and current account shows mild positive amounts during 2012-2013.

Based on our analysis, it is understandable that the world cannot revert back to a gold standard. If it does, then the value of gold would be much higher than today, maybe 10-20 times higher, at least in the current monetary circulation situation. Of course biases between countries in foreign trade continue as long as currencies, in general, sustain and other parties approve practices of deficit countries. Please, also do note that gold valuation has significantly increased, compared to the early 1970s, when it was valued to 35 USD per ounce. Gold, at the time of writing, is roughly 40 times more expensive than then.

The most probable scenario for the future is that some leading current account deficit countries face stiff currency devaluations. After this, massive debts need to be renegotiated with the debtors again-some sort of restructuring is needed (mostly due to massive debt load, which increases even more with devaluation). This is the only way for these deficit countries to spark again their manufacturing activity and performance, so as to achieve a trade balance. Going back to the gold standard would hurt the world's economy significantly, as currencies would again start to carry value too (and people could trust them without the fear of losing). Then the monetary circulation in the system would be constrained, loans would be difficult to acquire and again economies would face recessions or continued depressions as investments would be hindered by considerable delays.

3. Trade and Currency Perspective

For a long period of time, currency valuations of the Yuan have been on the agenda in the large trade deficit regions, such as USA and Europe (deficits in the last six years, which are stabile and high, see Tables 3 and 4). For example, USA has argued for a long time that China has kept currency valuations at artificially low levels, favoring Chinese manufacturing exports and doing great harm to the remaining USA manufacturing industries. In Europe, the financial turmoil has also resulted in manufacturing losing its attraction and lacking strong export industries. Germany still shares manufacturing performance and current account surpluses, but even this glorified EU country, in the industrial sense, is showing a deficit in trading with China (Table 3). Together with Germany, Japan is included in the old power triad (Ohmae, 1985). The Japanese Yen has been appreciating significantly over the past decades and this has partially affected its manufacturing growth to slow down. However, China's surplus was holding until 2012, when the first deficits were recorded (Table 4).

By observing Tables 3 and 4, it could be noted that the US trade deficit is still on a miserable growing trend and the European Union has leveled off to a very high-deficit position. Only Germany and Japan could be argued to be in a situation, where some control is still left on foreign trade and dependency is not only in one direction.

Table 3. Trade performance of European Union 27 and Germany with China (EU27 numbers in billion euros, Germany in bill. USD). Sources (data): Comtrade (2013), European Union (2013)

	European Union 27			Germany		
Year	Export	Import	Deficit	Export	Import	Deficit
2007	71.8	232.6	-160.8	41.11	75.05	-33.9
2008	78.2	247.9	-169.7	50.17	86.71	-36.5
2009	82.3	214.2	-131.9	51.09	77.50	-26.4
2010	113.3	282.5	-169.2	71.07	101.38	-30.3
2011	136.2	292.3	-156.1	90.50	112.18	-21.7
2012	143.8	289.7	-145.9	85.94	100.68	-14.7

Table 4. Trade performance of Japan and USA with China (all in bill. USD). Sources (data): Comtrade (2013).

	Japan			USA		
Year	Export	Import	Surplus	Export	Import	Deficit
2007	109.3	102.1	7.2	65.2	233.2	-167.9
2008	124.9	116.1	8.8	71.5	252.8	-181.4
2009	109.7	97.9	11.8	69.6	221.3	-151.7
2010	149.5	121.0	28.4	91.9	283.8	-191.9
2011	162.0	148.3	13.8	103.9	325.0	-221.1
2012	144.2	188.4	-44.2	110.6	444.4	-333.8

From a purely long-term currency change perspective (i.e. decade's long observation period) these arguments are more or less correct with regards to Europe, Japan and the USA (please see Figures 1-3 below). For both currencies, the Euro or the Japanese Yen against the Chinese Yuan, they have basically not changed at all during the last decade or so. Despite the gloomy European financial crisis, one Euro was purchased 4.4 percent less in July 2013 than in January 2000-for Japan the same minimal change was in place for a long time. However, recently, the Japanese Yen has lost much of its value and compared to January 2000, it is 23 % lower than the Chinese Yuan in August 2013. However, if the base period would be 1999, then the situation would still be of no change or even the opposite-the Yen has fluctuated quite much and in the late 1990s it was weak for a couple of years.

Basically the European Union is correct that emerging and high trade surplus driven by the Chinese economy is not that active to appreciate its currency against them. This would be a natural way out of the economic crisis in Europe, where the only remedies currently being offered are society-wide economic austerity packages and deflationary wage deals. These will eventually, and severely, hurt the Asian export countries as significantly lower consumption lowers the demand for foreign import. By lowering the overall consumption levels in the future, it will make Europe less attractive and less powerful, resulting in a lowering factor for Euro exchange rates in the future.

Interestingly, USA, as one of the most important trading partners of China (behind the EU), has been recently demanding a currency devaluation. However it has been noted that these valuations have not changed much. As an official tie between the US Dollar and the Chinese Yuan was broken down in July 2005, it is interesting to note that in eight years, the US Dollar has devaluated against the Chinese Yuan by more than 26 % (Figure 2). So, progress is being made in this area and trade pairing. However, its impact on the trade deficit is not what has been hoped for since deficits are only growing (Table 4). One reason might be that technological competitiveness has been lost in the USA and it is difficult to retain its world-class capabilities on high tech (Pisano & Shih, 2009). The USA might not have any other option but to continue acquiring products from China in the short-term-but with a higher amount of dollars demanded in exchange. So, based on this, the devaluation of the US Dollar should still continue to strengthen the export industry. The US Dollar does not only devaluate against the Chinese Yuan, but as Figure 1 shows, in the recent decade the Euro has gained considerable strength over the US Dollar, even if the economic challenges in Europe have been much discussed and negatively portrayed in the press (Lapavitsas et al., 2012).

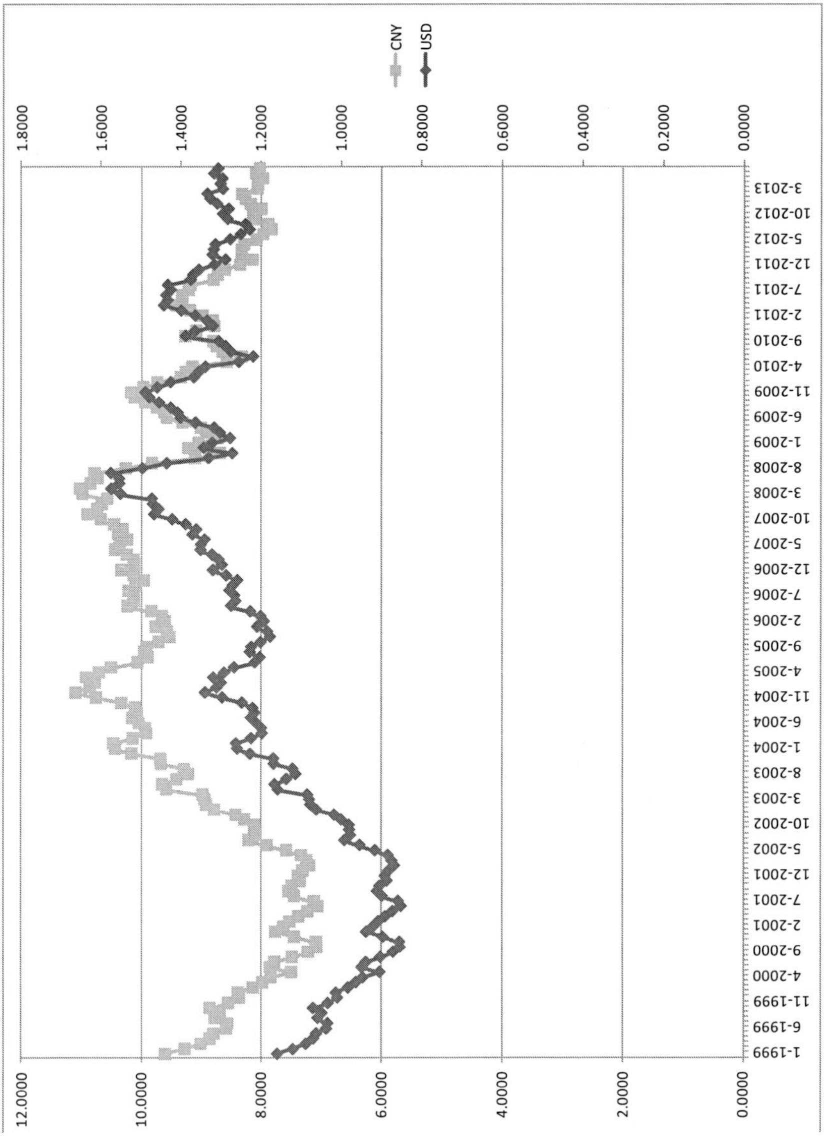

Figure 1. Chinese Yuan (CNY) and US dollar (USD) against Euro currency within period of Jan.1999-Aug.2013. Source: Bank of Finland (2013)

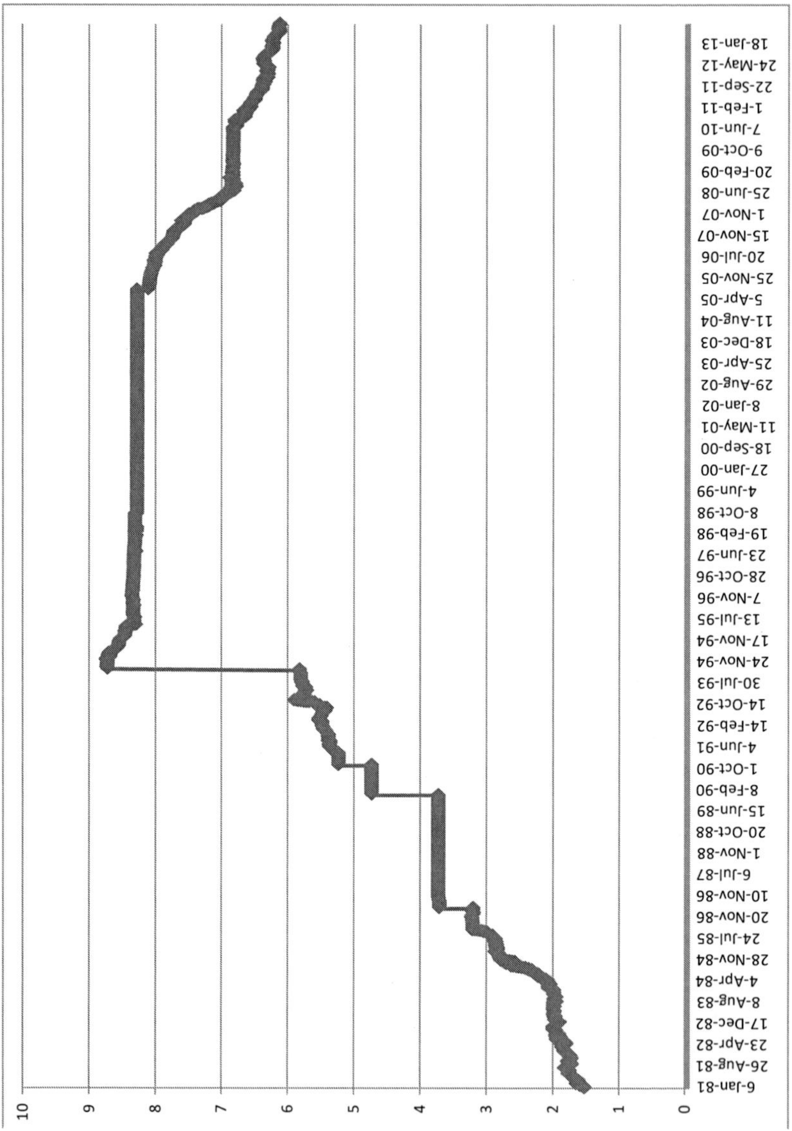

Figure 2. Chinese Yuan (CNY) against US dollar (USD) within period of Jan.1981-Aug.2013. Source: Bank of Finland (2013) and Federal Reserve (2013)

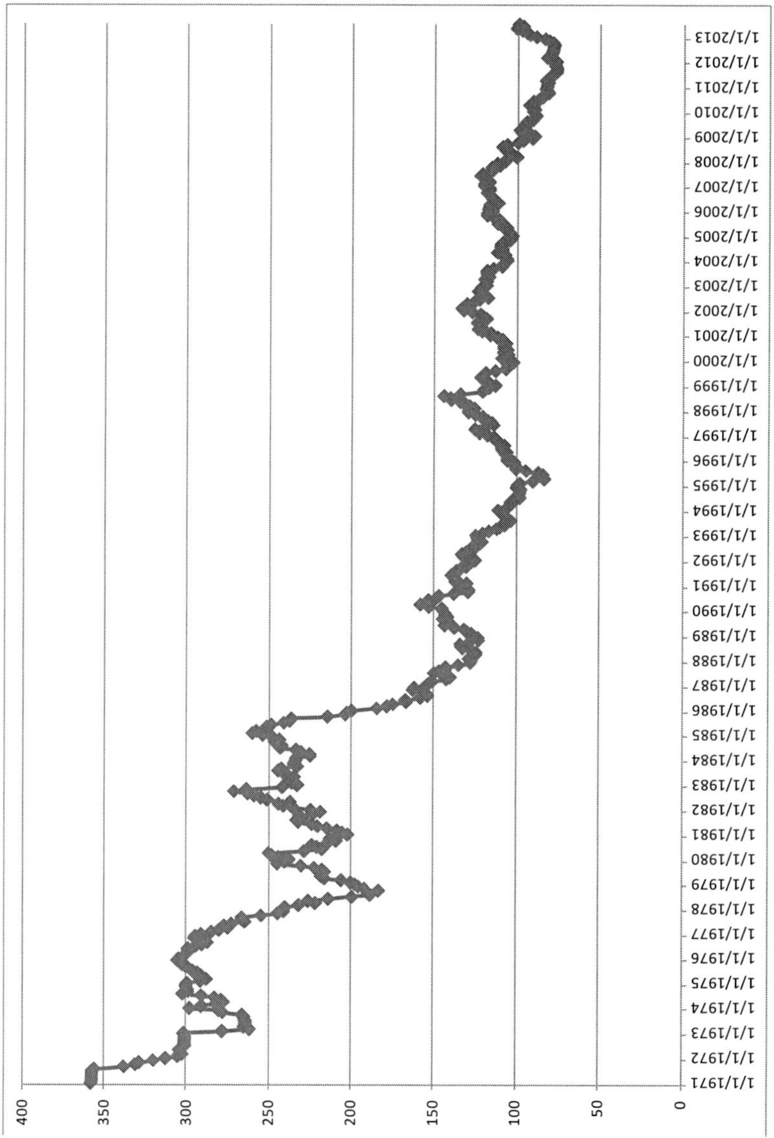

Figure 3. Japanese Yen against US dollar (USD) within period of Jan.1971-Aug.2013. Source: Federal Reserve (2013)

4. Container Flow Perspective

In terms of container export flows, China has been dominating the two old strong manufacturing exporters, the USA and Europe, for years. For example, China was dominating in a very significant manner, before the credit crunch took place in 2008-2009 (United Nations, 2006 & 2009). Actually in 2004 and 2007, full Asian containers (most of them from China) were transported with a nearly three-time volume than the USA was able to export back. This unbalance changed during the crisis and in 2010 for example, the USA was able to export 8.6 million TEU (Twenty feet Equivalent Unit) in full, while Asia exported to the USA 14.3 million TEU (United Nations, 2011). In 2011, the USA container export dropped to 6 million TEU and the Asian to 12.7 mill. TEU-the absolute difference is higher than in the previous year. Without doubt, the appreciation of the Yuan has improved this unbalanced situation. However this is not apparent in trade statistics measured in US Dollars-maybe Asian goods are being priced higher in the US markets. Increasing deficits as previously discussed would indicate so.

Europe was able to resist much longer against the Chinese export capability and actually in 2004, Europe was exporting 8.4 million TEU to Asia, while Asia was exporting back 5.6 million TEU (United Nations, 2006). This favorable situation could be partly explained by the huge investment activity and factory projects of European companies in Asia (and particularly in China). However, when these projects were completed, the surplus changed direction from Europe to Asia and China in a very short period of time. In 2007 Asia was already exporting 17.7 million TEU to Europe, while the latter had a mere export volume of 10 million TEU (United Nations, 2009). Thereafter, the Asian surplus developed to a similar situation; then was the situation with the USA and Asia before the credit crunch (and European companies are taking this into account in their logistics strategies, like Hilletofth et al., 2011 illustrate). So, Europe exported to Asia 5.6 million TEU in year 2010, while Asia was exporting to Europe 13.5 mill. TEU (United Nations, 2011). In most recent available statistics, the difference has remained, in an absolute sense, the same and both sides have increased their container trade. The situation within the European trade is, however, unsustainable in the long-run and as noted earlier, the currency policies of China have not changed much in the long-term, to that respect. Under these circumstances, it is very difficult for Europe to even build a fragile recovery in their export manufacturing industries.

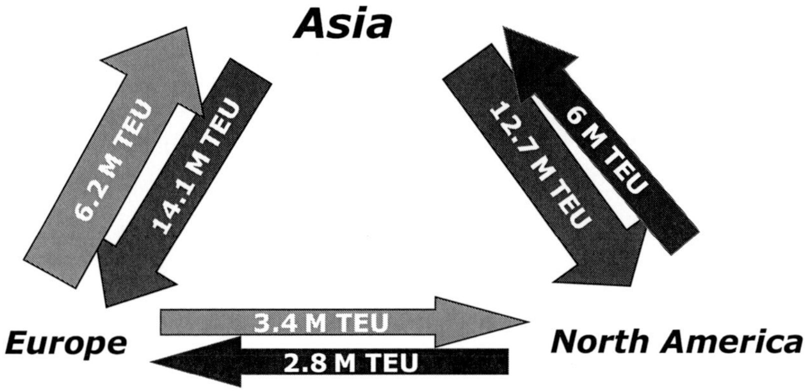

Figure 4. Container amounts and flows in Continental (Asia, Europe and USA) perspective during year 2011. Source: United Nations (2012)

Table 5. Container handling in leading Asian container countries and share of "To" / "From" USA and Europe. Source: United Nations (2012), United Nations (2006)

Country	2011	Country	2007
China	138,391,031	China	104,559,291
Singapore	30,722,470	Singapore	27,932,000
China (SAR HK)	24,404,000	China (SAR HK)	23,998,449
Japan	18,098,345	Japan	19,008,326
Korea	20,809,210	Korea	16,640,091
Malaysia	19,808,658	Malaysia	14,872,837
Taiwan	13,463,919	Taiwan	13,722,313
Total	265,697,633	Total	220,733,307
To USA+Europe	26,800,000	USA+Europe	33,100,000
Share (To)	10.1%	Share (To)	15.0%
From USA+Europe	12,200,000	From USA+Europe	14,900,000
Share (From)	4.6%	Share (From)	6.8%

If we leave out the continental perspective of container flows and take into account the internal Asian container markets, the bigger picture becomes much clearer (also argued in Stalk & Michael, 2011). As Table 5 illustrates, the largest Asian countries (from TOP 10 container handling countries in the world) are just a small fraction of the overall container handling, compared to the European and American volumes. Also container flows to these two continents are hardly growing, while inside Asia there is a clearly identifiable growth (Table 5). It is not surprising that the European market serving Singapore has been in trouble with its transshipment business growth-higher value is now a target instead of volume growth (Tan & Hilmola, 2012).

So, the Chinese Yuan and Asian currency development trends should be observed from a local perspective. It is important that trade facilitates and grows with the rest of the 85 % of container volume (rest of Asian sea port handling volume, mostly transported within the region). Should the Asian countries implement their own currency basket, then they should base their future on the strong Chinese Yuan. Basically the USA and Europe (and partly Japan) cannot return to consumption days fueled with debt finance and some manufacturing industries should return, so as to recover in the long-run. So, based on this argumentation, it could be stated that a stronger Asian currency basket or the Chinese Yuan is not a threat for the global economy-it is a must for sustainable recovery.

Even if this chapter argues that in the long term there has not been enough currency appreciation (e.g. the Yuan against the Euro), it should be stated that in the past five years (2008-2013) the trajectory has been developing in the right direction. The Euro has lost approximately 25 % to the Chinese Yuan (Figure 1), 20 % to the Singaporean Dollar, and 15 % to the Thai Baht. Similarly, but on a smaller scale, changes have occurred against the US Dollar. However, based on the abovementioned analysis, we think that this medium-term change should also continue in the long run, where Asian countries' trade increases more with each other and establishes a strong economic growth area for the whole world. The road with this scenario is not an easy one: Recently the Indian, Indonesian and Malaysian currencies have suffered from a considerable weakness due to fears that both Chinese and developed world markets would enter into a weaker economic growth, meaning that the less developed Asian economies would suffer even more.

5. Chinese-Led World or Internet Currency as Solution?

There is hardly anything new with demands to the Chinese Yuan to appreciate in value. A similar kind of dialogue was developing during the great recession in the 1930s-of course the importance of China then was much smaller. Instead of gold tied currencies in the late 1920s, the Chinese Yuan was tied to silver. Performance of silver against gold was very beneficial for China after the 1929 great crash. The devaluation of the Chinese Yuan against the US Dollar was 60 % in just a few years. However, appreciation followed shortly as UK removed the gold linkage in 1931 and the confiscation of gold in the USA, devaluating the dollar. Rapid appreciation, back to the starting level of 1929, did not bring much benefit to the world's economic problems. Both China's export and import declined (Burdekin, 2008). Similarly, we may argue that the world's structural trade problems were not solved by the strengthening of the Japanese Yen after abandoning the Bretton Woods contract in 1971 (Figure 3). The Japanese growth just started to ease and export-led growth had an impact on banks, the consumer sector and service economies. Also the Japanese demographical challenge did not support a further growth after the appreciation had started.

Somehow China is in a very similar position, like Japan during the 1970s. Based on Dent and Johnson (2011), China's demographical situation is repeating the same pattern in Japan-an increasing amount of older people and very few young. This is mostly the result of the one-child policy and getting increasingly wealthy. In the event of China's taking the lead in the world currency markets, the Yuan could appreciate 50-70 % against the US Dollar and the Euro. In this scenario, most probably, its export will be hurt; at least, their growth trajectories will be broken down. Consumption will not increase like it used to be, as older people in the economy are saving-oriented and social insurances are lacking from the governmental side. Export industries also consume lower amounts of imported items. So, the situation starts to repeat in the same pattern with Japan. The currency could be strong and stable, but the leading economy itself is not a growth engine for the world. In order to have a wage difference, dynamics and future growth, this currency needs to be expanded to a larger area in Asia, more young people need to be involved and societies with a healthy bias to young demographics.

It might be so that the entire world is getting tired of the fiat currency system and sudden devaluations and speculative forces very quickly influence the landscape. Also it is rather questionable, what central banks and single countries do different to benefit from the larger economic system. Typically in the fiat currency world, countries end up with massive debt spending (private consumption and public sector), followed by debt crises, deficits and printing increasingly more money. This is very natural, of course, as austerity and deflation is the least of what problematic countries would like to have on their plate. It is worth to try as long as the currency holds a comparative value against other world currencies. But maybe we have all seen this too many times-the current system doubtfully

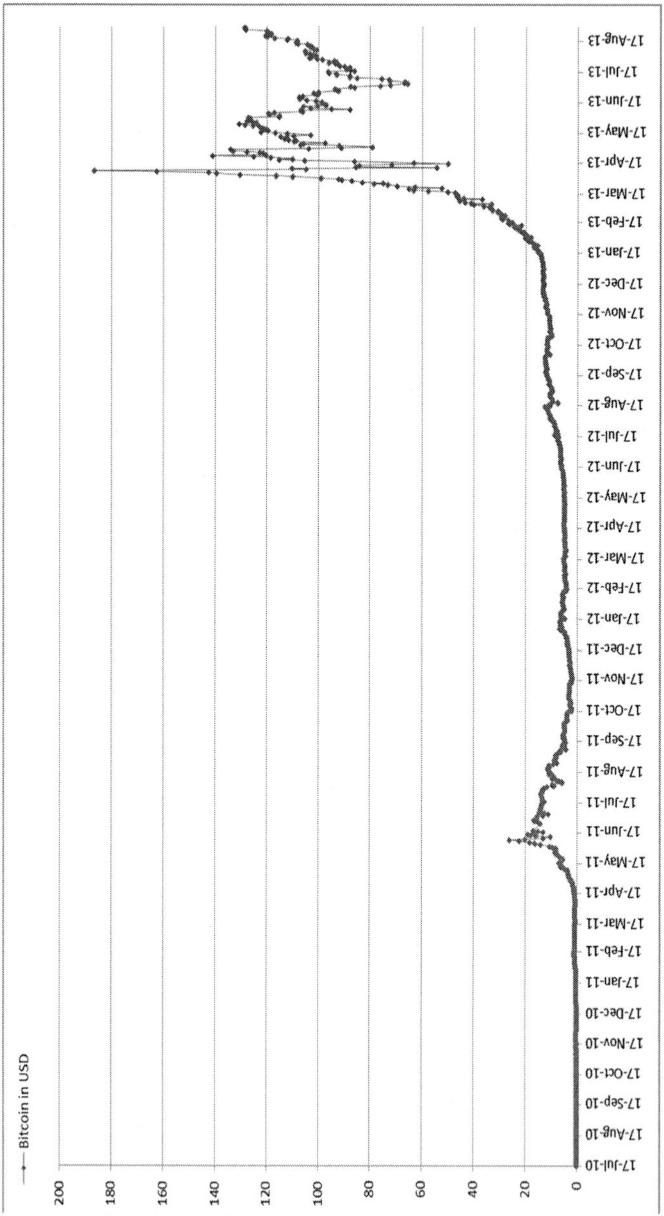

Figure 5. Bitcoin valuation in USD from its inauguration in July 2010 to 29th of August 2013. Source: Bitcoin Charts (2013)

benefits savers at all. Either they will hardly receive any interest on their savings or the value of their savings suddenly drops through devaluation.

One possible form of new currency to be used is Internet-based, central banker free, like Bitcoin. As Figure 5 shows, Bitcoin has shown a drastic valuation, increasing since its introduction in the mid-2010. The current valuation is 260 times higher than roughly three years ago (in US Dollar terms). What makes Bitcoin so good? It is first of all central-banker free and independent from any country (and respective debt problems and deficits). Bitcoin's amount cannot be increased by adding more Bitcoins to the system-actually its amount is going to be increased just very slightly, as people receive Bitcoins when computing power is shared in a peer to peer network. Otherwise money printing is not exercised. Bitcoins are also easy to be "carried" from country to country as the amounts of currency are just webpages where your wealth is stored (and ready to be spent, if an Internet access is available). Flexibility from the country of origin is an important feature for savers-think about the recent savings levy imposed in Cyprus. Bitcoins are not part of any current fiat-based banking system and cannot be taken by any government. Of course, as caveat Bitcoin is sharing the same weakness with gold-as its amounts do not grow-its availability will be a reason for concern in the forthcoming years and its value shall automatically increase (if the Bitcoin society is able to avoid the financial stress and current hostile approaches and law suits of different governments). If so, Bitcoin is going to be a good store of value but nothing else. The exchange element is not functioning, while the storage of value does (just the opposite of fiat currencies).

There is no final answer on the fiat vs. stabile currency worlds. Either one, taken to its extreme, is a poor system to be used. Internet technologies enable us to build more efficient and transparent currency systems and these are also favored by many people (as early success of Bitcoin demonstrates). However, being entirely fixed to some amount and providing no flexibility over economic cycles can result in anything good. Think about the European Euro rescue operations in recent years and keeping currency values high (Lapavitsas et al., 2012). Funding needs for the periphery countries are still on the agenda. One of the options is to implement currency (e.g. using Internet peer-to-peer technology) and tie that partially to gold or silver. However, this partial tie would be something, like 10-40 % of the currency value. The providing country would just assure that this currency is not going to collapse suddenly and lose all of its value. Also in its more advanced form, this physical tie could be implemented in a flexible manner, where it is said to fluctuate within some area. However, rules of the physical tie should be treated with great respect remain unchanged. Internet technologies would enable higher transparency and much lower transaction costs. It is all about trust and the current paper-based currencies can hardly achieve this status.

References

Bank of Finland (2013). Changes to the list of euro foreign exchange reference rates. Available at URL: http://www.suomenpankki.fi/en/tilastot/valuuttakurssit/Pages/taulukot.aspx Retrieved: August.2013

Bitcoin Charts (2013). Mt. Gox (USD) Bitcoin valuation. Available at URL: http://www.bitcoincharts.com/charts/mtgoxUSD#tgSzm1g10zm2g25 Retrieved: August.2013

Burdekin, Richard C.K. (2008). *China's Monetary Challenges – Past Experiences & Future Prospects*. Cambridge University Press, UK.

Comtrade (2013). *United Nations – International Merchandise Trade Statistics*. Available at URL: http://comtrade.un.org/ Accessed: August.2013

Containerization International (2011). *Containerization International Yearbook 2012*. Informa Publishers, UK, London.

Das, Satyajit (2012). *Traders, Guns and Money*. Financial Times Publishing, Great Britain.

Dent, Harry S. and Rodney Johnson (2011). *The Great Crash Ahead – Strategies for a World Turned Upside Down*. Free Press, New York.

European Union (2013). *China – Countries and Regions*. Available at URL: http://ec.europa.eu/trade/policy/countries-and-regions/countries/china/ Retrieved: August.2013

Federal Reserve (2013). *Foreign Exchange Rates - H.10*. Available at URL: http://www.federalreserve.gov/releases/h10/hist/ Retrieved: August.2013

Fergusson, Adam (1975). *When Money Dies: The Nightmare of the Weimar Collapse*. William Kimber & Co.: UK.

Hilletofth, Per, Olli-Pekka Hilmola and Frida Claesson (2011). In-transit Distribution Strategy: Solution for European Factory Competitiveness? *Industrial Management and Data Systems*, 111:1, pp. 20-40.

Hilmola, Olli-Pekka (2011). Logistics sector development potential of world's oil exporters. *International Journal of Energy Sector Management*, 5:2, pp. 256-270.

Lapavitsas, Costas, A. Kaltenbrunner, G. Labrinidis, D. Lindo, J. Meadway, J. Michell, J.P. Painceira, E. Pires, J. Powell, A. Stenfors, N. Teles & L. Vatikoitis (2012). *Crisis in the Eurozone*. Verso Press, UK, London.

Ohmae, K. (1985). *Triad Power*. Free Press, USA.

Pisano, G.P. & W.C. Shih (2009). Restoring American competitiveness. *Harvard Business Review*, July-August, pp. 114-125.

Richards, James (2012). *Currency Wars – The Making of the Next Global Crisis*. Penguin Press, New York, USA.

Sarnoff, Paul (1980). *Trading in Gold*. Woodhead-Faulkner: Cambridge.

Stalk, George & David Michael (2011). What the west doesn't get about China? *Harvard Business Review*, June, pp. 25-27.

Tan, Albert & Olli-Pekka Hilmola (2012). Future of transshipment in Singapore. *Industrial Management and Data Systems*, 112:7, pp. 1085-1100.

Turner, Graham (2008). *The Credit Crunch – Housing Bubbles, Globalisation and the Worldwide Economic Crisis*. Pluto Press, UK, London.

UNCTAD (2012). *Liner Shipping Connectivity Index*. United Nations, New York. Available at URL (data):
http://unctadstat.unctad.org/TableViewer/tableView.aspx?ReportId=92
Retrieved: March.2012

United Nations (2006). *Review of Maritime Transport 2005*. United Nations: New York and Geneva.

—. (2009). *Review of Maritime Transport 2008*. United Nations: New York and Geneva.

—. (2010). *Review of Maritime Transport 2010*. United Nations Conference on Trade and Development, New York and Geneva.

—. (2011). *Review of Maritime Transport 2011*. United Nations Conference on Trade and Development, New York and Geneva.

Vogel, Harold L. (2010). *Financial Market Bubbles and Crashes*. Cambridge University Press, UK.

Wener, Ed (2005). *A Look at Central Bank Gold Reserves*. Available at URL: http://www.gata.org/node/104 Retrieved: Aug.2013

World Bank (2013). *World Data Bank of World Bank*. Available at URL:
http://databank.worldbank.org/data/views/reports/tableview.aspx
Retrieved: Aug.2013

World Gold Council (2013). *Gold Demand Trends – Second Quarter 2013*. Available at URL:
https://www.gold.org/download/get/pub_archive/pdf/GDT_Q2_2013.pdf Retrieved: Aug.2013.

CHAPTER TWO

DRIVERS OF INNOVATION IN SINGAPORE'S FINANCIAL SERVICES SECTOR: AN EXPLORATION WITH PRACTITIONERS

STUART SMITH

1. Introduction

Financial services form a significant proportion of Singapore's economy, contributing to an estimated 11% of the country's GDP. (MAS, 2013)

Since the 2008 global financial crash, there have been renewed efforts by financial services organizations to adopt innovative practices in areas of their business. In particular, there is a perception that financial institutions are aiming to re-establish trust with customers and regulators alike by adopting more "customer centric" approaches and through the adoption of customer-enhancing digital technology.

This paper examines the perceived drivers of innovation through the eyes of practitioners in the financial services sector in Singapore. The paper also captures the various innovation tools and approaches that practitioners are utilizing within the Sector.

2. Methodology

This paper has been complied through in-depth qualitative interviews and group discussions with innovation practitioners in the financial services sector in Singapore during the first two quarters of 2013. In addition, the data gathered has been supported through further literature review.

This research is an early ethnographic exploration stage of a much larger research programme examining innovation practice in the Singapore and wider APAC financial services community. As such, it forms the basis of a more focused and quantitative research stage in the final quarters of 2013.

3. Financial Services in Singapore

The financial services sector in Singapore is one of the largest sectors in the country's economy. The sector is a large and diverse employer, ranging from major global banks through to small independent accountants and advisors.

The Monetary Authority of Singapore (MAS) indicates that over 600 major institutions offering a wide range of financial services can be found in Singapore and that the financial sector employs about 6% of the total workforce in Singapore. MAS suggests that the sector accounts for over 11% of the country's Gross Domestic Product. (MAS, 2013)

Whilst often perceived as "conservative", both from an internal and external perspective, the financial sector in Singapore is increasingly a home to several significant corporate innovation initiatives and some interesting finance startups.

4. Singapore and Innovation

Over the past decade it can be argued that Singapore has become synonymous to innovation in Asia. Recently ranked 7th in an INSEAD Global Innovation Index (INSEAD, 2013), the Singapore government has heavily invested in what may be termed as the "infrastructure of innovation" at all levels of its economy.

Investments have been made in physical infrastructure, universities, public and private R&D labs, as well as enabling infrastructure such as high speed broadband, wireless connectivity, security and transport.

In addition, large-scale education and workforce development programmes have been funded, focusing on providing a highly educated and skilled workforce. This is coupled with extensive inward investment activities, which encourage leading global companies to set up or establish activities in Singapore. (EDB, 2012). Over the past years several different innovation initiatives and 'innovation labs' have been set up in Singapore, by parties originally external to the country. These are across a diverse spectrum of innovation interests from security and policing (Interpol, 2013), food and drink (Food & Beverage Asia, 2013), technology and banking (Asian Scientist, 2012) .

The net economic impact of these internal and external initiatives is hard to disaggregate since it is probably too early to make a true judgment.

However, one thing is clear and that is the context in which many innovation practitioners we spoke to are highly attuned to innovation.

5. Drivers of Innovation in Financial Services in Singapore

In discussions with practitioners and from the wider literature review, we explored perceptions of the drivers behind innovation-both within the participants' own organizations and within the wider Singaporean financial services sector.

Through these explorations we could begin to discern emerging drivers of innovation that merit further discussion. Examining each of these in turn:

5.1 Consumerisation, Mobile & Data

The term "consumerisation", in relation to Information Technology (IT), is widely attributed to a 2004 report by CSC Ltd (Moschella D, 2004) and refers specifically to the growing tendency of IT to be popularized and developed in a consumer market *before* it reaches large corporates or organizations.

The implications of this is that financial service systems, which are almost solely dependent on ICT, are undergoing rapid transformation due to customer demands rather than through the organizations deciding 'consciously' to innovate. This "users as innovators" mode (Oliveria P, 2011), coupled with rapid technology changes, in particular the demand for mobile banking platforms, was from a practitioner's perspective driving many of the initiatives they were involved in.

Major Singaporean banks, such as DBS and OCBC, publically state that they are putting the customer experience and product/service innovation at the center of their strategies, as do overseas banks with heavy presence in Singapore such as Standard Chartered (DBS, 2013), (OCBC, 2011), (Standard Chartered , 2013) Several of the practitioners we spoke with were linked to or involved in groups looking at these items.

The sector also appears to be investing heavily in acquiring staff with skills such as User Experience Design (UXD), Customer Experience Design (CXD) and Digital Channel technologies (Hays, 2013), or training staff in new 'innovation' skills by using the Workforce Development Agency (WDA) Frameworks or through direct engagement with local institutes of Higher Education (WDA, 2013) (FICS, 2013).

One viewpoint expressed was that local and regional financial institutions were moving more rapidly into mobile technologies and customer experience platforms than some of the larger global institutions. For example, DBS highlights that it was recently voted the "*world's number 1 bank for mobile apps*" (DBS, 2013) whilst global banks such as HSBC are perceived to be lagging in their mobile offering to consumers (Finextra, 2013). Similarly, other Singaporean and SE Asian financial institutions such as OCBC, POSB, UoB and Maybank (Maybank, 2013) have all noticeably increased their mobile banking options in the past 18 months.

One of the by-products of the explosion in mobile devices and digital banking is the rise in the volumes of data that banks need to handle, keep secure and analyze. Financial institutions have long since recognized the power of data (Economist, 2012) and it appears that many financial institutions and technology vendors within Singapore are investing in this particular form of innovation. (CFO Innovation, 2013)

5.2 Innovation Zeitgeist

"*Innovation is fashionable. It's as simple as that*". This quote from one practitioner, summarizes of the most commonly expressed sentiments we found, which was that organizations are undertaking innovation quite simply because it is currently viewed as fashionable. This is a potentially cynical viewpoint, suggesting that decision makers in financial institutions are guilty of a 'herd' mentality.

However, the importance of prevailing narratives, the *zeitgeist* as it were, in contributing to innovation in organizations is an area that is gaining in academic attention (Andreas P. Müller, 2013). In addition we note that in the innovation literature of different eras, narratives around turbulence and responding to change through innovation are always present. For example the following is taken from the opening paragraph of a 1991 paper (Thwaites D, 1991) :

"*The financial services industry in the United States, Canada and the United Kingdom has experienced a period of rapid transition during the 1980's. The combination of increased global competitive activity, changing technology, new legislation and a more demanding consumer has led to a large increase in the number of new products launched*"

At this stage, from the qualitative perspective of practitioners, we can plausibly infer that a similar narrative is driving and influencing perceptions and understanding of the need for innovation in the financial services sector of Singapore.

Government Promotion & Regulation

The influence of the Singapore Government in driving innovation primarily appears to be perceived by practitioners in three dimensions: Regulatory, Industrial Policy, and Education, although clearly all of these areas are interlinked in some way:

Regulatory – practitioners often discussed "the regulator", MAS, and the role it has to play in constraining or encouraging innovation.

MAS itself, in its Tenets of Regulation document, states that it, "……… *seeks to establish sound regulation of a high standard that allows well-managed risk taking and innovation, and which emphasises the stable and sustainable development of the financial services sector*." (MAS, 2012)

Practitioners were, on the whole, not convinced that the regulator encourages what they would consider to be innovation. In addition, several mentioned that the regulator, or the threat of "the regulator", was enough to act as an internal barrier to taking innovations forward in their organizations.

Contrary to this view, opinion was also expressed that regulation often drove innovation in that it encouraged investment in new systems, technology or approaches to doing business. The constraining effect of the regulator in this regard could be argued to promote innovation.

Industrial Policy - The constant promotion by the Singapore Government of productivity and innovation through a number of policy channels, including inward investment, workforce skills, employer incentives, tax incentives and general advocacy, appears to be producing the desired effect in many areas. Reiterating the sentiments relating to zeitgeist, noted above, it is increasingly difficult to avoid mention of innovation in policy or industrial circles in Singapore. This was noted by practitioners to be helpful enabling them to gain acceptance for the work they are doing and for the senior management buy-in required.

Education – Singapore invests significantly in education and development of its skilled workforce. The Government has invested in a wide range of educational activities designed to encourage and embed innovative practice in the workforce. Agencies such as the Workforce Development Agency (WDA) play an important role in promoting business innovation through employee education and several practitioners spoke of attending courses on innovation at local universities or training centers.

5.3 Recovery from the 2008 Global Financial Crisis

In our conversation with practitioners perhaps one of the more unexpected drivers of innovation cited was the continued fallout from the 2008 Global Financial Crisis (GFC). Although in their work on financial crashes Reinhart and Roghoff indicate that it takes 4-6 years to fully recover after a financial crash, so perhaps this is not so surprising after all. (Reinhart C M, 2009)

It was clear that many *internal* innovation projects in institutions (as opposed to external customer facing projects or products) remained focused on recovering positions lost in the crash or improving systems and resilience. Examples given were: improving legacy systems for better transparency and visibility of assets; improving analytics and reporting infrastructures; and changing systems to cope with a refreshed and more stringent regulatory environment.

5.4 Globalisation & Market Forces

In an extension of the discussion around the financial crash, several practitioners proposed that innovation activity in the sector was simply a "*response to market forces*" or a more "*competitive global landscape*". As seen earlier these types of sentiments have been part of innovation narratives in the finance sector for some time. (Thwaites D, 1991).

Some participants suggested that the perceived economic rise of 'Asia' and shift in the economic balance of power from West to East meant that indigenous innovation in Singapore had become more prominent. Examples such as Prudential Insurance Company's recent profit announcement on the back of its SE Asia activities (Prudential PLC, 2012) were cited as evidence of this change, along with examples such as MasterCard establishing an innovation in Singapore (Asian Scientist, 2012).

Some practitioners felt that indigenous financial institutions were now showing "global leadership" in some aspects of innovation. This correlates with various commentarial pieces regarding the changing nature of innovation in Asia more broadly (Wagstyl, 2011) and the emergence of local advocates of banking innovation such as Next Bank Asia (Next Bank) that are taking these ideas out to a global audience.

6. Toolsets and Frameworks

In terms of responding to the drivers described in the previous section, practitioners were asked about the approaches they used, either personally or within their organizations, to address innovation challenges or bring forward new products and services.

Several broad approaches were mentioned and we have categorized them broadly below for discussion. Interestingly, several practitioners stated that they were not sure of what kind of approaches their institutions were using *beyond* what they themselves could see. This reflected the size and internal organizational structures of the institutions, with larger and more complex institutions potentially providing the least visibility in terms of innovation approaches.

- **Design Thinking, User Experience Design (UXD) and Agile**

Popularized by author/practitioners such as Tim Brown (Brown, 2009), David Kelly (Tom Kelly, 2005) and Roger Martin (Martin, 2009), "*Design Thinking*" was mentioned several times in the discussion with practitioners around tool kits and approaches they use.

In addition, related approaches such as User Experience Design (UXD) and Customer Experience Design (CX) were also mentioned as being important especially in the context of digital products and mobile apps.

'Agile' (Beck K, 2001) was also mentioned a lot by those involved in software and IT systems development and often generated debate as to whether it was being adopted correctly in financial organizations. Some practitioners viewed agile, as much as "a mindset", rather than a specific methodology. Others spoke of "Agile-like" approaches being championed, but were unclear as to whether these really helped innovation or "were that much different from how did things before."

- **Organizational Structures**

Some practitioners discussed the organizational structures and approaches that they were adopting in order to bring innovation forward.

Labs & Dedicated Innovation Teams - The idea of having dedicated teams to deliver innovation or New Product Development appears to be very popular and how these teams are structured varies from organization to organization, as does their role and purview.

Several of the large financial institutions in Singapore have some form of Customer or User Experience Laboratories (OCBC, 2011) (Bank, 2013), and other large financial institutions have invested in innovation labs within Singapore in recent years, notably MasterCard (Asian Scientist, 2012) and Citi Group (Citi, 2011). In the context of UXD and CXD then technology tools, such as eye tracking, appear to be gaining interest as part of a broader "*usability lab approach*"

Strategic Partnerships and Value Chains - Practitioners also spoke of partnerships in developing innovation. These partnerships might be with non-financial services sector players, such as retailers and telcos or with delivery partners such as consultants, design houses and technology vendors. For example, Visa Singapore recently announced a partnership with Singtel to bring mobile payments to customers who have NFC enabled smartphones (Visa, 2013). Similarly, OCBC worked with several different external partners to bring forward their "Gen Y" finance brand FRANK (The Financial Brand, 2011).

7. Summation

The financial services sector in Singapore is a significant contributor to the country's overall economic prosperity with approximately 11% of GDP coming from finance. The sector has grown within Singapore over the past decades and as such it seems a reasonable assumption that more innovation activity will emerge from the sector.

Whilst only a small qualitative snapshot, several drivers of innovation are evident in the narratives gathered from practitioners and the surrounding literature and these provide useful indicators of where research can progress.

The drivers included:

- consumerisation of IT, mobile and data – a move away from vendor or organizational led modes of technology innovation toward customer led approaches
- Government influence through regulation and promotion – in particular the maintenance of a nationwide meta-narrative on innovation and the role of MAS
- Fashion & Zeitgeist – linked in some way to Government activity but an acknowledgement of a general zeitgeist toward innovation
- Ongoing reaction to Global Financial Crisis of 2008
- Market forces & Globalization

In response to these drivers organizations appear to be adopting and, perhaps more interestingly, adapting a range of innovation approaches to suit their immediate needs. The primary factor in selecting particular approach appears to be a combination of organizational history, organizational acceptance and personal skillsets/experience of individual practitioners

This paper reflects the early stage of a wider research programme into finance innovation in Singapore. In terms of future research, several areas have emerged that merit further exploration including:

1. More detailed examination of approaches to innovation being adopted within Singapore's finance sector and the reasons for adoption
2. The relationship between the Singapore national meta-narrative on innovation and its effect on the finance sector in general
3. Knowledge and skills acquisition on innovation in the sector. How are organizations selecting and developing the new or innovative employees they need.
4. Exploration of the role and relationship that the regulator plays in promoting innovation in the sector

References

Andreas P. Müller, L. B. (2013). *Narrative & Innovation: New Ideas for Business Administration, Strategic Management and Entrepreneurship* (1st ed.). Springer.

Asian Scientist. (2012). *Asian Scientist*. Retrieved from http://www.asianscientist.com/tech-pharma/mastercard-launches-innovation-rnd-center-in-singapore-2012/

Bank, D. (2013). *MBFC Digital Innovations*. Retrieved from http://www.dbs.com/movingasia/mbfcbranch.html

Barras, R. (1990). Interactive Innovation in Financial & Business Services: The Vanguard of the service revolution. *Research Policy , 19*, 215-37.

Beck K, e. a. (2001). *Manifesto For Agile Software Development*. Retrieved from http://agilemanifesto.org/

Brown, T. (2009). *Change by Design.* HarperBusiness.

CFO Innovation. (2013, June 3rd). *Big Data Analytics Training Centre Opens in Singapore*. Retrieved from CFO Innovation: http://www.cfoinnovation.com/content/big-data-analytics-training-centre-opens-singapore

Citi. (2011). *Citi Launch Innovation Lab in Singapore.* Retrieved from http://www.citigroup.com/citi/press/2011/111206a.htm

DBS. (2013, April 29th). *DBS.* (DBS, Producer) Retrieved from DBS AGM Financial Presentation: http://www.dbs.com/investor/othermaterials/2013/FY2012%20AGM%20financial%20review.pdf

Economist. (2012, May 19th). Crunching the numbers. *The Economist* .

EDB. (2012). *Annual Report 2011-2012.* Singapore: Economic Development Board of Singapore.

FICS. (2013). *Financial Industry Competency Standards.* Retrieved from http://www.fics.org.sg/

Finextra. (2013, April 26th). *Chase and la Caixa top mobile banking study; HSBC bottom of the pile.* Retrieved from Finextra: http://www.finextra.com/News/FullStory.aspx?newsitemid=24766

Food & Beverage Asia. (2013). *Food & Beverage Asia.* Retrieved from http://www.foodbeverageasia.com/detail.php?tid=3563

Hays. (2013). *Hays Quarterly Skills Survey Singapore.* Retrieved from http://www.nextbank.org/

INSEAD. (2013). *INSEAD Global Innovation Index.* Retrieved from http://www.globalinnovationindex.org/content.aspx?page=GII-Home

Interpol. (2013). *Interpol Global Complex For Innovation.* Retrieved from http://www.interpol.int/About-INTERPOL/The-INTERPOL-Global-Complex-for-Innovation

Martin, R. (2009). *The Design of Business: Why Design Thinking is the Next Competitive Advantage* (3rd ed.). Harvard Business School Press.

MAS. (2013). *Singapore Financial Centre MAS Overview.* Retrieved from http://www.mas.gov.sg/Singapore-Financial-Centre/Overview.aspx

—. (2012). *Tenets of Effective Regulation.* Retrieved from http://www.mas.gov.sg/~/media/manual%20migration/Monographs/MAS_Monograph_Tenets_of_Effective_Regulation.pdf

Maybank. (2013). *Maybank2U.com : Maybank Mobile Banking Web Page.* Retrieved from http://www.maybank2u.com.my/mbb_info/m2u/public/personalList04.do?channelId=ACC-Accounts&programId=ACC08.03-MobileBanking&chCatId=/mbb/Personal/ACC-Accounts

Moschella D, N. O. (2004). *The 'Consumerization' of Information Technology.* Computer Sciences Corporation.

Next Bank. (n.d.). *Next Bank.org.* Retrieved from http://www.nextbank.org/

OCBC. (2011). *OCBC Bank Raises Bar With Brand New Online Banking Experience.* Retrieved from http://www.ocbc.com.sg/assets/pdf/Media/2011/oct/Media_Release_Tower_intranet.pdf

OCBC. (2011). *OCBC Quartelrly Results Presentation 2011*. Retrieved from http://www.ocbc.com.sg/assets/pdf/quarterly-results/2011/OCBC%202011%20New%20Horizons%20III%20Presentation.pdf

Oliveria P, v. H. (2011). Users as Service Innovators: The Case of Banking Services. *Research Policy , 40*, 806-818.

Prudential PLC. (2012). *Annual Results 2012.* Prudential PLC.

Reinhart C M, R. K. (2009). The Aftermath of the Financial Crisis. *NBER Working Paper Series* (Working Paper 14656).

Standard Chartered . (2013, April 30th). *Standard Chartered customises branches to cater to specific banking needs of customers.* Retrieved from http://www.standardchartered.com.sg/press-releases/en/_pdf/2013/PR_Standard_Chartered_customises_branches_to_cater_to_specific_banking_needs_of_customers_30Apr13_final.pdf

The Financial Brand. (2011, May 31st). *Meet FRANK, Maybe The Coolest Bank Gen-Y Has Ever Seen*. Retrieved from The Financial Brand: http://thefinancialbrand.com/18642/ocbc-frank-gen-y-banking-brand/

Thwaites D, E. S. (1991). Aspects of Innovation in a Turbulent Market Environment: Empirical Evidence from UK Building Societies. *The Service Industries Journal , 11* (3), 346-361.

Tom Kelly, J. L. (2005). *The Ten Faces of Innovation: IDEO's Strategies for Defeating the Devil's Advocate and Driving Creativity Throughout Your Organization* (1st ed.). Currency/Doubleday.

Visa. (2013, August 1st). *Press Release: Singtel and Visa Announce Mobile Payment Alliance.* Retrieved from http://www.visa.com.sg/ap/sg/aboutvisa/mediacenter/press.shtml

Wagstyl, S. (2011, January 5th). *Innovation: Replicators No More.* Retrieved from Finanical Times: http://www.ft.com/intl/cms/s/0/97a67340-1904-11e0-9c12-00144feab49a.html#axzz2cNEKt95O

WDA. (2013). *Workforce Development Agency*. Retrieved from http://www.wda.gov.sg/content/wdawebsite/L207-AboutWSQ/L301-WSQIndustryFramework-Finance.html

Acknowledgements

Acknowledgements to the innovation practitioners in the financial services sector who have given up lunch breaks, work time and evenings to contribute to these discussions.

CHAPTER THREE

INNOVATION AND FINANCIAL INCLUSION: THE BRAZILIAN BANK EXPERIENCE

MARISALVO DA SILVA

1. Introduction

The ability to innovate is currently considered as one of the essential faculties of competitive organizations. Within this context, the systematic search for radical innovations, or rather, those being both capable of creating new markets and at the same time provide rapid, productive expansion and economic growth, and by incremental innovations identified with processes of continued improvement, are fundamental to corporate survival.

Within the last years, the Brazilian banking market has gone through profound and rapid changes due to the stabilization of the economy, the reduction in the number of banks operating in the country, the arrival of foreign institutions and the reduction of state banks in operation. With the opening of markets and the subsequent growth within the wave of mergers and acquisitions that occurred during the last decade, the Brazilian banking sector has experienced significant impacts in terms of competition, leading it to adopt a posture of drawing closer to clients through a strategy of providing convenience and increasing profitability.

Brazil is a large, complex and diverse country in terms of its geography as well as its demographic and economic realities. It includes large sprawling urban conurbations in the Southeast, such as São Paulo and Rio de Janeiro, more remote and lightly populated areas, such as the Amazon rainforest, and arid rural regions in the central and northern parts of the country. The Brazilian financial system (SFN) represents the continuously evolving universe of regulated institutions in the Brazilian financial sector. Given the diversity of the Brazilian population, the SFN must cater for a variety of needs. This explains the broad range of institutions, from credit cooperatives and savings and loans associations, to large international banks and exchange brokerages. The National Monetary Council is the overarching entity responsible for issuing regulations and guidelines for the proper functioning of the SFN, operationalized through four regulatory and supervisory entities: The Central Bank of Brazil (BCB), The Securities and Exchange Commission, The Private Insurance Superintendence and The Complementary Pension Secretariat. These authorities regulate a diverse range of institutions in the following categories:

- Demand deposit-taking financial
- Other financial institutions (including micro-entrepreneur credit companies and development agencies)
- Financial intermediaries or auxiliaries
- Insurance and pension entities
- Portfolio management entities
- Liquidation and clearing systems.

There are a number of entities that are significant for financial inclusion, but at present are not actively supervised. For example, Civil Society Organizations of Public Interest (OSCIP) are registered with the Ministry of Justice and the Ministry of Labor and Employment and participate in the National Program for Productive Oriented Microcredit (PNMPO), a multi-ministry governmental program, but are not prudentially supervised. The same is true for other entities outside the SFN, such as public funds, NGOs involved in microcredit and factoring companies-a flexible form of loan that advances money to a company as it issues new invoices. This is different than overdrafts or more formal loans, which are usually applicable for a fixed amount (AFI, 2011).

2. Methodology

The present study is based on an exploratory research that seeks to gather information regarding a determined object and is limited, therefore, to a field of work that serves as a subsidy for the explanatory research to come later. The exploratory method is recommended for situations where knowledge about a topic under analysis is limited or demands new studies (Selltiz *et al.*, 1974). The case study method was used to understand the group of innovations implemented in the Brazilian financial sector.

> "The case study is an empirical investigation that investigates a contemporary phenomenon within its real-life context, especially when the

limits between the phenomenon and the context are not clearly defined" (Yin, 2005).

Specifically, the present project involves an analysis of cases that can be classified as exploratory, since they seek to increase understanding of the phenomenon studied. The study was construed from secondary data obtained from document research and from descriptive analyses of case studies available in the literature, following the recommendations presented by Yin (2005) for multiple case studies. In this project, the "approach by object" was used, which focuses on the characteristics of the innovation in an individualized way (OECD, 2005). Research using "approach by object" involves the collection of data about specific innovations, generally some type of "significant innovation" or the main innovation of an organization. Research begins with the identification of the report of successful innovations, frequently based on evaluations by specialists or advertisements for new products in specialized publications. The approach consists of collecting quantitative and qualitative data regarding the specific innovation under investigation and about the organizations being studied. The cases, object of the study, were selected based on representative criteria within the context of the theme under consideration as well as the consideration of convenience to the researcher, who works in the financial sector.

3. Innovation and Financial Inclusion

3.1 Innovation

Innovation has been highlighted and recognized as a critical factor in the success and competitiveness of organizations. Innovation, in terms of products, processes and services, is recognized as a critical factor for success in most companies and new products or services and constitutes a crucial leverage component to the performance of many companies. Thus, innovation should be the result of a conscious and intentional search for opportunities that can be found either in the internal or external environment.

The term "innovation" possesses different definitions depending on the author and context analyzed. Due to the scope and depth of the term "innovation", it was observed that authors used a guideline to present their definitions: the adoption of procedures, processes or services that were not used by the company and that are a novelty either to the company or to the market.

In general, innovation is associated with original, never-before-seen products or the use of cutting-edge technologies. However, innovations can include: (a) development and commercialization of new products or services; (b) development of new manufacturing processes or forms of service provider relationships; (c) drastically different concepts or completely new ways of setting apart existing business; (d) changing the company's organizational and management style and the administration of the production process; (e) ways of commercializing new products, new delivery methods and changes in packaging. (Rogers: 1995; OECD: 2005; Hamel: 2000; Van de Ven, Angle & Poole: 2000; Jaramillo, Lugones & Salazar: 2000).

Many attempts were made to build models that would shed light on how innovation is generated in companies and how it is influenced by the external environment. The conception of a conceptual model should seek to facilitate the understanding and manipulation of the relations that occur between the different variables that make up a system or process, abstracted from reality. For example, Silva and Ferreira (2005) conducted a study in thirteen Brazilian companies and developed a conceptual model, named Innovation Antecedents and Consequences (IAC Model), shown in Figure X.1, which covers three dimensions: internal and external antecedents, processes and consequences, formed by grouping constructs presented in theoretical discussions regarding market orientation, competitive intelligence, innovation, new product development and company performance. The generation and promulgation of information regarding clients, competitors and other market elements and the proper interpretation shared among members of the organization, in the literature called "market orientation", exerts a positive influence on business performance. Product and process innovation is recognized as a critical success factor by most companies. New products are a crucial component to the growth of the company. New product development essentially includes the process of research, development and engineering. The definition of strategic intent and the types of innovation strategies to be followed within the organization are considered as a crucial point towards the successful development of new products. Corporate performance has been broached as the result of competitive intelligence and innovation processes. Within the confines of performance proposals, market participation, sales volume, profit margins, new product success, investment returns and general performance; sales increase, increase in market participation, sales returns, outstanding debt returns, investment returns and general performance have set themselves apart. Competition intensity, technological changes and client demands were external factors considered in the model for the fact that they represent market forces and relevant variables in strategic terms. (Silva, 2010).

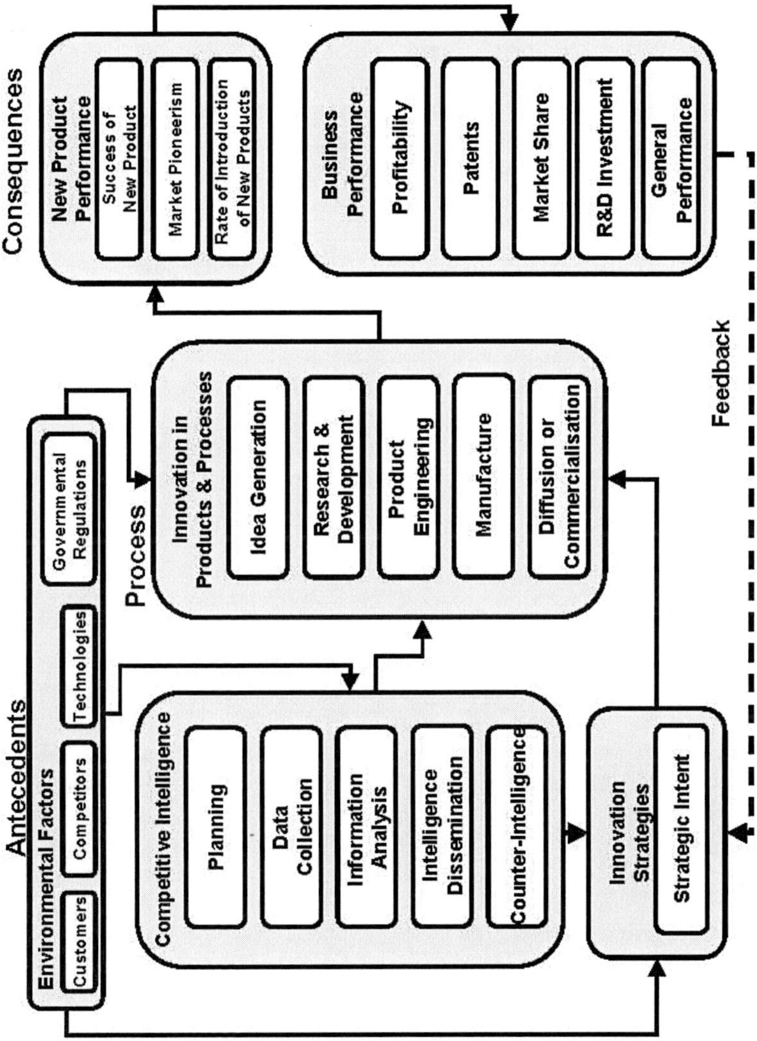

Figure 1. Innovation Antecedents and Consequences (IAC Model).
Source: Silva &Ferreira (2005).

3.2 Innovation in Services

An important topic, which has aroused growing interest during the last decade, is services innovation. The field of “service innovation studies” involves four different theoretical perspectives (assimilation, demarcation, inversion and integration), which reflect different conceptions of the relationship vis-à-vis the dominant field of (industrial) innovation studies. The assimilation of the “technologistic” perspective analyses innovation in services, just as innovation in manufacturing, focuses on their relationships with technological systems. Insofar as it mainly focuses on innovation adopted from manufacturing sectors, the assimilation perspective is also a subordination one. The differentiation (or demarcation) perspective focuses on service specificities and aims at capturing the innovation activity where the traditional (technologist or assimilation) gaze perceives nothing. The inversion perspective reflects the “revenge” of the service sector; it emphasizes the active role of KIBS in other sectors’ innovations. Finally, the integrative or synthetic perspective seeks to provide the same analytical frameworks for both goods and services and for both technological and non-technological forms of innovation (Gallouj and Weinstein, 1997; Djellal and Gallouj, 2012).

Based on Sundbo and Gallouj (1998), service innovations could be categorized into five types: product innovation, process innovation, organizational innovation, market innovation and ad hoc innovation. Organizational innovations are new general forms of organization or management such as the introduction of TQM or self-steering groups. Process innovations are renewals of the prescriptive procedures for producing and delivering the service. The innovation process could be divided into two categories: innovations in production processes ("back office") or in delivery processes ("front office"). Market innovations are new behaviors in the market, e.g. finding a new market segment, entering another industry and its market (e.g. retailing starting to sell bank deposit accounts). Ad hoc innovation is defined as the interactive (social) construction of a solution (strategic, organizational, social, legal, etc.) to a particular problem posed by a client. This type of innovation is co-produced by the client and the service provider. It is not reproducible, as such, but indirectly through the codification, the formalization of part of the experience and the competence.

3.3 Financial Inclusion

By definition, financial inclusion is the "process of effective access and use of financial services by the population that fits its needs and contributes to its quality of life" (BCB, 2011). It is a relatively new term on the international agenda and has attracted more attention in the debate and scope of cooperation. In the sphere of the G-20, the *Financial Inclusion Experts Group* as well as the *Access Through Innovation Subgroup* (ATISG) and *Small and Medium Enterprise Finance* were created. At the G-20 Summit held in Pittsburgh (U.S.A.) in September 2009, the leaders pledged to increase the level of financial inclusion in the world, based on successful financing models for small and mid-sized businesses, as well as on studies to identify lessons learned around the world regarding innovative approaches towards providing financial services to the less fortunate (Itamaraty, 2013). In 2010, the Central Bank of Brazil, together with the Australian Department of Treasury, led the ATISG subgroup activities that defined the G-20 Principles for Innovative Financial Inclusion, which were endorsed by the Summit leaders in Toronto in June 2010.

Table 1. G-20 Principles for Innovative Financial Inclusion

PRINCIPLES	
1. Leadership	Cultivate a broad-based government commitment to financial inclusion to help alleviate poverty.
2. Diversity	Implement policy approaches that promote competition and provide market-based incentives for the delivery of sustainable financial access and usage of a broad range of affordable services (savings, credit, payments and transfers, insurance) as well as a diversity of service providers.
3. Innovation	Promote technological and institutional innovation as a means of expanding financial system access and usage, including addressing infrastructure weaknesses.
4. Protection	Encourage a comprehensive approach to consumer protection that recognizes the roles of government, providers, and consumers.
5. Empowerment	Develop financial literacy and financial capability.
6. Cooperation	Create an institutional environment with clear lines of accountability and coordination within the government; and also encourage partnerships and direct consultation across government, business, and other stakeholders.

7. Knowledge	Utilize improved data to develop evidence-based policy, measure progress, and consider an incremental "test and learn" approach by both regulators and service providers.
8. Proportionality	Build a policy and regulatory framework that is proportionate to the risks involved in such innovative products and services, based on understanding the gaps and barriers in existing regulation.
9. Framework	Consider the following in the regulatory framework, reflecting international standards, national circumstances and support for a competitive landscape: a) An appropriate, flexible, risk-based AML/CFT regime; b) Conditions for the use of agents as a customer interface; c) A clear regulatory regime for electronically stored value; d) Market based incentives to achieve the long-term goal of broad interoperability and interconnection.

Source: GPFI (2010).

According to the Central Bank of Brazil (BCB, 2012), the effort to increase and improve access of the population to financial services in Brazil, along with the recently promoted debate and efforts to diagnose the Brazilian reality with regards to the situation, has culminated in the identification of new challenges to continue promoting financial inclusion, with a focus on:

- Continuing to adapt the offer of financial services to the needs of the economy and population
- Increasing the level of financial education among the population in order to combat indebtedness
- Stimulating savings
- Strengthening protection mechanisms for financial services users
- Stimulating the development of sustainable productive microcredit
- Guaranteeing stability and promoting perfection of the correspondent model in the country and
- Deepening knowledge regarding the Brazilian reality in relation to financial inclusion.

An analysis of microfinance characteristics in the Latin American and Caribbean countries, conducted by The Economist Intelligence Unit

(2012), indicates that among the 55 countries considered, Peru, with a score of 79.8, and Bolivia, with 71.8, have the most developed microfinance markets. Brazil came 16th in the general ranking, 49.2, 21st in regulatory structure, 50.0, 3rd in environmental investment, 87.5, and 15th in institutional development, 50.0. A recent Microfinance Information Exchange survey shows that 43% of microfinance clients in Latin America are people whose income is below the poverty threshold (MIF, 2013).

For financial inclusion to be, in fact, comprehensive, guaranteeing that all economic agents in the country-people and businesses-the opportunity to benefit from financial services, which are appropriate to their needs, it is not merely necessary to expand the access channels between the population and the SFN. Appropriateness and sustainability of the process should also be considered. As such, it is necessary to adopt measures relative to both the financial services offer and demand. In relation to offer, it is important to induce the reduction of regional asymmetries in the provision of financial services, adapt the services offered to the needs of the users and the sustainability of the process. Regarding demand, it is necessary to give attention to financial education and user protection in such a way so as to guarantee that the use of financial services is sustainable and that it beneficial for all (BCB, 2012).

4. Innovative Financial Inclusion in Brazil

4.1 Microcredit

The Brazilian microfinance experience, as in most Latin American cases, has some features that are distinct from those in other parts of the world. Contrary to most places, where most initiatives in the sector would have originated from the private sphere of society, those in Brazil primarily originate from public initiatives or the result of government incentives programs, which have stimulated credit to low income population. Brazil can be considered as a world pioneer in experimenting with microcredit in the informal, urban sector, using instant credit and real interest; conditions that are considered today as fundamental in order to operate in this sector. The experience has achieved a reasonable client portfolio and has rapidly reached self-sustainability.

In the context of this study, microcredit is considered as "the concession of small loans to small, informal businesses and microbusinesses that do not have access to the traditional financial system, mainly for not having a means of offering real guarantees". It is credit destined to production (working capital and investment) conceded by means of a specific methodology (Barone, Lima, Dantas, Rezende, 2002).

4.1.1 History of Microcredit in Brazil

By means of the initiative and technical assistance of the NGO, Accion International, at the time-and the participation of business entities and local banks, the *Northeastern Union for Assistance to Small Organizations* (União Nordestina de Assistência a Pequenas Organizações), known as UNO, was created in 1973.

UNO was a non-governmental organization specializing in microcredit and training for non-registered, low-income laborers, whose operations were guaranteed by a type of "moral surety". Financial resources came from international donations and were later increased by other lines of credit. Concurrent to the concession of credit, the UNO trained its clients in basic management skills. The UNO financed millions of small businesses in the Brazilian states of Pernambuco and Bahia, trained dozens of professional credit specialists for the informal sector and for many years, was the main reference regarding the expansion of microcredit programs in Latin America. Though successful in the technical area, the UNO disappeared eighteen years later for not considering self-sustainability as a fundamental factor in its policies.

The second Brazilian project began in 1987 as a government program named *Ana Terra Center for Small Business Support* or CEAPE, which rapidly became an NGO, integrated the business class into its administration and sought its own resources from international development organizations. To carry out its plan, it counted on UNICEF, giving birth to a national network of microcredit organizations-the CEAPE network. Founded over ten years ago, it is today one of the largest and oldest microcredit portfolios in the country. In 1990, the *National Federation for Small Business Support* or CEAPE Nacional was created. The CEAPE entities are independently joined in the CEAPE network, but use the same methods of production-oriented credit and guidance support to businesses excluded from the traditional financial system.

In 1995, the Brazilian government in partnership with the *Bank of Brasília* or BRB, launched a public productive credit program named *BRB-Work* (BRB Trabalho). It was at first a governmental initiative destined to provide credit to informal economic activities. Financial execution was under the responsibility of BRB and the credit agents were local government employees.

In 1996, with the technical support of the *German Society for Technical Cooperation* or GTZ, the government of the city of Porto

Alegre, in the state of Rio Grande do Sul, framed a model organization that, since its inception, established transparency and partnership as its principles. The Portosol project, designated the *Community Credit Institution*, performs its activities by means of public initiatives and resources. The Portosol experience has attracted national attention, arousing interest by governmental departments and the business community in the sector. It has also motivated development agencies and public institutions to support the creation and strengthening of institutions dedicated to alternative common credit. Initial resources for Portosol came from donations by the Porto Alegre City Government, the Government of the State of Rio Grande do Sul, the *German Society for Technical Cooperation*, the Inter-American Foundation (IAF), financing from the *Brazilian Development Bank* (BNDES), and the *Brazilian Micro and Small Business Support Service* (SEBRAE).

Since 1996, the BNDES has stimulated Brazilian microfinances and by means of the *Popular Productive Credit Program*, offers a line of credit to Brazilian *Microfinance Institutions*. Based on an agreement signed with the Inter-American Development Bank, the BNDES created the *Institutional Development Program* with the objective of strengthening the microfinance industry in Brasil.

In Brazil, the CrediAmigo of the *Bank of the Northeast of Brasil* or BNB, is the most successful example of production-oriented microcredit among the 58 institutions connected with the PNMPO. Officially created in 1998 in partnership with the World Bank, CrediAmigo operates in more than 1800 communities in the Northeast Region, the Brazilian states of Minas Gerais and Espírito Santo and the cities of Brasília and Rio de Janeiro. CrediAmigo operates under the group joint-liability method and along with the concession of credit, offers financial management training for borrowers. All operations, including hiring Credit Agents, is done independently from bank activities.

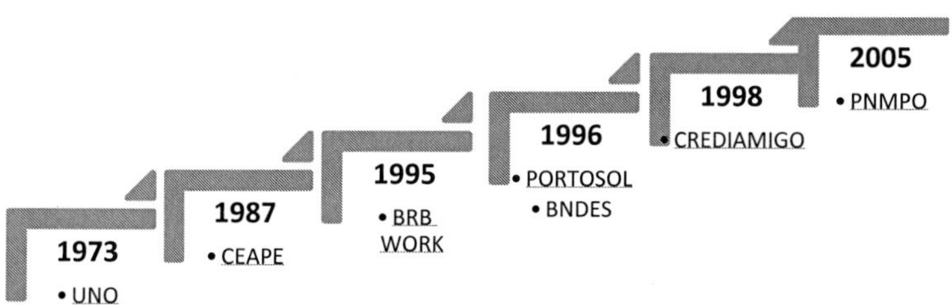

Figure 2. Timeline

4.1.2 The National Production-Oriented Microcredit Program (PNMPO)

Estimates regarding the potential Brazilian microcredit market reveal the existence of 9.5 million small businesses and about 13 million individuals that do not have access to credit through the traditional financial system. Thus, besides being an excellent business opportunity, microcredit is seen by national and international organizations as the most promising option to provide credit access to small business and, above all, those who need it at most (MTE, 2013a).

The evolving tendency in government policies over the last decades has been to stimulate a greater integration between formal financial institutions and those that offer microcredit, in order to guarantee low cost loan access to the population on the fringes of the financial system, make credit expansion possible by creating additional sources of microcredit finance and stimulate microcredit applications by public and private microcredit (Ribeiro, 2009). Production-oriented microcredit is credit given to meet the financial needs of individuals and small production companies, using methods based on a direct relationship to the business at the location where the economic activity is being carried out (MTE, 2013).

In production-oriented microcredit operations, it should be further considered that attending the business should be done by personnel trained to execute a socioeconomic analysis and give educational orientation about developing a business plan and defining credit and management needs directed towards the growing of the business. Contact with the entrepreneur should be maintained during the contract period under question, seeking the highest investment benefit as well as the growth and sustainability of the economic activity. The amount of the loan granted and credit conditions should be defined after an evaluation of the activity and credit worthiness of the borrower, in strict dialog with the same.

In April 2005, the *National Production Oriented Microcredit Program* or PNMPO was instituted under the authority of the Ministry of Employment and Labor or MTE. This program benefits all private and small production businesses, but with the differential of demanding a methodology based on the direct relationship between the credit agent and the micro-entrepreneur at the business location. Service is personalized and performed by people trained to advise the borrower regarding business management, credit needs, defining the loan amount and credit conditions after evaluating the activity and the ability to incur indebtedness. The main objectives of the PNMPO are to stimulate the generation of employment and income among informal micro-entrepreneurs, make resources available for production-oriented microcredit and offer technical support to production-oriented microcredit institutions, with a view of strengthening these institutions to provide lending services to informal entrepreneurs (MTE, 2013). The PNMPO is funded by resources from the *Labor Relief Fund* through the following institutions: the Bank of Brazil, Caixa Econômica Federal-Brazil's largest mortgage lender, Bank of the Northeast of Brazil, Bank of Amazonia and Brazilian Development Bank and by resources from deposits made via commercial banks and multiple banks with a commercial portfolio.

In 1999, through an initiative by the *Community Solidarity Council*-a governmental body tied to the Presidency of the Republic, regulation that establishes a certification process, which can be applied to a Non-Governmental Organization-NGO, in order to qualify it to become part of the *Public Interest Non-Governmental Organizations* (OSCIP) was developed. The microcredit NGO that obtains this certificate is not subject to the *Usury Law* (Lei da Usura), which prohibits non-regulated institutions from charging interest above one percent per month, or rather, well below the levels necessary to sustain a microcredit operation. This same law allows qualified organizations, such as OSCIP, to sign partnership agreements with governmental bodies, receive public funds for projects and use human resources from participants in volunteer programs without violating labor laws. Additionally, in 1999, the Central Bank of Brazil defined specific legislation that allows the creation of specialized, regulated entities: the *Micro-Entrepreneur Credit Societies* or SCM, which are closed capital, for profit, financial institutions that are exempt from the *Usury Law*.

Today, there is an increasing interest in the expansion of microcredit, especially in its "interiorization", since this service is practically non-existent in the North and Central-West regions of Brazil. Seeking to expand access to credit, SEBRAE has instituted a national microcredit support program focusing on the consolidation of institutions, securing resources to strengthen institutions, training human resources, funding and training micro-business entrepreneurs.

Between the creation of the PNMPO in April 2005 to December 2012, more than 13.7 million microcredit operations were performed for a total of R$ 19.4 billion. During the same period, there were 3.8 million Production-Oriented Microcredit operations by active clients, representing a total of R$ 6.2 billion. The average loans granted were for R$ 1,620.

Among active production-oriented microcredit clients, women have shown a strong presence as the principal group attended (62.6%). It is also worth noting that, considering the legal status of clients, informal laborers predominate (94.8%). In relation to the area of activity, a large concentration of clients is involved in commerce (72.7%). About 92 percent of Production-Oriented Microcredit resources are applied toward working capital.

Table 2. Active Portfolio by Legal Constitution in the 4th Quarter of 2012.

Legal Constitution	Value of Active Portfolio (R$ thousands)	
Factoring Agency	13,562	0.5%
Cooperative Bank	21,623	0.6%
Development Bank	1,619,932	49.0%
Credit Cooperative	100,181	3.0%
Financial Institutions	1,379,919	41.8%
OSCIP	169,525	5.1%
TOTAL	**3,304,742**	**100%**

Source: MTE (2013a)

Table 3. Production-Oriented Microcredit Clients by Credit Use-4th Quarter 2012.

Credit Use	Amount of Clients		Value (R$ thousands)	
Working Capital	1,997,522	91.9%	1,724	74.7%
Investment	156,064	7.2%	541	23.5%
Mixed	19,744	0.9%	42	1.8%
Total	**2,173,330**	**100%**	**2.306**	**100%**

Source: MTE (2013a)

4.1.3 The CrediAmigo Program

The CrediAmigo program of the Bank of the Northeast of Brazil (BNB) is the most successful example of production-oriented microcredit programs among the 58 institutions tied to the PNMPO. Officially created in 1998, in partnership with the World Bank, CrediAmigo operates in the Northeast region, the States of Minas Gerais and Espírito Santo and the cities of Brasília and Rio de Janeiro. CrediAmigo is a production-oriented microcredit program with the objective of providing easier access to credit for thousands of enterprises. Program establishment and client training occur by means of a partnership established between the Civil Society Organizations of Public Interest member *Northeast Citizenship Institute* (Instituto Nordeste Cidadania) and VivaCred. Based on the terms of partnership, the OSCIP are responsible for procuring businesses, from the first contact with the client through the post-sales follow-up.

Since 2003, the CrediAmigo/OSCIP *Northeast Citizenship Institute* partnership aims at contributing to the socioeconomic and cultural development of the urban and rural communities of the Northeast region and the States of Minas Gerais and Espírito Santo and the Federal District. In 2009 the partnership came to Rio de Janeiro by means of VivaCred. The main objective was the concession of credit to micro and small businesses, especially in the low income communities and their surrounding areas.

CrediAmigo made the Bank of the Northeast of Brazil the first public bank to have an operating model directed exclusively toward microcredit. Considered as an important tool for social inclusion and citizenship empowerment within its operational area, CrediAmigo uses a method based on the direct relationship with businesses and offers life insurance, loan insurance, business and environmental guidance and financial education to its checking clients (normal and simple).

The positive performance of CrediAmigo has become a reference for the sector, being chosen by the Federal Government as a model for the national microcredit program, (Programa Crescer). In 2011, CrediAmigo was responsible for 93% of the *Grow Program* contracts. Out of the 606 thousand operations, 565 thousand belong to the Bank productive microcredit, which lent R$ 565 million in the sphere of the program, launched by the Federal Government (BNB, 2012). CrediAmigo, as with a large portion of microcredit programs, has women as their main clients and 78% of the clients with a family income of less than R$ 1,500; showing its efficacy in attending those families with the lowest income. The program is present in over 1800 municipalities and, in April 2013, it reached about 1.4 million active clients, corresponding to the beneficiaries of resources conceded for informal production activities in the areas of industry, commerce and services. CrediAmigo has released resources above R$ 17 billion since its creation in 1998, having contracted more than 1 million in operations only in the period between January and April 2013 (BNB, 2013a).

4.2 Regional Sustainable Development Strategy

The *Regional Sustainable Development Strategy* or DRS, is a business strategy by the Bank of Brazil (BB) that seeks to stimulate the sustainable development of regions where the bank is present by means of mobilizing social and political economic agents to support economically, socially equitable and environmentally productive activities, while always observing and respecting cultural diversity. The DRS business strategy contributes to the generation of employment and income and the adoption of practices that permit an increase in social and environmental indicators with sustainable, inclusive solutions, always done together with partners within a process called "concertação" or "concertation" (BB, 2013).

Concertation, in the meaning of orchestration, is an integrated, harmonic action shared by several partners: economic agents, social agents, political agents and beneficiaries, promoting the articulation between persons and groups so as to act in synergy in favor of the sustainable development of the territory, involving all parts interested in the development of existing productive activities within their jurisdiction. Concertation is based on the participative principle and contributes to the mitigation of risks and reaching of positive results. It stimulates those involved to create solutions and conduct regional development initiatives under the perspective of sustainability, aggregating technical assistance, new technologies, training and consulting in all links of the value chain.

The desired results are the sustainable development of the regions involved, reduction of illiteracy, elimination of child and forced labor, professional training, access to information, and computerization, among others. The DRS business strategy proposes to promote social inclusion by means of the generation of work and income, the democratization of credit access, the stimulation of associations and cooperation, the contribution to the improvement of quality of life indicators and consolidation of business between rural and urban, micro and small businesses, whether formal or informal.

Currently, the DRS business strategy pursues productive activities such as agroforestry, tourism, hand crafts, ceramics from the Island of Marajoara, aquaculture, fruit growing, shoes, cotton growing, clothing, goat and sheep farming, beekeeping, horticulture, dairy and beef farming, manioc farming, mining, poultry farming and solid residue recycling.

4.2.1 DRS Business Strategy Methodology

The main success factor in the DRS business strategy is the participative and constructive principle in its methodology. Private initiatives, cooperatives, governments, universities, religious entities, and non-governmental organizations are partners in the planning, coordination and accompaniment in the process of sustainable regional development (BB, 2013a).

Table 4. DRS Business Strategy Methodology

Methodology		
Preparation Module	Sensitize and Train	This is the beginning of concertation. It covers contact with the actors that can enrich the process of considering the territory, understand its dynamics and identify local vocations and developed productive activities as well as its potentials and needs.
Preparation Module	Choose the Productive Activity	This consists of the participating group indicating the production activity that will be implemented under the guidance of the DRS strategy. The territory vision directs the study of potentials so the participating group can identify, among the existing production chains, the activities that are most in need of support and that present favorable conditions to implement the strategy. The choice of productive activity to be supported by the DRS strategy should favor the regional vocation and local knowledge while taking into consideration: economic viability, conditions to increase production or productivity, existence of a market able to absorb new products or a greater volume of production, ability of agents to use new technology and add value to products and potential of the activity to generate employment and income.
Preparation Module	Forming a Management Team	The management team should be composed of representatives of the beneficiaries and strategic partners and have as its main function the coordination of tasks, generation and implementation of the Business Plan and promotion of joint labor, division of tasks and planning in all phases of the process as well as integrating all other actors.
Structuring Module	Diagnostics	Diagnosis is construed from the collection of information that considers the internal processes (strengths and weaknesses) and external aspects (threats and opportunities) related to the chosen productive activity. Besides the collection of specific data regarding the activity, information regarding the territory, its economic, sociocultural, environmental, technological, infrastructure and market is researched. The data is systematized in such a way so as to permit a clear view of existing problems and potentials and allow the understanding of the current situation that is intended for change.
Structuring Module	DRS Business Plan	The Business Plan considers the description of scenarios, the intended objectives, budget, projected results, beneficiaries and actions to be implemented so as to promote the sustainable development of the chosen activity. Its preparation is done in a participative form based on the main questions identified in the analysis of the actual chain of production of the chosen activity.

Source: BB (2013a)

Table 4. DRS Business Strategy Methodology (Continued)

Methodology		
Structuring Module	Analysis and Reports	This covers analyses made before the implementation of the Business Plan, note: a) *Technical Analysis*-Performed by a professional, specialized in the areas of agronomy, veterinary medicine and zootechny. In cases of cattle farming, a report is sought regarding the technical viability of the proposed Plan, considering aspects of technical compatibility, production costs and budgets, market conditions, technical assistance and environmental impacts. b) *Bank Branch Report*-In this analysis, the manager expresses himself regarding the pertinence and consistency of information, the dedication of the partners to the proposed actions, the ability to execute the actions, the business perspective and adherence to the DRS objectives. c) *Adherence Analysis*-This is conducted by the bank operational area and has as its objective towards the evaluation of alignment of the proposal to the DRS concepts, premises and strategy objectives. d) *Risk Analysis*-This is done by the bank department responsible for evaluating business risk. The product of this analysis is the attribution of a risk index to the activity and the proposal of mitigating alternatives, if necessary. e) *Bank Superintendence Report*-Based on reports resulting from the different analyses; the superintendence defines orientation regarding the implementation or rejection of the proposed DRS Business Plan.
Management Module	Implementation of the DRS Business Plan	The materialization of what was planned and the signing of the Terms of Cooperation occur in this phase. Each partner is responsible for the planning and allocation of the required funds to bring about that is under their responsibility.
	Monitoring the DRS Business Plan	Monitoring and evaluation should be conducted in such a way so as to reveal inadequate operations, performance shortages or discrepancies between the established objectives and those obtained, making it possible to alter and redirect the actions in order to correct such deficiencies. To achieve the established objectives and performance levels, the monitoring and evaluation system should permit decision making, the maintenance of pre-established efficiency levels and project accompaniment.

Source: BB (2013a)

4.2.2 Results of the Regional Sustainable Development Strategy

In 2011, the volume of business done with beneficiaries of the DRS strategy, after the implementation of the Regional Sustainable Development Strategy Business Plan, reached a total of R$ 24,052 million. Seeking to improve the credit portfolio performance and contribute to the profitability of the DRS business strategy beneficiary clients, studies were conducted so as to identify the agencies, products, activities and beneficiaries with high exposure to credit loss and developed plans to mitigate the identified risks. Efficient activity in the DRS business portfolio repayment management resulted in a default rate of 0.6 percent in December 2011.

Table 5. DRS Business Results

Business Results	2008	2009	2010	2011
DRS Business Volume (in R$ millions)	4,676	7,803	13,299	24,052
Default (in %)	1.9	1.9	1.4	0.6

Source: BB (2013c).

By May 2013, the DRS strategy resulted in 4,098 Business Plans implemented in the 4,111 municipalities attended, serving about 1,470 thousand beneficiaries (BB, 2013b).

4.3 Banking Correspondents in Brazil

The offer of financial services by companies, whose main activity is not financial, has grown at an accelerated rate within the last years. New channels, such as banking, real-estate and fluvial correspondents, have significantly expanded their presentation in many ways, offering services through retail outlets, commercial establishments, lottery houses, post-offices, notary offices and water craft. Using partner infrastructures, banks amplify their presence in many geographic areas in order to offer financial services. The expansion of an alternative channel use, within the last years, can be explained by the fact that banks are making services available that are easy, convenient and secure; a fact that allows performing conventional banking operations without going to the bank branch.

4.3.1 Banking Correspondents

Banking correspondents offer to the population convenient access to banking services. Correspondents have become an alternative way of offering services and for retail banks to expand through new sales points, reaching a part of the population that, as of yet, does not have access to banking services and permitting geographic growth at a lower installation cost. The growth of an alternative channel use by clients means readapting the agency workforce, increasing focus on business and enlarging the fluidity of banks, as it permits attending the client by means of channels scattered to the most diverse points of the country.

Partnerships between banks and lottery houses, post-offices, supermarkets and drugstores are examples of banking correspondents that have low cost as an advantage over the traditional bank branch. According to the *Brazilian Banking Federation* or FEBRABAN (2013), in the period 2000-2012, the number of correspondents in the country increased from 19,000 to 161,000 service points.

Banking correspondents attend a population that does not require the services of a traditional bank branch and does not need a permanent relationship with a bank, such as in the maintenance of a checking account. According to the Central Bank of Brazil (2010), banking correspondents continue to be the principle channel by which bills and taxes are paid and credit transfers are executed. They are responsible for 36% of these types of transaction. The correspondent contract can have as its objective the following activities, while seeking to offer products and responsibility services by the contracted institution to its clients and users:

- Receive and forward proposals to open deposit, credit and savings accounts maintained by the contracting institution
- Receive deposits, payments and electronic transfers destined for the movement of deposit accounts maintained by the contracting institution and owned by clients
- Receipts and payments of any nature as well as other activities connected to the execution of contracts and agreements to provide services that are maintained by the contracting institution with third parties
- Active and passive execution of payment orders intermediated by the contracting institution when requested by clients and users
- Receive and forward proposals referent to credit and commercial lease conceded by the contracting institution
- Receipts and payments related to bills of exchange accepted by the contracting institution
- Execution of services related to extrajudicial collections relative to credit belonging to the contracting institution or its clients

- Receive and forward credit card proposals that will be the responsibility of the contracting institution and
- Perform exchange operations under the responsibility of the contracting institution.

Performing the complementary services of collecting application information and documentation, as well as the control and processing of data, can be included in the contract. The contracted acts on its own and within the policies of the contracting financial institution, which assumes entire responsibility for the customer service given to clients and users by means of the contracted company, which is responsible for guarantying the integrity, confidentiality, security and secrecy of the transactions performed, as well as the execution of legislation and regulations relative to these transactions.

4.3.2 Real-State Correspondents

Seeking to provide convenience to those clients who wish to finance their own home or grant easier credit concession, banks will transform real-estate agencies and builders into real-estate correspondents. These companies have the autonomy to receive and analyze the documentation necessary for home financing and perform the work that was previously done by bank employees. As a benefit, real-estate correspondents receive a percentage of the amount financed in order to bring in more clients. The companies answer all questions that clients may have regarding financing, perform simulations based on the buyer profile, complete the necessary forms and negotiate with the bank.

Work by correspondents reduces by half the time necessary to sign the financing contract. It is estimated that five days will be necessary to prepare the client documentation and that the contract can be signed at least ten days later. If the service were to be performed in a branch, the time needed would have been at least thirty days. Two reasons can explain part of the efficiency: the correspondent companies already know the process and avoid banal mistakes committed by clients and direct the documentation to those branches that have the least amount of contracts waiting to be signed.

4.3.3 Fluvial Correspondents

In November 2009, Bradesco Bank, Brazil's largest private bank, began to operate the first fluvial banking agency installed on the watercraft, *Voyager* III, which sails along the Solimões River in the Amazon region on a 1,600 km trajectory. It attends 50 communities and 11 municipalities with a population of about 250 thousand people. It is possible to open accounts, check balances, make withdrawals, deposits, transfers and account payments, apply for loans, buy pre-pay cell phone credits and receive credit cards. The watercraft makes the seven-day roundtrip up the Solimões River twice a month. Business is conducted on board by a manager, who also regularly visits residents in the communities situated along the banks of the river. He advises on how to open a bank account and how to use the bank products and services.

Analogously, in 2010, Caixa Econômica Federal, Brazil's largest mortgage lender, inaugurated the bank's first boat-branch. Its objective is to service the river populations that live in communities on the banks of the Amazon Basin, thereby increasing its service options and banking inclusion. The boat-branch will attend eight communities on the Solimões River between Manaus and Coari, covering an area larger than the States of Pernambuco and Sergipe together and a population of 253 thousand residents. Caixa Econômica Federal offers services such as opening accounts, providing social financial services, such as PIS payment and movement, Time of Service Guarantee Fund, Unemployment Insurance, and others, home financing, as well as production oriented microcredit and products such as Construcard (credit card for construction purposes) and consigned credit with payment deducted from the employee's payroll.

The Bank of Brazil, South America's largest retail bank, initiative to install correspondents on boats began in the State of Amazonas where three crafts have been in service since May 2011. In June 2012, the Bank of Brazil inaugurated the first fluvial correspondent in the State of Pará. The structure, which will make banking transactions possible, was set up on the Rodrigues Alves IV in partnership with Rede Ponto Certo. The craft, which serves as a means of public transport for the local population, sails 574 km on rivers in the Amazon Basin between the cities of Belém and Santarém, passing by the towns of Gurupá, Prainha, Breves and Monte Alegre. The population of the four cities, in which the ship docks, will have access to a branch located on the boat.

Using satellite communication technology, transactions with cash and debit cards can be executed, even with the boat being in motion, with the same convenience and security offered by conventional branches.

5. Conclusions

This chapter seeks to identify and characterize financial products and services offered by Brazilian banks that support the inclusion of segments of the population that are not served by the financial sector. The cases described in this chapter demonstrate that the use of innovative approaches can lower transaction costs for the banks and clients and enhance the efficiency and reliability of their delivery in products and services. In the context of innovative financial inclusion, this study contributes towards amplifying the understanding of the characteristics of innovations implemented in the Brazilian financial sector in order to set apart the offer of financial products and services.

Brazilian banking correspondents are known internationally as prime examples of branchless banking. The non-banking correspondent model has grown rapidly, with Brazil´s 165,000 correspondents now making it the world´s largest network of its kind. Brazil can be considered as the world's pioneer in experimenting with microcredit in the informal, urban sector, using instant credit and real interest, conditions that are today considered fundamental to operate in this sector. The DRS business strategy contributes to the generation of employment and income and the adoption of practices that permit an increase in social and environmental indicators with sustainable, inclusive solutions, always done together with partners in a process called "concertation".

The concept of financial inclusion remains under constant perfection regarding the variables used to define it as well as the incorporation of other pertinent factors. It is necessary to recognize that financial inclusion does not necessarily require the effective use of financial services by the public, but the real possibility of using such services if adapted to their needs. The decision to use them or not belongs to each individual. Another aspect to be considered, is related to the idea that the use of financial services should be sustainable, in the sense that they guarantee balance to society, the environment, the financial system and individually the users, while considering the concept of sustainability in its three dimensions: economic, social and environmental.

References

AFI. Alliance for Financial Inclusion, 2011. O 'Jeito Brasileiro' – The Brazilian Way: Brazil's engagement with standard setting bodies and the implications for financial inclusion. Retrieved from: http://www.gpfi.org/sites/default/files/documents/02%20Brazil.pdf.

ASBA. Association of Supervisors of Banks of the Americas, 2010. How to Contribute to Financial Inclusion? Inventory of Products and Services Available in the Region. Retrieved from: http://services.iadb.org/mifdoc/website/publications/9c6e93d5-7e00-4d60-904f-bcab92bd8fde.pdf.

Barone, F. M., Lima, P. F.; Dantas, V. & Rezende,V., 2002. Introduction to Microcredit (Introdução ao microcrédito). Brasília: Conselho da Comunidade Solidária.

BB. Banco do Brasil, 2013. Sustainability. What is DRS? (Sustentabilidade. O que é DRS.) Retrieved from: http://www.bb.com.br/portalbb/page3,8305,8369,0,0,1,6.bb

—. 2013a. Sustainability. Sustainable Regional Development (Sustentabilidade. Desenvolvimento Regional Sustentável – DRS). Retrieved from: http://www.bb.com.br/portalbb/page3,8305,8368,0,0,1,6.bb?codigoMenu=15244&codigoNoticia=28552&codigoRet=15306&bread=1

—. 2013b. DRS Goals and Results (Metas e Resultados DRS). Retrieved from: http://www50.bb.com.br/drs/jsp/consultas/consultarResultadosDPNPais/resultadosDPNPais.drs

—. 2013c. 2011 Annual Report. Sustainable Regional Development Strategy (Relatório Anual 2011. Estratégia Negocial Desenvolvimento Regional Sustentável). Retrieved from: http://www45.bb.com.br/docs/ri/ra2011/port/index.htm .

BCB. Banco Central do Brasil, 2010. Diagnosis of Retail Payment in Brazil – Statistic Addendum – 2009. Preliminary Version – July 2010 (Diagnóstico do Sistema de Pagamentos de Varejo do Brasil – Adendo Estatístico – 2009. Versão preliminar – Julho/2010). Retrieved from: http://www.bcb.gov.br/htms/SPB/Diagnostico-Adendo-2009.pdf.

—. 2011. *Financial Inclusion Report* (2011) (Relatório de Inclusão Financeira (2011). n.2. Retrieved from: http://www.bcb.gov.br/Nor/relincfin/RIF2011.pdf.

—. 2012. National Partnership for Action Plan for Institutional Environment Strengthening – 2012 (Parceria Nacional para Plano de Ação para Fortalecimento do Ambiente Institucional (2012). Retrieved from: http://www.bcb.gov.br/nor/relincfin/Plano_de_Acao_PNIF.pdf.

BNB. Banco do Nordeste, 2013. 2011 Crediamigo Annual Report (Relatório Anual Crediamigo 2011). Retrieved from: http://www.banconordeste.gov.br/content/aplicacao/produtos_e_servicos/crediamigo/docs/relatorio_2011_portugues.pdf

—. 2013a. Crediamigo – Results (Crediamigo – Resultados). Retrieved from:

http://www.banconordeste.gov.br/content/aplicacao/Produtos_e_Servicos/Crediamigo/gerados/Resultados.asp.

Djellal, F. & Gallouj, F, 2012. Two Decades of Research on Innovation in Services: which place for public services?. Proceedings of The International EIBURS-TAIPS TAIPS Conference on: "Innovation in the public sector and the development of e-services". University of Urbino. April 19-20, 2012.

Economist Intelligence Unit, 2012. Global microscope on the microfinance business environment. Retrieved from: http://www1.ifc.org/mwg-internal/de5fs23hu73ds/progress ?id=Bd9W17R5/Z

FEBRABAN. Federação Brasileira de Bancos, 2013. Banking Sector in Numbers 2013 (Setor bancário em números 2013). Retrieved from: http://www.febraban.org.br/7Rof7SWg6qmyvwJcFwF7I0aSDf9jyV/sitefebraban/Pesquisa%20FEBRABAN%20de%20Tecnologia%20Banc%E1ria%202013.pdf

Gallouj, F., Weinstein, O. (1997), Innovation in services. *Research Policy* 26 (4-5), p. 537-556.

GPFI. Global Partnership for Financial Inclusion. Innovative Financial Inclusion, 2010. Principles and Report on Innovative Financial Inclusion from the Access through Innovation Sub-Group of the G20 Financial Inclusion Experts Group (2010). Retrieved from: http://www.gpfi.org/sites/default/files/documents/Principles%20and%20Report%20on%20Innovative%20Financial%20Inclusion_0.pdf.

Hamel, G, 2000. Liderando a Revolução (Leading the Revolution). Rio de Janeiro: Campus.

ITAMARATY. Ministry of External Relations, 2013. G-20 Pittsburgh Summit – Leaders Declaration (Ministério das Relações Exteriores (2013). G-20 Cúpula de Pittsburgh – Declaração dos Líderes). Retrieved from: http://www.itamaraty.gov.br/temas/temas-multilaterais/governanca-global/g-20-financeiro/g-20-declaracao-de-pittsburgh.

Jaramillo, H. ; Lugones, G. & Salazar, M, 2000. Normalización de Indicadores de Innovación Tecnológica para América Latina Y el Caribe (Indicator Standardization in Innovative Technology for Latin America and the Caribbean) (Manual de Bogotá). Bogotá: OAS; COLCIENCIAS; RICYT y OcyT.

MIF. Multilateral Investment Fund, 2013. *Microfinance in China and Latin America*. Retrieved from: http://services.iadb.org/mifdoc/website/publications/b6bc2d1a-4724-4402-ae90-b73f49ef224f.pdf.

MTE. Ministério do Trabalho e Emprego, 2013. National Production Oriented Microcredit Program - PNMPO (Programa Nacional de Microcrédito Produtivo Orientado - PNMPO). Retrieved from: http://portal.mte.gov.br/pnmpo/esclareca-suas-duvidas.htm#quem.

—. 2013. Report on Microcredit Program Data – 4th Quarter 2012 (Relatório de Dados do Programa de Microcrédito – 4º. Trimestre de 2012). Retrieved from: http://portal.mte.gov.br/data/files/8A7C812D3D63BE8D013DAC992AC55317/Relat%C3%B3rio%204%C2%BA%20Trimestre%202012.pdf

OECD. Organisation for Economic Co-operation and Development, 2005. Oslo Manual: Proposed Guidelines for Collecting and Interpreting Technological Innovation Data, 3rd edition – Paris: OECD.

Ribeiro, D. A., 2009. Microcredit as a Means for Social Development (Microcrédito como Meio de Desenvolvimento Social). Dissertação. Curso de Mestrado em Direito Empresarial. Nova Lima: Faculdade de Direito Milton Campos.

Rogers, E. M, 1995. Diffusion of Innovations. 4th ed. New York: Free Press.

Selltiz, C, 1974. et al. Research Methods in Social Relations (Métodos de pesquisa nas relações sociais). São Paulo: Pedagógica e Universidade de São Paulo.

Silva, M. & Ferreira, J. J. A, 2005. A Contribution to the Study of Innovative Companies in Brazil. (Uma Contribuição ao Estudo das Empresas Inovadoras no Brasil). Tese. Curso de Doutorado em Engenharia da Produção. São Paulo: Escola Politécnica. Universidade de São Paulo.

Silva, M, 2010. A Contribution to the Study of Innovative Companies in Brazil. Proceedings of DRUID Summer Conference 2010. Imperial College London Business School, June 16 - 18, 2010. Retrieved from: http://www2.druid.dk/conferences/viewpaper.php?id=501969&cf=43.

Sundbo, J. & Gallouj, F, 1998. Innovation in Services. SI4S Project synthesis. Work package 3/4. European Commission. August, 1998.

Van De Ven, A.H.; Angle, H. L. & Poole, M. S, 2000. Research on the Management of Innovation: The Minnesota Studies. New York: Oxford.

Yin, R. K, 2005. Case Study: Planning and Methods (Estudo de Caso: Planejamento e métodos). 3ª ed. Porto Alegre: Bookman.

Acknowledgements

I would like to thank the following people and organizations that have contributed to the success and implementation of this project: my professors Dr. José Joaquim do Amaral Ferreira and Dr. Guilherme Ary Plonski of the Escola Politécnica at the University of São Paulo, for their valuable teaching and contributions along the journey; Dr. Anne-Laure Mention of the CRP Henri Tudor for the opportunity to put this project together; Mr. Mark Evans and all the independent reviewers for their comments and suggestions; my colleagues at the Banco do Brazil for their friendship and companionship; and my wife, Beth, and children, Jamile, Arthur and João Vitor, for their understanding, incentive and love.

CHAPTER FOUR

BANKS AND PATENTS IN THE U.S.[1]

FRANCESCA ARNABOLDI AND PETER CLAEYS

1. Introduction

Innovation benefits the economy as a whole and it is of particular relevance for the banking industry (Lerner and Tufano, 2011). The relationship between the development of an economy's financial structure and economic growth is well documented in the literature (Levine, 1997). The banking industry used to be seen as a general-purpose technology that supports investment in other productive sectors. Innovation in banking might therefore have potentially large effects on the overall economic progress. The financial crisis that started in 2007 dashed those beliefs, as excessive risk-taking in some specialized innovative products, like securitization, has brought down the financial system and produced the deepest and most prolonged economic crisis since the Great Depression. Recent studies now blame the excessive growth of financial economy as detrimental to the growth of the real economy (Levine, 2005). Innovation is a double edged-sword: favourable conditions that may spur banks to invest in new technologies can deliver growth, but too much of innovation can have serious consequences on a bank's risk profile (Beck et al., 2012).

The features of innovation in the banking sector are quite different from the characteristics usually encountered in other sectors. First, and in contrast to innovation in the manufacturing sector, financial innovation is hard to define. For Frame and White (2004, p. 118), "financial innovation represents something that reduces costs, reduces risks or provides an improved product/service/instruments". Financial innovation is primarily defined as product and organizational innovation, which allows cost or

[1] While the chapter is the result of intense collaboration between the two authors, sections 1 and 2 are attributable to F. Arnaboldi and section 3 to P. Claeys. Section 4 is a joint effort. The authors wish to thank V. Coppola for research assistance.

risk reduction for the single bank and/or an improvement of the services for the financial system as a whole. Banks do not usually have a research and development (R&D) department that launches new products and services. Most of new services are developed in an incremental way, often through "trial and error" and in all parts of the business. They are not always tangible and this complicates the registration of a new activity as innovation.

Second, banks are not the only developers of financial innovation. The banking sector is also an end-user of innovations developed in other sectors. Sometimes banks jointly develop innovations with non-financial firms, such as software houses or specialized technology firms. But very often, innovation happens thanks to the interaction with clients and so it is spread all over the departments. Like other firms, banks invest in innovation if they see this investment as a way of gaining a competitive advantage by reducing costs and raising profits. The product mix determines the choice of innovation (Berger and Mester, 2003). For instance, in order to stand out from the competitors, banks may have a stronger incentive to invent new products or to add new features to existing services in order to satisfy client's needs. The size of the firm can also play an integrative role. Larger banking groups receive a more stable flow of income, so they obtain a strategic advantage over other banks as it comes to innovation (Nickerson and Sullivan, 2003). Size makes it also easier to diversify business risk by starting up a variety of innovative projects (Corrocher, 2006). Larger banks can more easily assume the business risk of innovating. Innovation requires a large initial investment and is subject to technological, managerial and legal difficulties (Furst et al., 2002). A large bank is also more likely to possess the specialized complementary assets, necessary for the commercial success of innovation such as marketing and distributing services.

Both of the abovementioned features make the measurement of financial innovation a challenge. Because of the paucity of data, studies of financial innovation mostly concentrate on the cost savings or increased returns that financial intermediaries and clients may gain by the introduction of new products or processes. Frame and White (2004) identify only three studies that look at the origins of financial innovation: Ben-Horim and Silber (1977) and Lerner (2002, 2006a). Studies of manufacturing innovation traditionally focus on R&D spending. However, R&D is unlikely to be a satisfactory measure in banking, since banks rarely report such data (Lerner and Tufano, 2011). A count, based on the listings of new securities is not satisfactory either, since much of the innovation in financial services is not related to publicly traded securities, such as insurance and banking products (Lerner and Tufano, 2011). Furthermore, new securities are often minor variants of existing securities, issued by banks to differentiate themselves from competitors (Tufano, 2003). Lerner (2006a) develops a measure of financial innovation based on news items in the *Wall Street Journal* related to new financial products, services, or institutions. However, some innovation may not be reported in newspapers because it has no direct appeal to the reader. Some studies on innovation in the banking industry attempt to catalogue one particular type of innovation, such as credit default swaps or securitization (Tufano 2003). However these results cannot be easily generalized to other products.

A recent suggestion is to consider patents by financial institutions. Banks have started registering patents on their innovation activities only recently compared to manufacturing (Hall et al., 2009; Lerner, 2006b). A growing literature has emphasized the role of patent laws in creating incentives to invent, promoting innovation and encouraging economic growth (Moser, 2013). Patent system increases private incentives for innovation as it grants a temporary monopoly (Hall and Ziedonis, 2001). However, a patent system carries costs as well, because patenting may weaken incentives to invest in R&D for later generation (Scotchmer, 1991). Patentability protects innovation but does not discourage its diffusion *per se*.[2]

Financial innovation patentability is still in the making. A first reason is that historically legal protection of financial innovation has been weak relative to manufacturing, in particular because of the problem of clearly defining and identifying financial innovation. In the US, patents for financial formulas and methods could be awarded by the US Patent and Trademark Office (USPTO) since at least the early 1970s (Lerner, 2002). However, they have become increasingly frequent only since the 1998 trial decision in a lawsuit between Signature Financial Group and State Street Bank, which established the patentability of financial and other business methods "as such" (State Street vs. Signature Financial Group 149 F.3d 1368, Fed Cir 1998). In Europe, according to Article 52 of the European Patent Convention, business methods cannot be patented if they are not

[2] Lamoroeaux and Sokoloff (1999) link the increase in US patenting in the late nineteenth century with the emergence of professional patents agents whose role was to facilitate the trade in patented ideas. Investors may be more willing to share technical information to competitors if they feel protected by patents, especially in industries where secrecy is not effective, such as the banking industry (Moser, 2013). Recently Boldrin and Levine (2013) make a case against patents, pointing out that academic studies have typically failed to find much of a connection between patents, innovation and productivity growth.

related to other patentable topics, such as software (European Patent Office, 2000).[3] A second reason is that regulation of the banking industry has required a high level of transparency which, together with a weak appropriability regime, favours a rapid diffusion and imitation of innovations by competitors (Hunt, 2008). Financial services and in particular banking services are characterized by network externalities and a strong demand for standardization. A final reason is that litigation over patent validity is frequent and carries costs. Such high uncertainty about enforceability lowers incentives to invest in innovation but does not eliminate them completely (Hall et al., 2009). Against this background, patent counts have been used by Lerner (2006a) to measure innovation. The author uses patent counts as an alternative measure of innovation to address possible concerns about the originally proposed measure of news reports in the financial press. He investigates financial innovation and patents promoted by public entities in a wide variety of industries, ranging from computer programming and publishers to motor vehicle manufacturers. The most frequent innovators, according to the count of news stories, also appear in the list of leading patentees, confirming the validity of patent count as a viable solution to measure innovation.

Indeed, in contrast to manufacturing, legislation does not provide a precise definition of what it is meant by a financial patent and this shows up in the larger litigation rate on financial rather than on manufacturing patents (Lanjouw and Schankerman, 2001; Lerner, 2006b). Literature has tried to fill in the gap by defining financial patents as patents related to financial innovation. Broadly speaking, patents in class 705 are considered as financial patents (Hall et al., 2009). According to the United States Patent Classification System, this class includes data processing, financial, business practice and management or cost/price determination.[4]

---

[3] Article 52 on patentable inventions of the European Patent Convention states the following: "(1) European patents shall be granted for any inventions, in all fields of technology, provided that they are new, involve an inventive step and are susceptible of industrial application. (2) The following in particular shall not be regarded as inventions within the meaning of paragraph 1: (a) discoveries, scientific theories and mathematical methods; (b) aesthetic creations; (c) schemes, rules and methods for performing mental acts, playing games or doing business, and programs for computers; (d) presentations of information. (3) Paragraph 2 shall exclude the patentability of the subject-matter or activities referred to therein only to the extent to which a European patent application or European patent relates to such subject matter or activities as such."

[4] According to the January 2012 classification definitions available on the US Patent and Trademark Office (USPTO) website, class 705 "is the generic class for apparatus and corresponding methods for performing data processing operations,

Furthermore, banks have been awarded non-financial patents, defined as patents classified in any classes but 705. In addition to these two groups of patents (financial vs. non-financial) a third one, formed by non-financial patents which may have additional financial content, is investigated. Indeed, the US Patent and Trademark Office (USPTO) may provide not only the original class and subclass where innovation has been registered but also cross-reference class and subclass. Thus a patent not originally registered in class 705 may be cross-referenced to class 705. The subject matter of these patents can be additionally considered as financial.

Against this background, we analyse patents awarded to the US banking sector starting from the change in business methods patentability, introduced by the State Street case in 1998, and the relationship between patents and bank performance. First, we compile an original dataset which includes all patents granted to banks in the US over the period 1998-2012 as reported by the US Patent and Trademark Office. We depart from previous studies in three ways: (a) we do not focus on applications but on patents awarded, thus limiting our investigation to successful applicants; (b) we exclusively investigate the banking sector, because of its distinctive features; (c) we consider both public and private banks and both financial and non-financial patents.

Then we analyse the main features of patents. We identify in our sample those patents registered in class 705 and the relative subclasses, and describe their contents. In addition, we investigate which kind of non-financial patents have been granted to banks. We do so by analysing the US class and subclass codes which differ from class 705.

We examine the relationship between patents and bank performance, using several indicators. We look at the cross-section features of patentees and see what characterises them. We also compare bank size, risk, performance, and efficiency across patentees, merging the patent dataset with bank data from Fitch-Bureau Van Dijck Bankscope.

Our contribution to the existing literature is twofold: to our knowledge, this is the first study to examine, in detail, patents awarded since 1998 by

---

in which there is a significant change in the data or for performing calculation operations wherein the apparatus or method is uniquely designed for or utilized in the practice, administration, or management of an enterprise, or in the processing of financial data. This class also provides for apparatus and corresponding methods for performing data processing or calculating operations in which a charge for goods or services is determined. This class additionally provides for the subject matter described in the two previous paragraphs together with "cryptographic apparatus or method" (http://www.uspto.gov/web/patents/classification/selectnumwithtitle.htm).

the US Patent and Trademark Office to financial institutions. We believe patenting has unique features in the banking sector, because of its peculiarity in terms of regulation, network externalities and standardisation. Second we investigate the relationship between patenting and bank risk-adjusted performance, which has been deeply affected by the recent financial crisis.

The remainder of this work is structured as follows: section 2 describes the newly compiled dataset, with particular reference to the number and classification of patents. Section 3 offers an insight on patents granted to banks in the US, taking into account bank-specific features. Finally, section 4 concludes.

2. Dataset

To select the sample we perform a search on the US Patent and Trademark Office website and look for all the assignee names that pertain to financial institutions from 1976 to 2012. A general consensus in the productivity literature is that the filing date of patent applications, rather than their award dates matters. Unfortunately, the processing time for these awards varies over time (Lerner, 2006a) and would limit the time period over which we can examine patents. Moreover, applications are often held confidential in the United States prior to award, so we cannot determine how many applications each bank has made per year. This also implies that the number of patents may result slightly lower for banks that have merged or been taken over, as the patent has been attributed to the bidder bank.

We detect a total of 1,487 granted patents over this period.[5] Just 510 patents were granted between 1976 and 1997. As bank-specific data from Bankscope are scarcely available on comparable standards before 1998, we exclude patents granted before this date. The final sample is formed by 977 patents from 58 patentees. The sample includes banks classified as commercial banks, savings banks, bank holding and holding companies in Bankscope.[6] They can be fairly referred to as deposit taking and loan

[5] This number is smaller compared to the number of patents released in previous studies, such as in Lerner (2006a), because we focus on patents granted to banks. In fact financial institutions have a small share of patents: 26% in the US and 11% in the EU (Tufano, 2003; Hall et al., 2009).

[6] According to Bankscope classification, commercial banks are mainly active in a combination of retail banking (individuals, SMEs), wholesale banking (large corporates) and private banking (not belonging to groups of saving banks, co-operative banks). Savings banks are mainly active in retail banking (individuals,

making institutions. The sample starts with the State Street case, and includes the beginning of the liquidity crisis (August 2007), the Lehman failure (September 2008) and the unfolding of the crisis as it infected the financial system globally (Brunnermeier, 2009).

Figure 1 reports the total number of granted patents per year. Following the decision in the lawsuit between Signature Financial Group and State Street Bank, the number of patents granted to banks has started to rise continuously. A first wave of awards occurs in the years after the 2001 economic crisis, but then declines after 2005. A second wave, which reaches its peak in 2008, with 127 awarded patents, can be reasonably explained by the higher number of applications before the crisis. Indeed, studies in manufacturing suggest that the lag between the patent application filing and the R&D activity is minimal (Hall et al., 1986). The effects of the financial crisis have been felt on patenting activity. Only 5 patents have been granted in 2012, well below the annual average of the entire period (65 patents per year). The strong decline of granted patents after 2008 has been caused by shifts in the tax burden, regulatory changes, and the overall economic environment. A tax policy change may prevent the introduction of new financial instruments geared to taxpayers' particular needs or reduce bank profitability from the sale of innovative products. Regulatory changes may impose limits to the negotiations of new financial products or introduce heavy reporting requirements. A deterioration of the overall economic environment may reduce bank expenditure in new financial products. The general idea is that innovative banks engaged in excessive risk taking, causing them to make larger losses during the crisis (Diamond and Rajan, 2009, Bebchuk and Spamann, 2010; Beltratti and Stulz, 2012). In addition, some banks were required to take over illiquid peers, like JP Morgan acquiring Bear Stearns.

SMEs) and usually belonging to a group of savings banks. Bank holdings and holding companies are typically holding companies of bank groups, which may have limited business activities. We are aware of differences among these groups and we further investigate such differences in the next section, but for the sake of readability, we refer to them as commercial banks in the remaining of this section. Central banks supervise the national banking systems.

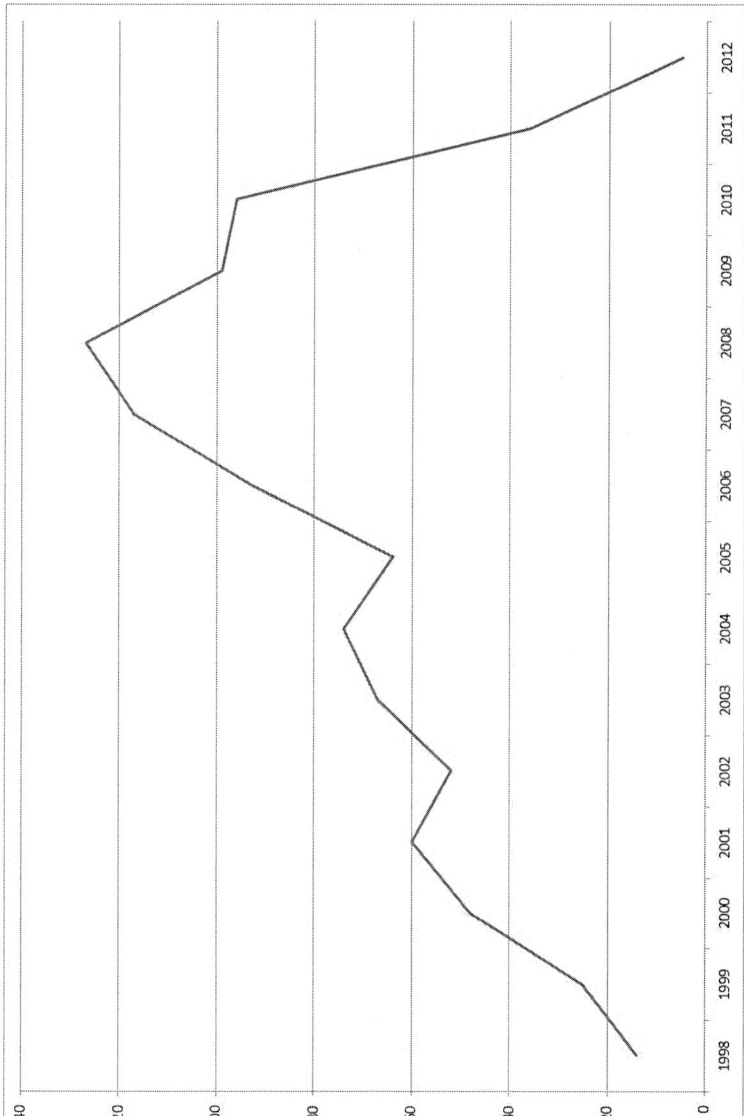

Figure 1. Patent grants per year (1998-2012). Source: Developed by authors based on http://www.uspto.gov

As previously mentioned, the sample includes both financial and non-financial patents and they are almost equivalent in percentage (49.5 vs. 50.1 percent respectively). Considering financial patents, banks patent innovations in about 60 different subclasses of class 705. However, more than 50 percent of financial patents are classified in only four subclasses out of 60. The most frequent subclass is finance e.g., banking, investment or credit (subclass 35). This subclass refers to computerized arrangements for planning the disposition or use of funds or securities, or extension of credit. Under this subclass definition, subclass 38, 36R and 39 are indented. They refer respectively to credit risk processing or loan processing, such as the computerized arrangement for evaluation of the risk factors in a mortgage; to portfolio selection, planning or analysis, referring to computerized arrangement for planning the selection or evaluation of securities or other investments; and to funds transfer or credit transaction.

In the other relevant subclasses, subject matters are the programming of a portable memory device, like for instance the "electronic purse"; the trading or exchange of securities or commodities within an organized system; the bill distribution or payment; risk analysis; the processing of a paper document authorizing the transaction check as part of the funds transfer operation; and the computerized arrangement to accept for deposit or convey for withdrawal, a financial document or currency. Table 1 lists the pre-eminent US subclass codes, the number of financial patents and the cumulative percentage. We do not report all subclasses of class 705, because it would excessively burden the table, but we list the subclasses where at least ten patents had been registered.

Table 1. Financial patents (class 705): most frequent subclass codes

US subclass code	US subclass label: Automated electrical financial or business practice or management arrangement	Number of patents	Cumulative percentage
35	Finance	92	18,9%
38	Credit (risk) processing or loan processing	66	32,6%
36R	Portfolio selection, planning or analysis	51	43,2%
39	Including funds transfer or credit transaction	46	52,7%
41	Having programming of a portable memory device	30	58,9%
37	Trading, matching or bidding	29	64,8%

40	Bill distribution or payment	28	70,5%
7.28	Risk analysis	13	73,1%
45	With paper check handling	12	75,6%
43	Including Automatic Teller Machine	10	77,6%

Source: Developed by authors based on http://www.uspto.gov

Turning to non-financial patents, the sample comprises patents awarded to 77 different classes. However, once again the first five classes account for about 50 percent of non-financial patents. Class 235 includes registers, class 707 is for computerized data processing systems and corresponding methods for the retrieval of records stored in a database or as computer files, class 382 is for automated image analysis or recognition of a pattern, class 709 provides for an electrical computer or digital data processing system or corresponding data processing between a plurality of computers, and class D14 refers to design patents claiming ornamental designs for, among others, computer, data processor, facsimile, and telegraph equipment. These classes refer to equipment and systems that can have a variety of applications in banking. For example, cash registers are classified in class 235. Even if the machine is not a financial innovation *per se*, its purpose of keeping a check upon the financial transactions is a good fit to the banking business. Table 2 reports the most relevant US class codes for non-financial patents, the number of patents granted to each class and the cumulative percentage.

Table 2. Non-financial patents: most frequent class codes

US class code	US class label	Number of patents	Cumulative percentage
235	Registers	89	18,0%
707	Data processing: database, data mining, and file management or data structures	47	27,6%
382	Image analysis	42	36,2%
709	Electrical computers and digital processing systems: multicomputer data transferring	37	43,8%
D14	Recording, communication, or information retrieval equipment	37	51,3%
726	Information security	27	56,7%
D19	Office supplies, artists' and teachers' materials	26	61,9%

713	Electrical computers and digital processing systems: support	22	66,3%
715	Data processing: presentation processing of document, operator interface processing and screen saver display processing	12	68,7%
714	Error detection/correction and fault detection/recovery	11	70,9%
340	Communications: electrical	10	72,9%

Source: Developed by authors based on http://www.uspto.gov

We further investigate the issue of non-financial patents which may have an additional financial content by checking the cross-reference class of patents in the USPTO database. Seventy-five non-financial patents (about 15 percent of the non-financial patents subsample) provide class 705 as cross-reference class.[7] Most of these patents are related to automated electrical financial or business practice, including remote banking, automatic teller machine, or with paper check handling. Thus innovation related to physical equipment is combined with financial innovation.

We now investigate the main features of patenting banks. Following the literature, the most frequent patentees (recurrent patentees) are those banks that were awarded more than six patents over the period of 1998-2012. Figure 2 reports the distribution of both financial and non-financial patents awarded to recurrent and occasional patentees. Recurrent patentees accumulate 93 percent of all patents and their importance is growing over time. Indeed in the last seven years they have been awarded 96 percent of all patents, whereas from 1998 to 2004 the figure was lower (87 percent). Occasional patentees only account for seven percent of the total number of patents.

The list of recurrent patentees is reported in Table 3 below. On a total of 58 patentees, the two leading patentees, Bank of America Co. and JP Morgan Chase, together account for 84 percent of all patents awarded. There are a few other financial institutions that obtain the remaining 16 percent of patents. Wells Fargo and Bank One have been granted more than

---

[7] The remaining 75 per cent of the non-financial patents subsample (more than 400 patents) either has been patented only in one class-for instance class 15, subclass 352: "Brushing, scrubbing, and general cleaning machines with air blast or suction, with dust or dirt handling or storing or separating (e.g. filter bags) and separator element cleaning in situ and/or storage or removal of retained dirt" – or has been patented in more than one class but the cross-reference class differs from class 705.

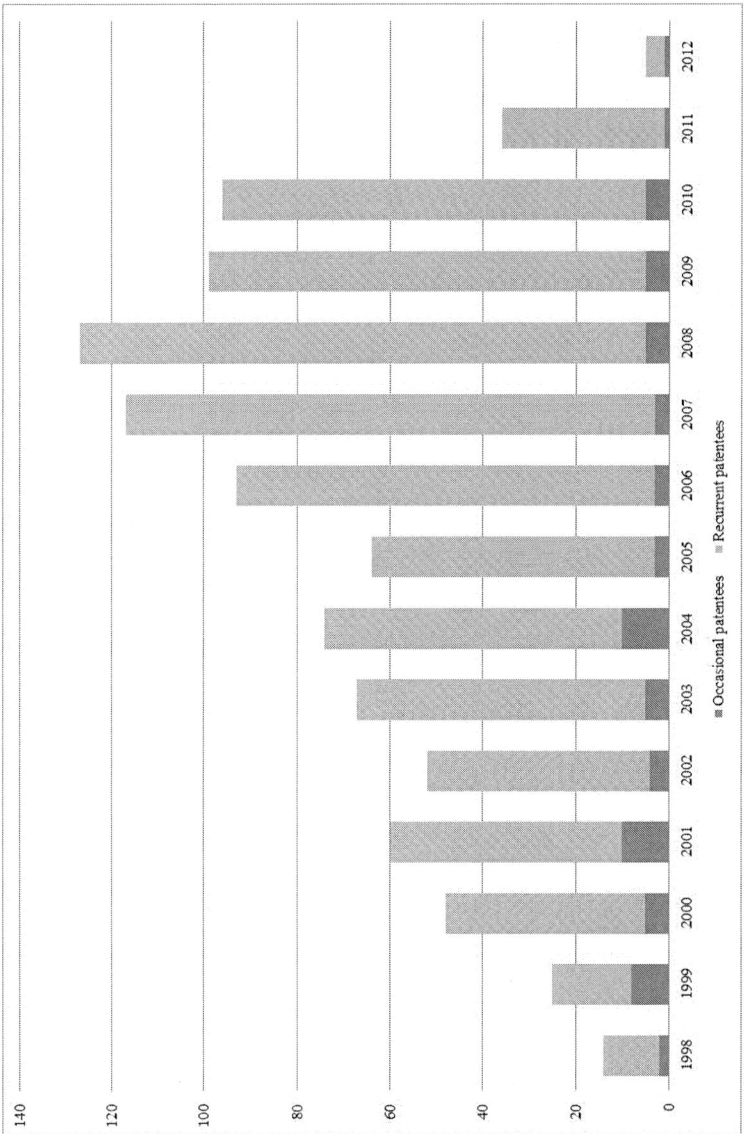

Figure 2. Distribution of patents awarded to recurrent and occasional patentees (1998-2012). Source: Developed by authors based on http://www.uspto.gov

20 patents each (59 and 23 patents, respectively). Four of the 12 District Banks of the Federal Reserve System are also among the main patentees. Together, the Federal Reserve banks have been awarded four percent of all patents. At first sight this may seem surprising, since the Federal Reserve banks are subsidiaries of the US central bank and are clearly not profit-oriented commercial banks, which may receive economic benefits from innovation patenting. However, the Federal Reserve banks have been granted patents related to their monitoring and fraud prevention activities, like for example patents to prevent duplicative electronic check processing or on methods and systems for screening financial transactions. More information is provided later in this section. Also, two foreign banks, Bank of Tokyo-Mitsubishi and Barclays Bank have been continuously active in US patenting, yet they barely reach two percent of the patent sample.

Table 3. Recurrent patentees (1998-2012)

Patentee	Total patents
Bank of America	387
JP Morgan	362
Wells Fargo Bank	59
Bank One	23
Federal Reserve Bank of Atlanta	15
Federal Reserve Bank of Kansas City	11
Bank of Tokyo - Mitsubishi UFJ Ltd	11
Federal Reserve Bank of Cleveland	10
Barclays Bank	8
Federal Reserve Bank of Dallas	7
Silicon Valley Bank	7
Bank of New York Mellon Corporation	7
Total	907
Percentage of the full sample	93%

Source: Developed by authors based on http://www.uspto.gov

Among the 58 patentees, 41 banks are incorporated in the US, while 17 are foreign banks. The latter are incorporated in various countries, such as Australia, Canada, China, Japan, Great Britain and the Netherlands but run part of their business in the US banking market. British and Japanese banks account for 82 percent of all foreign patentees. They applied for patent recognition in the US for various reasons. First in the US the legal protection of innovation is stronger than in other countries. Banks may prefer to apply for patenting where their invention could be more easily ascertained and protected. Analysing the content of those patents, indeed most of them are related to business methods and systems, which are protected by the US legal framework. Second, foreign banks patent their innovation in the US because they are global players. Patenting in the US is a mean to protect their innovation from local competitors and run their business smoothly. Figure 3 shows that the distribution of patents awarded to foreign banks is always a marginal phenomenon. From 1998 to 2012 only 26 patents have been awarded to foreign banks (about 3 percent of the sample). The distribution of foreign patentees is skewed. The two main foreign patentees, The Bank of Tokyo-Mitsubishi and Barclays Bank, account for 63 percent of all patents awarded to foreign institutions. Foreign banks have been granted patents in the US from the second half of the 2000s but stopped doing so in 2010, when the crisis became global and affected the country of origin of foreign banks as well.

If we now consider the subject matter of patents granted to foreign banks, 50 percent are financial patents, as in the full sample. They are related to portfolio selection, planning or analysis, to trading and to funds transfer or credit transactions. On the other hand, non-financial patents include, among others, electrical computers and digital processing systems between a plurality of computers, recording, communication or information retrieval equipment, furnishings, or dynamic magnetic information storage or retrieval.

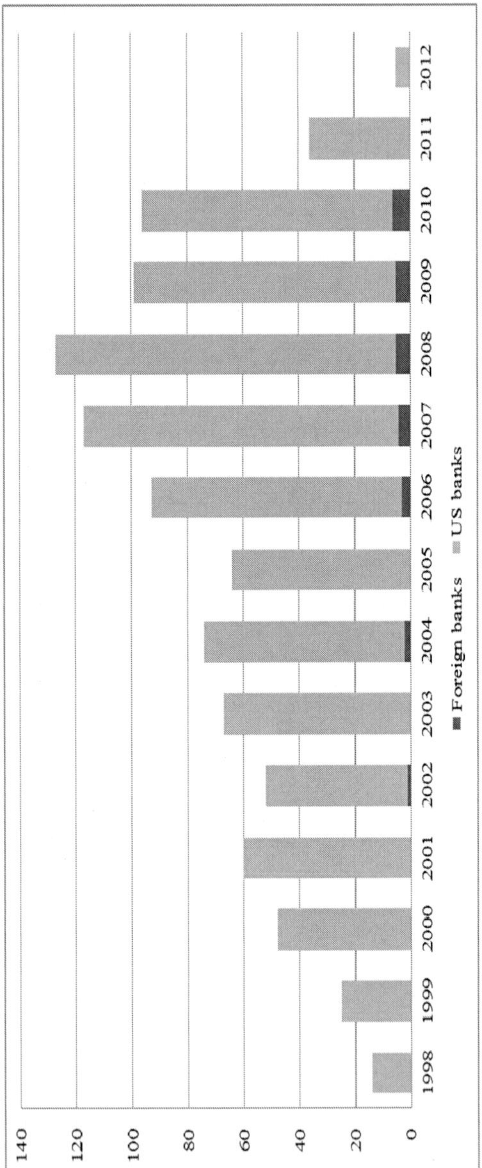

Figure 3. Distribution of patents awarded to US and foreign banks (1998-2012). Source: Developed by authors based on http://www.uspto.gov

As previously mentioned, we also include patents awarded to central banks. Figure 4 summarises the distribution of patents awarded to commercial banks and Federal Reserve Banks over the sample period. Federal Reserve banks have been particularly active in patenting from 2003 to 2010, although their overall contribution is always limited as compared to that of commercial banks. Because of their scope and functions, the Federal Reserve banks are interested in patenting innovations on very specific matters, in particular to fraud prevention. Besides, in contrast to commercial banks, central banks simultaneously patent the same innovation in more than one District. For instance, the same five innovations have been patented in three different Districts and five in two Districts. The variety of topics is therefore very limited but it is not exclusively related to financial innovation. In fact, financial patents account for 34 percent of all patents granted to Federal Reserve banks. As for the subject matter patented by the Federal Reserve banks, financial patents are especially related to automated electrical financial or business practice with paper check handling, to credit risk or loan processing and to funds transfer or credit transactions. Non-financial patents belong to class 235, which includes registers to sense a data-bearing record in combination with a system or apparatus to utilize or be activated or controlled by the information sensed from the record and to class 382, that includes documents, like for example paper money or bank checks, analyzed or verified by information content, such as patterns or alphanumeric characters.

From Table 3 we recall that 12 banks absorb 93 percent of all patents. The large majority of banks have received just a few. Indeed 31 have been awarded just a single patent. Figure 5 shows the distribution of the number of patents per bank. Only a quarter of all banks have been granted five patents or more. This stands in contrast to the extremely high number of patents awarded to the Bank of America Co. and JP Morgan Chase (387 and 362 patents, respectively). Experience plays a central role in successful patenting application; hence recurrent patenting may prove that previous experience with patenting application enhances the probability of success. Hall et al. (2009) show that patenting experience matters a great deal: a doubling of the firm's patent portfolio is associated with a 16% increment in the probability that a financial patent is granted.

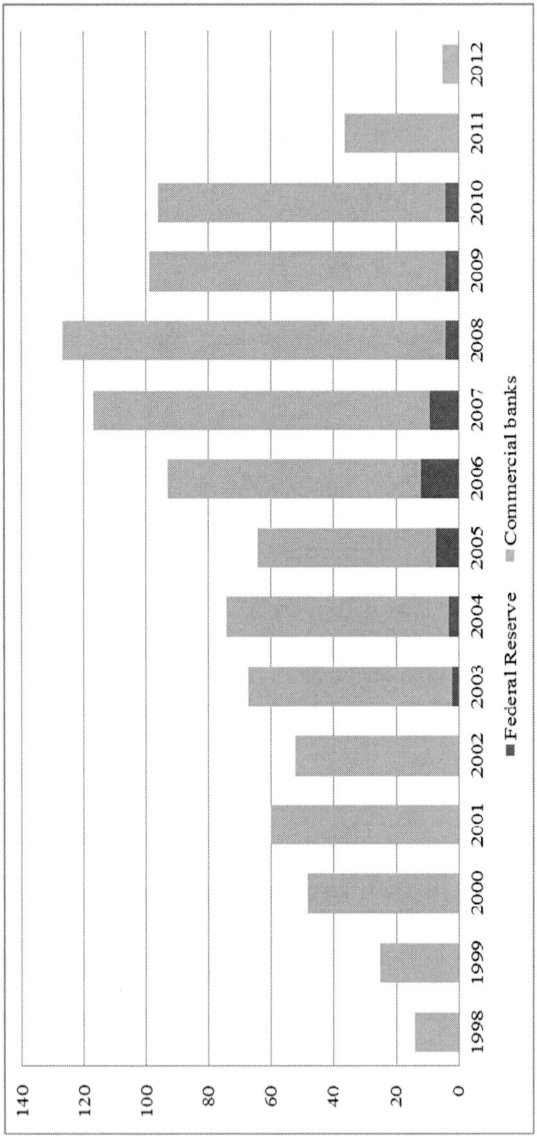

Figure 4. Distribution of patents granted to commercial and Federal Reserve banks (1998-2012). Source: Developed by authors based on http://www.uspto.gov

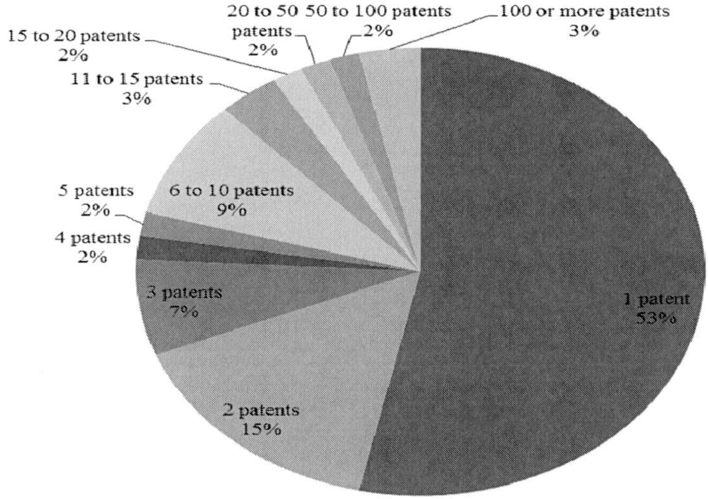

Figure 5. Distribution of number of patents per bank (all years). Source: Developed by authors based on http://www.uspto.gov

Few patents have been awarded jointly to banks and to non-financial institutions. Joint patents account for less than two percent of the sample and involve only US and Japanese banks. Indeed, JP Morgan Chase and the Bank of Tokyo-Mitsubishi account for two third of the joint patents. Apparently network externalities and standard setting processes do not seem as relevant in banking as we would expect. Banks prefer to patent innovation independently. Otherwise, banks choose the partnering with non-financial firms on a patent-by-patent basis. Banks seek external help on a variety of patent contents such as switched charge voltage driver, settlement systems, systems for extracting information from documents, and circuits for distributed electrical power, with partners in the manufacturing sector.

3. Patents and bank risk-adjusted performance

We now look at the characteristics of those banks that patented innovation in the US from 1998 to 2012 and compare them by their size, risk, performance, and efficiency. All data are taken from Bankscope. Table 4 lists the variables we consider.

Table 4. Bank balance sheet and income statement variables

Bank-specific variables		Definition
Size		Log (total asset)
Risk	Total asset growth (%)	(Total assets$_t$ – total assets$_{t-1}$)/total assets$_{t-1}$
	Liquidity	Net loans/customer and short term funding
		Net loans/total assets
Risk-adjusted performance	ROE to ROE volatility	Mean ROE/standard deviation ROE
	ROA to ROA volatility	Mean ROA/standard deviation ROA
	Net interest margin to quality of loan portfolio	Net interest margin/(loan loss reserves/gross loans)
	Net income to capital employed	Net income/(equity/total asset)
Efficiency	Cost to income ratio	Overheads/(net interest revenue + other operating income)
	Branch network	Number of branches/total assets

Source: Developed by authors

As reported in the previous section, the sample is homogeneously formed by banks that are mainly active in the traditional deposit taking and loan making business.

Table 5 below summarises the sample mean for the various characteristics, and tests for the difference between the group of occasional and recurrent patentees. In line with the patenting literature, we define occasional patentees as commercial banks that obtained less than 6 patents over the sample period (Lerner, 2006a; Hall et al., 2009). We do not include the Federal Reserve banks, because their scope significantly differs from those of commercial banks. This results in a sample of 52 commercial banks.

Manufacturing patents are usually promoted by large firms. The same is true for banks: JP Morgan Chase, Bank of America Co. and Barclays Bank totalized assets for more than two trillion dollars in 2011. Larger banks have more resources to invest in patent application, increasing chances of award. If the patent is infringed, larger patentees can sue the infringer to recover lost profits or obtain a court order that prevents the alleged infringer from continuing to make, use, or sell the patented invention (Hunt, 2008). Smaller banks do not have a comparable legal support. This difference is confirmed by the data: the recurrent patentees are significantly larger in terms of total assets.

Recent literature argues that banks particularly active in innovation have been riskier than their less innovative peers (Diamond and Rajan, 2009, and Bebchuk and Spamann, 2010). If we assume that patents are a proxy for bank innovation, we would expect the recurrent patentees to be riskier than the occasional ones. We first measure the risk computing banks' total asset growth. Asset growth should be funded by a commensurate amount of additional capital. Persistently high growth of assets can be an alarming signal. Excessive asset growth can imply excessive risk-taking and a building-up of vulnerabilities, which would eventually jeopardise sustainable growth (ECB, 2010). In fact recurrent patentees experiment a slower total asset growth, probably because they have already reached a considerable size and further growth may add more complexity than benefits.

The crisis has highlighted the crucial importance of banks' liquidity and funding capacity. The deregulation and financial innovation developments led banks to increase their dependence on financial markets for their funding. This has involved borrowing more intensively from wholesale markets, where funds are usually raised on a rollover basis through instruments such as mortgage bonds, repurchase agreements and commercial paper (Altunbas et al., 2011). An alternative source of funding is represented by retail deposits, which tend to be more stable during periods of crisis (Shleifer and Vishny, 2010). Recent evidence suggests that when funding from financial markets became unavailable, or prohibitively expensive, the market valued more positively those institutions that were more heavily funded via customers' deposits (Demirguc-Kunt et al., 2010; Beltratti and Stultz, 2012). As a second measure for risk, we therefore include the net loans-to-customer and short term funding ratio, in order to assess the relative funding strength of a bank. Once more, recurrent patentees show a significant lower risk and greater liquidity. The loan-to-total-asset ratio, an additional measure for liquidity which indicates the relevance of the loan portfolio as a percentage of bank's total asset or, alternatively, the percentage of total assets tied up in loans, does not provide significant information.

The crisis has highlighted the relevance of risk also when investigating banks' performance. Therefore, simple performance measures, such as return on equity, are limited because they are not risk-sensitive. Return on equity failed to discriminate the best performing banks from the others in terms of sustainability of their results during the crisis (ECB, 2010). One possible refinement to our performance analysis would be to rely on risk-adjusted returns instead of plain returns. Indicators could be related to the total return of an investment, the most popular one being the economic value added (EVA), or to the underlying level of risk associated with banks' activity, such as the risk-adjusted return on capital (RAROC). However, it is difficult to calculate these indicators without having access to banks' internal data, this being out of the scope of the present work. We therefore use a good proxy and compute the ratio of return on equity to its volatility for each bank over the sample period. Recurrent patentees show a lower risk-adjusted performance than banks that have been awarded patents occasionally. The ratio is not significant any longer when we substitute the return on equity with the return on assets.[8]

Alternative approaches to measuring banks' risk-adjusted performance may require a deeper analysis of the way in which banks run their business. We compute the ratio of the net interest margin to the quality of loan portfolio, measured as the ratio of loan loss reserves to gross loans. This latter ratio indicates how much of total portfolio has been provided but not charged off. Banks that have been awarded fewer patents show a higher ratio, which is usually associated to higher margins and better quality of loan portfolio. Higher margins and profitability are desirable as long as an adequate capitalisation is being maintained. Investigating now the net income to capital employed ratio, occasional patentees have a higher ratio than the recurrent ones. Revenues could be higher, confirming a positive performance. However, an alternative explanation is that the capital employed is lower, indicating a lower equity protection against asset malfunction.

Finally, we compute the cost to income ratio, which shows the ability of the institution to generate profits from a given revenue stream. The cost to income ratio is considered one of the most important efficiency based indicators (ECB, 2010). On average, recurrent patentees are more efficient, but the difference among the two groups of patentees is not statistically significant. Different levels of efficiency could be partially explained by the size of the physical network, which is significantly smaller for recurrent patentees. Excessive number of branches could cause overstaffing and an increase in overheads.

Overall, occasional patentees show higher risk, but also higher risk-adjusted performance than recurrent patentees. The diversification and specialisation of banks' activities is a relevant issue in that respect. There is much literature on this topic, but the empirical evidence is mixed (ECB, 2010). In theory, diversification (including product diversification) should

---

[8] Traditionally, ROA is considered a more reliable profitability indicator than ROE, in terms of efficiency performance, since it is adjusted for the leverage effect. However, this ratio is quite flat across time and so its predictive power is weak (ECB, 2010).

lead to reduced volatility of earnings. Thus we would expect that larger and well diversified banks show a higher risk-adjusted performance. However, earnings arising from non-interest activities of banks are much more volatile than net interest income. A large part of these gains is considered non-recurring, such as trading income and non-retail fee income. Our results seem to confirm this second hypothesis, since recurrent patentees deliver lower risk, measured in terms of asset growth and liquidity, but lower performance as adjusted for earnings volatility. Thus the profits of non-recurring activities seem not sufficient to make up for increased volatility.

4. Conclusions

Examining the source of financial innovation is of primary interest. Financial innovation has been both appraised for its economy-wide growth effects and blamed for causing the downfall of the financial system. Even if financial innovation escapes easy classification, several papers have argued that it can be measured by patenting activity.

We examine in detail the patents awarded since 1998 by the US Patent and Trademark Office to financial institutions. We limit our analysis to the banking sector, because of its peculiarity in terms of regulation, network externalities and standardisation.

Three major findings come out of our descriptive analysis. First, the number of patents has increased substantially since the State Street case in 1998. The upward trend is due to an increase in patenting both by US and foreign banks. The crunch in the number of bank patents since 2010 seems to indicate that the financial crisis has a significant effect not only on various bank-specific features extensively studied in the recent literature but also on the bank's capacity to innovate. Forced by the liquidity crisis, by the banking crisis and by the economic downturn, banks cut on innovation first.

Second, recurrent patentees, defined as banks that have been awarded at least six patents over the sample period, do not show higher risk, as compared to occasional patentees, both in terms of asset growth rate and liquidity. Indeed, recurrent patentees may be further divided in sub-groups, according to the number of patents awarded. JP Morgan and Bank of America show an extreme patenting activity, being awarded more than 350 patents over the last 15 years. These banks can be defined as extra-recurrent patentees. Wells Fargo and Bank One, fall in an intermediate category, whereas the remaining eight banks have been granted seven to 15 patents. Thus, patenting is concentrated in a few large commercial banks. They may be the innovation leaders that other banks just follow. Experience plays a central role in successful patenting application; hence, extra-recurrent patenting may prove that previous experience with patenting application enhances the probability of success. In addition extra-recurrent patentees are on average larger than other recurrent patentees or occasional patentees. Larger banks may invest a larger amount of resources in patent application to increase chances of award. Besides, larger patentees can enforce and protect their rights more effectively. Case studies of innovation at JP Morgan or Bank of America may provide additional information to the aggregate analysis on patenting activity, which, is of course, limited by such a skewed distribution of patents among banks.

Third, the Federal Reserve banks also participate in patenting activities. These banks have been granted patents related to their monitoring and fraud prevention activities. The same innovation is usually patented in more Fed Districts, to enforce its validity. However, the financial crisis has halted more patenting.

We finally investigate patentees according to various risk, performance and efficiency measures. Recurrent applicants show distinctive features in terms of lower risk, as measured by total assets growth and liquidity, but lower risk-adjusted performance, when the volatility of earnings is investigated, compared to occasional patentees.

Table 5. Comparison of patentees for different characteristics

	N. of banks	Bank size	Growth total assets (%)	Net loans to customer and short term funding	Net loans to total assets	Mean ROE/ vari-ance ROE	Mean ROA/ vari-ance ROA	Net interest margin to quality of loan portfolio	Net income to capital employ-ed	Cost to income ratio	N. of branches/ total assets
Occasional patentees	44	16.45	66.6	70.21	0.48	5.43	0.73	2.50	17.56	57.72	0.01
Recurrent patentees	8	19.52	17.77	45.45	0.33	2.80	1.55	1.80	7.37	51.59	0.00
(p-value)		0.00	0.01	0.00	0.14	0.02	0.07	0.00	0.00	0.10	0.00
Foreign banks	17	18.34	20.03	52.01	0.39	3.46	1.32	2.10	10.48	53.41	0.00
US banks	41	20.39	23.71	95.32	0.26	0.75	-0.10	0.84	22.25	60.48	0.01
(p-value)		0.04	0.10	0.01	0.19	0.22	0.18	0.04	0.05	0.41	-
Commercial bank	32	17.90	15.96	65.07	0.49	2.11	0.77	2.27	13.64	63.75	0.01
Savings bank	7	14.51	.	92.09	0.70	.	0.68	3.21	8.68	68.02	.
Bank holding	7	20.32	14.48	64.10	0.40	1.44	0.78	1.47	12.03	61.30	0.00
Governmental credit institutions	5	19.04	.	.	0.79	.	0.19	.	4.30	37.12	.

Notes: Recurrent patentees obtained more than six patents over the sample period; p-value is for the test of significance of difference between both groups.

Governmental credit institutions act on privileged or protected segments or benefit from governmental guarantee or sponsoring.

Bibliography

Altunbas, Y., Manganelli S., Marques-Ibanez D. (2011) Bank Risk during the Financial Crisis. Do Business Models Matter? ECB Working Paper Series No 1394, November.

Bebchuk, L., Spamann, H. (2010) Regulating banker's pay, Georgetown Law Review 98, 247–287.

Beck, T., Chen, T., Lin, C. and Song, F. (2012) Financial Innovation: The Bright and the Dark Sides, Working Papers 052012, Hong Kong Institute for Monetary Research.

Beltratti, A., Stulz, R. M. (2012) The credit crisis around the globe: Why did some banks perform better?, Journal of Financial Economics.

Ben-Horim M, Silber W. (1977) Financial Innovation: A Linear Programming Approach, Journal of Banking and Finance 1, 277-96.

Berger, A., Mester L. (2003) Explaining the dramatic changes in performance of US banks: technological change, deregulation, and dynamic changes in competition, Journal of Financial Intermediation 12(1), 57-95.

Boldrin, M., Levine D.K. (2013) The Case Against Patents, Journal of Economic Perspectives 27 (1), 3–22.

Brunnermeier, M. (2009) Deciphering the Liquidity and Credit Crunch 2007-2008, Journal of Economic Perspectives 23 (1), 77–100.

Corrocher N. (2006) Internet adoption in Italian banks: an empirical investigation, Research Policy 35, 533-544.

Demirguc-Kunt, A., Detragiache E., Merrouche O. (2010) Bank Capital: Lessons from the Financial Crisis, The World Bank Policy Research Working Paper Series 5473.

Diamond, D.W., Rajan, R.G. (2009) The credit crisis: conjectures about causes and remedies, American Economic Review 99, 606–610.

European Central Bank, (2010) Beyond ROE – How to measure bank performance, Appendix to the report on EU banking structures, September.

European Patent Office, (2000) Convention on the Grant of European Patents (European Patent Convention) of 5 October 1973 as revised by the Act revising Article 63 EPC of 17 December 1991 and the Act revising the EPC of 29 November 2000, available online at: http://www.epo.org/law-practice/legal-texts/html/epc/2010/e/ma1.html

Frame W.S., White L. (2004) Empirical studies of financial innovation: lots of talk, little action?, Journal of Economic Literature 42, 116-144.

Furst K., Lang W., Nolle D. (2002) Internet banking: developments and prospects, Center for Information Policy Research, mimeo, Harvard University.

Hall, B.H., Griliches, Z., Hausman, J.A. (1986) Patents and R and D: is there a lag? International Economic Review 27, 265–283.

Hall, B.H., Thoma G., Torrisi S. (2009) Financial patenting in Europe, European Management Review 00, 1–19.

Hall, B H., Ziedonis R.H. (2001) The Patent Paradox Revisited: An Empirical Study of Patenting in the US Semiconductor Industry, 1979–1995, RAND Journal of Economics 32(1), 101–128.

Hunt R. (2008) Ten Years After: What Are the Effects of Business Method Patents in Financial Services?, Business Review Q3 2008, 21-34.

Lamoreaux, N.R., Sokoloff K.L. (1999) Inventors, Firms, and the Market for Technology in the Late Nineteenth and Early Twentieth Centuries, In Learning by Doing in Markets, Firms and Countries, edited by N.R. Lamoreaux, D.M.G. Raff, and P. Temin, University of Chicago Press.

Lanjouw, J. O., Schankerman M. (2001) Characteristics of patent litigation: A window on competition, Rand Journal of Economics 32, 129–151.

Lerner, J. (2002) Where Does State Street Lead? A First Look at Finance Patents, 1971-2000, Journal of Finance 57, 901-30.

—. (2006a) The New New Financial Thing: The Origins of Financial Innovations, Journal of Financial Economics 79, 233-55.

—. (2006b) Trolls on State Street? The Litigation of Financial Patents, 1976-2005, mimeo, Harvard Business School.

—. (2010) The Litigation of Financial Innovations, Journal of Law and Economics 53(4), 807-831.

Lerner J., Tufano P. (2011) The Consequences of Financial Innovation: A Counterfactual Research Agenda, NBER Working Paper 16780, February.

Levine, R. (1997) Financial development and economic growth, Journal of Economic Perspectives 35, 688–726.

—. (2005) Finance and Growth: Theory and Evidence. In: P. Aghion and S. Durlauf, Handbook of Economic Growth, Elsevier.

Moser P. (2013) Patents and Innovation: Evidence from Economic History, Journal of Economic Perspectives 27 (1), 23-44.

Nickerson D., and Sullivan R. (2003) Financial Innovation, Strategic Real Options and Endogenous Competition: Theory and an Application to internet Banking, Federal Reserve Bank of Kansas City, Payments System Research Working Paper 1.

Scotchmer, S. (1991) Standing on the Shoulders of Giants: Cumulative Research and the Patent Law, Journal of Economic Perspectives 5(1), 29–41.

Shleifer, A., Vishny R.W. (2010) Unstable Banking, Journal of Financial Economics 97(3), 306-318.

Tufano, P. (2003) Financial Innovation, in G.M. Constantines, M. Harris, and R. Stulz, eds. Handbook of the Economics of Finance, Vol. 1a: Corporate Finance, Amsterdam, Elsevier.

CHAPTER FIVE

INTELLECTUAL PROPERTY AND APPROPRIABILITY REGIME OF INNOVATION IN FINANCIAL SERVICES

RAHUL KAPOOR

1. Introduction

A patent contract requires inventors to disclose their inventions to the public, in return for protection against its unsolicited commercial use. This disclosure of invention details is systematically stored in worldwide patent databases. The stored information has given rise to the field of patent statistics that has been used to predict science and technological activities of firms and nations. This ability to predict, offers the financial services industry opportunities to use patent data in making investment, strategy, policy and valuation decisions.

OECD (2009) reports the first use of patent statistics in the 1950s by Jakob Schmookler, a United States scholar, who used patent counts as indicators of technological change in certain industries. Since then, parallel to the rise of computing power, the use of patent data expanded dramatically. The rise of patent statistics is in-line with the tremendous increase in the number of patent applications filed worldwide. Patent statistics thus became an active area of research, which has resulted in a myriad of patent value indicators to assess the quality of patents. Researchers (Trajtenberg, 1990; Hall, Jaffe & Trajtenberg, 2005; Baron & Delcamp, 2010) have, in the last two decades, devised many patent value indicators. As the field of patent statistics matured, researchers started integrating market-based information with patent-based indicators.

Along with the rise in the number of patent applications, patents became an important aspect of the core strategy for some firms or industries. Successful companies are associated with having well managed intellectual property (IP) portfolios. The management of their IP is designed to maximize revenues through licenses, royalties and robust business alliances. A survey of the Fortune 500 companies estimated that 45%-75% of the wealth of individual companies comes from their intellectual property rights (Cockburn, 2004). In an in-depth single-case study of Swiss Re, Bader (2007) delineates the opportunities and risks associated with managing intellectual property in the financial services industry. Swiss Re is one of the first European financial services firm that created its own patent department and systematically engaged in managing intellectual property.

The literature has viewed appropriability as one of the major drawbacks of innovation in the financial services industry. Financial innovations are easily imitable and their diffusion across institutions is fast (Roberts and Amit, 2003). Conventionally, most innovations from financial services were not considered eligible for patent protection (Kumar and Turnbull, 2006; Lerner, 2006). The Swiss Re example, however, shows that the premise of financial services patents not meeting the traditional criteria of patentability is somewhat disproved. Investment in intellectual property is now of an increasing strategic importance. Better protected service innovations can lead to reduced imitation and second mover advantages. The increased importance of IP management is further confirmed by Lerner (2010), who provides evidence that financial services patents are being litigated at a much higher rate than patents in general.

This chapter aims at developing the field of patent statistics and use it to obtain insights within the financial services industry. The chapter will use the existing literature on patent value indicators to build new patent citation-based indicators that can be helpful in studying infringing levels and appropriability potential. Views of experts in the field of intellectual property are considered in various instances, within the chapter, so as to make assumptions, develop hypothesis and understand results. The new measures developed, will be used in the context of the financial services industry, first, at a macro level and then at the firm level. The analysis can provide useful insights regarding encroachment levels among industry players. Key players in the European market will be identified in the process.

The new indicators created, based on citation categories, can help in understanding the nature of patenting in the financial services industry, along with a possibility to improve appropriability. The results can be beneficial for financial analysts, finance managers, industry regulators, policy makers and patent analysts.

2. The patent system

The data collected in patent databases is generated at various stages of the patenting process. A brief idea of the evolution of a patent application is necessary to understand, which value indicators are most suitable at different stages. Figure 1 gives a glimpse of a simple timeline for the applicant to consider when making a patent application.

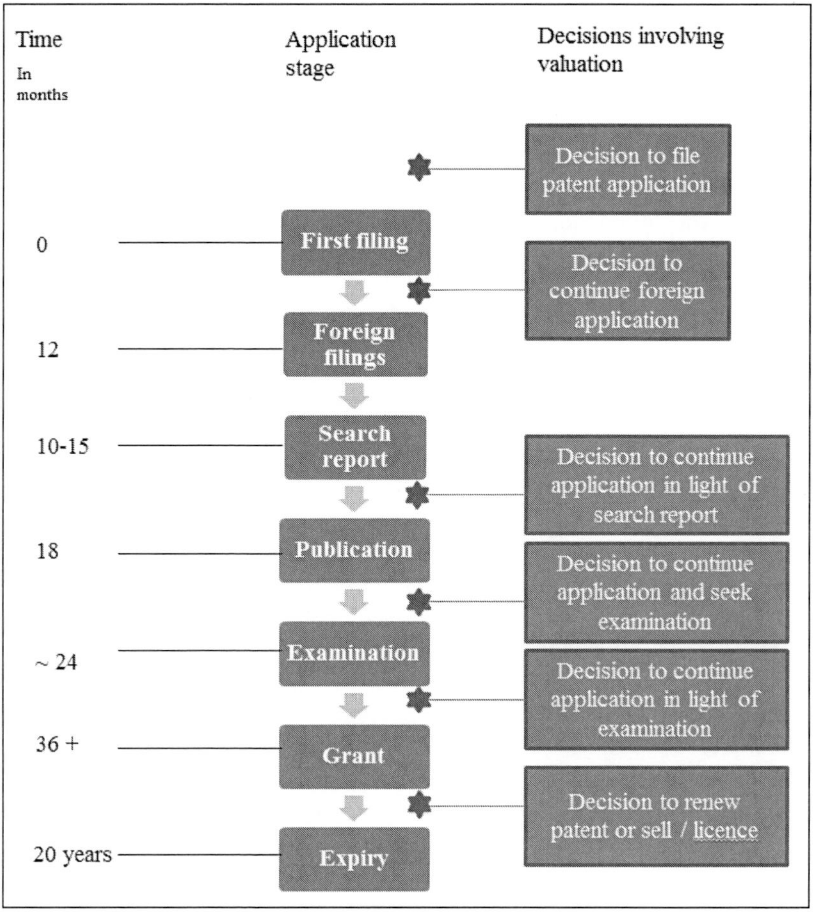

Figure 1. Patent timeline and decision points (Adapted from Pitkethly, 1997)

An applicant generally faces many decision points, where there is a need for weighing the feasibility of continuing the patent application. There is a cost involved at each decision point and the applicant decides whether the invention, at that stage, is worth the costs incurred, or not.

Eighteen months after the first filing, the patent application is first published along with the search report in patent databases. This is the earliest when patent statisticians can make use of patent databases to analyse inventions. This stage also makes the invention public and competitors can view the invention details in public databases. An interview with the R&D manager of a large corporation indicated that the biggest risk for them is when the patent is made public and their competitors get too much information. R&D managers and patent strategists consider the timing of making an invention public to be the key in the battle for technological dominance. When the invention is not totally ready and too much information is divulged in patent databases, competitors can work around the claims in certain ways to use new inventions.

Typically, an inventor/applicant in Europe has three routes to follow in the process of a patent application; namely, national, regional (EPO) or PCT route. The dataset considered for citation analysis consists of EPO patents in this analysis. The European patent convention (EPC) was signed in 1973 and entered into force in 1977. EPO was created as a result, which could grant a patent through a centralised examination procedure. It is possible to obtain patent rights in all 38 EPC signatory countries (EPO, 2010a). Patents can be filed in any of the three official languages English, French or German. When the application is extended to individual countries, their national offices may require translations. The EPO route is a fast way of getting patent rights in many European markets. Deng (2007) found, based on renewal behaviour that EPO patents are substantially more valuable than patents obtained through the national route. This procedure is more expensive if the applicant targets only a few countries, but cheaper if the number of countries targeted are more. (OECD, 2009)

3. Review of patent value indicators

The rationale behind the use of patents in predicting economic performance is the fact that getting exclusive rights to superior technology can enable innovators to reap above normal benefits. There are many studies that have looked, in retrospect, at this phenomenon of strong patent characteristics leading to strong financial performance. However, there are very few studies that have attempted to use patent statistics in foresight or prediction. The primary reason for this, as seen in the last section, is that a patent application is normally a long and tedious process. It can take more than three years from first filing to get a patent granted. The data collected in patent databases is generated at various stages of the patenting process. The first availability of any information is usually 18 months after first filing. Some of the indicators developed in the literature (like forward citations) require a significant time to have passed before they acquire any predictive power. For the field of patent statistics to be useful in financial decision making, there is a need to identify value determinants early in the lifecycle of an invention. The following sections will show the use of patent statistics and describe the most important patent value indicators along with their rationale.

Deng et al., (1999) showed that patent counts, forward citations and closeness of R&D to basic research are associated with future firm performance. The patent value indicators are significantly correlated with the market value of firms holding patent stocks (Hall et al., 2005). This view was backed by Neuhäusler et al., (2011) who used patent characteristics data along with data on R&D expenditure and market capitalization to indicate that patent family size and forward citations positively influence market value. Research on the pharmaceutical industry by Chen and Chang (2010) found that patent citations were positively correlated with a firm's corporate market value. Häussler et al., (2008) studied the role of patents in venture capital (VC) financing. They found that in the presence of patent applications, VC financing occurs earlier. Also, successful ventures produce patents, which have a better quality of value indicators.

3.1 Patent family size

Among the most authentic indicator backed by expert interviews and research studies (Guellec and van Pottelsberghe, 2000; Lanjouw and Schankerman, 2004) is patent family size. This number indicates how many patents have been filed in different countries through their national offices to protect the same invention. Patenting the same invention in many countries is a sign of a large market size. A large family size is a depiction of the willingness of the patent applicant to incur high patent application and maintenance costs. This shows a corresponding level of returns, which the applicant expects from the invention. There are a number of relevant definitions of patent families as described by (Martinez, 2011). The most common definition is that of equivalent patent families. It refers to patent documents that share exactly the same priority application. Equivalent patent family applications are usually related to family members, very closely, and are most likely to be protecting the same invention (OECD, 2009).

3.2 Renewal and litigation

Patents are renewed only if the value of keeping it alive is higher than the cost of its maintenance fee. The renewal fee of patents generally keeps increasing as the patent approaches near its full term, although the extent varies between patent offices. The first models, which used renewal behaviour to estimate distribution of patent value, were developed by Pakes and Schankerman (1984) and Pakes (1986). There are numerous limitations associated with using patent renewal as a value indicator. The renewal information comes late in the patent lifecycle, which makes it impossible to analyse more recent patents. Sometimes, the decision to renew or not to renew can be based on circumstances beyond the scope of the economic patent value like change in goals or maintenance of patent stocks.

In opposite, a patent is a costly procedure and it has been hypothesized in the literature that only patents, which are economically valuable are opposed, thus making opposition a strong sign of patent value. Harhoff et al., (2003) have found that a patent right, which has withstood opposition, is a very strong predictor of patent value. Opposition rates in different patent systems were compared by Graham et al., (2002), which revealed that the average re-examination rate in EPO is much higher than the United States Patent and Trademarks Office (USPTO).

3.3 Number of claims

The average number of patent claims can help in determining the breadth and scope of the invention. A study by Lerner (2010) shows that financial patents are being litigated at a high rate, especially the ones with high number of citations and claims are disproportionally susceptible to litigation. Experts opine that the legal proceedings related to patent infringements are invariably solved by an evaluation of the claims. This makes publication claims an important factor in determining the quality of the patent portfolio. The EPO allows up to 15 claims in the published patent. Any extra claim that a patentee wants to add has to be paid for (EPO, 2013). If an inventor is willing to pay for the extra claims, it can be inferred that the relevance of the patent in question is high, or at least the applicant feels paying extra money will enhance the core scope of the invention. One of the major advantages of assessing the number of claims is the fact that this indicator is available early in time as soon as the patent is published (Reitzig, 2004). This makes it useful to use a number of claims as an indicator for evaluating emerging industries.

3.4 International patent classification

Each granted patent is technically classified by specific technology areas of the invention. It is a hierarchical way of assigning the category to which a patent belongs and is known as International Patent Classification (IPC) classes. An example of the hierarchical way of classification is shown in Table 1 below. The nNumber of IPC classes attributed to a patent application has been used as a proxy for the scope and hence the market value of a patent (Lerner, 1994). It has also been argued in the literature that IPC classes have little or no association with the value of the patent rights (Harhoff et al., 2003; Lanjouw and Schankerman, 1997).

Table 1. International Patent Classification system

Subdivision	**Example of an IPC code**	
	Symbol	**Title**
Section	G	Physics
Class	G06	Computing; calculating; counting
Sub-class	G06Q	Data processing systems or methods, specially adapted for administrative, commercial, financial, managerial, supervisory or forecasting purposes
Main group	G06Q 20/00	Payment architectures, schemes or protocols
Sub group	G06Q 20/10	...specially adapted for electronic funds transfer [EFT] systems

Karvonen et. al. (2010) used IPC classes to plot industry convergence in the paper industry and information and communication technologies (ICT) industry. The financial services industry, itself is going through a lot of change and IPC analysis can be a good way to identify new entrants patenting in the same technology fields.

4. Review of citation based indicators

Patent citations are references provided in the search report, which are used to judge the novelty and the inventive step of a patent. The history of citations in patents dates back to 1947 when examiners in the United States Patent and Trademarks Office (USPTO) began citing references considered during the examination process (List, 2010). These references are referred to as prior art and the final list is prepared by the examiner of the respective patent office. The list can contain previous patents in the same field, non-patent scientific literature, internet links for describing state of the art and other documents. Citations made to previous patents are called backward citations and citations received from future patents are called forward citations (see Figure 2 below).

4.1 Forward citations

Forward citations are found to be the most stable value determinant regarded by researchers (Zeebroeck and van Pottelsberghe, 2011). Studies have shown that forward citations are strongly correlated with the economic value of patents (Trajtenberg, 1990), as well as the social value of inventions (Scherer et al., 2000). It was reported that patent renewal is correlated with high count of forward citations (Putnam, 1996). Lanjouw and Schankerman (1997) showed that patents, which receive more citations than average, are more likely to be opposed or litigated. Despite being the most important indicator explaining patent value, studies have shown (Gambardella et al., 2008) that it explains very little of the actual variance in patent value.

4.2 Backward citations

Backward citations, or the references put in the patent document during the patent examination process, reflect the importance that is put in the field on particular documents but may not be a valid indicator of ‘channels of influence’ (Griliches, 1998). Backward citation analysis can potentially provide insights into the exploration process of new technologies or radical search behaviour (Jaffe, Trajtenberg and Fogarty, 2000; Lukach and Plasmans, 2002). The idea behind utilizing backward citations as a

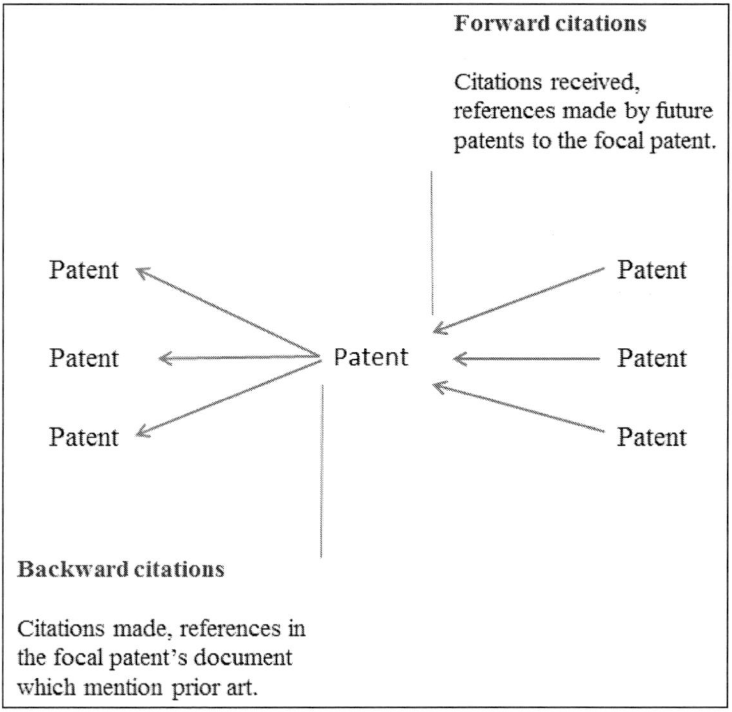

Figure 2. Understanding patent citations

value determinant is in assumption that combinations and knowledge transfer from other technological domains would lead to more valuable patents (Nemet and Johnson, 2012). Backward citations have been a subject of debate among patent value researchers. The results of using backward citations as a value determinant have provided ambiguous results (Hall et al., 2001; Zeebroeck et al., 2011).

4.3 Derived citation indicators

Other indicators developed based on citations make use of the spread of forward or backward citations over technology classes. Measure of generality combines forward citations and their International Patent Classification (IPC) codes to give a measure of how widespread the impact of the invention is in a variety of fields. The originality of a patent makes use of backward citations and their IPC classes. If a patent cites a narrow set of technology classes, it will have a low originality score. (Hall et al., 2001; Trajtenberg, Henderson and Jaffe, 1997)

4.4 Limitations of citation indicators

Michel and Bettels (2001) advised caution in the use of simple patent citation counts in statistical analysis without an in-depth knowledge of search reports and idiosyncrasies of patent offices. It was also seen that USPTO cites far more than their European or Japanese counterparts. There is a home bias among examiners who tend to cite more patents from their own country. Language barrier sometimes results in examiners being unable to cite relevant prior art in languages they are unaware of. This necessitates wariness in the sampling stage when doing any kind of analysis using patent citation information. In order to get uniformity in the sample of patents, only European Patent Office (EPO) applications are evaluated for the respective case companies. Any kind of asymmetry in patent regulations is nullified making the sample befitting for citation analysis. Some of the main limitations adapted from Hall et al., (2001) are listed below:

1. Number of citations received (forward citations) is truncated because only citations received so far are known. More recent patents cannot be evaluated as there is not enough time for future patents to cite.
2. Differences in patent office practices produce differences in citation intensities.
3. Since the number of patents filed has steeply increased, in the last decade or so, there are also differences in comparing citations of old and new patents.
4. Number of citations made, varies significantly across technology field or maturity of technology/industry.

5. Concept of citation categories

The analysis presented makes use of citation categories which are assigned to patent references by the examiners of the European Patent Office (EPO). The EPO examination guidelines (EPO, 2010 b) require all documents cited in the search report to be identified by a certain letter or a combination of letters, where appropriate. The search report is made public by the EPO examiners with the publication after 18 months of the patent filing date (also called priority date).

After a patent is filed and all the administrative formalities are complete, the first step for the patent examiner is to judge the novelty and inventive step of an invention. This is done by a prior art search and the relevant references are cited in the search report. Each reference that is cited in the search report is assigned a citation category. Citation categories are a useful way of assigning relevance to a cited document in terms of its impact on the claims of the applied patent. Each claim of the applied patent is assigned a citation category which judges the novelty of the claim with respect to relevant prior art. Figure 3 below explains the concept using a sample search report.

Three main citation categories are considered in this research, namely, X, Y and A. Related documents assigned 'X' in the search report indicate a clear similarity between the claimed invention and the cited document's contents. 'Y' refers to documents which can be combined with other documents by a person skilled in the art to develop a concept as claimed by the patent applicant. Documents ascribed 'A' refer to records, which define the state of the art, but no aspect of the document can challenge the claimed invention. Table 2 carries the definition of less used citation categories as well as the main categories X, Y and A.

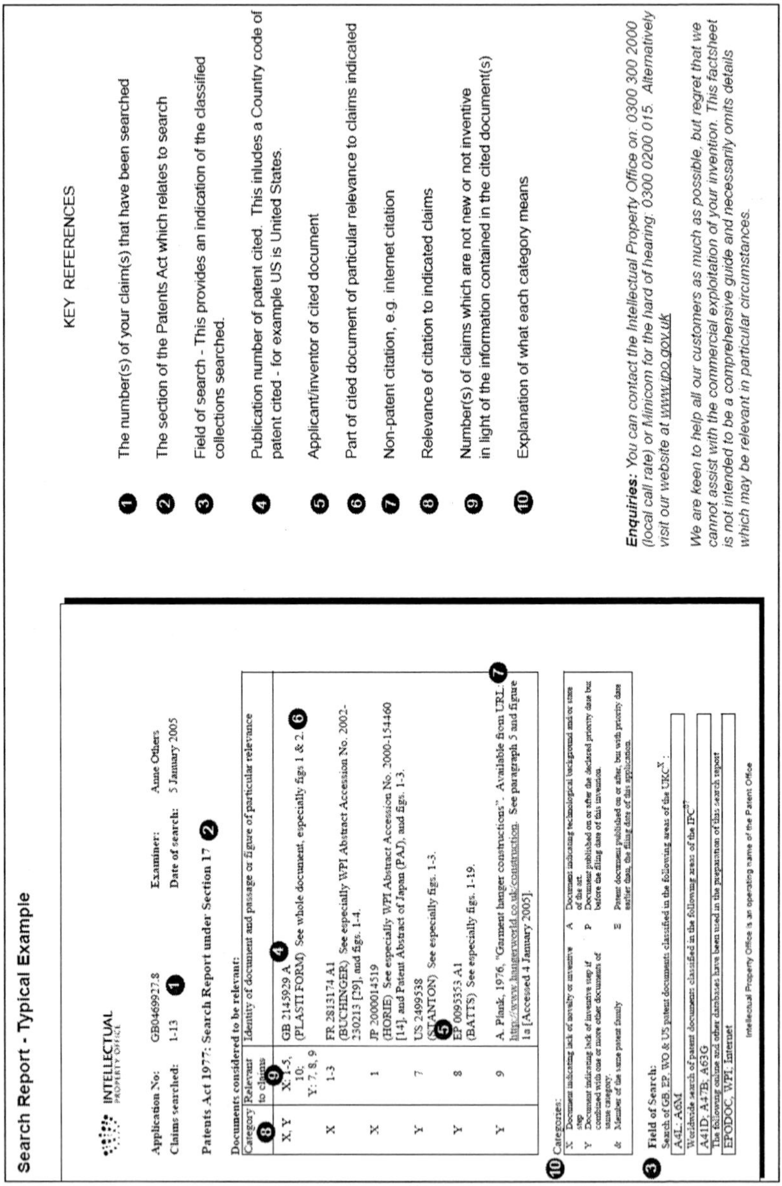

Search Report - Typical Example

INTELLECTUAL PROPERTY OFFICE

Application No: GB0469927.8 **Examiner:** Anne Others
Claims searched: 1-13 (1) **Date of search:** 5 January 2005

Patents Act 1977: Search Report under Section 17 (2)

Documents considered to be relevant:

Category (8)	Relevant to claims (9)	Identity of document and passage or figure of particular relevance
X, Y	X: 1-5, 10; Y: 7, 8, 9	GB 2145929 A (4) (PLASTI FORM) See whole document, especially figs 1 & 2. (6)
X	1-3	FR 2813174 A1 (BUCHINGER) See especially WPI Abstract Accession No. 2002-230213 [29], and figs. 1-4.
X	1	JP 2000014519 (HORIE) See especially WPI Abstract Accession No. 2000-154460 [14], and Patent Abstract of Japan (PAJ), and figs. 1-3.
Y	7	US 2499538 (STANTON) (5) See especially figs. 1-3.
Y	8	EP 0095353 A1 (BATTS) See especially figs. 1-19.
Y	9	A. Plank, 1976, "Garment hanger constructions". Available from URL: (7) http://www.hangerworld.co.uk/construction. See paragraph 5 and figure 1a [Accessed 4 January 2005].

(10) Categories:

X	Document indicating lack of novelty or inventive step	A	Document indicating technological background and/or state of the art.
Y	Document indicating lack of inventive step if combined with one or more other documents of same category.	P	Document published on or after the declared priority date but before the filing date of this invention.
&	Member of the same patent family	E	Patent document published on or after, but with priority date earlier than, the filing date of this application.

(3) **Field of Search:**
Search of GB, EP, WO & US patent documents classified in the following areas of the UKC^{X} :
A4L; A6M
Worldwide search of patent documents classified in the following areas of the IPC^{07}
A41D; A47B; A63G
The following online and other databases have been used in the preparation of this search report
EPODOC, WPI; Internet

Intellectual Property Office is an operating name of the Patent Office

KEY REFERENCES

1. The number(s) of your claim(s) that have been searched
2. The section of the Patents Act which relates to search
3. Field of search - This provides an indication of the classified collections searched.
4. Publication number of patent cited. This inludes a Country code of patent cited - for example US is United States.
5. Applicant/inventor of cited document
6. Part of cited document of particular relevance to claims indicated
7. Non-patent citation, e.g. internet citation
8. Relevance of citation to indicated claims
9. Number(s) of claims which are not new or not inventive in light of the information contained in the cited document(s)
10. Explanation of what each category means

Enquiries: *You can contact the Intellectual Property Office on: 0300 300 2000 (local call rate) or Minicom for the hard of hearing: 0300 0200 015. Alternatively visit our website at* *www.ipo.gov.uk*

We are keen to help all our customers as much as possible, but regret that we cannot assist with the commercial exploitation of your invention. This factsheet is not intended to be a comprehensive guide and necessarily omits details which may be relevant in particular circumstances.

Figure 3. Search report description

Table 2. Description of commonly used citation categories (OECD, 2009)

Citation Category	Description
X	Particularly relevant documents when taken alone (a claimed invention cannot be considered novel or cannot be considered to involve an inventive step)
Y	Particularly relevant if combined with another document of the same category
A	Documents defining the general state of the art
O	Documents referring to non-written disclosure
P	Intermediate documents (documents published between the date of filing and the priority date)
T	Documents relating to theory or principle underlying the invention (documents which were published after the filing date and are not in conflict with the application, but were cited for a better understanding of the invention)
E	Potentially conflicting patent documents, published on or after the filing date of the underlying invention
D	Document already cited in the application (provided by the applicant)
L	Document cited for other reasons (e.g. a document which may cast doubt on a priority claim)

The search report is prepared by the examiner to make the applicant aware of the chances of a successful patent grant. Knowledge of search reports is a pre-requisite for carrying out citation analysis. Michel and Bettels (2001) showcase the intricacies of citation categories and other factors related to the heterogeneity of patent offices. Cited documents categorized as 'X' are considered to be particularly relevant and can potentially damage the chances of a patent being granted, if the claims are not suitably modified. This notion has been backed by a study on the economic value of R&D intensive firms in the US, Europe and Japan (Czarnitzki, Hussinger & Leten, 2011). The owners of the patent cited 'X' can infringe on the citing patent, and thus, are in a stronger position to exploit the value of their intellectual property. This view has been seconded by Harhoff and Wagner (2009) who maintain that patents, which receive a larger share of 'X' and 'Y' citations, are more valuable than otherwise.

Interviews with patent examiners in the field of nano-technology revealed that the presence of 'X' and 'Y' citations in the search report of a patent can be an indication of an important business area. It can be inferred from the comments below that the business area of 'X' and 'Y' citations in the search report can be commercially valuable. As opposed to other patent based indicators, like grant, forward citations and renewals, citation categories come early in the lifecycle of a patent. This makes analysis of relatively new patents possible which is useful in the context of fast track industries.

> "...It [patent] might be very limited on technical part if you have X's and Y's, but maybe it is good for doing business. Value still depends on the markets. The nature of citations is more important than the amount of them... If you have a lot of A's then it can mean that you are in a new territory. It may be the case that there is no point of inventing in this region as there is no market. So even if you find a tiny place in the existing scope of invention coverage (more X's and Y's) it can mean more value."

The advantage of making analysis based on citation categories is that they can be used to evaluate newly published patents. In the views of a patent attorney dealing with software patents *"sometimes an applied patent can be more valuable than a granted patent. If somebody is interested in the business area and wishes to buy the patent, they prefer to buy during the application stage so that they can proceed with the application in a way that suits their needs."* The early advantage results in one limitation that the patent claims can change from the time the search report is released to the time of patent grant. The examiners might ask the applicant to modify claims based on the categories provided or restrict them altogether. Once the patent is granted, the value is judged solely by the breadth and scope of the claims and not based on citation categories. Nevertheless, citation categories are a useful way of understanding the learning process behind inventions. An 'X' or 'Y' citation surely represents the fact that the invention has used some parts of the cited document.

6. Data collection and methodology

The empirical part of the study makes use of the theory of citation categories to see the encroachment levels in the financial services industry. Measure of encroachment is proposed by the author to study the infringing levels in financial services industries. Citation category analysis can be better than simple citation analysis as they can enable the weighing of citations. The value weighing of citations can lead to a more refined usage of patent citations in determining value potential of patent portfolios. The research based on citation categories is in the early stages and this explorative study evaluates its usefulness in technology management studies.

Patent data for the financial services industry was collected using the EPO PATSTAT database. The PATSTAT contains bibliographic data provided to the EPO by over 90 countries (EPO, 2012 p. 163). The time span of the analysis is the period 2001-2010.

Patents in the field of financial services are filtered using the International Patent Classification (IPC) four-digit code 'G06Q'. The IPC sub-class 'G06Q' stands for *"data processing systems or methods, specially adapted for administrative, commercial, financial, managerial, supervisory or forecasting purposes; systems or methods specially adapted for administrative, commercial, financial, managerial, supervisory or forecasting purposes, not otherwise provided for"* (WIPO, 2013).

The dataset contained only patents filed through the European Patent Office (EPO) as citation categories are assigned only by EPO examiners. Backward citations of all the patents in the dataset are found next. The backward citations, thus obtained, are divided into two categories: the ones that belong to the same industry (also having IPC class 'G06Q') and the ones that belong to other industries. This split can give us an estimate of patents that are citing patents from the same industry and patents that are citing patents from a different industry. It can also reveal the learning process or technology diffusion in industries. The backward citation data was further filtered by finding only the backward citations, which received 'X' and 'Y' references from the patent dataset. The 'X' and 'Y' backward citations would refer to infringing patent citations. The backward citations, thus obtained, are again split into the ones belonging to the same industry and the ones belonging to other industries. The methodology is depicted in Figure 4 below.

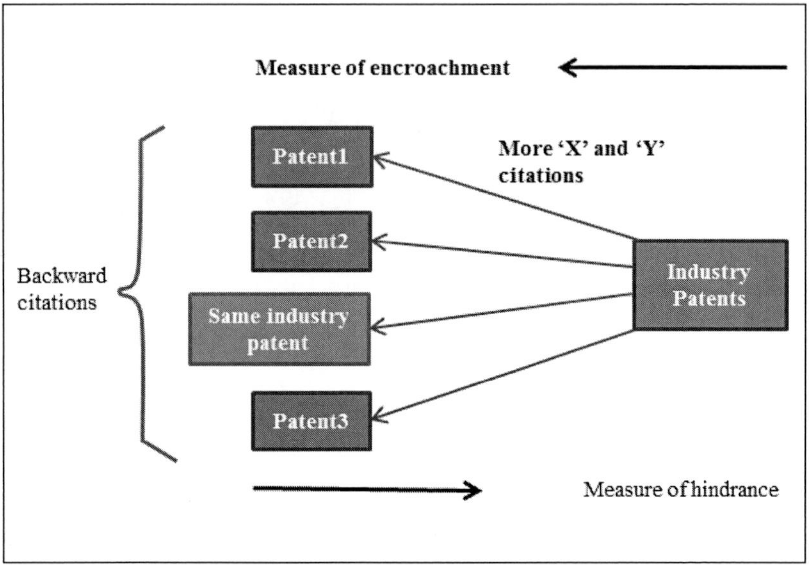

Figure 4. Measure of encroachment

Citations made to the same industry are considered as more important in this analysis as they can represent a possible conflict of interest. The 'X' and 'Y' category citations are also considered as more important as there is a possible overlap between the claims. Based on interviews with patent attorneys it was found that in terms of patent value, it is only the text of the claims, which matters. In their view, if matters have to be settled in the court, the decisions are solely made on the scope of the patent right as delineated by the text of the claims. In this analysis, encroachment refers to higher 'X' and 'Y' citations made to the same industry. Measure of encroachment of an industry is defined as the ratio of 'X' and 'Y' citations made to the same industry (or competitors) and all 'X' and 'Y' citations made.

$$\text{Measure of encroachment} = \frac{\sum \text{'X' and 'Y' cit. to competitors}}{\sum \text{All 'X' and 'Y' cit. made}}$$

Measure of encroachment can take any value between 0 and 1. A value closer to one would indicate that there are too many 'X' and 'Y' citations made within the same industry, which can result in increased infringing and thus legal expenses. For example, a measure of encroachment value of

0.5 will mean that 50% of the 'X' and 'Y' citations made are within the same industry or among competitors. Measure of hindrance can be seen in the same way, except that it would require data on forward citations. Analysis related to the measure of hindrance is not considered in this study.

7. Findings and discussion

The dataset created contained a set of 17232 patent applications having at least one IPC sub-class 'G06Q', applied through the European Patent Office (EPO) and belonging to the period 2001-2010. The dataset of patents belonging to the IPC class 'G06Q' crudely represents patents filed in the domain of financial services. This can be seen by the trend in patenting in Europe (1996-2010). The rise and fall in 'G06Q' patent applications coincides with the 2001 dot-com bubble and the 2008 financial crisis (see Figure 5 below).

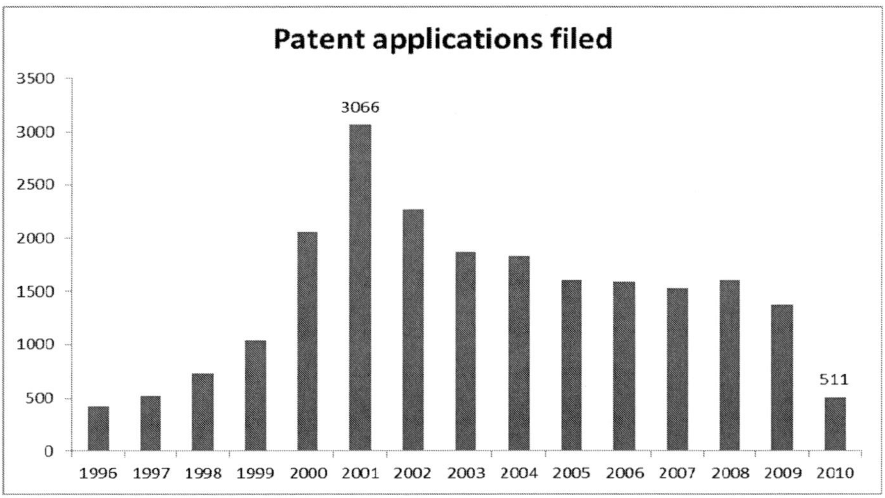

Figure 5. EPO patent applications filed in IPC class 'G06Q'

The following analysis will consider the dataset (2001-2010) of 'G06Q' to be patents in the field of financial services. The patent count and backward citation data are presented in Table 3 below. Only the patent references were considered, all non-patent references were left out from the analysis.

Table 3. Backward citation information (EPO Patent applications made 2001-2010)

No. of financial services patents	No. of unique backward patent citations	No. of backward citations in same field
17232	23303	9594 (41%)

Citation category analysis was carried out next. Table 3 gives the figure for the total number of unique backward citations (23303). However, one patent can receive citations from many patents. When the unique filter was removed, it was found that all the financial services patents (17232) had made 32544 backward citations. Citation categories were assigned to 30487 of these 32544 backward citations. Out of the 30487 citation categories assigned, 14487 were in the same industry. Data for citation categories is tabulated in Table 4 below.

Table 4. 'X', 'Y' and 'A' citations made by 'G06Q' patents

	'X' citations	'Y' citations	'A' citations	Other categories	Total
All backward citations	15391	2615	10947	1534	30487
Same industry citations	7863	1014	4853	757	14487

The measure of encroachment value for the above table is 0.49. This means that almost 50% of the 'X' and 'Y' citations are made within the same industry.

The citation category analysis presented is done at a macro level. The insights can reveal the level of competition within industries. A cross-industry analysis can assist industry regulators in decision making. For example, a high value of measure of encroachment can mean it is better for industry players to engage in cross-licensing rather than going through high costs related to IP lawsuits. A similar analysis can be performed at a micro level, which will show the extent of infringing within firms. The analysis can benefit firms in terms of knowing the areas where there is a possibility to appropriate returns through licensing. It can also lead to the identification of key patents which receive more 'X' and 'Y' citations from competitors.

The analysis was extended to a more specific set of patents related to the financial services industry. WIPO (2012) IPC classifications were used to form three main sections related to financial services patents. These are (i) Payment architectures and protocols, (ii) Shopping or e-commerce and (iii) Finance, insurance and tax. The number of European patents filed in these categories is shown in Table 5 below.

Table 5. No. of EP patent applications (2001-2010)

Payment architectures and protocols	Shopping or e-commerce	Finance, insurance and tax
2181	6669	1895

Patenting activity in the field of commerce (shopping or e-commerce) was seen to be significantly higher than other segments. The key players having the highest number of patent applications in each category are tabulated in Table 6 below.

Table 6. Top patenting players by category (EPO patents between 2001-2010)

Payment architectures and protocols	**Shopping or e-commerce**	**Finance, insurance and tax**
Siemens AG	Sony Corp	Espeed Inc
Sony Corp	Microsoft Corp	Trading Tech Int Inc
Nokia Corp	Koninkl Philips Electronics NV	SAP AG
Visa Int Service Ass	SAP AG	Swiss Reinsurance Co
Ericsson Telefon Ab L M	Accenture Global Services Gmbh	Accenture Global Services Gmbh
NTT Docomo Inc	Matsushita Electric Ind Co Ltd	Chicago Mercantile Exchange
First Data Corp	Nokia Corp	Goldman Sachs & Co
France Telecom	Hewlett Packard Co	Bank Of America
Fujitsu Ltd	IBM	Siemens AG
Mastercard International	Google Inc	OMX Technology

Microsoft Corp	Bidamic Inc	UBS AG
Koninkl Philips Electronics NV	Nec Corp	Sony Corp
Giesecke & Devrient Gmbh	Fujitsu Ltd	Visa Int Service Ass

Sony was the only firm to feature among the top patentees in all three categories. Presence of a large number of non-European firms in the above list is an indication that they are more patent-aware than European firms. This can be because the European Patent Office is more restrictive in patenting business methods. Patenting of financial service innovations is a relatively new phenomenon among European organizations and only 10% of the patent applications filed at the EPO come from European organizations (Bader, 2007). An analysis of the patents, which were classified in multiple categories, revealed that there was no significant overlap between the patents of the above categories. The Venn diagram in Figure 6 below shows the number of patent applications, which belonged to all the categories. Only 88 patent applications belonged to all three categories. There was more overlap between patents related to commerce and payment architectures. Each of the three categories is fairly independent in themselves.

The measure of encroachment analysis was extended to firm level instead of a more macro analysis at the industry level. Measure of encroachment was found for each firm against its competitors. Patent citations analysed were made to the same industry field. For example, Siemens' patents in 'payment architectures and protocols' were reviewed for citations made in the same category. The firm level analysis was carried out for all three categories. Backward citations of each firm made by patents of the time period 2001-2010 were considered. The analysis only considered references or citations made to patent applications. In the process, all non-patent citations like research articles, internet links, etc. were left out. The set of backward citations were then filtered into the ones coming from other competitors in the same technological class. The patent count considered only the European applications made by the patentees while the citations include all patents worldwide.

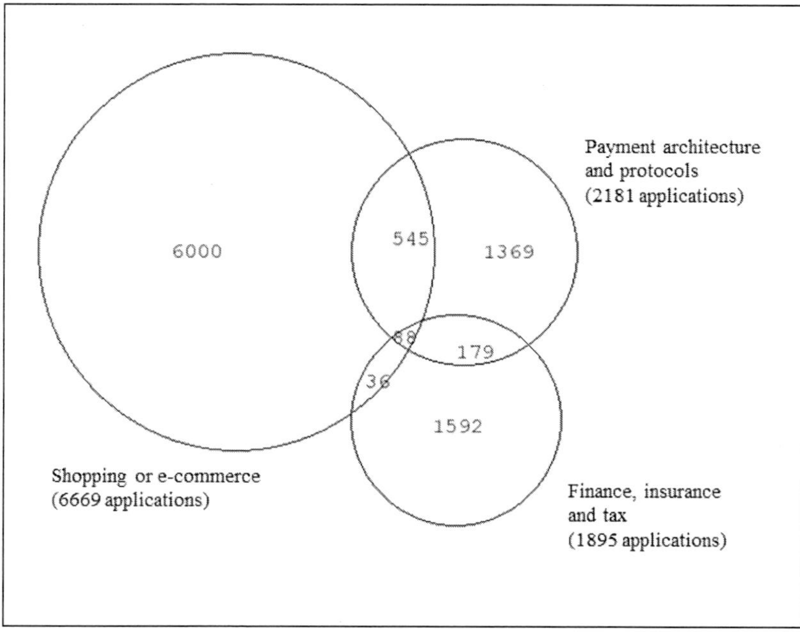

Figure 6. Overlap of patents in the three categories

7.1 Trend analysis: payment architectures and protocols

The IPC main group associated with payment architectures and protocols is 'G06Q 20/00'. Citation analysis was done for the top ten patenting firms in this IPC class. The list of top patenting firms includes mainly telecom giants. The basic backward citation data are presented in Table 7 below.

Table 7. Backward citation data (payment architectures and protocols)

Firm name	Patent count	Backward citations	Backward citations to same technology class	% citations made to same technology class
Siemens AG	62	219	151	68,95
Sony Corp	57	184	83	45,11

Nokia Corp	43	137	56	40,88
Visa Int Service	41	97	66	68,04
Ericsson Telefon	37	90	67	74,44
NTT Docomo Inc	29	122	70	57,38
First Data Corp	28	91	50	54,95
France Telecom	27	66	30	45,45
Fujitsu Ltd	27	110	70	63,64
Mastercard International	25	44	27	61,36

The numbers in Table 7 suggest that Nokia, Sony and France Telecom are relatively more diversified in their innovative activity as compared to their top ten peers. Table 8 below presents the citation category analysis for 'payment architectures and protocols'.

Table 8. citation category data and MoE (payment architectures and protocols)

Firm name	**Total 'A' citations**	**Total 'X' and 'Y' citations**	**'X' and 'Y' to competitors**	**Measure of encroachment**
Siemens AG	96	110	76	0,69
Sony Corp	63	110	57	0,52
Nokia Corp	63	60	30	0,50
Visa Int Service	26	67	47	0,70
Ericsson Telefon	46	38	27	0,71
NTT Docomo Inc	65	49	30	0,61
First Data Corp	48	43	24	0,56
France Telecom	33	29	12	0,41
Fujitsu Ltd	55	46	30	0,65
Mastercard International	19	24	17	0,71
Average	**51,40**	**57,60**	**35,00**	**0,61**

The measure of encroachment values for most of the players are on the higher side for the segment 'payment architectures and protocols'. The average measure of encroachment was 0.61, which is higher than 0.49 for the whole financial services industry. A lower value can suggest that the learning process is diverse and research is not too focused. For example, France Telecom makes almost 60% of their 'X' and 'Y' patent citations to other technology classes than their own, making their learning process more diverse. A high value for measure of encroachment can be an indication that there is a possibility of research collaboration and cross licensing. A larger share of 'A' citations compared to 'X' and 'Y' citations made can indicate more novel research or first movers in the field.

7.2 Trend analysis: shopping or e-commerce

The 'shopping and e-commerce' category is associated with IPC main group 'G06Q 20/00'. The list of top patenting firms includes all information and communication technology (ICT) firms. A relatively high-patent count in this segment is due to the fact that the ICT industry has traditionally been a patent-intensive sector (Bessen and Hunt, 2007). Table 9 below presents the backward citation data for the top patenting firms.

Table 9. Backward citation data (shopping and e-commerce)

Firm name	Patent count	Backward citations	Backward citations to competitors	% citations made to competitors
Sony Corp	215	552	184	33,33
Microsoft Corp	153	174	50	28,74
Koninkl Philips Electronics	152	98	32	32,65
SAP AG	121	118	46	38,98
Accenture	120	205	72	35,12
Matsushita Electric Ind	100	170	57	33,53
Nokia Corp	83	146	35	23,97
Hewlett Packard	79	169	53	31,36
IBM	76	141	50	35,46
Google Inc	74	69	61	88,41

With the exception of Google, the segment seems to be more diverse in terms of citing patents from other industries. All other firms show similar figures for patent citations in the same field. Citation category analysis is depicted in Table 10 below for the segment 'commerce'.

Table 10. Citation category data and MoE (shopping and e-commerce)

Firm name	**Total 'A' citations**	**Total 'X' and 'Y' citations**	**'X' and 'Y' to competitors**	**Measure of encroachment**
Sony Corp	176	317	116	0,37
Microsoft Corp	59	98	33	0,34
Koninkl Philips Electronics	26	58	18	0,31
SAP AG	42	72	28	0,39
Accenture	63	107	48	0,45
Matsushita Electric Ind	60	100	31	0,31
Nokia Corp	55	77	18	0,23
Hewlett Packard	62	95	23	0,24
IBM	54	77	32	0,42
Google Inc	8	61	55	0,90
Average	**60,50**	**106,20**	**40,20**	**0,40**

The measure of encroachment values were lower in the 'commerce' category with the exception of Google, which had an alarmingly high ratio of 'X' and 'Y' citations made to the same segment patents. The average MoE value for this segment was 0.40 as opposed to 0.49 for the financial industry in general. A low number of 'A' citations made by Google is also representative of the lack of original research in the field.

7.3 Trend analysis: finance, insurance and tax

The 'finance, tax and insurance' category is associated with IPC main group 'G06Q 40/00'. The nature of firms in the top patenting companies is mainly related to banking and trading. The backward citation data is tabulated in Table 11 below.

Table 11. Backward citation data (finance, tax and insurance)

Firm name	Patent count	Backward citations	Backward citations to competitors	% citations made to competitors
Espeed	60	34	20	58,82
Trading Tech	46	35	24	68,57
SAP AG	42	38	7	18,42
Swiss Re	39	59	24	40,68
Accenture	33	8	2	25,00
CME	31	8	8	100,00
Goldman Sachs	31	27	15	55,56
Bank of America	23	18	9	50,00
Siemens AG	23	58	8	13,79
OMX Technology	22	23	14	60,87

Siemens, Accenture and SAP had the lowest ratio of citations made to same industry patents. Trading firms have higher average backward citations to competitors than other firms on the list. The analysis was advanced by finding the citation categories assigned to the backward citations by the examiners.

Table 12 suggests that the segment 'finance, insurance and tax' is characterized by fewer 'A' citations made by players that can signify a lack of fundamental research. Fewer A's compared to X's and Y's can mean that it is a 'greenfield' area of research and that there is a lot of potential to develop novel technologies in the field.

The players in this segment are more inexperienced compared to players in other segments. This is because the business method patent is still a relatively new phenomenon in Europe. Kumar and Turnbull (2006) have advised caution in patenting in this category as it can be detrimental to long-term profits. The main reason cited is that institutions invite other institutions to participate in product innovation to diversify risks. The end user also has to be educated on the product, which undermines the idea of patenting. Licensing, as a tool for appropriability, has still not matured fully due to complications due to pricing and antitrust laws.

Table 12. citation category data and MoE (finance, tax and insurance)

Firm name	Total 'A' citations	Total 'X' and 'Y' citations	'X' and 'Y' to competitors	Measure of encroachment
Espeed	7	22	15	0,68
Trading Tech	9	24	18	0,75
SAP AG	3	33	7	0,21
Swiss Re	6	24	12	0,50
Accenture	1	0	0	--
CME	0	5	5	1,00
Goldman Sachs	4	17	9	0,53
Bank of America	8	10	4	0,40
Siemens AG	22	21	2	0,10
OMX Technology	10	13	9	0,69
Average	**7,67**	**18,78**	**9,00**	**0,54**

7.4 Discussion of results

A number of inferences can be drawn from the above tables. A low score in measure of encroachment can suggest that the firm learns from a varied set of industries. A high number of 'A' citations can indicate a more fundamental approach in research and development. Having a high ratio of 'A' citations can help a firm avoid infringement related lawsuits. In this case, it is also possible that the invention is speculative and there are no direct commercial areas where the invention can be utilized. The top patenting players analysed in the study are all big firms or multi-industry conglomerates. Earlier studies by Dow (2007) and Furst et al., (2002) have found a positive relationship between size and the likelihood of adopting new technologies in the context of the financial services industry.

The measure of encroachment figure (0.61) is highest for 'payment architectures and protocols' compared to other categories in the financial services patents. This segment operates in the presence of standards because the presence of standards can create substantial network effects that significantly increase the value of a patented technology. Lemley (2007) estimated that US patents covering an industry standard were 13 times more likely to be litigated than other general US patents. Hunt et al., (2009) considered the complicated goals of standard setting and IP appropriability a reason for conflicting intersection. The goal of IP is to exclude competitors from using proprietary technology while the goal of standards is to stimulate the use of technology as a standard. This can be a reason for a high measure of encroachment in the payment architecture segment. Hunt et al., (2009) used the example of Single Euro Payments Area (SEPA) to emphasize the importance of encompassing intellectual property in influencing the design and implementation of SEPA.

8. Conclusions

The financial services industry does not have as many patents as traditional industries, like mechanical, chemical or pharmaceutical, have. They are still in a stage where effective portfolios are being built. As the restrictions related to business methods patents become lax, we are going to see more patents in the field and more importance associated with their effective management. As portfolios grow, technology transfer and licensing become more and more important.

This chapter looked at the field of patent statistics and the various patent value indicators in use by researchers. Measure of encroachment was introduced as a novel way to use patent citations to study the infringing levels to firms and industries. The list of top patenting companies as shown in Table 6 shows the widespread diffusion of the financial industry. The players belong to a range of core competences. Financial innovation is seen to have a strong bond with IT and telecommunications industries (Lener and Tufano 2011). The results also indicate a close presence of ICT firms in the top patenting firms in the financial services industry. There is lesser encroachment in the field of 'commerce' than in 'payment architectures' and 'finance, tax and insurance'. A high value of measure of encroachment in general for individual firms, especially Chicago Mercantile Exchange (CME), Trading Technologies and Google, can indicate second mover benefits.

8.1 Managerial implications

The analysis presented can help firms in identifying key patents which receive more 'X' and 'Y' citations than others. The technique can help find partners in research collaborations and act as a technology scouting tool. It is also possible to identify potential sources of licensing income. A similar analysis based on a more narrow set of technologies can enable firms identify potential buyers and sellers of certain technologies.

An interview with a software patent attorney revealed that there are fewer cases of litigation among software patents than other traditional industries. The implications seem relevant even to patents related to financial service. Software companies are more into cross-licensing, which saves the need for opposition. A brief excerpt is reproduced below:

> "…by the time it [software patent] is granted, the technology may already be old which makes software patents have fewer opposition proceedings. Software companies are into cross licensing which saves the need of opposition. In traditional industries however, the technology lifecycle is quite long, which gives value to a patent for many years, this is why there is more opposition in, say, the paper industry."

The 'X' and 'Y' citation analysis, when carried out at a more micro level can help in identifying new market entrants who may not strictly belong to the financial service industry but carry products, which perform the same functions. The method presented can be replicated for other industries using relevant IPC classes and used to evaluate infringing levels in other industries. The patent value indicators from the field of patent statistics can be used in financial valuation and decision making. They can provide insights, which can lead to predicting success of firms and thus enable better investment decisions for financial services firms.

The method proposed in this study can be particularly useful for intellectual property managers in evaluating patent portfolios in competitive industries. Use of 'X' and 'Y' citations received can be a better method to identify core patents of a firm. The use of 'A' citations, on the other hand, can be a better way of assessing knowledge spill overs. There are very few studies based on citation categories and this study can attract more attention of researchers towards this potential patent value determinant.

8.2 Future possibilities

Measure of hindrance was introduced earlier as a tool to study the blocking power of firms with respect to their IP portfolios. An extension of the analysis to citations received rather than citations made, can help understand the potential for obtaining licensing income from patent portfolios. A patent, which receives a lot of 'X' and 'Y' patent citations, has the ability to restrict subsequent patents or extract royalties and licensing incomes.

The current analysis checked for 'X' and 'Y' citations made to patents in the same segment. Furthering the analysis to find in which segments the firms are making most 'X' and 'Y' citations can reveal the focus areas of players in the financial services industry. Text mining of patent descriptions can reveal similarities between patents. Combined with a citation category analysis, it can be possible to narrow down on more relevant patents.

References

Bader, M.A. "Managing intellectual property in the financial services industry sector: learning from Swiss Re". *Technovation* 28.4 (2007):196–207.

Baron, J. and Delcamp, H. "The private and social value of patents in discrete and cumulative innovation". *Scientometrics* 90.2 (2012): 581-606.

Bessen, J. and Hunt, R. M. "An empirical look at software patents". *Journal of Economics and Management Strategy* 16.1 (2007): 157-189.

Chen, Y. and Chang, K. "The relationship between a firm's patent quality and its market value — The case of US pharmaceutical industry". *Technological Forecasting and Social Change* 77.1 (2010): 20-33.

Cockburn, I. "Valuing Patents" (2004) [www-document]. [Accessed 25 May 2013]. Available at: http://www.piperpat.com/LinkClick.aspx?link=articles/brands/Value.pdf

Czarnitzki, D., Hussinger, K. and Leten, B. "The market value of blocking patent citations". ZEW - Centre for European economic research. Mannheim, Germany: *Discussion paper no. 11-021* (2011).

Deng, Z., Lev, B. and Narin, F. "Science and technology as predictors of stock performance", *Financial Analysts Journal* 55.3 (1999): 20-32.

Deng, Y. "Private value of European patents". *European Economic Review* 51.7 (2007): 1785-1812.

Dow, J.P. Jr. "The adoption of web banking at credit unions". The *Quarterly Review of Economics and Finance* 47.3 (2007): 435–448.

EPO. "List of Contracting States sorted according to the date of accession" (2010 a) [www-document]. [Accessed 5 May 2013] Available at: http://www.epo.org/about-us/organisation/member-states/date.html

—. "Guidelines for Examination in the European Patent Office" (2010 b). [www-document]. [Accessed 7 June 2013]. Available at: http://documents.epo.org/projects/babylon/eponet.nsf/0/7ffc755ad943703dc12576f00054cacc/$FILE/guidelines_2010_complete_en.pdf

—. "Data Catalog - EPO Worldwide patent statistical Database" (2012). European Patent office [Online document]. [Accessed 24 May 2013]. Available at: http://documents.epo.org/projects/babylon/eponet.nsf/0/830d207d355f3af2c1257aa1002d0cfb/$FILE/data_catalog_v4.41_en.pdf

—. "Schedule of fees" (2013). [www-document]. [Accessed 24 June 2013]. Available at: http://www.epoline.org/portal/portal/default/epoline.Scheduleoffees

Furst, K., Lang, W.W. and Nolle, D.E. "Internet banking". Journal of *Financial Services Research* 22.1/2 (2002): 95–117.

Gambardella, A., Harhoff, D. and Verspagen, B. "The value of European patents". *European Management Review* 5.2 (2008): 69-84.

Graham, S. J. H., Hall, B. H., Harhoff, D. and Mowery, D. C. "Post-Issue Patent Quality Control: A Comparative Study of US Patent Re-examinations and European Patent Oppositions". National Bureau of Economic Research. Cambridge, MA. *NBER Working Paper 8807* (2002).

Guellec, D. and van Pottelsberghe, B. "Applications, grants and value of patents", *Economics Letters* 69.1 (2000): 109-114.

Hall, B. H., Jaffe, A. B. and Trajtenberg, M. "Market value and patent citations". *The RAND Journal of Economics* 36.1 (2005): 16-38.

Hall, B. H., Jaffe, A. B. and Trajtenberg, M. "The NBER Patent Citations Data File: Lessons, Insights, and Methodological tools". Cambridge: The MIT Press. *NBER Working Paper no. 8498* (2001).

Harhoff, D., Scherer, F. M. and Vopel, K. "Citations, family size, opposition and the value of patent rights". *Research Policy* 32.8 (2003): 1343-1363.

Harhoff, D. and Wagner, S. "The Duration of Patent Examination at the European Patent Office". *Management Science* 55.12 (2009): 1969-1984.

Häussler, C., Harhoff, D. and Mueller, E. "The role of patents for VC financing". *Frontiers of entrepreneurship research* 28.3 (2008): 1-17.

Hunt, R.M., Simojoki, S. and Takalo, T. "Intellectual property rights and standards setting in financial services: the case of the single European payments area", in Anderloni, L., Llewellyn, D.T. and Schmidt, R.H. (Eds.): *Financial Innovation in Retail and Corporate Banking* (2009): 170–198, Edward Elgar, Cheltenham.

Jaffe, A. B., Trajtenberg, M. & Fogarty, M. S. "Knowledge spillovers and patent citations: Evidence from a survey of inventors". The American Economic Review 90.2 (2000): 215-218.

Karvonen, M., Kässi, T. and Kapoor, R. "Technological innovation strategies in converging industries". *International Journal of Business Innovation and Research* 4.5 (2010): 391-410.

Kumar, P. and Turnbull, S.M. "Patenting and licensing of financial innovations", *Working paper*, July, CT Bauer College of Business, University of Houston (2006).

Lanjouw, J. O. and Schankerman, M. "Stylized facts of patent litigation: Value, scope and ownership". Cambridge: The MIT Press. *NBER Working Paper no. 6297* (1997).

Lanjouw, J. O. and Schankerman, M. "Patent quality and research productivity". *The Economic Journal* 114.495 (2004): 441-465.

Lemley, M. A. "Ten things to do about patent hold-up of standards (and one not to)". *Boston College Law Review* 48 (2007): 149-168.

Lerner, J. "The Importance of Patent Scope: An Empirical Analysis", *RAND Journal of Economics* 25.2 (1994): 319-333.

—. "The new new financial thing: the origins of financial innovations", *Journal of Financial Economics* 79.2 (2006): 223–255.

—. "The litigation of financial innovations", Journal of Law and Economics 53.4 (2010): 807–831.

Lerner, J. and Tufano P. "The consequences of financial innovation: a counterfactual research agenda", *Annual Review of Financial Economics* 3 (2011): 41–85.

List, J. "An A to X of patent citations for searching". *World Patent Information* 32.4 (2010): 306-312.

Lukach, R. and Plasmans, J. "Measuring Knowledge Spillovers Using Patent Citations: Evidence from the Belgian Firm's Data". Center for Economic Studies & Ifo Institute for Economic Research. Munich, Germany. *CESifo Working Paper No. 754* (2002).

Martinez, C. "Patent families. When do different definitions really matter?" *Scientometrics* 86.1 (2011): 39-63.

Michel, J. and Bettels, B. "Patent citation analysis. A closer look at the basic input data from patent search reports". *Scientometrics* 51.1 (2001): 185–201.

Nemet, G.F. and Johnson, E. "Do important inventions benefit from knowledge originating in other technological domains?" *Research Policy* 41.1 (2012): 190–200.

Neuhäusler, P., Frietsch, R., Schubert, T. and Blind, K. "Patents and financial performance of firms – An analysis based on stock market data". Fraunhofer ISI, Karlsruhe, *Discussion Papers Innovation Systems and Policy Analysis No. 28* (2011).

OECD. Patent Statistics Manual (2009) France: *OECD Publications*.

Pakes, A. and Schankerman, M. "The rate of obsolescence of patents, research gestation lags, and the private rate of return to research resources". In: Griliches, Z. R&D, Patents, and Productivity. University of Chicago Press, Chicago (1984): 73–88.

Pakes, A. "Patents as options: some estimates of the value of holding European patent stocks". *Econometrica* 54.4 (1986): 755–784.

Pitkethly, R. "The valuation of patents: A review of patent valuation methods with consideration of option based methods and potential for future research" (1997). Judge Institute of Management Studies. Cambridge. *Working Paper WP21/97*.

Putnam, J. "The value of international patent rights". *Doctoral dissertation*. Yale University, New Haven, CT (1996).

Reitzig, M. "Improving Patent Valuations for Management Purposes: Validating New Indicators by Analyzing Application Rationales". *Research Policy* 33.6-7 (2004): 939-957.

Roberts, P.W. and Amit, R. "The dynamics of innovative activity and competitive advantage: the case of Australian retail banking, 1981 to 1995", *Organization Science* 14.2 (2003): 107–122.

Scherer, F. M. and Harhoff, D. "Technology policy for a world of skew-distributed outcomes". Research Policy 29.4-5 (2000): 559-566.

Trajtenberg, M. "A Penny for Your Quotes: Patent Citations and the Value of Innovations". *The Rand Journal of Economics* 21.1 (1990): 172-187.

Trajtenberg, M., Henderson, R. and Jaffe, A. "University versus Corporate Patents: A Window on the Basicness of Invention". *Economics of Innovation and New Technology* 5.1 (1997): 19-50.

World Bank. "Patent applications, residents" (2012). [www-document]. [Accessed 31 July 2012]. Available at: http://data.worldbank.org/indicator/IP.PAT.RESD

WIPO. "International Patent Classification (IPC) Official Publication" (2013). [Online document]. [Accessed 14 Aug 2013]. Available at: http://web2.wipo.int/ipcpub/#refresh=page&notion=scheme&version=20130101&symbol=G06Q&viewmode=a&lang=en

Zeebroeck, N. and van Pottelsberghe de la Potterie, B. "The vulnerability of patent value determinants". *Economics of innovation and new technology* 20.3 (2011): 283-308.

CHAPTER SIX

BUSINESS MODEL DESIGN ISSUES: THE CASE OF MOBILE PAYMENTS

DENIS DENNEHY, FREDERIC ADAM AND FERGAL CARTON

1. Introduction

Any new form of payment channel faces the classic "chicken and egg" dilemma; to attract consumers a suitable infrastructure (e.g. point-of-sales) must be implemented; but to attract merchants a critical mass is required before they will invest in the infrastructure (Begonha et al., 2002; Boer and Boer 2010; Contini et al., 2011; Dahlberg et al., 2007; De Bel and Gâza 2011). This would suggest that it is essential to generate sufficient awareness and demand by both consumers and merchants (Ondrus and Lyytinen 2011). Critical mass is closely linked to universality because a vital indication of critical mass is how universal the payment system is (Van der Heijden 2002). To realise its potential, m-payment solutions need to fulfil key requirements for their adoption to reach critical mass. These requirements are: simplicity and usability, universality, interoperability, security, privacy and trust, cost, speed and cross border payments (Antovski and Gusev 2003; Dahlberg et al., 2007; Karnouskos and Fokus 2004; Pousttchi 2003).

Although m-payment solutions have become a fashionable and novel topic in recent years, it has thus far, failed to attract critical levels for mass adoption by consumers and merchants (Mallat 2006; Pousttchi et al., 2009), as well as being overshadowed by a number of publicised failed m-payment initiatives. For example, many of the initiatives that were launched in EU countries have been discontinued, including Paiement CB sur mobile in France, PayBox in Germany and Mpark in Ireland (Dahlberg et al., 2007; Karnouskos and Fokus 2004). In contrast, m-payment services (i.e. Octopus, Mobile Suica) have been successfully launched in Asian countries such as Japan and South Korea (Ondrus and Pigneur 2007) and in developing countries such as M-Pesa in Kenya.

While the adoption of m-payments has been slower than initially expected, there is a growing consumer appetite for a new payment instrument due to a decline in the use of cash at point-of-sales (Kreyer et al., 2003; Mallat 2006; Mallat and Tuunainen 2008). Yet, there is a growing evidence of inertia by key players in the m-payments industry due to issues of poor revenue sharing amongst stakeholders (Ballon and Van Bossuyt 2006), static business models being used in dynamic environments (Coursaris et al., 2006) and that "partnership management" has become a central competence for stakeholders in the m-payments ecosystem (Pigneur, 2002). The absence of coherent definitions and mutually shared terminology across the industry are also attributed to restricting stakeholder cooperation (Boer and Boer 2010; Ondrus and Pigneur 2005). These obstacles may explain why m-payments have not lived up to the hype as promised by its proponents (Damsgaard and Hedman 2009).

To understand how organisations can develop "balanced" or "sustainable" business models, designers need to understand business model "design issues". These issues include: partner selection, orchestration of activities, valuing contributions and benefits of each partner, acceptable risks, acceptable division of roles, acceptable profitability and their interdependencies (De Reuver et al., 2008). Building on this knowledge, the authors designed and evaluated a PMC that can assist practitioners to approach such issues. The structure of the PMC is also influenced by the work of Stähler (2002, p. 8) who states that part of a business model is the *"deliberate decision which value steps the firm sources from external partners and which are conducted internally"*. In the PMC, the internal and external partners are represented under two main sections, the "Internal Partner Value Architecture" and the "External Partner Value Architecture".

The study is motivated after the authors tracked a failed real-world m-payment initiative in Ireland which was in collaboration with a leading mobile network operator (MNO) and various integration partners (i.e. SIM card manufacturer and SIM card integration team, the mobile wallet application developers, the funding account and card issuer, the payment transaction processor, the NFC terminal provider) from the retail and payments industries. After eighteen months of investing resources (e.g. people, technology, financial) and three missed launch dates the MNO withdrew and the initiative collapsed in April 2012. Having identified the absence of "*a common platform to identify, discuss and address partnership challenges*" (Dennehy *et al*., 2012, p.3) as an underlying cause for the collapse of this m-payment initiative, the authors subsequently developed a visualisation tool in the form of a PMC. The aim of the PMC is to assist multiple stakeholders to achieve a shared understanding and a shared commitment at the early stage of forming an m-payment solution. Undertaking the study also answers to the call by Zolnowski et al., (2011, p. 10) who state that future research "... *should thus focus on developing a simple representation of the participation and integration of multiple actors in a business model*" and that the main focus of such research "*should consider the impact of the actors on the business model*".

The structure of our chapter is as follows: First the evolution of value-networks and the associated partnership challenges are presented (Section 2). Following this, is a detailed discussion on the value of business models and how the use visualisation tools encourage creativity, pre-emptive problem solving and controlled implementation (Section 3). A description of the final version of the PMC is also discussed in this section. The next section (Section 4) justifies why a design science research approach and the focus group technique was adopted, as well as the evaluation process of the PMC as a prototype. Next is a summary of the key findings that emerged during the evaluation process (Section 5). The final section (Section 6) provides a conclusion of the study and is implications for practice. Limitations and how future research can overcome such limitions are also discussed here.

2. Value Creation in Value-Networks

Historically innovation was primarily equated with the development of new products or technology. More recently, innovation is being viewed as the development of new service offerings, business models, pricing plans, entry to market plans and management practices (Birkinshaw et al., 2011; Sawhney et al., 2007). Innovation is essentially about identifying and using opportunities to create new products, practices, or services that challenge the status quo and is perceived as 'new' by an individual or group (De Ven 1986; Rogers 1995; Subramaniam and Youndt 2005).

As the ability of organisations to continuously generate innovations is one of the most important capabilities in today's business environment, the ability to innovate is idiosyncratic, even among organisations that operate under the exact same environmental conditions (Ellonen et al., 2009). While there is no shortage of literature dedicated to innovation, much of it is based on the assumption that all organisations face the same challenges to develop new products, practices or services. As a result, adopting a 'one size fits all' approach can be detrimental to a company's survival as in reality, innovation challenges differ from organisation to organisation. Managers need to take an end-to-end view of their innovation activities, identify their specific strengths and weaknesses and tailor 'best practices' of innovation where appropriately needed (Birkinshaw et al., 2011; Hansen and Birkinshaw 2007).

With advances in mobile technology and the emergence of the "digital economy" firms are increasingly experimenting with new forms of value creating techniques such as using a value-network of partners to create value for multiple users (Currie and Parikh 2006; Zott et al., 2011), as well as achieving competitive advantage. As such, the value-chain has evolved to a value-network or value-web, which are characterised by a complex network of direct and indirect relationships between various actors (partners), all delivering value to either the end-consumer or to their immediate customer (Basole and Rouse 2008; Kothandaraman and Wilson 2001). A value-network is a combination of firms (i.e. banks, insurance, telecoms) that can be modelled as value-networks, which depend on a "mediating technology" (Thompson 1967) that facilitates an exchange of interdependent relationships among customers distributed in space and time (Stabell and Fjeldstad 1998). Most organisations are part of a wider value-network, which is *"the set of inter-organisational links and relationships that are necessary to create a product or service"* and is useful in terms of understanding the strategic position of the organisation (Johnson et al., 2011, p. 97). Unlike the traditional, linear value-chain, value-networks are flexible and dynamic and each stakeholder will possess different capabilities and resources which will lead to innovative solutions, when combined together (Faber et al., 2004; Moschella 2003). Such value-networks most often have a leader who manages the network (Kothandaraman and Wilson 2001), as well as, specialisation of roles amongst the actors within the value-network (Johnson et al., 2011). Subsequently, the value-network approach shifts the focus of the firm to a more holistic perspective in which examining the actor-network relationships, transactions costs and resource dependency is crucial (Basole and Rouse 2008).

While a value-network can lead to successful innovations (i.e. m-payment solutions) it presents a number of challenges. For example, as there are various stakeholders in an m-payment value-network: consumers, merchants, mobile network operators, mobile device manufacturers, financial institutions, software and technology providers and governments (Dahlberg et al. 2007), each stakeholder brings their own unique strengths and expectations (Au and Kauffman 2008), which adds another layer of complexity to the network (Carr 2007; Karnouskos and Fokus 2004).

Consequently, the value-network becomes even more complex as each stakeholder has different incentives and strategies, which may result in conflicts and disruption of the ecosystem (Antovski and Gusev 2003; Carr 2007; Gao et al., 2005).

In a complex value-network where the organisations are engaged in inter-organisational investments, they are connected through intended relationships and interdependencies, which involve considerable risks, problem solving, collective-decision making and having access to complimentary knowledge (Bouwman and Ham 2003; Dahlberg et al., 2007). As a result, investment decisions will extend beyond a single organisation and the value implications extend to a network (Kohli and Grover 2008). As organisations shift from single firm revenue generation to multi-firm control and revenue sharing issues, not only are control and value issues of most relevance to business modelling, but two key questions emerge *"Who controls the value network and the system design?"* and *"Is substantial value being produced by this model or not?"* (Ballon 2007, p. 2). Creating value for actors in a value-network is both challenging and complex due to their conflicting strategic interests such as generating transactions and extending services to new customer segments (De Reuver et al., 2008).

Cooperation in a value-network is also challenging, as there is evidence that organisations experience significant difficulties in attaining mutual benefits and because the partners are from different industries (i.e. retailers, network providers), there is potential that the diversity could disrupt the network and revenue sharing issues (Ballon 2007; Faber et al., 2004). For example, in order to increase competitive advantage, organisations will exploit their market position, negotiating power and access to critical resources (Bouwman and Ham 2003). These challenges can be partly attributed to explaining why the success of m-payment platforms remain hampered by recurring and fundamental social, institutional and business challenges that requires a multi-level and multi-perspective approach as it provides a richer picture of the phenomenon (Currie and Parikh 2006; Dahlberg et al., 2007; Dahlberg et al.,2008; Gao and Damsgaard 2007; Ondrus and Lyytinen 2011). This would suggest that researching m-payment adoption issues without assessing the institutional and business context will not provide sufficient explanations into a complex value-network such as m-payments (Ondrus and Lyytinen 2011; Zmijewska and Lawrence 2005).

Since business model innovation can be viewed as *"reconfiguring the value-network...based on actor change"* (Wu and Zhang, 2009, p. 4), it would be prudent to use the business model literature as a lens to further understand the m-payment phenomenon which is discussed in the next section.

3. New Business Models for Mobile Channels

Business models are an important locus of innovation and are a critical source of value creation and competitive advantage for an organisation, its suppliers, partners, and customers (Amit and Zott 2001; Mitchell and Coles 2003). Business models also have an important role in business practice (Bodker et al., 2009) as they answer two fundamental questions of organisations: How do we make money in this business? What is the underlying logic that explains how we can deliver value to our customers at an appropriate cost? (Magretta 2002). However, the business model concept and strategy are often used interchangeably in business practice even though they have different meanings. For example, business models describe how the different elements of a business fit together, as a whole system, but it does not factor in competition, which is an essential aspect of performance (*ibid*). This is an important point because even though a firm may have a business model it is the competitive strategy that explains how the organisation will do things better than its competitors. Aligning the business model with the market environment as well as the industry environment, is crucial (Ondrus et al., 2009).

Although the ultimate aim of designing a business model is to create sufficient economic and customer value, the challenge is that it requires connecting and balancing design choices in different business model domains while taking into account technical, market and legal developments (Faber et al., 2004). In many instances, the customer value envisaged in the initial design of a business model has little to do with the value as perceived by the end-customer (e.g. the end-user) as it depends on the customers' personal and consumption context (Chen and Dubinsky 2003; Wieringa and Gordijn 2005). However, financial institutions are being forced to change their attitude to deliver compelling value propositions due to increased demand by the end-consumers. This is particularly evident with a new costumer segment known as "Generation Y" or the "Millennia's" that have emerged in the past decade. These baby boomers of the mid 1980s are a mobile savvy customer segment that are being touted as the cohort, which will be the catalyst for driving m-payments into mainstream banking services by using their mobile phones to make m-payments their preferred method of payment (Au and Kauffman 2008; Britton and McGonegal 2007; Goswami and Raghavendran 2009; Jacob 2007). Financial institutions also have a long tradition of cooperating with merchants, whereas cooperating with telecoms and technology vendors is a new experience for them (Dahlberg et al., 2007). Nevertheless, the overall value of a business model is measured by its return to all stakeholders, financial performance, market share, brand and reputation, and the return to the company (Hedman and Kalling 2003).

There are weaknesses in the creation and use of business models, which include: flawed assumptions underlying the core logic of the business model if based on weak assumptions about the future (i.e. financial crises), too much focus on the value creation and minimising the value capture component of the model can result in the corresponding return on investment (ROI) not being captured and assuming that the existing value-network will remain unchanged in the future, can be detrimental to the organisations profitability (Shafer et al., 2005). Although business models are a vital source of innovation for an organisation, these short-comings indicate that even the best business model does not guarantee organisational sustainability. Specific to m-payments, the uncertainty around establishing a sustainable economic business model that can be agreed by the multiple stakeholders has been identified as a contributing factor for the delayed launch of m-payment initiatives (Chaix and Torre 2010). Pousttchi et al., (2009) express a similar view that the interrelations within an m-payment business model have been ignored by service providers, which has resulted in failed initiatives. In addition, stakeholders in the m-payment value-network need to agree on acceptable revenue and cost sharing amongst stakeholders (Mallat and Tuunainen 2008; Varshney 2002).

Withstanding such weaknesses, the business model provides many practical benefits. For example, when managers consciously operate from a model of how the entire business systems will work, every decision, initiative and measurement provides valuable feedback (Magretta 2002). Business models are beneficial in determining the underlying logic that explains how an organisation creates and delivers value to their customers, while also capturing returns from the value itself (Magretta 2002; Shafer et al., 2005). Business models also offer a high level of abstraction, which is the correct starting point when creating or redefining business processes rather than analysing the business processes themselves (Weigand et al., 2006). Yet, a majority of managers find the business model concept difficult as they either don't understand their current model enough when to know it needs changing or how to make that change (Chesbrough and Schwartz 2007; Johnson et al., 2008). In response to this knowledge gap between academia and practice, Osterwalder and Pignuer (2010) proposed the Business Model Canvas which was based on Osterwalder's earlier work on Business Model Ontology. The Business Model Canvas is one example of how practitioners and academics can leverage the use of visualisation tools, which are briefly discussed in the next section.

3.1 Leveraging Visualisation Tools

The use of visualisation tools (i.e. business model canvas, service blue printing) have been critical in the analysis of complex systems such as service value-networks (Brandes et al., 2001). Unlike verbal definitions, design techniques (i.e. service blueprints, business modelling) are more accurate, are less likely to be misinterpreted and can reduce the potential for failure as they encourage creativity, pre-emptive problem solving and controlled implementation (Shostack 1984). For example, although service blueprinting shares similar characteristics (i.e. using visual notations to represent actors and activities) with other process modelling techniques (i.e. Unified Modelling Language, Business Process Modelling Notation), it is less formal and complex, enabling all stakeholders to meet particular requirements (Bitner et al., 2008). Service designers see the design of service (e.g. service innovation) as intertwined with the business strategy (e.g. business model innovation), because they are continuously moving between the design of a service and the business model (Kimbell 2008). In the absence of modelling service systems and because services are intangible, people frequently use words only to specify them, which results in over generalisation and incompleteness (Bitner et al., 2008). Building on this body of knowledge the authors propose a visualisation tool in the form of a PMC, which is discussed in the next section.

3.2 The Partnership Management Canvas

This section explains the three main sections of the final version of the PMC which is presented in Fig 3-1 below. The top section (green) is the starting point as it focuses on the internal and external partnership value architecture as there can be multiple internal partners (i.e. departments such as legal, sales, IT), as well as multiple external partners (i.e. integration partners, merchants, telecoms), the middle section (blue) emphasises the partners' position within the value-network and the bottom section (red) explicitly identifies and prioritises risks.

Within each of these sections, there are a number of elements. The top (green) section includes; the partner's name, their contribution to the business model (i.e. branding, financial, customer access), their role within the network, the benefits gained by each partner (i.e. new or increased revenue streams) and the impact that each partner will have on the business model of the "focal" company that is initiating the new service (i.e. a telecom or bank led business model or a business model with a neutral entity). By starting in the top (green) section, each partner is assigned a coloured "Post-it" and move through the three sections where they position a post-it that has been filled with key words. For example, an internal partner name could be the "Sales & Marketing" department and their contribution would be informing consumers of the new mobile service prior to and after the launch phase. Their role may be supporting the overall business model and their expertise will highlight potential risks that may have been overlooked by other stakeholders.

The middle (blue) section highlights where each partner can be strategically positioned within the three phases of the network, these being the concept development phase, the testing/pre-launch phase and post-launch phase. In this section, each partner is positioned at three possible levels, level one (Lead), level two (Contribute) and level three (Support). Such positioning is important as it clarifies any misconceptions that a partner may have about themselves or the other partners and exemplifies that even the focal organisation does not necessarily have to lead each phase.

The final (red) section prioritises risks, their impact domain (e.g. time, cost, quality, scope), action plan, who is responsible and the desired outcome (i.e. risk eliminated or minimised).

The PMC is a practical tool that can be used by key decision-makers and strategists when they are designing innovative business models, which involve multiple stakeholders. Due to the iterative "design and evaluate" nature of the study, adopting a design science research approach was deemed highly suitable and is justified in the next section.

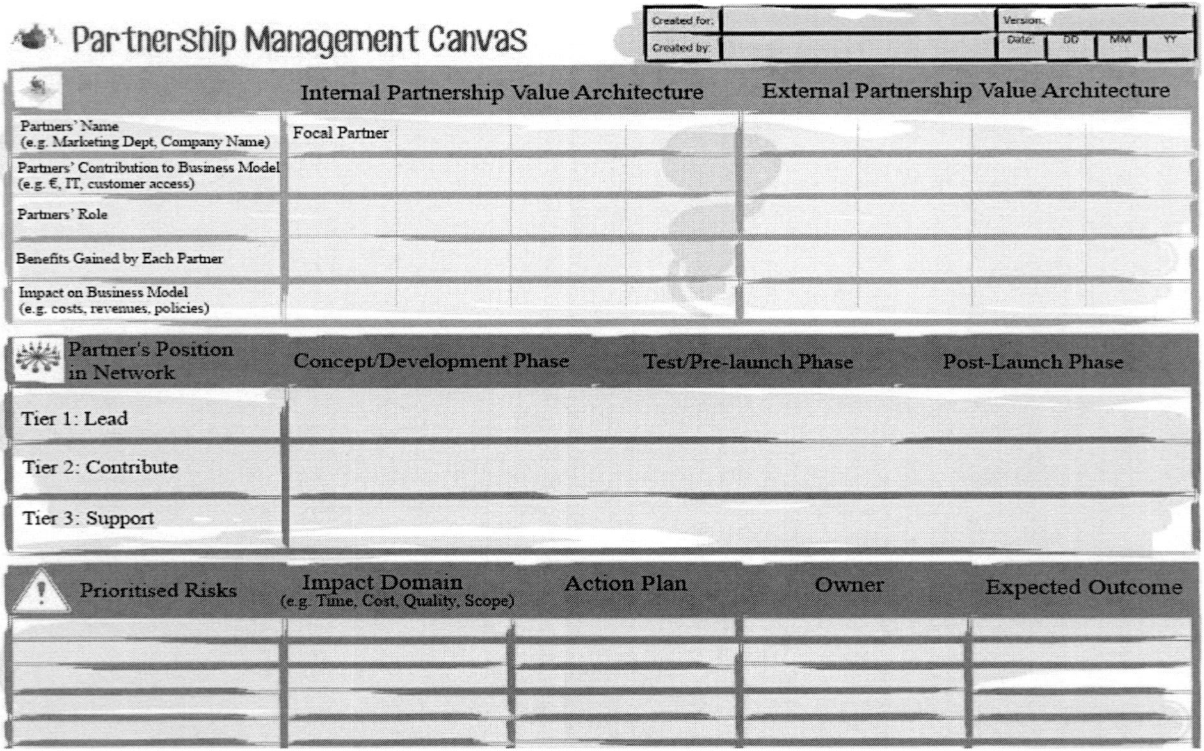

Figure 1. Partnership Management Canvas ©

4. Adopting a Design Science Research Approach

Design science research (DSR) addresses what are considered to be wicked problems, or using Simon's (1973) terminology, "ill-structured" (Brooks Jr 1987; Rittel and Webber 1974). Design thinking assumes the human experience is always messy and sees true objectivity as an illusion (Liedtka and Ogilvie 2011). This research paradigm is about understanding and solving a "real world" problem (Baskerville 2008) by developing artifacts in the form of constructs (e.g. concepts, terminologies), models, methods, and instantiations, which are solutions implemented as prototypes or production systems (Österle et al., 2010). For example, enterprise resource planning systems (ERPs), activity-based costing (ABC), radio-frequency identification (RFID) are artifacts that have been created to solve managerial problems, as well as business models, guidelines and frameworks (Holmström et al., 2009; Österle et al., 2010). Although design is central to the activities of design science research, it is more than just design practice, since design science is a "knowledge producing activity" while design practice is a "knowledge using activity (Baskerville 2008; Hevner et al., 2004; March and Smith 1995).

4.1 Research Methodology

To ensure that the research results are both rigorous and relevant, the study followed a design science research method, as proposed by Peffers et al., (2006), which involves six key activities. The first activity is to "identify the problem and motivation" for the study, which we outlined in the introduction section. The second activity concerns the "objective of the solution": our objective is to address the above mentioned research gap and facilitate a better understanding of partnership issues within value-networks by conceptualising these issues in the form of a PMC and to derive design principles that can inform practice and academia. The third activity involved the "design and development", which in this study resulted in a PMC. The fourth activity is to "demonstrate" a proof of concept by finding a suitable context (e.g. m-payment value-networks) so that the use of the PMC can be employed so as to address instances of the problem. The fifth activity is the "evaluation" of the PMC which was achieved by observing its efficiency and effectiveness through a number of iterations starting from the third activity. This iterative evaluation process was informed by feedback provided by practitioners who participated in a series of focus groups and is discussed in the following section. The sixth and final activity is to disseminate the insights gained from the study to practitioner and academic audiences.

4.2 The Focus Group Technique

Focus groups are a type of group interviewing technique, which relies on interaction within a group. In contrast the group interview is about interviewing a number of people at the same time and the emphasis is on the questions and answers between the interviewer and participants (Gibbs 1997; Morgan 1997). The focus group technique is historically based on the classic literature of Merton who in 1956 wrote a paper titled "The focused interview" (Robinson, 1999). The focused interview was primarily used to *"... provide some basis for interpreting statistically significant effects of mass communication"* (Merton and Kendall 1946, p. 542). More recently though, researchers are increasingly advocating for the adoption of the "interactionist approach" within focus groups as it *"strives to integrate the various stakeholder interests and perspectives when determining the value of socially embedded systems"* (O'Raghallaigh et al., 2011, p. 3).

Leveraging focus groups fits with the aims of the study as this technique can be used for exploratory and confirmatory research methods, because the nature of the data generated (e.g. emic and etic) is different to that of other research methods. For example, "emic" data are data that emerge in a natural form that are minimally imposed by the researcher or the research setting, while "etic" data are data that are imposed by the researcher (Stewart et al., 2007). While neither emic and etic data are better or worse than each other, when little is understood about the phenomenon, tools that generate more emic data are usually first used and as the knowledge accumulates, tools that generate more etic data are employed (*ibid*). There are numerous reasons why focus groups are highly suited to this study. For example, the researcher has direct contact with domain experts and potential users of the design artifact (e.g. PMC), the interactions between participants allows for the emergence of ideas or opinions that are not usually uncovered in individual face-to-face interviews and focus groups produce a very rich body of data expressed in the respondents own words and context (Peffers and Tuunanen, 2005; Stewart et al, 2007; Tremblay et al., 2010; Wilkinson, 2004).

Although the recommended group size in a focus group can range between six to twelve people (Mallat 2006; Stewart et al., 2007), a focus group can have as little as two participants (Wilkinson 2004). The group sizes in this study ranged from eight to ten people, with the exception of one focus group, which consisted of three people. The dynamics of small and large groups differ, as with smaller groups, participants must contribute more, while with the larger groups there is the risk of "social loafing" (Stewart et al., 2007; Tremblay et al., 2010).

As the process of design science research requires the frequent iteration between the development and evaluation of the artifact, Tremblay et al., (2010, p. 600) propose two types of focus groups; exploratory focus groups (EFGs), which are used for the *"design and refinement of the artifact"* and confirmatory focus groups (CFGs) which are used for the *" confirmatory proof of an artifact's utility in the field"*. The next section reports on the iterative "design and evaluate" process of the study, which includes a pilot focus group, three exploratory focus groups and a confirmatory focus group.

4.3 Evaluating the Partnership Management Canvas

The focus groups commenced in January 2013 with a ninety-minute informal pilot focus group with eight undergraduate students from the Business Information Systems Department in University College Cork (UCC), Ireland. All students were in their final year of studies and had a range of business and technological competencies, as well as having industry placement experience. The benefit of running an informal pilot focus group (where one could and did use students) is that the researcher can identify timing issues, refine the questioning route and the moderators style (Tremblay et al., 2010).

Following the pilot study, three exploratory focus groups took place between February and May with practitioners who were completing Executive education programmes with UCC and the Irish Management Institute (IMI). Table 4-1 below provides a range of the participant profiles who participated in the exploratory and confirmatory focus groups.

Table 1. Range of Participant Profiles

Participant Titles	
Vice President Payment Services	Global Technical Support Director
Chief Business Development Officer	Head of IT Corporate Systems
Chief Technology Officer	Service Operations Manager
Product Specialist - New Product Introduction Management	Head of Finance
Senior Development Manager	Senior Operations Manager
Senior Finance Manager	European Sales Manager

As the practitioners possessed a wide range of expertise and were from diverse industry backgrounds, it was possible to reflect the real-world challenges (e.g. negotiation, communication, and managing partnerships) faced by practitioners during the focus group sessions. The duration of the exploratory and confirmatory focus group was two hours, during, which participants were presented with an m-payment scenario and were required to approach this scenario by role playing the various stakeholders in a typical m-payment value-network. Initially the groups worked without the PMC and then approached the same scenario using the canvas prototype. On completion of this activity participants individually filled in an evaluation form which enabled them to document their experience of using the PMC and the overall process of interaction between the other group members. The questions contained in the evaluation form focused on utility measurements such as communication, positioning and contribution of stakeholders within the value-network, identification of any issues that emerged in their group and any benefits observed while using the PMC. Participants were also asked to provide suggestions to improve the usefulness and ease-of-use of the canvas.

The focus groups were strategically conducted at least four weeks apart as this provided the researchers with sufficient time to analyse the feedback provided from each focus group. This feedback coupled with the observations of the focus group facilitators informed the iterative "build and evaluate" nature of the study, which resulted in elements of the PMC undergoing a number of changes. For example, the terminology in some elements of the PMC was changed and additional lines were added as this made the canvas more user-friendly. Such changes were necessary as this ensured that the design and utility of the PMC was sufficiently robust before progressing to the confirmatory focus group.

In June, a confirmatory focus group was carried out in Luxembourg with senior executives from an indigenous company that currently provides an m-payment service. A top-level executive from a leading bank in Luxembourg also participated in this focus group as it is a key supporting partner within the business model of this focal company. Although the participants of this focus group were partners in a successful m-payment business model, they were presented with the partnership issues associated with m-payment value-networks. These issues were informed by academic literature and the insights gained from the failed m-payment initiative, which was highlighted in the introduction section. In order to extract rich data from this focus group, the researchers ensured that the information provided would be treated confidentially and as a result we have integrated this data with the exploratory focus group data which is presented in the next section.

As the participants from the exploratory and confirmatory focus groups possessed a wide range of expertise, skills and terminology specific to their business backgrounds, using the PMC to create a common platform for discussion was essential in order to approach stakeholder issues. By observing how practitioners used the PMC, coupled with the individual evaluation forms, the researchers were able to gain empirical evidence on the benefits gained by the use of this visualisation tool and are summarised in the next section.

5. Key Findings

Taking into consideration the iterative nature of the study, which was informed by the feedback, provided by over eighty practitioners, this section provides a summary of our key findings indicating that the utility of the PMC was achieved. The findings would also support the claim by Moody (2009, p. 756) who states that the "*use of visual representations are deemed to be effective because they tap into the capabilities of the powerful and highly parallel human visual system*".

As highlighted in the literature, one of the challenges that emerge when forming an m-payment value-network, is how multiple stakeholders perceive their own (and the other stakeholders) position and contribution to a value-network. By using the PMC, participants stated that not only did they use the canvas "*focus and simplify relationships*" but it also provided them with a *"clear view of each partner" and a "clear delineation of impact of various stakeholders."* The PMC also helped the partners *"identify if certain partners make unreasonable demands regarding returns that are not proportional to their contribution*".

In relation to the positioning of the stakeholders in the value-network, participants commented that by using the PMC it supported *"the creation of a hierarchy [which] ensured the correct level of involvement [of stakeholders] at the right time" and that it* "*could be used to exclude unnecessary stakeholders" as* "*trade-off positions become clearer".* One participant noted that although their group initially discussed their position in the network, it was not until their positions were in a *"diagram format [that] it became clearer as to where everybody else saw themselves and others.* Similar supporting views were expressed by other participants who stated that by using the canvas, they *"identified the players who were or wanted to lead this project"* and that it gave them *"a greater understanding of which stakeholders I needed to engage with more".*

Using the PMC as a visualisation tool provided a *"clearer view of the role of each stakeholder and particularly the leadership [that is] expected or not"*.

The literature also revealed that the absence of a mutually shared terminology across the industry was also attributed to restricting stakeholder cooperation. Participants expressed their belief that using the PMC provided a common platform as a "*basis for discussion" which in turn helped to* provide a structure to finding solutions as it "focused [our] thinking" and *"focused all stakeholder's understanding of the process*", which in turn "*helped to focus all stakeholders on reaching agreements"*. The relevance and utility of the PMC was noted by a participant who stated that *"if adopted early in the process, its helps to gain buy-in of stakeholders"*. By using the PMC it created a common platform for multiple stakeholders from diverse backgrounds to communicate. For example, a number of participants stated that it was *"good to have a model to bring together all parties"* so that *"everyone had a voice"* as the PMC provided a *"common language"* for the stakeholders. Participants also commented that the PMC acted as *"a vehicle for brainstorming"* and that it provided the opportunity to *"identify gaps"*, as well as *"highlighting issues that had not surfaced before using the visualisation tool"*.

Introducing the PMC during the focus group, rather than at the beginning, was important, as it revealed that although the groups believed that they had performed well without using the canvas, once it was introduced *"more issues were highlighted"* and *"it put a framework on all the issues we discussed and as a result there was a clearer understanding of where everybody fitted into the process"*.

These findings suggest that introducing the PMC at the early stages, when forming an m-payment value-network, is highly beneficial as it enables multiple stakeholders to achieve "a shared understanding and shared commitment". Even though the PMC was evaluated in the context of an m-payment value-network, the study revealed a number of implications for practice and is discussed in the next section.

6. Conclusions

The potential benefits of m-payments remain limited until a universal m-payment solution that delivers a compelling value proposition is adopted by merchants and consumers. To achieve this potential, collaboration with multiple stakeholders from diverse industries is essential and inevitably requires partnership management. Yet partnership management has been identified in the literature as a core competence that organisations need to develop in order to bring m-payment solutions into mainstream financial services. Failure to develop this core competence can and does result in failed m-payment initiatives. Rather than providing another theoretical perspective to this challenge, the authors adopted a design science research approach to design and evaluate a visualisation tool in the form of a PMC. The aim of the PMC is to assist practitioners to approach partnership issues when forming an m-payment value-network. By providing a simple representation of how multiple actors participate and integrate in a business model and their impact on the business model, we answered to the call of Zolnowski et al., (2011).

While elements of the initial PMC prototype were informed by extant literature on business models and value-networks, the prototypes were evaluated by over eighty practitioners who participated in a series of exploratory and confirmatory focus groups. As managing partnerships is a core competence for stakeholders engaging in m-payments, leveraging the PMC supports managers to develop this proficiency while also increasing their potential to design sustainable business models for value-networked initiatives. The authors discuss the implications for practice in the next section.

6.1 Managerial Implications

Although the jury is out on, which business model (bank or telecom led or a neutral entity) will ultimately win the race to achieving a universal m-payment solution, the authors believe that organisations that want to engage in sustainable value-networks will need to practice "co-leadership" rather than assuming that a single leadership role is necessary.

The findings suggest that by leveraging design thinking and the use of innovative visualisation tools, such as the PMC, communication and decision-making between multiple stakeholders improves, which increases the potential to design a sustainable business model. Further, by utilising the PMC, stakeholders can pre-empt potential partnership issues that may undermine the sustainability of the value-network, while also using the PMC to pre-empt mutually agreeable solutions. By understanding the roles, contributions and positions of the various stakeholders in the value-network, stakeholders can focus on how best to design and deliver a compelling value proposition that has been adapted to meet the needs of the end-consumer.

By adopting a design science research approach, the study revealed that although the business model canvas has been frequently criticised for being "static" in a dynamic environment (e.g. m-payments), such criticisms should focus on the manager's inability to manage a dynamic process. Managers and other decision-makers should also incorporate more "decision-making by design" into their work practices as visual representations are two-dimensional (spatial) while textual representations are one-dimensional (linear) (Moody, 2009). The insight gained from the research suggests that the sooner multi-stakeholder initiatives use visualisation tools such as the PMC, a common platform can be created to identify, discuss and address partnership challenges (i.e. contributions, roles and responsibilities). In doing so, practitioners can identify sooner, rather than later, if a sustainable value-network can be realised or not, thus saving time, resources, finances and even personal reputations.

As with any research project there are limitations, hence, the limitations of our study and how to overcome such limitations with future research are presented in the next and final section.

6.2 Limitations and Future Research

In order to demonstrate a proof of concept, the PMC was evaluated in the context of m-payment value-networks. Future research in other value-networked industries would provide new knowledge. In addition, by upgrading the current PMC paper prototype into a digital format would provide new insights into how practitioners can leverage visualisation tools on-line for multi-stakeholder collaboration.

References

Amit, R., and Zott. C. 2001. Value creation in E-business. *Strategic Management Journal* 22 (6 7):493-520.

Antovski, L. and Gusev, M., 2003. M-payments. *Proceedings of the 25th International Conference on Information Technology Interfaces*, vol., no., pp. 95, 100, DOI: 10.1109/ITI.2003.1225328

Au, Y.A. and Kauffman, R.J., 2008. The economics of mobile payments: Understanding stakeholder issues in an emerging financial technological application, *Electronic Commerce Research and Applications* Vol/Issue: 7 (2), p. 141

Ballon, P., 2007. Business modelling revisited: the configuration of control and value. *Info* 9 (5):6-19.

Ballon, P. and van Bossuyt, M., 2006. Comparing business models for multimedia content distribution platforms.

Baskerville, R., 2008. What design science is not. *European Journal of Information Systems* 17 (5):441-443.

Basole, RC. and Rouse, WB., 2008. Complexity of service value networks: conceptualization and empirical investigation. *IBM Systems Journal* 47 (1):53-70.

Begonha, D.B, Hoffmann, A. and Melin, P., 2002. M-Payments: Hang up, try again. *Credit Card Management* 15 (10):40-44.

Birkinshaw, J., Bouquet, C. and Barsoux. J., 2011. The 5 Myths of Innovation. *MIT Sloan Management Review* 52 (2):43.

Bitner, M.J., Ostrom, A.L. and Morgan. F.N., 2008. Service blueprinting: A practical technique for service innovation. *California Management Review* 50 (3):66.

Bodker, M., Gimpel, G. and Hedman, J., 2009. Smart Phones and Their Substitutes: Task-Medium Fit and Business Models. *Eighth International Conference on Mobile Business*, 27-28 June.

Boer, R. and Boer, T., 2010. Mobile payments 2010: Market analysis and overview. *Innopay BV and Telecompaper BV,* https://www.ebaportal.eu/_Download/ResearchandAnalysis/2010/Mobile_payments_2010_Innopay.pdf

Bouwman, H. and Ham, E., 2003. Designing metrics for business models describing Mobile services delivered by networked organisations. In Workshop on concepts, metrics and visualization at the *16th Bled Electronic Commerce Conference eTransformation, Bled, Slovenia*.

Brandes, U., Raab, J. and Wagner, D., 2001. Exploratory network visualization: Simultaneous display of actor status and connections. *Journal of Social Structure* 2 (4):1.

Britton, D.B. and McGonegal. S., 2007. The digital economy fact book. *The Progress and Freedom Foundation,* Washington DC.

Brooks Jr, F.P., 1987. No silver bullet essence and accidents of software engineering. *IEEE Computer* 20 (4):10-19.

Carr, M., 2007. Mobile Payment Systems and Services: An introduction. In *Mobile Payment Forum*, pp. 1-12

Chaix, L. and Torre, D., 2010. Different models for mobile payments. *Different models for mobile payments*. Working Paper University of Nice Sophia-Antipolis

Chen, Z. and Dubinsky. A.J., 2003. A conceptual model of perceived customer value in e-commerce: A preliminary investigation. *Psychology and Marketing* 20 (4):323-347.

Chesbrough, H. and Schwartz. K., 2007. Innovating business models with co-development partnerships. *Research-Technology Management* 50 (1):55-59.

Contini, D., Crowe, M., Merritt, M., Oliver, R. and Mott S., 2011. Mobile Payments in the United States: Mapping Out the Road Ahead. *In proceedings of the Mobile Payments Industry Workshop,* Federal Reserve Banks.

Coursaris, C., Hassanein, K. and Head, M., 2006. Mobile Technologies and the Value Chain: Participants, Activities and Value Creation. Paper read *International Conference on Mobile Business*, pp. 26-27.

Currie, W.L. and Parikh, M.A., 2006. Value creation in web services: an integrative model. *The Journal of Strategic Information Systems* 15 (2):153-174.

Dahlberg, T., Huurros, M. and Ainamo, A., 2008. Lost Opportunity Why Has Dominant Design Failed to Emerge for the Mobile Payment Services Market in Finland? In *Hawaii International Conference on System Sciences, Proceedings of the 41st Annual*, pp. 83-83 IEEE

Dahlberg, T., Mallat, N. ., Ondrus, J. and Zmijewska, A., 2007. Past, present and future of mobile payments research: A literature review. *Electronic Commerce Research and Applications* 7 (2):165-181.

Damsgaard, J. and Hedman, J., 2009. Mobile Services Revisited: an Analysis of ICMB 2006. *Center for Applied ICT (CAICT),* CBS, Frederiksberg

Dennehy, D., Carton, F., and Adam, F. (2012), M-payments: Exploring the process of creating and delivering value - *Proceedings of the 2nd Innovation for Financial Services Summit* (ISPIM), Luxembourg

De Bel, J. and Gâza. M., 2011. Mobile Payments 2012 - My mobile, my wallet? http://www.innopay.com/publications/mobile-payments-2012-my-mobile-my-wallet

De Reuver, M., Bouwman, H. and Haaker. T. , 2008. Capturing value from mobile business models: design issues that matter. *21st Bled eConference, eCollaboration: Overcoming boundaries through multi-channel interaction.*

Ellonen, H.K., Wikström, P. and Jantunen. A., 2009. Linking dynamic-capability portfolios and innovation outcomes. *Technovation* 29 (11):753-762.

Faber, E., Haaker, T. and Bouwman. H., 2004. Balancing requirements for customer value of mobile services. *International Journal of Mobile Communications* 4, no. 6 (2006): 645-661.

Gao, J., Edunuru, K., Cai, J. and Shim. S.P.D., 2005. P2P-paid: a peer-to-peer wireless payment system. In t*he Second IEEE International Workshop on Mobile Commerce and Services, WMCS'05.* IEEE, pp. 102-111.

Gao, P. and Damsgaard. J. , 2007. A framework for understanding mobile telecommunications market innovation: A case of China. *Journal of Electronic Commerce Research* 8 (3):184-195.

Gibbs, A., 1997. Focus groups. *Social research update* 19 (8).
Goswami, D. and Raghavendran. S., 2009. Mobile-banking: can elephants and hippos tango? *Journal of Business Strategy* 30 (1):14-20.
Hansen, M.T. and Birkinshaw. J., 2007. The innovation value chain. *Harvard Business Review* 85 (6):121.
Hedman, J. and Kalling. T., 2003. The business model concept: theoretical underpinnings and empirical illustrations. *European Journal of Information Systems* 12 (1):49-59.
Hevner, A.R., March, S., Park, J. and Ram. S., 2004. Design Science in Information Systems Research. *MIS Quarterly* 28 (1):75-105.
Holmström, J., Ketokivi, M. and Hameri. A.P., 2009. Bridging practice and theory: a design science approach. *Decision Sciences* 40 (1):65-87.
Jacob, K., 2007. Are mobile payments the smart cards of the aughts? *Chicago Fed Letter*:1-4.
Johnson, G., Whittington, R., Scholes, K. and Pyle. S., 2011. *Exploring Strategy: text & cases*: Financial Times Prentice Hall.
Johnson, M. W., Christensen, C. M., and Kagermann, H., 2008. Reinventing your business model. *Harvard Business Review*, *86*(12), 57-68.
Karnouskos, S. and Fokus. F., 2004. Mobile payment: a journey through existing procedures and standardization initiatives. *Communications Surveys & Tutorials, IEEE* 6 (4):44-66.
Kimbell, L., 2008. Service design: a 21st century interdsicipline. *Designing for Services-Multidisciplinary Perspectives*:53-54.
Kohli, R. and Grover. V., 2008. Business value of IT: An essay on expanding research directions to keep up with the times. *Journal of the Association for Information Systems* 9 (1):23-39.
Kothandaraman, P. and Wilson. D.T., 2001. The Future of Competition: Value-Creating Networks. *Industrial Marketing Management* 30 (4):379-389.
Kreyer, N., Turowski, K. and Pousttchi. K., 2003. Mobile payment procedures: scope and characteristics. *E-Service Journal* 2 (3):7-22.
Liedtka, J. and Ogilvie. T., 2011. *Designing for Growth - a design thinking toolkit for managers*: Columbia University Press.
Magretta, J., 2002. Why business models matter. *Harvard Business Review* 80 (5):86-93.
Mallat, N., 2006. Exploring consumer adoption of mobile payments - A qualitative study. *The Journal of Strategic Information Systems* 16 (4):413-432.

Mallat, N. and Tuunainen. V.K., 2008. Exploring merchant adoption of mobile payment systems: an empirical study. *E-Service Journal* 6 (2):24-57.
March, S.T. and Smith. G.F., 1995. Design and natural science research on information technology. *Decision Support Systems* 15 (4):251-266.
Merton, R. and Kendall. P., 1946. The Focused Interview. *American Journal of Sociology* 51 (6):541-557.
Mitchell, D. and Coles. C., 2003. The ultimate competitive advantage of continuing business model innovation. *Journal of Business Strategy* 24 (5):15-21.
Moody, D., 2009. The "physics" of notations: toward a scientific basis for constructing visual notations in software engineering. *Software Engineering, IEEE Transactions on* 35 (6):756-779.
Morgan, D., 1997. *Focus groups as qualitative research*. Vol. 16: Sage.
Moschella, D., 2003. Customer-driven IT. *Harvard Business School Press, Boston*.
Ondrus, J. and Pigneur. Y., 2007. An assessment of NFC for future mobile payment systems. In *Management of Mobile Business, International Conference on Mobile Business (ICMB)*, pp. 43-43. IEEE.
Ondrus, J., and Lyytinen. K., 2011. Mobile Payments Market: Towards Another Clash of the Titans? *Paper read at Mobile Business, Tenth International Conference on Mobile Business (ICMB)*, 20-21 June 2011.
Ondrus, J., Lyytinen, K. and Pigneur. Y., 2009. Why mobile payments fail? Towards a dynamic and multi-perspective explanation. In *System Sciences, 2009. 42nd Hawaii International Conference on System Sciences (HICSS)*, pp. 1-10. IEEE.
Ondrus, J. and Pigneur. Y., 2005. A disruption analysis in the mobile payment market. In *System Sciences, 2005. Proceedings of the 38th Annual Hawaii International Conference on System Sciences (HICSS)*, pp. 84c-84c IEEE.
Österle, H., Becker, J., Ulrich, F., Hess, T., Karagiannis, D., Krcmar, H., Loos, P., Mertens, P., Oberweis, A. and Sinz. E., 2010. Memorandum on design-oriented information systems research. *European Journal of Information Systems* 20 (1):7-10.
Osterwalder, A. and Pigneur. Y., 2010. *Business model generation: a handbook for visionaries, game changers, and challengers*: Wiley. com.
Peffers, K., Tuunanen, T., Gengler, C.E., Rossi, M., Hui, W., Virtanen, V. and Bragge. J., 2006. The design science research process: a model for producing and presenting information systems research. In

Proceedings of the first international conference on design science research in information systems and technology (DESRIST), pp. 83-106.

Pigneur, Y., 2003. An ontology for m-business models. In *Conceptual Modeling—ER 2002* (pp. 3-6). Springer Berlin Heidelberg.

Pousttchi, K. 2003. Conditions for acceptance and usage of mobile payment procedures: 201-210.

Pousttchi, K., Schiessler, M. and Wiedemann. D.G., 2009. Proposing a comprehensive framework for analysis and engineering of mobile payment business models. *Information Systems and E-Business Management* 7 (3):363-393.

O'Raghallaigh, P., Sammon, S. and Murphy, M. 2011.Building towards a Software Based Innovation Modelling Tool. In *Enterprise and Organizational Modeling and Simulation*, pp. 192-213. Springer Berlin Heidelberg.

Rittel, HWJ. and Webber. MM., 1974. Wicked problems. *Man-made Futures*:272-280.

Robinson, N., 1999. The use of focus group methodology -with selected examples from sexual health research. *Journal of Advanced Nursing*, Blackwell Science.

Rogers, E.M., 1995. Diffusion of innovations. *Free Press*. 4th Edition, New York

Sawhney, M., Wolcott, R.C. and Arroniz. I., 2007. The 12 different ways for companies to innovate. *IEEE Engineering Management Review* 35 (1):45.

Shafer, S.M., Smith, H.J. and Linder. J.C., 2005. The power of business models. *Business Horizons* 48 (3):199-207.

Shostack, G.L., 1984. Designing services that deliver. *Harvard Business Review* 62 (1):133-139.

Simon, H.A., 1973. Does scientific discovery have a logic? *Philosophy of Science*:471-480.

Stabell, C.B. and Fjeldstad. Ø.D., 1998. Configuring value for competitive advantage: on chains, shops, and networks. *Strategic Management Journal* 19 (5):413-437.

Stähler, P., 2002. Business models as an unit of analysis for strategizing. *Paper read at International Workshop on Business Models,* Lausanne, Switzerland.

Stewart, D.W., Rook, D.W. and Shamdasani. P.N., 2007. *Focus groups: Theory and practice*. Vol. 20: Sage Publications, Incorporated.

Subramaniam, M. and Youndt. M.A., 2005. The influence of intellectual capital on the types of innovative capabilities. *Academy of Management Journal* 48 (3):450.

Thompson, J., 1967. *Organizations in action.*: McGraw-Hill, New York.

Tremblay, M.C., Hevner, A.R. and D.J. Berndt. D.J., 2010. Focus groups for artifact refinement and evaluation in design research. *Communications of the Association for Information Systems* 26 (1):27.

Van de Ven, A.H. 1986. Central problems in the management of innovation. *Management Science* 32 (5):590-607.

Van der Heijden, H., 2002. Factors affecting the successful introduction of mobile payment systems. In *15th Bled Electronic Commerce Conference* (Bled 2002), Bled, Slovenia.

Varshney, U., 2002. Mobile payments. *Computer* 35 (12):120-121. *IEEE Engineering Management Review*

Weigand, H., Johannesson, P., Andersson, B., Bergholtz, M., Edirisuriya, A. and Ilayperuma. T., 2006. On the notion of value object. In *Conceptual Modeling-ER 2006*, pp. 482-496. Springer Berlin Heidelberg,

Wieringa, R.J. and Gordijn. J., 2005. Value-oriented design of service coordination processes: correctness and trust. In *Proceedings of the 2005 ACM symposium on Applied computing*, pp. 1320-1327. ACM,

Wilkinson, S., 2004. Focus Group Research. *Qualitative research: Theory, method and practice*:177.

Zmijewska, A. and Lawrence. E., 2005. Reshaping the framework for analysing success of mobile payment solutions. In *IADIS International Conference on E-Commerce, Porto, Portugal.*

Zolnowski, A., Semmann, M. and Böhmann. T., 2011. Metamodels for Representing Service Business Models.

Zott, C., Amit, R. and Massa. L., 2011. The Business Model: Recent Developments and Future Research. *Journal of Management* 37 (4):1019.

CHAPTER SEVEN

DEFINING A FRAMEWORK FOR DEVELOPING A MASS CUSTOMIZATION STRATEGY FOR ONLINE BANKING

TEEMU SANTONEN

1. Introduction

Due to recent events such as the collapse of Lehman Brothers (Hines *et al.*, 2011) and the Euro crises (e.g. Welfens, 2011; Candelon and Palm, 2010) or the banking crises in individual countries including Iceland (Vaiman *et al.*, 2011), Ireland (Ryan, 2011), Greece (Paris et al., 2011, Abboushi, 2011) and most recently Cyprus (Forelle *et al.*, 2013), the banking sector is definitely going through a turbulent market condition for the past few years (Pine, 1993; Slater and Narver, 1994). In such a turbulent market environment, the former cradle-to-grave commitment of customers to one universal bank is under threat (Revell, 1991). Traditionally, the better coverage of channels and products was increasing the likelihood of market coverage (Chandler *et al.*, 1984), but now in consequence of electronic banking services (e.g. Karjaluoto *et al.*, 2002) and globalization of financial market (Cihák, 2012), the effect of distance on banking can be weakened (Berger 2003, Degryse and Ongena, 2004), emphasising the importance of online banking (Chong, 2010).

In the Internet the closest competitors are only one click away and the customers do not necessarily respect the national borders, but instead are the best offers and service providers. Thus, the lethargy of universal banks has opened the doors for new niche market players (e.g. Gordon, 2010) and non-banks, including disruptive value brands, such as Virgin, which operate across diverse consumer sectors (Worthington and Welch, 2011) and are trying to captivate consumer's share of wallet not only limited to banking (Baumann *et al.*, 2012). Without the burden of tradition, these new players are in a better position to introduce more innovative low-cost business models (Kachaner *et al.,* 2011) grounded e.g. on flexible product range and distribution channel mixes. As a result they can significantly reduce their cost structure comparing to established actors and unbalance the industry, like in the case of aviation due to low-cost airlines (Pereira and dos Reis, 2011).

Moreover, due to the European integration, also known as Europeanization (Lynggaard, 2011), new mechanisms, such as the Single Euro Payments Area (SEPA), have been introduced, which are suggested to provide multiple benefits including reduced transaction times, lower costs of cash management and thus pushing consumers to use new payment technologies (Calabrese, 2010). Hence, one could expect the intensifying of cross-border competition within the banking sector in the forthcoming years.

A good coverage of channels and products can have a downfall for the overall profitability, if there are overlapping efforts caused by poor hybrid marketing systems management (Moriarty and Moran, 1990). Therefore, for retail banks, it is important to discover efficient means to secure continuous competitive advantage without losing the cost-effectiveness. Porter (1985) has defined two primary types of competitive strategy that can provide a source of competitive advantage: differentiation and low cost strategy.

The low cost strategy can, however, lead to price wars and ultimately only one company can be the price leader. Furthermore, universal banks might not be able to challenge the innovative low-cost business models, which are implemented by the new market entrants (Kachaner *et. al.*, 2011). Also in the digital domain, products can easily be copied and distributed through the Internet at almost zero cost (Choi *et al.*, 1997; Shapiro and Varian, 1998), which makes fast reaction easy for competitors. As a result, the novel product and service innovations are often soon copied by competitors in online banking. Therefore, it has been argued that banks should rather focus on making harder-to-copy features like service quality, satisfaction and cradle-to-grave customer management strategies (Garland, 2002; Worcester, 1997; Yavas and Shemwell, 1996).

2. Objectives of this study

The management system grounded on mass production of customized products is called mass customization (Pine, 1993). It is enabling companies to customize products and services in high volumes at a relatively low cost (Gilmore and Pine, 1997). By following the footsteps of authors in banking and other digital domains (e.g. Kalakota and

Whinston 1996; Wells *et al.,* 2000; Santonen, 2004), mass customization is presented as a way to implement a product differentiation strategy in the context of immaterial digital products, in general, and especially in online banking. According to Kalyanaraman and Sundar (2006), the greater levels of personalized content in a website, should engender more positive attitudes, thus making customization an attractive option for an online bank. Moreover, within a turbulent market environment the industry is moving more likely towards mass customization (Pine, 1993), thus making this a suggested strategy especially valid for today's banking industry, which is evidently facing turbulence.

On the contrary, among the various alternatives to differentiate in retail and online banking, the mass customization, or also sometimes known as personalization (Sunikka and Bragge, 2012), is one of the promising approaches not yet extensively empirically studied as a strategy or business model for online banks (Al-debei and Avison, 2010). In general, the rare empirical customization studies in banking have focused on the value of customization in general, the privacy and trust issues of customization or personalized marketing messages in the online banking context (Coner, 2003; Serino *e. al.*, 2005, Sunikka *et al.*, 2011; Bragge *et al.,* 2012). One study by Fung (2008) had a similar focus than in this revised study, which was originally proposed by Santonen (2007). According to Fung (2008), some customization approaches enable higher commitment and higher tendency to stay with the website than in a site without any customization.

Therefore in this study we are especially interested in evaluating the perceived value of different customization approaches from an end-user point of view in the context of online banking. In this study the empirical ranking will be loosely based on the Technology Acceptance Model (i.e. TAM), which has been validated as a suitable instrument for evaluating the software application usage in the World Wide Web environment, such as online bank (e.g. Davis 1989; Davis *et al.*, 1989; Moon and Kim, 2000). In addition, we are also interested in analyzing whether, as suggested, better business success is achieved, or not, by applying the mass customization strategy (Pine 1993; Kalakota and Whinston, 1996; Ihlström and Palmer, 2002; Santonen, 2004). Based on these research objectives, the following generic research questions were formulated:

RQ A: Which customization approaches the online bank end-users are valuing the most?

RQ B: Which online bank services are the most suitable for customization?

RQ C: Are the end-users willing to pay more for the customized online banking service experience?

The paper is structured as follows. In section 2 we define the mass customization management system in more detail and introduce the different fundamental and practical approaches of customization. In section 3 we describe our research methodology. Section 4 explains the results of our empirical analyses and in section 5 we propose a conceptual framework for evaluating the rationality of implementing the mass customization management system in digital domain. Finally, in section 6 we draw conclusions from our observations.

3. Literature review

3.1 Mass Customization as a differentiation and a customer orientation strategy

The product differentiation strategy has been suggested as the main source of competitive advantage for most high-technology companies (Porter 1985; McGrath, 1995). The management system grounded on mass production of customized products is called as mass customization, which is one option to execute a differentiation strategy (Pine, 1993). The evolving customization literature is mainly grounded on physical product manufacturing and it has an extensive history, which goes back over thirty years (Toffler, 1970; Davis, 1987; Pine, 1993). In the mass customization management system, the goal is to develop, produce, market, and deliver affordable goods and services with enough variety and customization that nearly everyone finds exactly what they want (Pine, 1993), yet with the shorter cycle times (Hart, 1995; Anderson, 1998).

In marketing literature the strong desire to identify customer needs and the ability to answer these recognized needs is defined as a customer orientation strategy (Narver and Slater, 1990; Rohit *et al.*, 1993; Gatignon *e. al.*, 1997). In most cases, as a result of heterogeneous customer needs, the true desire and willingness to listen to the customer needs (i.e. customer orientation) should probably lead to customized products and services.

Most importantly, the mass customization management system, in addition to the urge to fulfil the identified customer needs, emphasizes the cost effectiveness of the production process, whereas customer orientation strategies in general do not stress this particular aspect. Both the presented theories are grounded on the basic belief that the company that better satisfies its customers' individual wants and needs will eventually have greater sales (Pine, 1993).

3.2 Challenges in implementing customization strategy

In retrospective, performance estimations researchers and managers have noticed that as a result of increased complexity, the poorly formulated and implemented mass customization strategy can generate cost ineffectiveness (Gilmore and Pine, 1997). This unwanted setback is against the fundamental foundations of the mass customization management system, since although the mass customization theory emphasizes the fulfilment of customer needs, the achievement of this goal cannot be done at the cause of cost effectiveness. In addition to complexity related problems, which are usually increasing the costs, other failure causes have also been suggested.

Manber *et al.* (2000) focused on demand curve and identified that the utilization rate of the customized features is often very low, since the majority of the end-users in the Internet never uses the given customization possibilities. They offered the following causes for this: 1) the default mass produced web pages are already so good that from an end-user point of view, there is no real reason to invest more efforts in order to create a customized user experience, 2) the customization approaches, which are available, are too difficult to use or 3) there is no genuine customer need for complex customization. Santonen (2004) on the other hand pointed out that some service providers, in the field of digital information products, believed that the low interest towards customization is caused by the loss of communal interaction between different end-users. Furthermore, Zipkin (2001) suggested limits of mass customization including requirement of a highly flexible production technology, an elaborate system for eliciting customers' wants and needs, a strong direct-to-customer logistics system and the unwillingness of customers to pay for customization.

These identified reasons clearly indicate that the managers in charge of the failure projects did not do their homework properly, but instead they were actually applying a hit-or-miss customization strategy as identified by Gilmore and Pine (1997). The fundamental starting point of customer orientation strategy-the identification and satisfaction customer needs-was definitely neglected.

3.3 Customization vs. personalization

In the Internet environment the term personalization is often replacing the customization or more specific the mass customization term, although the definitions of these terms in our opinion are very alike. Some authors share this opinion (e.g. Miceli *et al.*, 2007; Peppers and Rogers, 1997) while others disagree and claim that they are different concepts (Arora *et al.,* 2008; Gilmore and Pine, 1997; Kumar, 2007; Montgomery and Smith, 2009). Recently, Sunikka and Bragge (2012) conducted an extensive review regarding customization and personalization literature suggesting that personalization research has a stronger focus on technology and internet, while customization, as an older domain, is related to tangible products, although it has lately shown interest also in the field of services. Moreover, they suggested a framework in which concepts of personalization, customization and mass customization can be clarified. However, as stated in this research setting we consider that the customization and the personalization term definitions for our research purposes are close enough and a special distribution between the terms is needless.

3.4 Fundamental approaches to customization

In practice, mass customization means that customers can select, order, and receive a specially configured product-often choosing from among hundreds of product options-to meet their specific needs (Bourke and Kempfer, 1999). For example, Shapiro and Varian (1998) discussed on selling the information in a smart way and identified twelve different version sources. In principal, Anderson (1997) pointed out that there are four types of variety (i.e. options): 1) external variety, which is seen by customers, 2) internal variety, which is only experienced inside the manufacturing and distributions operations, 3) useful variety, which is appreciated by customers and 4) useless variety, which is transparent, unimportant, or even confusing. External variety is often, but not always, good; but the internal variety is suggested to be always a bad thing (Anderson, 1997).

At the extreme level of mass customization, a company can produce and market the unique products for all customers. Pepper and Rodgers (1996) determined this approach as one-to-one marketing, while defining the differences between individual customers and customer segments, which more commonly are related to a mass customization management system. Most interestingly, the authors of mass customization and one-to-one marketing (Pine *et al.*, 1995) joined forces and argued that a company hoping to deliver to customers exactly what they want (i.e. implement the extreme customer orientation strategy), must utilize both mass customization and one-to-one marketing management systems. Contrary to physical products and manufacturing achieving the level of uniqueness, in digital domain is not necessarily a big problem. As a result of fundamental features of digital products-indestructibility, transmutability and reproducibility (Choi *et al.*, 1997)-the number of possible configuration alternatives, e.g. as result of modularity, might easily expand exponentially (Schilling, 2000).

Gilmore and Pine (1997) defined four distinct approaches to product customization and named them as collaborative, adaptive, cosmetic and transparent approach. According to Gilmore and Pine (1997) the collaborative customization occurs when an employee of the company is directly interacting with customer and based on this interactive dialogue, the customized product that fulfils the identified user needs is made. Contrary to collaborative customization, in adaptive customization there is no direct dialogue between customer and an employee of the company in order to change the design of the product. The actual product is already designed or constructed in a way that customers can adjust or modify it themselves. The possibility of customization in this case is grounded on the product design, while in the case of collaborative customization the design of the product might be altered, as a result of the dialog between the company and consumer. Two other approaches introduced by Gilmore and Pine (1997)-cosmetic and transparent-are distinctly different from the two above-mentioned approaches. A cosmetic customizer in the online banking environment changes only the representation of the online bank (e.g., colours or font size), while the functionality of the web site remains the same to all end-users. The transparent customizer on the other hand provides customized service experience without letting the end-users know explicitly that the website have been modified for them. According to Gilmore and Pine (1997) many companies are actually combining multiple approaches in order to better match the individual customer needs.

Moreover, Lampel and Mintzberg (1996) argued that customization and the previous dominant strategy-standardization management strategy-are not alternative models but rather a continuum of real-world strategies. The authors classified the following five stages in this continuum: 1) pure standardization, which is based on dominant standard design (i.e. one-size-fits-all approach), 2) segmented standardization, where basic design is modified and various standard options are offered to end-users, but not at the request of the individual end-user, 3) customized standardization, where end-users can alter or configure the product by selecting even from hundreds of predefined modules, 4) tailored customization, where a company is presenting a prototype to the end-user and then alters the product features, but not the original design, in order to fulfil the individual needs and finally 5) pure customization, where end-users are deeply participating already into the design process of the product.

While evaluating the impact of web site customization on commitment, Fung (2008) conceptualized the following three customization types: *First*, remembering-type in which information is collected from the user in order to customize the website without the website necessarily knowing the meaning of the information. *Second*, comprehension-type referring to customized features that are assigned to user behaviour and then making pendent adjustments, which are aiming to satisfy the user needs. *Third*, association-type, which is linking user behaviour with similar user behaviour, in order to reflect what the particular user wants.

The father of mass customization management systems himself (Pine 1993) introduced five fundamental methods for customization: 1) service customization, where the person-to-person service experience is customized, but the offered products and services are standardized, 2) creation of customized products and services, 3) point-of-delivery customization, 4) quick response throughout the value chain in order to produce customized experiences and finally 5) the modular approach, which end-users can modify products and services by selecting predefined components. Pine (1993) also claimed that the modular approach might be one of the best methods to produce customized products and services and in more detailed defined five different types of modularity.

We conclude our introduction to fundamental customization approaches in Wells *et al.* (2000) observations, who identified that two generic approaches of customization are emerging in the Internet: 1) some websites offer users the ability to become Graphical User Interface (i.e. GUI) designer and while others are 2) customizing on the basis of the information held about customers.

3.5 Comparing the practical approaches of customization

We argue that the previously presented classifications are too generic to properly and practically evaluate the perceived value of different customization approaches (or personalization as some authors like to state). Therefore, we present a list of more down-to-earth web customization approaches, which have been identified from the evolving customization and personalization literature or as a result of becoming familiar with different web sites on the Internet (Appendix 2 - Table 1).

First, our interest was focused on the data collection process of the end-user profile, which usually must be generated in order to provide the customized application or content (Wells *et al.,* 2000). Two main principles of data collection will be placed under head-to-head comparison: the simple and wizard form. In the case of the wizard forms, the end-users preferences are clarified with help of sequence forms, which are taking notice of previous selections of the respondent. On the contrary the simple forms are based on plain and simple one page or even one field form. The comparison need was derived from the suggestions of authors of the high-variety strategy studies, which argue that the process of learning one's own preferences will increase customer satisfaction (Huffman and Kahn, 1998; Kahn, 1998). This same assumption led us to compare the differences between the fundamental approaches of customization as presented by Gilmore and Pine (1997). We wondered if the direct user driven customization would generate greater success than customization approaches, which are based on automation (i.e. when the website is automatically adjusting itself without any direct interaction with the end-user). Since the automatic customization might easily lead in to transparent customization, this approach was also added to this comparison.

By following Wells *et al.* (2000) observations, the remained customization approaches were classified in recommendation (i.e. customization on the basis of the information held about end-users) and technical gadgets groups (i.e. the ability to become GUI designer). The recommendation group included the following approaches: Recommendation based on 1) usage or click-through history, 2) pre or user defined keywords (Mobasher *et al.*, 2000), 3) simultaneous versions (Lampel and Minzberg, 1996), 4) purchase history (e.g. www.amazon.com), and 5) user performed rating (Balabanovic and Shoham, 1997).

The technical gadgets group contained 1) search agents (Palmer and Eriksen, 1999) 2) user defined link list or navigation, 3) modular customization or my page (Manber *et al.*, 2000) and 4) cosmetic customization (Gilmore and Pine, 1997).

4. Research method

4.1 Data collection and response

Our empirical survey was carried out in Finland, which is one of the world leading countries regarding the usage of online banking services (Karjaluoto *et al.*, 2002). At the time of the study in Finland, the majority of all retail banking transactions was made over Internet (The Finnish Banker association, 2003). In addition, Finland is also one of the globally leading countries regarding the national IT infrastructure available for online services. The survey questionnaire-especially the formulation of the customization statements in Finnish-was somewhat based on the previous empirical customization study proposed by Santonen (2004) in the online newspaper environment. Therefore, in this study only a light instrument validation process was conducted. We finalized and pre-tested the paper copy survey questionnaire in a few interviews with specialists of one Finnish bank (a partner of our study) to make sure that all our questions were semantically precise and understandable also in the online banking environment from the end-user point of view. With the help of the bank's marketing department all together 1.358 questionnaires were sent to the bank's customers which had been identified as online bank users.

In one month, we received 386 acceptable responses, which gave us a very nice overall response rate (about. 28 percent), considering the fact that no follow-up letters were sent or reminder phone calls were made. According to the demographic profile presented in Appendix 1 Table 1, we were convinced that our data was adequate enough in order to look for answers to our research questions A, B and C: A) which customization approaches the online bank end-users are valuing the most, B) which online bank services are the most suitable for customization and C) are the end-users willing to pay more for the customized online banking service experience?

4.2 Construction of key measures

The Technology Acceptance Model (later TAM) has previously been validated as a suitable instrument to measure and evaluate software application usage also in the World Wide Web environment (e.g. Davis 1989; Davis *et al.* 1989; Moon and Kim, 2000). In the original TAM theory, the perceived ease of use and usefulness are suggested to affect the attitude towards using a particular software application. Further on, the attitude towards using application is suggested to affect the end-user's behavioural intention to use the application. Finally, behavioural intention on the other hand is argued to correlate with the actual software usage. In general the TAM model is refereed and agreed to be a solid construct, although it is not fully without criticism (Legris *et al.*, 2003). In the case of each identified customization approach (Appendix 2 Table 2), respondents were presented with the following TAM related statements:

- Using the presented customization approach would be entertaining (adapted from Moon and Kim, 2000)
- Using the presented customization approach would be useful
- I would take up a positive attitude towards using the presented customization approach
- I would use the presented customization approach

Since the usage of the particular customization approach in the website is often very similar (basically first filling different kinds of forms, then based on the generated profile, the customized content or user interface is presented to the end-user) and because of the limited space in the questionnaire, the perceived ease of the use item included in the original TAM-model was not implemented within our questionnaire.

All four statements within each sixteen individual customization approaches were measured by using a 7-point Likert-scale, ranging from 1 (=completely disagree) to 7 (=completely agree). The average value of these four statements was used as the ranking criteria of each individual customization approach. By measuring four different aspects of each individual customization approach, we could increase the reliability of our study, comparing to the research setting where only one statement would have been included into each customization approach. The average value of these sixteen combined customization measures was defined as the overall approach based on customization attitude. The level of internal consistency of the defined combined customization measures was evaluated with the help of the Cronbach's alpha test (Cronbach and Meehl, 1955). In the series of Cronbach's alpha tests it appeared that all combined reliability coefficients within each variable were clearly above the suggested limiting value 0.700 (Nunnally 1978; O'Rourke, 2005). Based on these results we were assured that all the defined customization measures were logically solid.

In addition to abovementioned customization measures, the additional generic customization attitude measure was constructed. Following four 7-point Likert-scale statements were presented to respondents: In my opinion customization of online banking is 1) bad vs. good idea, 2) silly vs. wise idea, 3) unpleasant vs. pleasant idea and 4) negative vs. positive idea. The average value of these four attitude statements was used as an overall customization attitude measure.

In order to evaluate the most suitable banking products and services for customization, the following products and services were listed to the respondents: 1) savings, 2) investments, 3) home mortgages, 4) insurances, 5) credit and debit cards, 6) inquiries, questions and guidance in general, and 7) news and bulletins. Also these customization statements were measured by using a 7-point Likert-scale. Moreover, the respondent's price elasticity for customized online banking service was estimated by using seven different price categories ranging from no more than now to over 3 €/month more than now. Finally, extensive demographic and Internet usage profiles were collected from the respondents.

5. Results

5.1 RQ A: Ranking the different customization approaches

Based on the literature review we identified sixteen different web customization approaches, which were classified into four logical groups in order to compare and rank the approaches in question (Appendix 3 Table 3a and 3b).

Group 1: Data collection. Based on the literature review we had identified two different data collection methods: the simple and wizard forms. In our initial assumptions we thought that the wizard form would achieve greater rank in comparison to simple forms, since the deeper and more detailed involvement of end-user in product's co-design process should result into a higher match to the end-user's individual needs. However, in contrast to our initial assumptions, the end-users appeared to appreciate the ease of use and effort free data feeding, which are more closely related to simple forms. The mean value difference 0.231 was statistically significant (at the level of 0.000 2-tailed) but still rather modest. The higher standard deviation value in the case of wizard forms indicated a bit higher division of opinion.

Group 2: Fundamental methods. Another logical head-to-head comparison was made between the user-driven and automatic customization approaches. This comparison resulted in a bit stronger support to the user-driven customization approach (mean difference was 0.346, sig. 0.000). When this result is compared to the previous data collection comparison, it is suggested that although the end-users in general favour the smoothness of data feeding process, some end-users will feel a stronger alienation if full automatization is implemented. It is suggested that too strong automatization might weaken the perceived value of customization as a result of unclear visibility. This point of view is argued to be justified, since the perceived value of transparent customization was ranked below both the user-driven and automatic customization approaches. The mean value difference in the case of the user driven customization approach was 0.601 (sig. 0.000) and in the case of automatic customization it was 0.252 (sig. 0.001). To create the higher value for the end-users, it is suggested that web site designers must make it fully clear, when the content or the functionality is customized for individuals. This on the other hand might decrease the fear of privacy violations, which is proposed as an alternative explanation for the mean difference of the user driven and automatic customization approaches.

Group 3: Recommendation. In all, seven different recommendation approaches were submitted under detailed evaluation. It turned out that the recommendations based on 1) usage history and 2) pre or user defined keywords together were the most valued among our respondents, since the identified minor mean difference between them was not statistically significant. Although the mean difference between these two first ranking recommendation approaches and the five follow-up approaches was statistically significant, the absolute difference remained relatively minor. The identified mean difference values ranged between 0.146 and 0.391. Also all the standard deviation values in each customization approaches were at the same magnitude level. Based on these observations we suggest that in general the different recommendation approaches should generate nearly the same amount of perceived value to the end-users. Therefore, other decision criterions (e.g. implementation costs) might turn out being more vital, in order to become successful in a mass customization management system.

Group 4: Technical gadgets. Our final group-the technical gadgets-included four individual customization approaches, which all, in our opinion, had a stronger technical orientation. It appeared that the search agent approach was ranked the first. The search agent approach even outperformed all the previously presented recommendation approaches, which in a way are based on the same kind of filtering logic. However, the "search results" in those cases are rendered directly to the web page, which is obligating the end-user to visit at the actual web page in each "search result". Based on this observation it is even stronger, suggested that the end-users will put great value not only on the effort free data feeding, but also on the effort free data receiving. Most importantly, the end-users want to be in charge and receive only the content or services, which they have directly indicated to be fond of. The two runner-up approaches-the customized link list and the modular page approaches-received a similar interest level. The same level of perceived value was not a big surprise, since both approaches are basically rising from the GUI development trend, which was identified by Wells *et al.* (2000). Finally, the crown of the loser was admitted to the cosmetic customization approach without any doubts. This customization method appeared to be the least tempting approach of all customization approaches and therefore it is not recommended to apply it within an online banking environment.

To shortly summarize the abovementioned results, we suggest that in order to become successful in mass customization management systems, online bank managers should rather put weight on simple and effort free end-user driven customization approaches than a more complex often even invisible automatic customization.

5.2 RQ B: Finding the most suitable online bank services to customization

In this section, we will evaluate, which online banking services would most likely gain the greatest value throughout the identified and ranked customization approaches. In order to evaluate the most suitable online banking products and services for customization Appendix 4, Table 4 was constructed.

It appeared that the investments related services and content were considered clearly the most suitable for customization, whereas the information and services affiliated to home mortgages and insurances gained the least popularity. The hectic investments environment often demands fast actions, but also requires efficient management of the complex and multidimensional information. Therefore, filtered information and tailor made applications are almost a necessity in order to become a successful online banker. Home mortgages and insurances are opposite by nature. The frequency of true involvement is short-lived. In general e.g. home mortgages are mostly applied only few times per lifetime of a customer and moreover as a result of a direct payment mechanism in Finland, the loan shortenings can be automatized, which makes the banking service nearly invisible to the end-user. Other standard online banking products and services including cards, customer guidance, savings and news, received a somewhat similar level of interest for customization. It is suggested that this observation denotes that the presumptive frequency of usage of services or information might be related to the end-user's customization interest.

5.3 RQ C: Is the better business success achieved by applying the mass customization strategy?

Our final research question speculated if the end-users are willing to pay more for the customized online banking service experience. In order to look for an answer, a simple correlation analysis presented in Table 5 was conducted.

Table 5: Correlation analysis between generic customization and price elasticity measures (N=370-376), **Significant at the 0.01 level (2-tailed).

	1. Approach based general customization attitude	2. Overall customization attitude
1. Approach based general customization attitude		
2. Overall customization attitude	0.700**	
3. Price elasticity	0.218**	0.261**

First of all there was an expected and strong relationship between our two generic customization attitude measures (0.700**). This on the other hand validated that our data collected and the customization research model in general was valid. Interestingly, the correlation between price elasticity measure and both generic customization measures remained under 0.300 limiting value for a statistically weak correlation. This outcome does not support our initial expectation, which argued that the end-users are willing to pay more for the customized online banking service experience.

6. Defining a conceptual framework for evaluating the rationality of mass customization

It is suggested that our research findings indicate that 1) the rate and the frequency of the online service usage and 2) the requirement of mandatory end-user participation in order to create individual service experience are both affecting the acceptance of online bank customization. When online banking applications or information are used on a regular basis and in high quantities, it is more likely for the end-users to start developing and identifying their individual needs. In the case of rarely used online services, the learning curve and TAM related ease of use factor are entering into picture. The additional efforts, which the majority of customization approaches undeniably require, are not appearing as a tempting alternative. Although, the additional customization might result in a higher value to the end-users, based on our research findings, we suggest that the majority of the online bank end-users are more likely selecting the free of effort option. This suggestion is somewhat in conflict with the previous findings in literature, which argued that the higher end-user involvement will result in higher perceived value for customers. We agree with this suggestion, only partially, and define that the high-user participation is a valid strategy in the online banking environment only when the application or service usage is expected to be a large-scale. To illustrate our customization results, the framework in Figure 1 is presented (see next page).

Based on our observations, it is suggested that an online bank manager should not apply customization in the quadrant Q1 where the implemented customization approach(es) would require a considerable amount of end-user involvement in order to create more individual service experience, but the level and frequency of service usage would probably be low. In the opposite quadrant Q4, where service usage is expected to be high and the applied customization approaches are free of effort by nature, it is proposed that a customization strategy is more than justified and probably the most risk free decision.

The sensibility of the customization strategy in quadrants Q2 and Q3 is more blurry. From a cost effectiveness point of view, the implementation of a customization approach is usually expensive (i.e. at least more expensive than the implementation of a standard approach). Therefore, the online banking managers should ask themselves if they really need to invest more on customization of the services, which anyway are in low running (Q3). On the other hand if the main objective is to increase the usage level of that particular service, the customization strategy might turn out to be a good decision.

The customization of online services in the quadrant Q2 is not risk-free but might result in the best outcome. If the requirement of the end-user involvement is too demanding and requires too much effort, it is likely that only a small number of end-users will adopt the customized approach. Then the cost effectiveness of customization strategy might be lost, if the business model is based on higher usage fees. However, the higher risk might be worth to take. It is likely that the necessary extra efforts will engage the end-users more deeply into the service provider. This again is increasing the switching cost and will diminish the probability of customer defection and create stronger lock-in. Therefore, although it was suggested that the customization strategy in quadrant Q4 is justified, and most likely successful, the total outcome is probably less compared to successful customization projects in quadrant Q2.

Figure1: Suggested framework for evaluating the rationality of implementation of a mass customization management system within an online banking environment

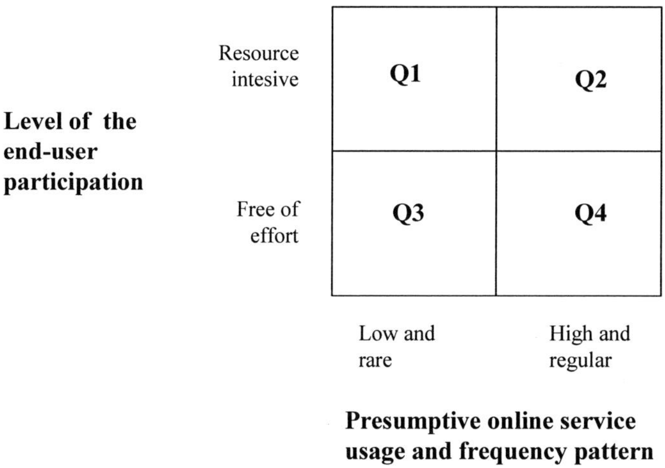

7. Conclusion

In addition to empirically ranking the sixteen identified customization approaches, we evaluated, which seven typical online banking services would most likely gain the highest value throughout customization. It appeared that there were truly statistically significant differences between the perceived values of different customization approaches although the overall evaluation of customization seemed to dominate the evaluations of individual customization approaches. Over and above it was discovered that some online banking services areas were more suitable for customization than other. However, the empirical results did not clearly support the previous suggestions that the end-users are willing to pay more for the customized online banking service experience. Based on these observations it was suggested that the success of mass customization management system in online banking might depend on the level of end-user participation and the rate and the frequency of the customized service usage. A conceptual framework was defined in order to help the practitioners evaluate the rationality of mass customization and clarify their thought incorporated within a mass customization management system in the online banking environment.

The outcome of this study should also be valuable for practitioners, since, in general, the implementation and running of a mass customization management system often requires an outstanding amount of financial and human resources. With the help of this study online banking managers could more solidly estimate the cost-performance in relation to different customization practices, before actually implementing the different approaches, which is always a challenging task and definitely not a risk-free strategy.

It has been argued that online banks cannot fully substitute traditional channels, but it can be an important choice criterion especially for young and well-educated individuals who are seeking enhanced convenience and increased control (Ioannou and Zolkiewski, 2009). Moreover, banks should not any more focus only on providing useful and informative content (Pikkarainen *et al.*, 2004) but highlight their role as effective relationship managers by offering online services, which pay attention to customer's preferences and behaviour also at individual level (Liang and Chen, 2009). However, when providing a customized online experience, banks should emphasise the trustworthiness and the security features to enforce customer's confidence (Yap *et al.*, 2010). Anyhow, we argue that taking the risk might be profitable especially when free of effort customization approaches are applied to high-usage services. The value of personalization has been argued to be more influential than customer's concerns regarding privacy issues (Chellappa and Sin, 2005) and therefore a well-done customized service should overcome the trust related suspicions. Although, a high-quality online service ability to improve customer relationships can be questioned, user-friendly and effective features such as well-focused customization can support loyalty (Herington and Weaven, 2007).

As a marketing strategy we suggest that customized services should be targeted to innovative customers (Midgley and Dowling, 1978) who can act as early adopters (Rogers, 2010) and positively influence non-users to adopt the novel services (Aldás-Manzano, 2008). Today, in practice, a modern smartphone instead of a traditional computer could be a more appropriate platform for customized features. Especially customers having already the tendency to customize their smartphones via Apple App Store or Google play downloads could be an ideal target group since they have the willingness and skills to create an individual user-experience.

This study is subject to the following limitations. First, the evaluations and rankings of different customization approaches were based on user perceptions, not the actual real life experiences. The longitudinal usage based experiments might generate more accurate ranking orders since free of effort, usefulness and easy to use issues might affect more precise in the case of actual usage. Second, concerning the nature of the rather homogeneous sample group (only one nationality and bank) we can see that the generalizability of the findings calls for further research. In the following studies the sample should include different kinds of market environments, operating regions and companies with different kinds of product and service range. Also the demographic profile of the respondents was a little bit over weighed in favour for older and higher educated males with higher than average annual incomes. Third, this study neglected the bank's standpoint, which might be significantly different than the end-user point of view. Only by evaluating the customization approaches from all key players' point of view can one generate a comprehensive understanding of the ranking order of different customization approaches. The final remark on the limitations of this study, concerns the statistical methods used. It would be valuable to rank the customization approaches with the help of different statistical methods e.g. conjoint analysis, which is commonly used in marketing studies, in order to rank the different alternatives. By validating or rejecting the current ranking order with different methods, would minimize the possibility of a false conclusion. We conclude that as a result of these limitations this study and especially the defined framework must be seen more as a tentative concept rather than as a universal theory for mass customization in different business environments.

References

Abboushi, S. (2011). Analysis and outlook of the greek financial crisis. Journal of Global Business Management, 7(1), pp. 1-8.

Aldás-Manzano, J., Lassala-Navarré, C., Ruiz-Mafé, C., & Sanz-Blas, S. (2009). The role of consumer innovativeness and perceived risk in online banking usage. International Journal of Bank Marketing, 27(1), 53-75.

Al-debei, M., & Avison, D. (2010). Developing a unified framework of the business model concept. European Journal of Information Systems, 19(3), pp. 359-376.

Anderson, D. M., (1998), Agile Product Development for Mass Customization: How to develop and deliver products for Mass

Customization, Niche Markets, JIT, Build-to Order and Flexible Manufacturing, McGraw-Hill.

Arora, N., Dreze, X., Ghose, A., Hess, J. D., Iyengar, R., Jing, B. (2008). Putting one-to-one marketing to work: Personalization, customization, and choice. Marketing Letters, 19(3–4), pp. 305–321.

Balabanovic M., Shoham Y., (1997), Fab: Content-based, collaborative recommendation, Association for Computing Machiner, Communications of the ACM, New York.

Baumann, C., Hamin, H., & Tung, R. L. (2012). Share of wallet in retail banking. The International Journal of Bank Marketing, 30(2), pp. 88-101.

Bourke R.; Kempfer L., (1999), Achieving Success with Mass Customization: The vital contribution of engineering Computer - Aided Engineering, Cleveland.

Bragge, J., Sunikka, A., & Kallio, H. (2012). An exploratory study on customer responses to personalized banner messages in the online banking context. JITTA : Journal of Information Technology Theory and Application, 13(3), pp. 5-18.

Calabrese, A., Gastaldi, M., Iacovelli, I., & Ghiron, N. L. (2010). New technologies in the payment system industries: The SEPA project. American Journal of Economics and Business Administration, 2(4), pp. 384-394.

Cameron, G. (2011). Competing in global niche markets: The case of macquarie bank. The International Journal of Bank Marketing, 29(4), pp. 293-307.

Candelon, B., & Palm, F. C. (2010). Banking and debt crises in europe: The dangerous liaisons? De Economist, 158(1), pp. 81-99.

Chellappa, R. K., & Sin, R. G. (2005). Personalization versus privacy: An empirical examination of the online consumer's dilemma. Information Technology and Management, 6(2-3), 181-202.

Choi, S-Y, Stahl D. O., Whinston A. B., (1997), The Economics of Electronic Commerce: The Essential Economics of Doing Business in the Electronic Marketplace, Macmillan Technical Publishing.

Chong, A. Y., Keng-Boon Ooi, Lin, B., & Tan, B. (2010). Online banking adoption: An empirical analysis. The International Journal of Bank Marketing, 28(4), pp. 267-287.

Cihák, M., Muñoz, S., & Scuzzarella, R. (2012). The bright and the dark side of cross-border banking linkages. Finance a Uver, 62(3), pp. 200-225.

Cronbach, L.J., Meehl, P.E., (1955), Construct validity in psychological tests. Psychological Bulletin, 52, pp. 281-302.

Davis S.M., (1987), Future Perfect, Reading, Mass.: Addision-Wesley.
Davis, F.D., (1989), Perceived Usefulness, Perceived Ease of Use, and User Acceptance of Information Technology. MIS Quarterly / September 1989.
Davis, F.D., Bagozzi, R., Warshaw, P.R, (1989), User acceptance of computer technology: a comparison of two theoretical models, Management Science 35 (8), pp. 982-1003.
Forelle, C., Stevis, M., & Enrich, D. (2013, Mar 22). Clock ticks on Cyprus—nation aims to restructure bank to secure aid, stay in euro. Wall Street Journal.
Fung, T. K. F. (2008). Banking with a personalized touch: Examining the impact of website customization on commitment. Journal of Electronic Commerce Research, 9(4), pp. 296-309.
Garland, R., (2002), "Non-financial drivers of customer profitability in personal retail banking", Journal of Targeting, Measurement and Analysis in Marketing, Vol. 7 No. 4, pp. 27-42.
Gatignon, H.; Xuereb, J-M; (1997) Strategic orientation of the firm new product performance JMR, Journal of Marketing Research; Chicago.
Gilmore J.H., Pine J., (1997), The Four Faces of Mass Customization, Harvard Business Review, 75, January/February.
Hart C. W.L., (1995), Mass customization: conceptual underpinnings, opportunities and limits, International Journal of Service Industry Management, Vol. 6, Issue 2.
Herington, C., & Weaven, S. (2007). Can banks improve customer relationships with high quality online services?. Managing Service Quality, 17(4), 404-427.
Hines, C., Kreuze, J., & Langsam, S. (2011). An analysis of lehman brothers bankruptcy and repo 105 transactions. American Journal of Business, 26(1), pp. 40-49.
Huffman, C., Kahn B.E., (1998), Variety for sale: Mass customization or mass confusion? Journal of Retailing, Winter, Vol. 74 (4), pp. 491-513
Ihlström, C., Palmer, J., (2002), Revenues for Online Newspapers: Owner and User Perceptions, Electronic Markets, Vol.12, No 4.
Ioannou, M., & Zolkiewski, J. (2009). Can retail bank-client relationships be developed online?. EuroMed Journal of Business, 4(3), 254-269.
Kachaner, N., Lindgardt, Z., & David, M. (2011). Innovating low-cost business models. Strategy & Leadership, 39(2), pp. 43-48.
Kahn B. E, 1998, Dynamic relationships with customers: High-variety strategies Academy of Marketing Science. Journal, Greenvale, Vol. 26, Issue 1, Winter, pp. 45-53.

Kalakota, R., Whinston, A.B., (1996), Frontiers of Electronic Commerce, Addison-Wesley Publishing Company, USA

Kalyanaraman, S., Sundar, S.S., (2006), The Psychological Appeal of Personalized Content in Web Portals: Does Customization Affect Attitudes and Behavior? Journal of Communication Volume 56, Issue 1, pp. 110–132.

Karjaluoto, H., Mattila, M., Pento, T., (2002), Electronic banking in Finland: Consumer beliefs and reactions to a new delivery channel, Journal of Service Marketing, Jun, London

Kumar, A. (2007). From mass customization to mass personalization: A strategic transformation. International Journal of Flexible Manufacturing System, 19(4), pp. 533–547.

Lampel, J., Mintzberg, H., (1996) Customizing Customization, Sloan Management Review, Fall, Vol. 38, No. 1, pp. 21–30

Legris, P., Ingham, J., Collerette (2003), Why do people use information technology? A critical review of the technology acceptance model, Information & Management, pp. 191-204.

Liang, C. J., & Chen, H. J. (2009). How to lengthen, deepen and broaden customer–firm relationships with online financial services & quest. Journal of Financial Services Marketing, 14(3), 218-231.

Lynggaard, K. (2011). Domestic change in the face of european integration and globalization: Methodological pitfalls and pathways. Comparative European Politics, 9(1), pp. 18-37.

Manber U., Patel A., Robison J., (2000), Experience with personalization on Yahoo! Association for Computing Machinery. Communications of the ACM, New York.

McGrath, M.E., (1995), Product Strategy for High-Technology Companies. McGraw-Hill

Miceli, G. N., Ricotta, F., & Costabile, M. (2007). Customizing customization: A conceptual framework for interactive personalization. Journal of Interactive Marketing, 21(2), pp. 6–25.

Midgley, D.F. and Dowling, G.R. (1978), “Innovativeness: the concept and its measurement”, Journal of Consumer Research, Vol. 4, March, pp. 229-42.

Mobasher B., Cooley R., Srivastava J., (2000), Automatic personalization based on Web usage mining, Association for Computing Machinery. Communications of the ACM, New York.

Montgomery, A. M., & Smith, M. D. (2009). Prospects for personalization on the internet. Journal of Interactive Marketing, 23(2), pp. 130–137.

Moon, J-W., Kim, Y-G., (2001). Extending the TAM for a World-Wide-Web context. Information & Management 38

Narver, J., Slater S., (1990), The Effect of a Market Orientation on Business Profitability, Journal of Marketing, 54 (4), pp. 20-35.

Nunnally, J.C., (1978), Psychometric theory. New York: McGraw-Hill.

O'Rourke, N., Hatcher, L., Stepanski, E.J., (2005), A step-by-Step Approach to using SAS for Univariate and Multivariate Statistics (Second edition ed.). Cary, North Carolina: SAS Institute Inc.

Palmer, J.W., Eriksen, L.B., (1999), Digital newspapers explore marketing on the Internet Association for Computing Machinery. Communications of the ACM, New York, Sep, Vol. 42, Issue 9, pp. 33-40.

Paris, A., Dedes, S., & Lampridis, N. (2011). Greek financial crisis. Global Business and Management Research, 3(3), pp. 319-341.

Peppers, D., & Rogers, M. (1997). The one-to-one future. New York: Double Day Publications.

Pereira, C. F., & dos Reis, F. L. (2011). Regular airlines flying towards A low cost strategy. International Business Research, 4(1), pp. 93-99.

Pikkarainen, T., Pikkarainen, K., Karjaluoto, H., & Pahnila, S. (2004). Consumer acceptance of online banking: an extension of the technology acceptance model. Internet research, 14(3), 224-235.

Pine J., (1993), Mass Customization, The new Forntier in Business Competition, Harvard Business School Press.

Pine, J.B., Peppers, D., Rogers, M., (1995), Do you want to keep your customers forever? Harvard Business Review; Boston.

Porter, M., (1985), Competitive Advantage: Creating and Sustaining Superior Performance, New York: The Free Press

Rogers, E. M. (2010). Diffusion of innovations. Simon and Schuster.

Rohit, D., Farley, J. U., Webster, F.E., (1993), "Corporate Culture, Customer Orientation, and Innovativeness in Japanese Firms: A Quadrad Analysis," Journal of Marketing, 57 (January), pp. 23-37.

Ryan, C. (2011). The euro crisis and crisis management: Big lessons from a small island. International Economics and Economic Policy, 8(1), pp. 31-43

Santonen, T., (2004), Four essays studying the effect of customization and market environment on the business success of online newspapers, Helsinki School of Economics, A-242

Schilling M.A, (2000), Toward a general modular systems theory and its application to interfirm product modularity, Academy of Management, The Academy of Management Review; Mississippi State.

Serino, C.M., Furner, C.P., Smatt, C., (2005), "Making it Personal: How Personalization Affects Trust Over Time," hicss, p. 170a, Proceedings of the 38th Annual Hawaii International Conference on System Sciences (HICSS'05)

Shapiro C., Varian H. R., (1998), Information Rules: A Strategic Guide to the Network Economy, Harvard Business School Press Boston, Massachusetts.

Sunikka, A., and J. Bragge, "Applying text-mining to personalization and customization research literature—Who, what and where?" Expert Systems with Applications, 2012, 39:11, pp. 10049–10058.

Sunikka, A., Bragge, J., & Kallio, H. (2011). The effectiveness of personalized marketing in online banking: A comparison between search and experience offerings. Journal of Financial Services Marketing, 16(3-4), pp. 183-194.

The Finnish banker association, (2003), Banking Year 2003, pp.13-15, http://www.suomenpankki.fi

Toffler A., (1970), Future Shock, New York: Bantam Books.

Vaiman, V., Sigurjonsson, T. O., & Davídsson, P. Á. (2011). Weak business culture as an antecedent of economic crisis: The case of Iceland. Journal of Business Ethics, 98(2), pp. 259-272.

Welfens, P.J.J. (2011). From the transatlantic banking crisis to the euro crisis? International Economics and Economic Policy, 8(1), pp. 15-29.

Wells, N., Wolfers, J., Riecken, R.C., (2000), Finance with a personalized touch, Association for Computing Machinery. Communications of the ACM; New York

Worcester, R.M., (1997), managing the image of your bank: the glue that binds", International Journal of Bank Marketing, Vol. 15 No. 5, pp.146-52.

Worthington, S., & Welch, P. (2011). Banking without the banks. The International Journal of Bank Marketing, 29(2), pp. 190-201.

Yap, K. B., Wong, D. H., Loh, C., & Bak, R. (2010). Offline and online banking–where to draw the line when building trust in e-banking?. International Journal of Bank Marketing, 28(1), 27-46.

Yavas, U., Shemwell, D.J., (1996), "Bank image: exposition and illustration of correspondence analysis", International Journal of Bank Marketing, Vol. 14 No. 1, pp.15-21.

Zipkin, P. (2001). The limits of mass customization. MIT Sloan Management Review, 42(3), pp. 81-87.

Appendix 1

Table 1. The demographic profile of the respondents

Demographic characterictics	Freq.	Valid percent	Demographic characterictics	Freq.	Valid percent
Gender			*Education*		
Male	298	78.4	Comprehensive school	39	10.3
Female	82	21.6	Vocation school	63	16.7
Missing	6		Secondary school	18	4.8
			Technical college	95	25.1
			University or polytechnic degree	163	43.1
			Missing	8	
Household income			*Age*		
< 20.000 €	7	1.9	< 30	8	2.2
20.001-40.000	79	21.4	30 – 39	25	6.8
40.001-60.000	101	27.3	40-49	117	31.8
60.001-80.000	68	18.4	50 -59	194	52.7
> 80.001	115	31.1	> 60	24	6.5
Missing	16		Missing	18	
Start using Internet			*Start using online banking*		
< 1996	113	30.2	< 1996 (prior web banking)	66	17.8
1996-1997	86	23.0	1996-1997	53	14.3
1998-1999	110	29.4	1998-1999	125	33.7
2000-2001	62	16.6	2000-2001	118	31.8
2002 -	3	0.8	2002 -	9	2.4
Missing	12		Missing	15	
Internet usage frequency			*Online banking frequency*		
Once a week or less	32	8.4	Once a month or less	4	1.0
2-3 times per week	68	17.8	2-3 times per month	58	15.2
4-6 times per week	47	12.3	Once a week	191	50.0
Once a day	76	19.9	3-4 times per week	82	21.5
Many times per day	158	41.5	Every day	47	12.3
Missing	5		Missing	4	

Internet usage (hours in a week)			*Online banking per visit*		
1 hour or less	74	19.5	Less than 5 min.	34	8.9
1-5 hours	208	54.9	5- 10 min	147	38.5
5-10 hours	56	14.8	10-15 min.	111	29.1
10-15 hours	10	2.6	15-30 min	78	20.4
15 hours or more	31	8.2	over 30 min	12	3.1
Missing	7		Missing	4	

Appendix 2

Table 2. Description of the ranked customization approach

Variable name	Description of the customization approach
Data collection	
D1. Simple/one page forms	End-user preferences are clarified with help of one form.
D2. Wizard forms	End-users preferences are clarified with help of sequence forms which are taking notice of previous selections of respondent.
Fundamental methods	
F1. End-user driven customization	The web site is customizing or adjusting itself only based on direct end-user interaction. End-users can themselves influence what kind of customized content and services they receive
F2. Automatic customization	The web site is automatically customizing or adjusting itself without any direct interaction with end-user (e.g. meeting the requirements of different kinds of browsers, operating systems and screen resolutions).
F3. Transparent customization	The end-user will receive customized web pages without explicitly knowing that the pages have been modified for him/her
Recommendation	
R1. Usage/click-through history	End-user received customized content based on a profile, which has been generated by analyzing the previously visited web pages.
R2. Pre/user def. keywords	End-users can choose specific interest areas (e.g. by selecting predefined keywords or by giving open-ended words). Based on this profile and specified rules end-user received customized content.

R3. Simultaneous versions	There are several simultaneous web site versions which all are designed for different target groups e.g. for youth, senior citizens, families with children. End-users can select the most suitable version for them.
R4. Purchase history	End-user received customized content based on a profile, which has been generated by analyzing the products and services the end-user has previously bought.
R5. User performed rating	A pure content-based recommendation system. End-user received customized content based on a profile, which has been generated by analyzing the content that the end-user has rated in the past
R6. Demographic profile	Web site content and services are filtered based on user's demographic profile (e.g. age, sex, place of residence)
R7. Collaborative	A pure collaborative recommendation system. End-user received customized content which other end-users having similar tastes, as him/her have previously liked.
Technical gadgets	.
G1. Modular customization or my page	End-users can modify web page or pages in the web site by using predefined modules like in the case of my.yahoo
G2. Search agents	Search agents technologies are used to transmit filtered information from single or multiple sources to the end-users via email or through mobile channels
G3. Customized link list or navigation	End-users can create their own customized link list or navigation bars.
G4. Cosmetic customization	A cosmetic customization changes only the representation of the web site (e.g. colors, background picture and fonts), while the functionality or content of the web site remains the same to all users

Appendix 3

Table 3a. Ranking of identified customization approaches

	Mean	**Std. Dev**	**Mean difference**	
Data collection			D1. Simple form	
D1. Simple/One page forms	4.259	1.556		
D2. Wizard forms	4.046	1.616	0.231**	
Fundamental methods			F1. User driven	F2. Automatic
F1. End-user driven customization	4.755	1.503		
F2. Automatic customization	4.407	1.687	0.346**	
F3. Transparent customization	4.162	1.698	0.601**	0.252**

*Significant at the 0.05 level (2-tailed), **Significant at the 0.01 level (2-tailed).

Table 3b. Ranking of identified customization approaches

	Mean	Std. Dev	Mean difference				
Recommendation			R1. Usage history	R2. Pre/user def. keywords	R3. Simultaneous versions	R4. Purchase history	R5. User performed rating
R1. Usage/click-through history	4.337	1.560					
R2. Pre/user def. keywords	4.270	1.538	0.066				
R3. Simultaneous versions	4.119	1.584	0.227**	0.146*			
R4. Purchase history	4.052	1.476	0.289**	0.214**	0.071		
R5. User performed rating	4.006	1.466	0.330**	0.264**	0.106	0.049	
R6. Demographic profile	3.969	1.580	0.363**	0.301**	0.150*	0.071	0.013
R7. Collaborative	3.935	1.569	0.391**	0.333**	0.183**	0.103	0.043
Technical gadgets			G1. Search agent	G2. Link list	G3. My page	G4.. Cosmetic	
G1. Search agents	4.742	1.577					
G2. Customized link list	4.411	1.592	0.337**				
G3. Modular customization or my page	4.361	1.649	0.387**	0.050			
G4. Cosmetic customization	3.373	1.503	1.395**	1.061**	0.993**		

*Significant at the 0.05 level (2-tailed), **Significant at the 0.01 level (2-tailed).

Appendix 4

Table 4. Ranking of identified customization approaches

Service area	**Mean**	**Std. Dev.**	**Mean difference**					
			Investments	Credit and debit cards	Inquiries, questions, guidance	Savings	News and bulletins	Insurances
1. Investments	5.442	1.481						
2. Credit and debit cards	5.071	1.499	0.375**					
3. Inquiries, questions, guidance	5.063	1.529	0.384**	0.003				
4. Savings	4.942	1.480	0.503**	0.129*	0.121			
5. News and bulletins	4.822	1.549	0.621**	0.245**	0.241**	0.121		
6. Insurances	4.061	1.618	1.377**	1.005**	1.000**	0.882**	0.761**	
7. Home mortgages	4.037	1.469	1.395**	1.024**	1.016**	0.894**	0.772**	0.008

The rank of the most suitable online banking products and services for customization (N=381-378),
*Significant at the 0.05 level (2-tailed), **Significant at the 0.01 level (2-tailed).

CHAPTER EIGHT

ICT-BASED FINANCIAL INNOVATIONS

SERGEY YABLONSKY

1. Introduction

A major focus of writings on financial innovations has been the attempt to categorize them. There are almost as many schemes as authors, but many of these share the feature of looking through to the underlying functions performed by the innovations. Not surprisingly, no classification scheme is perfect, and more importantly, given their complexity of design and use; many innovations span multiple categories in known schemes and their alternatives (Lerner and Tufano, 2011a,b).

Turning to the question of what motivates financial innovation, the literature has focused on the following drivers, common both to the manufacturing and service industries (Fagerberg et al, 2005; Anderloni et al., 2009):

- availability of new technology
- competition
- evolving customer needs.

Technological progress in corporate finance and banking has multiple dimensions. Although product innovation and process innovation are crucial elements of technological change, improvements in the organization of financial intermediaries and financial networks have also been important.

We agree with Mention (2011) and Mention and Torkkeli (2012) that the concept of “financial innovation” can be defined as making and promoting new financial products and services, developing new processes to facilitate financial activities, to interact with customers and to design new structures for financial institutions.

Information technologies, including the Internet and other related technologies, are changing the way companies do business. As a result, new ways of doing business in the digital economy have opened up (Peitz and Waldfogel, 2012). Globalization, increasingly, leads to a network economy (Liezenberg and Lycklama, 2012) and forces electronic infrastructures, enabling industries to cooperate in networks, in real-time. Digital or electronic business (e-business) conducts business through electronic and mobile networks, being one of the most innovative sectors of the global economy. E-Business usually refers to a business conducted over the Internet, but in general, any network, public or private, can be included. E-Business is a term that has a broader definition of e-commerce, which includes servicing customers, collaborating with business partners and conducting electronic transactions within an organization, as well as buying and selling. Digital business is increasingly important in our networked world of global transactions and global competition (Meier and Stormer, 2009).

Our research was motivated by the observation that various descriptions of e-finance innovation services implement the concept of an e-finance service on similar core concepts with distinct features. The scope is Global economy and a large emerging economy, namely Russia. The goal is to capture the common core of different approaches to facilitate research in e-finance Multi-Sided Platforms (henceforth, MSPs). Thus we illustrate how the e-finance innovative services taxonomy can be complemented by the real instances in the emerging market of Russia. E-finance innovative services in Russia are in the early phase of development and the research in this field will bring more understanding of the Russian e-finance market perspectives in the next decade.

The qualitative research presented in this chapter aims at collecting and analysing quality data, regarding the current status and prospective evolution of e-finance services offered by Global and Russia's leading e-business and banking companies that are running businesses in the e-business sector. The analysis proposes classification and examination of the current status of e-finance services and possible ways of further evolution of e-finance technology and services both for the banks and their customers.

The analysis methodology incorporates information from different but interrelated sources that form a representative sample of the domain:

- Reported and observed trends and e-finance activity. This study incorporates data from 2001 up to 2010 from Internet (blogs, web conferences, etc.)

- E-finance services briefings, press releases, market and company reports and other publicly available information
- Research and text books, published from 2001 up to 2010
- Open ontologies and taxonomies including e-business, finance and service domains.

The methodology, classification and organization of domain concepts, validation issues and the first pilot version of an e-finance innovation services ontology (taxonomy) are discussed. Then an e-finance innovation services detailed analysis is developed. Finally, we summarize the main results of the study.

2. E-finance innovation services

E-finance is a part of e-business and provides financial services through electronic channels (Apte and Vepsäläinen, 1993; Bátiz-Lazo, 2004; Nsouli and Schaechter, 2002; Park and Campbell, 2001; Risk management principles for electronic banking, 2003; Worthy et al, 2003). Financial services are electronic infrastructures-enabled industries. Mobile Internet is developing into a true transaction channel, creating new transaction contexts that require new transaction services and new options emerge in existing contexts (King, 2010; Liezenberg and Lycklama, 2012). At the same time financial transaction services are part of many-sided markets, with sophisticated network effects. So, future innovations in financial services require a thorough understanding of the platform context in which transactions take place.

The finance industry is at the forefront of innovation, both to reduce the costs of bank operations and to improve services to customers. Electronic financial services (e-finance services) have spread quickly in recent years. There are several branches that come from e-finance. They cover the sectors of e-banking, e-brokerage, e-payment and many other activities. Both banks and customers (individuals, companies or government) benefit from the use of alternative channels and e-banking services (Claessens et al., 2002). These services offer consumers a great deal of convenience, saving time when managing financial matters and also lowering costs, reducing service charges. However, advantages come together with disadvantages, which banks and customers must take into account in order to make e-finance services a valuable alternative and not a catastrophe.

What exactly is e-finance? The definition that is used as the basis of this study is: the provision of financial services and markets through electronic channels (Bank for International Settlements, 2000; Claessens et al, 2002; Franklin et al., 2001; Friedman, 2000; Lee et al., 2008; Nsouli, and Schaechter, 2002; Schaechter, 2002; Shahrokhi, 2008).

During the late-2000s (decade) economic recession (Bordo and Haubrich, 2012), the way in which a financial organization applies innovation to routine activities gains greater importance. The overheads and associated costs, once acceptable under normal conditions of moderate growth, need to be brought into line. To achieve this, a financial organization will need to adapt its current business processes and IT infrastructures so as to maintain competitiveness both nationally and internationally. Innovative alignment of business processes and services technologies can be built upon the organization's existing systems in order to achieve higher levels of efficiency and productivity.

E-finance is rapidly changing the structure and the nature of financial services (Frame and Lawrence, 2002; Herfurth and Weib, 2010; Karakostas et al., 2005; Liebena and Khiaonarong, 2009; Moshirian, 2004; Service Innovation Yearbook 2010-2011, 2010). Despite the differences between countries in the availability of telecommunications infrastructure and the quality of the rules, there are many promising and similar to the distribution of e-finance.

The term electronic banking (e-banking, internet banking, virtual banking, or online banking) and e-payments, usually refers to all forms of banking services and transactions performed through electronic means (Cronin, 1997; ISACA Internet Banking Guideline). E-banking includes the systems that enable financial institution customers, individuals or businesses, to access accounts, transact business, or obtain information on financial products and services through a public or private network, including the internet (Joshi, 2010). Nowadays, financial transactions executed by ATM, direct deposits and payments and debit card transactions are recorded and verified instantly from a distant location via the Internet, which reduces the further need for brick-and-mortar banking institution visits.

E-finance has numerous e-payment services; however, numerous problems continue to be left unresolved (Anderloni et al., 2009; Joshi, 2010; King, 2010, 2012; Rezaee, 2011; Shahrokhi, 2008; Yablonsky, 2014):

- Users still have no trust. Because of this, banking cards in some countries/regions are seldom, if ever used, for online payments. Therefore Cash on Delivery is commonly used in e-commerce. The absence of trust can influence, as well, SMS payments, due to a variety of swindling offers.

- Additional option solutions for online payments complicate user experience. Working with electronic currencies requires the following of several, sometimes uneasy, steps. Offline terminals are much more user-friendly although they stop the online buying experience.
- Users and merchants are often charged in some countries with significant fees. Fees are unreasonably high with telephone-based payment means; they can be essential with offline terminals and electronic currencies too.
- Merchants have to aggregate numerous payment services, which may cause complex processes or to the necessity of paying for additional aggregation services.
- By default, e-wallets are secure with double password authentication required for every online payment. Consumers can opt for even stronger protection with advanced authentication-instead of a single payment password; they can use a table of codes or an e-token to generate unique passwords for each transaction.

Internet banking using mobile devices is known as mobile banking (m-banking). For customers, m-banking provides a very convenient and effective means of managing personal finances, supporting seamless anytime, anywhere connectivity (Riivari, 2005). M-banking can be considered as one of the most significant financial service innovations, which is emerging as a key platform for expanding access to banking transactions via mobile devices (Sulaiman et al., 2007).

Mobile payment services (see fig.1) in m-banking allow operators, banks and financial institutions to introduce new service offerings, such as micropayments, bill pay and top-ups. This payment method makes it possible to purchase goods from merchants, top-off credit balances for airtime, or make person-to-person payments, loan payments, bill payments and more. Thus, it introduces a new channel to interact with customers. Usually m-payment services are adapted to all networks, mobile devices, languages, currencies and deliver communications across multiple mobile channels, including SMS, USSD, mobile Web browser and mobile client applications. Financial institutions in developed and emerging markets can rely on m-payment services for a complete mobile banking solution that supports all mobile transactions conducted by a mobile phone.

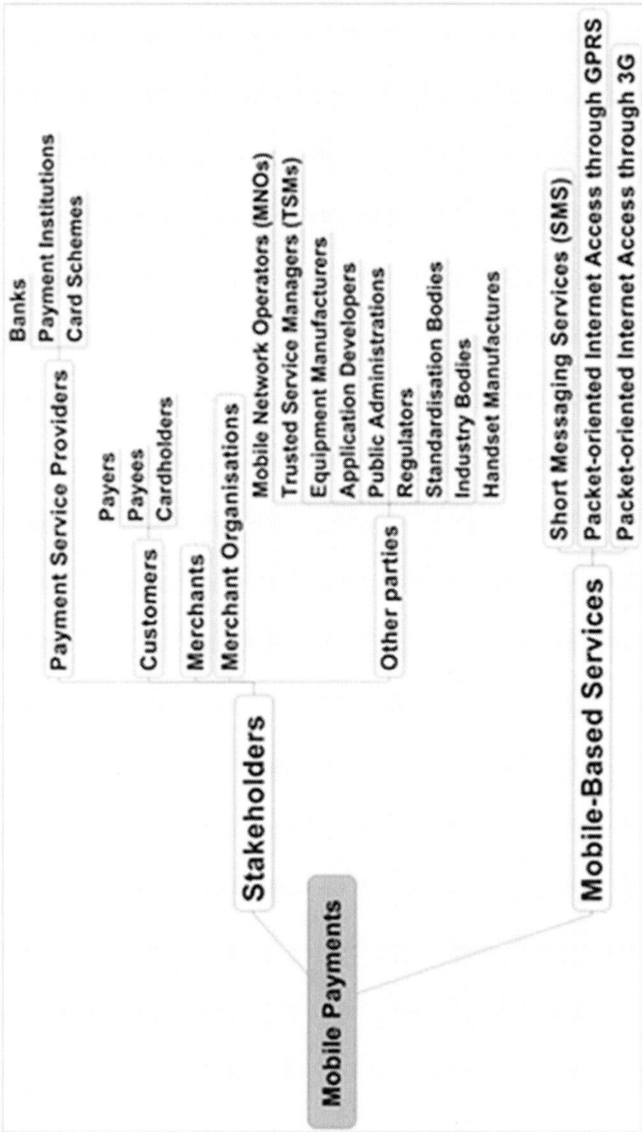

Figure 1. Mobile payments taxonomy (part of the e-finance innovation services taxonomy)

M-payments are at the centre of m-banking and mobile commerce. M-banking and m-payments bring financial banking services closer to the demand-creation point through the use of the mobile phone's unique features like Location-Based Services (henceforth, LBS), voice control, camera, complete availability, constant Internet connectivity and Quick Response (henceforth, QR).

Mobile banking is more than just a channel; it provides a new way of thinking about old processes (Tiwari et al., 2006). Banks that can conceptualize bank interaction through a mobile device, beyond simple transaction order taking, can help differentiate your bank and provide unique client experiences.

Mobile banking, together with mobile business, is induced by some unique features that enhance it with several positive aspects against classical forms of commercial transactions, including Electronic Commerce (Tiwari et al., 2006; Turban and King, 2011):

- Ubiquity: Ubiquity means that the user can take advantage of services and perform transactions largely independent of his current geographic location (the "anywhere" feature).
- Immediacy: Strongly related to the feature of ubiquity is the possibility of a real-time advantage of services (the "anytime" feature). This feature is mainly attractive for services that are time-critical and require a swift reaction, e.g. stock market information.
- Localization: Positioning technologies, such as the Global Positioning System (henceforth, GPS), allows companies to promote goods and services to the user targeted to his current location.
- Instant connectivity: Based on the latest available technology, such as General Packet Radio Service (henceforth, GPRS), 4G or so, mobile devices are constantly "online" (the "always-on" feature). This feature gives advantage to the user, as time-consuming dialup or boot processes are not needed.
- Pro-active functionality: The user may choose the products and services, which he/she wants to be kept informed about.
- Mobile Banking provides to prospective clients such new innovation services (Turban and King, 2011).
- Customers can use their mobile handsets to access account balances, pay bills and transfer funds using SMS.
- Wireless Electronic Payment Systems. Wireless payment systems transform mobile phones into secure, self-contained purchasing-

support tools, capable of instantly authorizing payments over the cellular network.

- M-wallet (mobile wallet). Technologies that enable cardholders to make purchases with a single click from their wireless device.

In 2013, e-banking and m-banking, are viewed as a sustainable innovation in its maturity stage, reaching to the late majority in the diffusion process.

While e-commerce and e-payments extended, buying from the shop and mail-order catalogue to the PC and laptop at home, enabling tickets and digital content to be fulfilled directly to the desk, m-commerce and m-payments carry this evolution further, still by making the smartphone the point where demand is created and supply fulfilled outside the home, workplace and shop. The take up of individual applications such as m-commerce and e-shopping apps, social commerce, location-based commerce, price comparison, daily deals and quick response is increasing rapidly.

E-insurance in the broad sense can be defined as the use of the Internet and related ICT in production and distribution of insurance services. In a more narrow sense, E-insurance can be defined as the provision of insurance coverage via the Internet, resulting in requesting and delivering online of the insurance police, as well as carrying online negotiations and contracts (Joshi, 2010).

Table 1. Typology and characteristics of electronic payment systems

(Adopted and updated from Brousseau, and Curien, 2007)

Type of EPS	Example	Market structure	Monetary form	Keeping of accounts	Monetary base	Integration with the banking system	Type of transaction
Secured payment	SSL	Competitive	Scriptural	Bank	Institutional	Complement	B2C
Order protocols with bank card	SET	Oligopoly	Scriptural	Bank	Institutional	Complement	B2C
Trusted systems	PayPal	Oligopoly	Scriptural	Non-bank	Institutional	Substitute	B2C / C2C/P2P/A2A
	E-gold	Monopoly	Scriptural	Non-bank	Private	Substitute	B2C / C2C P2P/A2A
Loyalty systems	Beenz	Competitive	Scriptural	Non-bank	Private	Substitute	B2C
Billing systems	I-pin	Oligopoly	Scriptural	Non-bank	Institutional	Complement[*]	B2C
Electronic purse	Proton, Mondex	Oligopoly	Electronic (hardware)	Bank	Institutional	Complement	B2C / C2C P2P/A2A
Virtual purse	Ecash, Millicent	—	Electronic (software)	Bank	Institutional	Complement	B2C

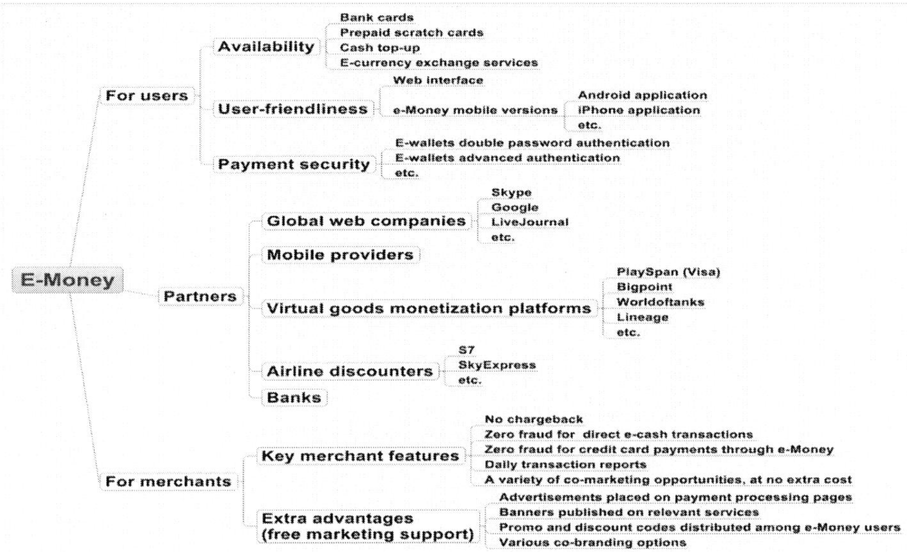

Figure 2. E-money features taxonomy (part of the e-finance innovation services taxonomy)

E-trading is defined as the provision of some or all of the following services (Joshi, 2010):

- Electronic exchange of data between users and the system.
- Automated execution of orders.
- Formation of post-trade information (transaction price and volume data).
- Electronic distribution of quotas on supply/demand.

E-acquiring is a service payment carried out by using credit cards over the Internet. Nowadays, bank cards are a common form of payment for goods and services. In recent years, along with the development of the Internet, credit cards have grown in popularity in terms of paying for goods and services online. Using the e-acquiring, the company gets access to new segments of customers who prefer to pay for goods and services over the Internet and thus provides an additional service to their current customers. Apart from the growth in customer base, using the Internet reduces the costs of acquiring, related to the processing of cash, such as costs of conducting transactions on the Internet disproportionately lower than the cost of rent, staff salaries in the sales area, collection, etc.

The question of payments on the Internet refers to the Electronic Payment Systems (EPS) and is associated with the rise of a new monetary form, electronic money, sometimes issued by non-banks. (Brousseau and Curien, 2007). Payments on the Internet are carried out by means of EPS. Typology and characteristics of electronic payment systems are shown on Table 1 (Brousseau and Curien, 2007). E-money or e-currency is stored-value or prepaid payment mechanisms (fig.2). The difference between e-money and e-banking is that with e-money, balances are not kept in financial accounts with banks (Nsouli and Schaechter, 2002). All purchases are provided by online or mobile services.

3. Ontology of e-finance innovation services

The financial services industry is one of the most data-rich environments on the Web today; although access to this data is very often inhibited by the poor adoption of standards by the industry. Using semantic technologies in the financial services sector will help to clarify the discourse surrounding the financial instruments to a wider audience, including regulators who want to deal with the risks of conceptual issues that played a big role in the financial crisis.

The current standards activities that are likely to be of interest for the financial services industry include (A Discussion of the Role of Standards in the Financial Services Industry, 2011):

- Accredited Standards Committee X9 (ASC X9)
- North American Security Standards Productions Organization (NASPO)
- Standards in the areas of payments, securities and related security technologies-International Organization for Standardization Technical Committee 68 (ISO TC 68)
- Standards and tools for assessing IT outsource vendors-The Santa Fe Group
- Payment Card Information (PCI) Security Standards Council.

A clear and precise description and structuring of the information in the e-finance domain are the prerequisites for a common understanding of the information exchanged among different partners of e-finance. It also fosters semantic interoperability in the context of pan-European data exchanges among public administrations, facilitates electronic interoperability among e-finance businesses (ebXML, XBRL, FpML) and improves statistics on e-finance. Taxonomies and other types of controlled vocabularies are the preferred means to achieve such a common understanding by specifying the terms of the domain, disambiguating them from each other, controlling synonyms and structuring the domain via term relationships. There are many approaches to the classification of goods, ranging from rather coarse taxonomies, created for customs purposes and statistics of economic activities, like the North American Industry Classification System (NAICS) to expressive descriptive languages for products and services, like UNSPSC/NAPCS, eCl@ss, eOTD, or RNTD (Hepp et al., 2006). It is out of the scope of this chapter to list and compare all available standards in this area, but one can say that services categorization standards, like UNSPSC, eCl@ss2, eOTD3, or the RosettaNet Technical Dictionary, reflect some degree of community consensus and contain, readily available, a wealth of concept definitions plus a hierarchy. Products and Services Categorization Standards (PSCS) and taxonomic standards UNSPSC/NAPCS, eCl@ss and eOTD are currently the most important horizontal standards (i.e. covering a broad range of industries) and RNTD is a high-degree detailed standard, albeit limited to a narrow segment of products (Hepp et al., 2006; Hepp et al., 2007). Standard taxonomy for products and services, often referred to as a business ontology, UNSPSC contains 20,789 categories and eCl@ss, a similar but more expressive standard, contains 25,658 categories plus 5,525 precisely defined object and data type properties (Hepp et al., 2007).

A taxonomy is comprised of a hierarchy of concepts linked by a transitive generic relation (often called isA or subClassOf) whereby each instance of a class can be inferred to be an instance of all parent classes. Taxonomies are strict hierarchies: each class has at most one parent. A lightweight ontology typically consists of a hierarchy of concepts and a set of relations holding between those concepts. If we specify only a hierarchy of concepts related using an is-A relationship (is-A is a relationship where one class A is a subclass of another class B), then we have taxonomy. Heavyweight ontologies add classes (concepts), instances (objects) of classes or concepts, attributes (aspects, properties, features, characteristics, or parameters that objects and classes can have), relations and more (Poli et al., 2010).

Ontologies are typically divided into foundational (or top-level), domain and application ontologies (Poli et al., 2010). Foundational ontologies cover the most general concepts that can be expected to be common to all domains, such as “individuals” vs. “universals”. Domain ontologies are tailored for a specific area of human activity, e.g. medicine or business. Application ontologies further restrict attention to a particular activity in a domain, e.g. a computer-based order handling system in business. Some of foundational ontologies include domain and application knowledge (ex.: OpenCyc, SUMO).

The Semantic Web, a Web with the meaning or Web 3.0, produces new specific XML-based standards for semantics, such as Web Ontology Language (OWL) (W3C, 2004). It is demonstrated that more expressive forms of semantic structures for knowledge management encompass simpler forms and extend their capabilities (Küster et al., 2008).

For example, the OWL comprises the ability to represent glossaries, taxonomies, thesauri, subject ontologies and the semantics of specific XML schemas, database schemas, entity-relationship and UML models.

Deployment and development of ontologies in the domain of innovation e-finance services management demonstrate the applicability of the method to this field and it's potential. The methodological insight into innovation ontology development was shown by several researchers (Bullinger, 2009; Hafkesbrink et al., 2010; Hafkesbrink and Schroll, 2011; Osterwalder and Pigneur, 2002; Riedl et al., 2009; Sheth, 2011; Yablonsky, 2009; Yablonsky, 2010, 2014). In various recent works, it was demonstrated how the ontology can be used to achieve interoperability between innovation tools and to answer questions relevant for innovation managers that demonstrate the advantages of semantic reasoning (Hepp et al., 2006; Hepp et al., 2007; Riedl et al., 2009; Yablonsky, 2009). Today many taxonomies and ontologies are transformed or created in Semantic Web OWL (W3C, 2004) standard representation (Hepp, 2006, 2007, 2008; Hepp and de Bruijn, 2007; IEEE Suggested Upper Merged Ontology, 2013; Protege Ontology Library, 2013). For example, eClassOWL (eClassOWL, 2013), is one of the most comprehensive and mature Web ontology for types of products and services. It defines classes for more than 30,000 product/services types and more than 5,000 properties for product/service features.

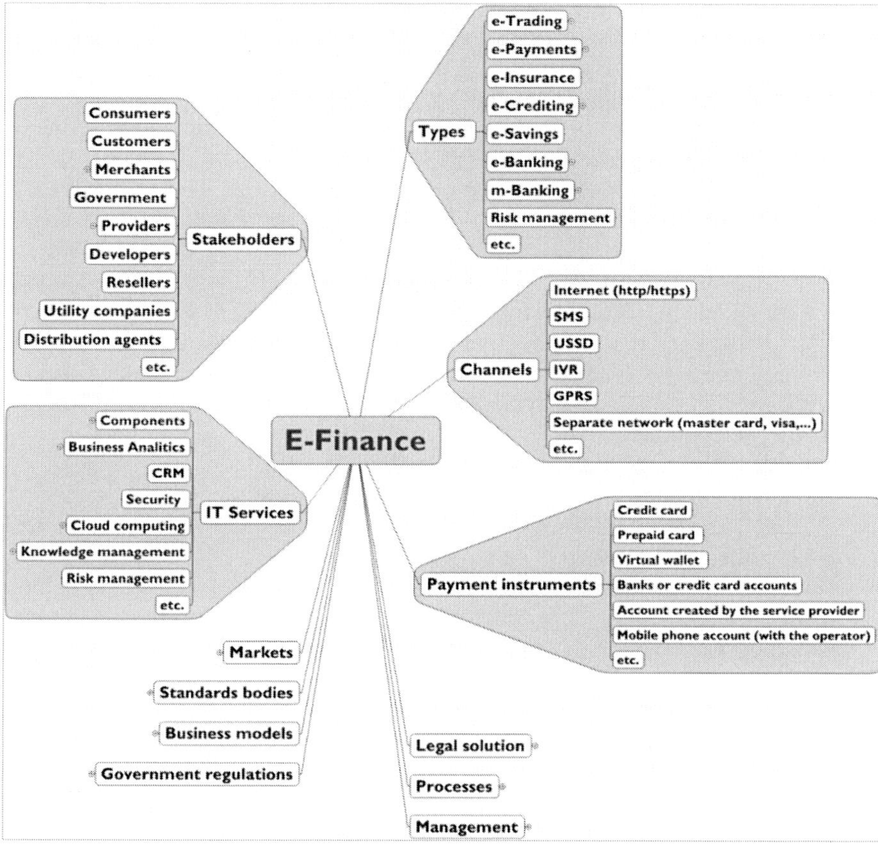

Figure 3. The e-finance innovation services taxonomy (first level)

In the domain of finance such ontologies and implementations of Semantic Web based applications exist.

- ISDA-approved (International Swaps and Derivatives Association) standard contract template.
- Financial Industry Business Ontology (FIBO) based on Semantic Web standards of World Wide Web Consortium (W3C)-for financial services transactions (Financial Industry Business Ontology (FIBO), 2013).
- Finance ontology (Vanderlinden, 2011) follows ISO standards and covers several aspects (classification of financial instruments,

currencies, markets, parties involved in financial transactions, countries etc.). Suggested Upper Merged Ontology (SUMO) also includes a subset related to finance domain, which is richly axiomatized, not just taxonomic information but with terms formally defined.
- There are also several contributions in financial investments and trading systems (Mellouli et al., 2010; Qin and Taffet, 2004; Zhang et al., 2000).

The Financial Industry Business Ontology (FIBO) standard, a joint effort between OMG and the Enterprise Data Management Council, is an industry initiative to define and standardize financial industry terms, using semantic web principals and OMG modelling standards. FIBO model can be adequately used to satisfy:

- Regulatory governance
- Data standardization
- Risk management
- Data analytics requirements.

As it was expressed by (Zaino, 2012), while each money related exchange takes after a standard contract pattern, ISDA-sanction (International Swaps and Derivatives Association) contract parts could be assembled and there has been no scientific classification of budgetary instruments to enhance cognizance of their items or to decipher risks. Along these lines, plus a normal vocabulary industry needs ontology to classify instruments as per the agreement parts they have. This is the place semantic innovation outperforms, for making meanings of classifications through OWL and utilizing reasoners to take cases of contracts and sort them into different classes. Alternately XML exchange messages could be made as RDF with OWL reasoners then amassing all subsidiaries that have an agreement example into a solitary class; computations might be performed that could prompt findings-for instance, that some gathering has taken a position for which it doesn't have the possessions available to make the needed pay-outs, may as well circumstances require that (Zaino, 2012).

The qualitative research presented in this chapter aims at collecting and analysing quality data regarding the current status and prospective evolution of IT-based e-finance innovations offered by leading e-business and banking companies. The analysis proposes a classification and an examination of the current status of e-finance IT services and possible ways of further evolution of e-finance technology and services both for the banks and their customers.

A few points should be noted concerning the methodology. They include the method in which knowledge was extracted from a particular domain, the classification and organization of domain concepts, validation issues and development tools. An appropriate knowledge source consists of documents that constitute the entire knowledge domain (for example, text books: Gup, 2011; Haan et al., 2009; Rezaee, 2011 etc. published from 2001 up to 2010; foundational RDF/OWL ontologies and taxonomies, for example, OpenCyc, SUMO, Linking Open Data (LOD), UNSPSC, eCl@ssOWL, WordNet), a set of documents that form a representative sample of the domain (for example, domain ontologies and taxonomies; reported and observed trends and e-finance activity from 2001 up to 2010, e-finance services briefings, press releases, market and company's reports and other publicly-available information; web documents (blogs, web conferences, etc.), market and company reports. On the other hand, depending on the nature of the knowledge domain and the ontology's purpose, physical analysis of source documents and the validation of the first pilot version of ontology by experts in the field, can result into a superior identification and organization of concepts.

The structuring of the e-finance services ontology is roused by the need to give three essential types of knowledge about e-finance services using a modification of a known OWL-S notation (Semantic Markup for Web Services, 2013), each characterized by the question it answers:

- What does the service provide for prospective clients? The answer to this question is given in the each instance of the class Service that presents a ServiceProfile.
- How is it used? The answer to this question is given in the "process model". This perspective is captured by the ServiceModel class. Instances of the class Service use the property describedBy to refer to the service's ServiceModel.
- How does one interact with it? The answer to this question is given in the "grounding". Grounding provides the needed details about transport protocols. Instances of the class Service supports property referring to a ServiceGrounding.

The class Service provides an organizational point of reference for a declared e-finance service; one instance of Service will exist for each distinct published service. The properties presents, described by and supports are properties of Service.

The pilot version of lightweight ontology e-finance service ontology (hierarchy of taxonomy concepts-is shown on fig.3, a set of relations holding between those concepts-for example: one can relate stakeholders to IT services, stating for example: (developer) develops (IT-service), (customer) buys (IT service), relations IsPartOf, etc. and a set of instances-international and local regional companies, services, etc.; the total number of all ontology features-400) is too complex to be represented here in its entirety, but an example of taxonomy is provided in order to demonstrate both the process of classification and the intermediate result (Yablonsky, 2014).

The e-finance service ontology offers a complete and effective framework for describing and managing e-finance services innovations in the research area. It will also favour market description and enactment, by means of composition of multiple resources, emerged as a fundamental requirement in the Web, mobile and e-finance context. Using the ontology one can create complex queries, for example: to see what the customers of the Customer Relationship Management (CRM) application from a specific developer are.

The e-finance service ontology adds to the current understanding of:

– E-finance services innovation workflow and service model foundations
– Organization of e-finance innovation services domain knowledge in ontological form
– Ontology design principles and validation issues development
– Identification and organization of the concepts and instances (or examples) of concepts in a manner that achieves the ontology's purpose
– The types of e-finance services
– E-finance innovation services metrics and indicators
– Prediction, modelling, and design of new e-financial innovations types.

The next stage of ontology development is its evaluation and correction by the group of experts from the domain.

4. Platform-based financial innovations

Terms multi-sided market, two-sided market and platform-based market are used sometimes inter-changeably. We shall use such definition

(Evans et al, 2008; Hagiu and Wright, 2011): a multi-sided market exists, when at any point in time there are

- two or more distinct groups of customers
- the value obtained by one kind of customers increases with the number of the other kind of customers, and
- an intermediary is necessary for internalizing the externalities created by one group for the other group.

Products and services that bring together groups of users in multi-sided markets are multi-sided platforms-MSPs (Hagiu and Wright, 2011; Järvi et al., 2011; Peitz and Waldfogel, 2012). Economists use the terms ''two-sided market'', ''two-sided platform'' or ''multi-sided platform'', to refer to the mediating role of service platforms between two or more groups of agents (Evans et al., 2006; Rochet and Tirole, 2003). We argue that only the proposed (Hagiu and Wright, 2011) definition provides a more precise notion of MSPs by requiring that they enable direct interactions between the multiple customer types which are affiliated to them.

Platforms are defined (Gawer, 2009) as building blocks (products, technologies or services) that act as a foundation upon which an array of firms (a business ecosystem) develops complementary products, technologies or services, proposing such requirements for a platform:

- it should perform a critical function of the overall system or should solve a crucial technological issue of an industry
- it should be easy to connect to, ''build upon'' and provide space for new and unplanned usage.

Platforms enable new services due to the reuse of platform components. They have lower fixed costs and enable shorter time to market for service providers.

In two-sided and many-sided markets, the value creation and appropriation logic is different (Hagiu, and Wright, 2011); the linear and transitive value chain and value-creation thinking is outdated. Often this duality, of both sides representing cost and revenue is neglected, and the other side is treated as a profit on and the other either as loss or financially neutral (Hagiu, and Wright, 2011). Figure 4 represents in a simple way the key distinctions between MSPs and input suppliers on the one hand and between MSPs and re-sellers on the other hand (Hagiu, and Wright, 2011). An intermediary can choose between functioning as a marketplace, on which suppliers sell their products directly to buyers, or as a reseller, purchasing products from suppliers and selling them to buyers (Hagiu, and Wright, 2013). In Hagiu and Wright model, this choice comes down to whether residual control rights over non-contractible decision variables are better held by suppliers (the marketplace mode) or by the intermediary (the reseller mode). They focus on a single non-contractible decision variable-the level of demand-enhancing marketing activities. The reseller is better able to coordinate these activities across products, whereas the marketplace mode benefits from allowing independent suppliers to tailor their marketing activities to local information about buyer demand. In the benchmark setting, the marketplace mode is preferred, if and only if, the variance of local information exceeds the squared value of spillovers from marketing activities across products. Hagiu and Wright explore several generalizations, showing how the benchmark trade-off is modified in different settings.

We consider finance intermediaries MSPs and markets (Evans et al, 2008). The role of financial intermediary is to:

– minimize transaction costs through matchmaking and audience making
– minimize costs through the elimination of duplication
– permit value-creating exchanges that would not take place otherwise
– enforce innovation.

MSPs include different organizations in finance, banking and other industries such as debit and credit card payment schemes, which cater for cardholders and merchants (American Express, Visa, MasterCard), stock markets which cater for companies wishing to list and to investors/traders (through brokers), financial intermediations, insurance, securities, online and mobile banks, auctions, shops, social services, e-payment services (Amazon, eBay, Facebook, Apple, Mall of America, PayPal etc.) in their current forms (Gawer, 2009; Gawer and Cusumano, 2012; Hagiu and Wright, 2011; Peitz and Waldfogel, 2012). For emerging market's MSPs the main threat is disintermediation: by replicating the platform side services, rivals may be able to clone the platform itself and compete with it directly (Baldwin and Woodard, 2008; Yablonsky, 2013).

The driving force behind multi-sided markets and platforms is the need to induce coordination among two or more groups of affiliated customers and what they coordinate on is precisely a fixed point in the architecture of transactions in which they collectively participate (Baldwin and Woodard, 2008). That fixed point may be a particular financial service, for example the Visa payment-processing service, which both issues cards to consumers and approves transactions on behalf of merchants. Finally, all platforms of services or products exhibit tensions between platform owners and complimentary. These tensions are variously expressed.

Playing with multisided platforms soon will be a fact of life for all finance and banking companies. MSPs reduce search and transaction costs and give companies vastly broader access to markets than they could achieve on their own. But over the past 10 years, we've also seen powerful owners of MSPs like Microsoft, Google, American Express, Visa, MasterCard and Apple extract most of the value from platforms, because companies that played with them didn't adequately understand their motives and operating strategies.

Several papers (Gawer and Henderson, 2007; Gawer, 2009; Gawer and Cusumano, 2012) have discussed some of the major differences between internal and external platforms and have suggested how both types of platforms can impact product and service innovation. It is stated that MSPs facilitate the generation of a potentially very large number of complementary innovations by tapping into the innovative capabilities of many external actors and function as a technological foundation at the heart of innovative business ecosystems. MSPs guide technological innovation trajectories and stimulate innovation on complements. It was reviewed in the literature (economics, innovation, operations and strategy), that MSPs are associated with a positive impact on innovation. The positive effect stems from the fact that by offering unified and easy ways to connect to common components and foundational technologies, platform leaders help reduce the cost of entry in complementary markets and provide demand for complements, often fuelled by network effects. MSPs offer a setting where it is in the interest of private firms to elicit and encourage innovation by others.

A successful coordination of MSP-based innovations has become a major pillar in sustaining competitive advantage and long-term increase of company value in platform markets, characterized by indirect network externalities (Scholten and Scholten, 2010, 2012). Leading ICT-based platform owners have put a strong focus on attracting and tying external complementarities to their platforms by applying several distinct types of control mechanisms along their external innovation process (Scholten and Scholten, 2012).

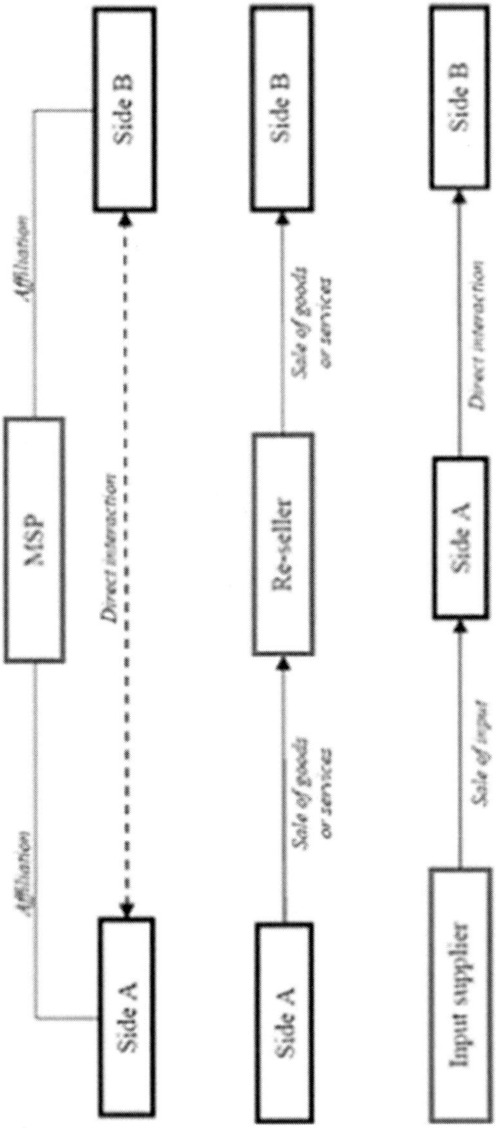

Figure 4. Difference between input suppliers, MSP's and re-sellers caption (Hagiu, and Wright, 2011).

Platform openness has been discussed from the perspective of strategic management and leadership, complementary markets and network externalities. Making a decision on how much to open or close a platform is critical for the growth and sustainability of the platform (Boudreau, 2006). ‘‘A platform is open to the extent that: (1) restrictions are not placed on participation in its development, commercialization or use; and (2) any restrictions are reasonable and non- discriminatory, i.e. they are applied uniformly to all potential platform participants’’ (Eisenmann et al., 2008, p.1).

There are two types of platform competition. One type of competition happens between dissimilar incompatible platforms for the market, while another one often occurs between compatible platforms and technologies in the market (Church and Gandal, 2004). Competitions for the market usually occur between closed platforms whereby platform providers tend to internalize network effects, use design or intellectual property rights (IPR) to restrain rival firms from developing compatible complementary products in the hope of becoming dominant and maintaining power and profits. How to dominate a service platform, while attracting and maintaining the interest of both sides of the market, is a core issue. The concept of platform leadership refers to strategies deployed by platform providers to control critical components or interfaces and to facilitate the participation of other firms for innovative development and growth. Typically, platform leaders deploy various social and political strategies to deal with competition challenges that they face in mobilizing cooperation around the platform. Such strategies play a role in persuading or hampering third-parties to join and persist in the platform. Typically, platform leaders design and modify technical implementation, coordinate supply-side user investment and provide tools to support innovation in complementary products and services (Greenstein, 2009).

With regards to motivating complementary providers (banking, agriculture, healthcare) there are several leadership strategies that are used to encourage the participation. For instance, sharing technical specifications, developing enabling tools and technologies, APIs and SDKs to assist third-parties to develop complementary services, providing subsidizing and funding opportunities and employing IPRs are commonly discussed to encourage partnership (Huang et al., 2009).

It is important to focus the research on the same problems in e-financial MSPs. Each of these control mechanisms can be applied at dedicated phases of the platform-based innovation process in order to steer external complementary innovation efforts on top of the platform.

We argue that nowadays the main part of e-finance sector innovations are MSP-based multi-sided platform open or closed innovations (Armstrong, 2006; Baldwin and Woodard, 2008; Caillaud and Jullien, 2003; Chesbrough, 2006; Chesbrough, 2011; Evans, 2003; Rochet and Tirole, 2003).

Such main e-finance innovative services form different sides of e-financial MSPs:

- credit/debit cards
- e-banking
- mobile banking (including sms-banking)
- e-acquiring
- e-trading
- e-money
- Web 2.0 services (P2P services).

We agree with the IDC Financial Insights (IDC 2012) that in the nearest future:

- "Proximity payments will ride upgrades in point-of-sale and mobile device technology to become the second-largest category of mobile payments spending, about evenly divided between the two methods.
- Person-to-person or point-to-point (P2P) fund transfers will be a distant third, mainly due to a lack of common standards for sending money across borders using mobile devices as well as a lack of locations for adding cash to and withdrawing cash from the system".

5. E-finance MSPs in emerging markets

The level of the development activity and the level of innovation in channels are rapidly increasing in emerging markets. E-finance services will lead to much lower costs and greater competition in financial services on the emerging markets too, through both greater competition among incumbent financial services and new entries from the global financial sector. Accordingly, incumbent financial institutions will probably experience a sharp decline in revenues.

For example, the mobile financial services portfolio for emerging markets has grown in recent years using Short Message Service ((henceforth, SMS), mobile web, Radio-Frequency Identification (henceforth, RFID), Near

Field Communication (henceforth, NFC), smart cards, micro-transactions, macro-transactions for mobile banking transactions (Karippacheril et al., 2013; Yablonsky, 2014). Mobile services for financial inclusion are enabling widespread use of money transfers, credit and savings. Platforms can play a crucial role in making services available in an easy and affordable way for local providers, developers and communities, not only for feature and smart phones, but also for very low cost phones.

Mobile service MSPs can create the ecosystem for services to low-income users (Karippacheril et al., 2013). The poor are incredibly resourceful and this is best displayed by mobile services that enable cost sharing and device sharing. Devices are mostly very low-cost phones, which are capable of voice, text messaging and basic pre-installed applications.

M-banking MSPs have the possibility to bring basic banking and electronic transactions services to unbanked consumers in emerging and developing markets (Karippacheril et al., 2013). M-banking solutions also provide telecommunications industry regulators with specific concerns. Regulators need to address if the elements are in place for m-banking networks to tip towards a single platform, especially in markets with dominant operators that hold significant market share.

6. Findings and Discussion

In this explorative study we have attempted to clarify advantages and disadvantages of IT-based e-finance innovations. They will expedite much easier expenses and more stupendous rivalry in financial and banking industries on the worldwide market through both new sections from the global financial sector and greater competition among incumbent financial service providers. As it was expressed by Claessens et al. (2002) these advancements will compel banks to lower charges and requisitions, as providing e-finance is much cheaper than providing traditional financial services. Therefore, incumbent financials will probably experience a sharp decrease in income. Consequently, Internet and identified advances are more than just new conveyance channels: they are a totally diverse method for providing financial services. We can agree with (Claessens et al., 2002) that these developments will force banks to lower fees and commissions, as providing e-finance is much cheaper than providing traditional financial services. As a result, incumbent financial institutions will likely experience a sharp decline in revenue. Thus, Internet and related technologies are more than just new delivery channels: they are a completely different way of providing financial services.

In summary, we can conclude the following. E-finance is a term used to collectively describe many different delivery channels available to banks and other key players in order to attract new customers and retain the existing ones. The level of the development activity and the level of innovation in channels are rapidly increasing all over the world. Most of this activity is focused on alternative distribution channels, but some branch innovations are also taking place (Innovation in Retail Banking, 2009). The e-finance innovation service ontology for global markets is deduced from qualitative empirical research and offers a means of structuring the understanding of the e-finance innovation services, in particular the stakeholders, payment instruments, types, channels etc. ICT-based innovations, the backbone of financial innovations and the capacity for analytics, have reformed the way in which companies conduct their business. There is an extensive variety of e-financial ICT-based innovations in the market (Table 2).

Summarising, we can distinguish such main types of ICT-based financial innovations.

Product innovations

Integration. Banks are developing a single contract to empower clients to open diverse accounts with the bank in an impressively simpler manner and without the need to experience the same procedure every time. (Innovation in Retail Banking, 2009).

Payments. Banks are developing different remittance products, which enable users to send money by SMS and other electronic channels.

Personalization. A user can select a photo to put into their credit card.

New card concepts. Several world banks developed new concepts based on interactivity and simplicity. A new customer can design its day-to-day banking cart, by means of simulation on the Internet or with his bank adviser in a branch, benefiting from permanent discounts on the standard rate of each product, which increase according to the number of products and paying services subscribed (Innovation in Retail Banking, 2009).

Service innovations

The technological e-financial service innovations. Nowadays customers can perform a variety of transactions at a lower cost and without time and location limits by simply using its fixed phone (phone banking), personal computer (PC and Internet banking) or mobile device (either phone, PDA or tablet). Cloud computing (private clouds) is a perspective e-finance IT platform.

Self-Service Kiosks and ATM. Banks are significantly expanding the range of services that can be delivered by ATMs in many markets and also experimenting with more targeted marketing to ATM users (Innovation in Retail Banking, 2009). Bill payment, cash deposits, contactless card operations and multiple operations, without having an ATM card are all examples.

Internet. E-banking functionality is constantly improving, but mainly in an incremental way. E-banking functionality is continually enhancing, yet, mainly in an incremental way.

The focus and the principle interest seem to be on how to use the Internet not just as a service channel, but as a sales channel, improving user interfaces, and exploiting Web 2.0 opportunities (Innovation in Retail Banking, 2009).

Mobile. SMS alerts service is also frequently offered by banks, but SMS banking is much less common. Mobile P2P and contactless payments are offered by only 5-20% of banks (depends on country). This proportion will continue growing within the next 3-5 years.

Call centres. The primary innovation here is the growing use of voice over internet protocol and collaboration software to empower customers to speak to an adviser interactively, either from their own PC, or from a branch terminal, or mobile device. This innovation has the possibility to significantly change the way service and advice is provided to customers. It is not simply a call centre innovation but more broadly a customer service innovation (Innovation in Retail Banking, 2009).

E-financial customer relationship service innovation. Nevertheless customers benefit from easiness in use, lower costs and nonexistence of time and location limitations.

Platform-based innovations

Since most world banks believe innovation is extremely significant for growing revenues and improving efficiency, it makes sense to look at the barriers to innovation and also at the steps banks are taking to increase their level of innovation (Innovation in Retail Banking, 2009). E-finance services implementation shares the main problem: design and implementation of security and privacy guarding systems. The lack of trust or smartphones can also affect SMS payments due to a number of swindling offers.

Today there are several examples of successful adoption and implementation of e-finance services by global MSPs (banks, telecommunication and search companies) and national MSPs. It mediates the activities of the e-finance ecosystem.

Table 2. Advantages and disadvantages of ICT-based financial innovations

Innovation	Advantages	Disadvantages
ICT-based financial innovations (general)	– Generate revenues from selling services and products (Lichtenthaler, 2007). – Improvement of quality of services and products (Rigby and Zook, 2002). – Development of new business technologies (Harianto and Pennings, 1990). – Guarantee of technological leadership by focusing solely on a firm's core competences (Koruna, 2004; Lichtenthaler, 2007).	*Risks* – ICT-based financial innovations mostly do not cause new kinds of risks and disadvantages, but bring in new dimensions to other types of risks (Ghosh, 2012). The creation of online channels for providing product/services has added another dimension to financial firm's risk profile. – Technology risk arises from the vendors from whom the technological systems are procured. Most of the banks outsource information technology services due to the lack of in-house capabilities and the need for continuous updating of the systems. Technology risk increases substantially when a bank entrusts the entire responsibility of designing and developing the technological systems to an outside agency (Ghosh, 2012). – The limitations of the internal staff to absorb new technologies at frequent intervals add to the risk (Ghosh, 2012). – Lack of sufficiently timely availability of services from the vendors when the technological system develops problems is a potential source of high risk (Ghosh, 2012).

		Security – Security Breaches. Since financial firms and clients store their data on private remote (cloud) servers which can be accessed with a user name and password, they risk losing that data due to wrong minded bank's employees, hackers or viruses that can harm data. – Security issues. For the merchant to process an order online, a consumer has to provide dedicated financial details. Experienced hackers can use this lop hole to channel this information and use it for their own needs. *Employees* – Job Elimination. ICT has replaced some bank and financial positions which humans used to occupy. For example, accounting is now being done by software, so some of accountants run out of opportunities (van de Vrande et al., 2009). *Privacy* – Websites and mobile sites collect personal data using cookies to know more about clients and suggest products based on that information. This data is collected without any notice, but with a potentially selfish intent. *Costs and Expenses* – Transaction costs (van de Vrande et al., 2009). – Implementation Expenses. Small businesses fail to afford this expense.

		Regulations – Banking and supervision regulations are missing in some countries.
Product innovations.	*Revenues* – Generate revenues from selling products (Lichtenthaler, 2007). – Improvement of quality of products (Rigby and Zook, 2002). – Development of new business technologies (Harianto and Pennings, 1990).	– Employees may lack commitment (King, 2010, 2012; van de Vrande et al., 2009). – Employees may lack knowledge and competences needed to exploit knowledge externally (King, 2010, 2012; van de Vrande et al., 2009).
Service innovations	– Generate revenues from selling services (Lichtenthaler, 2007). – Improvement of quality of services (Rigby and Zook, 2002). – Development of new financial service technologies (Harianto and Pennings, 1990). – Building dynamic capabilities for open innovation (Kutvonen et al., 2011).	– Risk of leaking internal resources to competitors in case of revealing (Laursen and Salter, 2006). – Risk of enveloping of the business platform (Coles and Edelman, 2012). – Risk of excessive use from impeding transactions (Coles and Edelman, 2012). – Risks of participation (Coles and Edelman, 2012).
Platform innovations	– Driving co-created value through Global networks (Prahalad and Krishnan, 2008). – Building dynamic capabilities for open innovation (Kutvonen et al., 2011). – Innovation risk diversification (Hoffman and Schlosser, 2001; Mention and Asikainen, 2012).	- Risk of leaking internal resources to competitors in case of revealing (Laursen and Salter, 2006). - Risk of enveloping of the business platform (Coles and Edelman, 2012). - Risk of excessive use from impeding transactions (Coles and Edelman, 2012). - Risks of participation (Coles and Edelman, 2012).

	– Improvement of innovation process (van de Vrande et al., 2009). – Shortening time-to-market (Rigby and Zook, 2002). – Accelerating internal innovation (Chesbrough et al., 2006). – Access to partners' networks (Mention and Asikainen, 2012). – Guarantee of technological leadership by focusing solely on a firm's core competences (Koruna, 2004; Lichtenthaler, 2007). *Regulation and Government Policy* – Broad protection for harmful user submissions (Coles and Edelman, 2012). – Antitrust scrutiny (Coles and Edelman, 2012).	
Integration innovations	*Performance* – Improvement of performance and flexibility of backstage operations. *Employees* – Learning new skills (Baum et al., 2000). *Competitive position* – Clarify core business of a firm (Rigby and Zook, 2002). – Guarantee of technological leadership by focusing solely on a firm's core competences (Koruna, 2004; Lichtenthaler, 2007).	*Employees* – Integrating ICT requires increasing levels of managerial and employee skills to deliver and use effectively (Ward and Daniel, 2012). – Adoption of the financial integration IT (ERP) applications impacts more people inside the organization and needs relationships with external trading partners and customers. Achieving benefits relies on the active cooperation of a wide range of enterprise ecosystem stakeholders (Ward and Daniel, 2012).

The most significant motivators for banks to implement MSPs are the attainment of competitive advantage, the tracking of technological developments and the lower transaction costs.

M-banking MSPs have the possibility to bring basic banking and electronic-transactions services to unbanked consumers in emerging and developing markets (Karippacheril et al., 2013). Be that as it may in empowering two-sided markets, m-banking solutions also provide telecommunications industry regulators with particular concerns (Anderson, 2010). Regulators need to address if the elements are in place for m-banking networks to tip towards a single platform, especially in markets with dominant operators that hold significant market share.

In view of the multi-homing expenses inherent in most existing m-banking MSPs, these platforms present both economic and psychological switching costs for consumers. In turn, these switching costs can have the effect of reinforcing existing network effects in markets where the incumbent already holds significant market share for voice traffic. There are various choices accessible to telecommunication regulators in responding to the emergence of m-banking MSPs and authorities should take a measured approach towards achieving optimal social and industry results.

Integrating Financial Front/Back-Office Systems

The difficulty in consolidating and synchronizing financial data is evident. For this reason, financial organizations need to employ integration solutions for back and front offices. Ensure corporate and governmental rules and regulations are represented to support the security and management of corporate information. The enterprise universal Internet/Intranet/Extranet network is a key enabler of business readiness. Employees and customers expect instant access, from any location on any device. Internet/Intranet/Extranet enterprise network services provide both scale and flexibility critical to responding to real-time demands and create a foundation for sustainable growth.

7. Conclusions

The major contributions and findings of this chapter include the description of all areas of e-finance, application of technology to e-finance, growth of the e-finance in the financial services. The chapter provides areas of ICT-based e-finance innovations that face many different challenges and calls for further research in a number of areas related to e-finance technology and financial MSPs.

Today every business is, basically, an e-business (Prahalad and Krishnan, 2008). We can claim that today, mostly every provision of financial services and markets is done through electronic channels. Hence, senior managers need to pay attention to the quality and capabilities of the ICT-based financial innovations. While the hardware and connectivity part of ICT architecture can be entrusted to the IT departments and vendors, CEOs and line managers cannot delegate strategic decisions on the business applications, analytic capabilities, data warehousing, and multi-sided platforms (Prahalad and Krishnan, 2008). In order to compete effectively, financial firms need to develop forward-looking ICT platforms.

References

A Discussion of the Role of Standards in the Financial Services Industry, 2011. *The Innovator*, 4(2).

Abernathy, W., and Clark, K.B., 1985. Mapping the Winds of Creative Destruction. *Research Policy* 14(1), pp.3-22.

Armstrong, M. (2006) 'Competition in Two-Sided Markets', RAND Journal of Economics, 37(3), pp.668–691.

Anderloni, L., Llewellyn, D., and Schmidt, R., 2009. *Financial Innovation in Retail and Corporate Banking.* Edward Elgar Publishing Limited, UK, 352 pages.

Anderson, J., 2010. *M-banking in developing markets: competitive and regulatory implications.* Info 12(1), pp.18-25.

Apte, M., and Vepsäläinen, A., 1993. High tech or high touch? Efficient channel strategies for delivering financial services. *The Journal of Strategic Information Systems* 2(1), pp.39-54.

Baldwin, C., and Woodard, C., 2008. *"The Architecture of Platforms: A Unified View".* Harvard Business School Finance Working Paper No. 09-034.

Bank for International Settlements, 2000. Basel Committee on Banking Supervision. Electronic Banking Group Initiatives and White Papers, Basel. *http://www.bis.org/publ/bcbs76.htm* (accessed August, 3rd 2013).

Bátiz-Lazo, B., 2004. Benchmarking financial services and online innovations benchmarking. *An International Journal* 11(5), pp.431-446.

Baum, E., 2000. Engineering accreditation in the United States of America – Criteria 2000. Proc. 2nd Global Congress on Engng. Educ., Wismar, Germany, 17-20.

Bordo, M.D., and Haubrich, J.G., 2012. *Deep Recessions, Fast Recoveries, and Financial Crises: Evidence from the American Record*, NBER Working Papers 18194. National Bureau of Economic Research, Inc.

Brousseau, E., and Curien, N., 2007. Internet and Digital Economics. Cambridge University Press.

Bullinger, A.C., 2009. *Innovation and Ontologies. Structuring the Early Stages of Innovation.* Gabler Edition Wissenschaft.

Caillaud, B., Jullien B., 2003. 'Chicken and Egg: Competition among Intermediation Service Providers', RAND Journal of Economics, vol. 34, pp.521–552.

Chesbrough, H., 2006. 'Open Innovation: A New Paradigm for Understanding Industrial Innovation', In: Chesbrough, H., Vanhaverbeke, W., West, J., eds., Open Innovation: Researching a New Paradigm. Oxford: Oxford University Press, pp.1-12.

Chesbrough, H., Crowther, A., 2006. Beyond high tech: early adopters of open innovation in other industries. R and D Management, 36(3), pp.229-236.

Chesbrough, H., 2011. Open Services Innovation: Rethinking Your Business to Grow and Compete in a New Era, Jossey-Bass, 256 p.Carbó, S., Humphrey, D., and López, R., 2007. Opening the black box: finding the source of cost inefficiency, *Journal of Productivity Analysis*, 27 (3), pp. 209–220.

Chorafas, D. (2011). *Cloud Computing Strategies*, Auerbach Publications, 354 pages.

Christensen, C., 1997. *The Innovator's Dilemma: When New Technologies Cause Great Firms to Fail*, Boston: Harvard Business School Press.

Church, Jeffrey & Gandal, Neil, 2004. "Platform Competition in Telecommunications," CEPR Discussion Papers 4659, C.E.P.R. Discussion Papers.

Claessens, S., Glaessner, T., and Klingebiel, D., 2002. Electronic Finance: Reshaping the Financial Landscape around the World. *Journal of Financial Services Research* 22(1/2), pp.29-61.

Coles, P.A., and Edelman, B., 2012. The Online Economy: Strategy and Entrepreneurship, Course Architecture Note, *Harvard Business School Course Overview Note 911-069*, May 2012.

Cronin M. (Ed.) 1997. *Banking and Finance on the Internet*, Wiley, 352 pages.

DeYoung, R., 2001. The financial performance of pure play internet banks, Federal Reserve Bank of Chicago Economic Perspectives, 25 (1), pp. 60–75.

Donze, J., and I. Dubec (2006), The role of interchange fees in ATM networks, International Journal of Industrial Organization, 24 (1), pp. 29–43.

eClassOWL., 2013. The Web Ontology for Products and Services. *http://www.heppnetz.de/projects/eclassowl/#gentax-classes* (accessed August, 3rd 2013).

Eisenmann,T., Parker, G., and Van Alstyne, M., 2006. Strategies for Two-Sided Markets. *Harvard Business Review* 84(10), pp.92-101.

Evans, D., 2003. 'The Antitrust Economics of Multi–Sided Platform Markets', Yale Journal on Regulation, vol. 20, pp. 325–381.

Evans, D., Hagiu, A., and Schmalensee, R., 2006. Invisible Engines. How Software Platforms Drive Innovation and Transform Industries, The MIT Press Cambridge, Massachusetts, London, 408 pages.

Evans, D., Schmalensee, R., 2007. Industrial Organization of Markets with Two-Sided Platforms, *Competition Policy International*, Vol. 3, No. 1.

Evans, D., Hagiu, A., and Schmalensee, R., 2008. *Invisible Engines: How Software Platforms Drive Innovation and Transform Industries*, MIT Press.

Fagerberg, J., Mowery, D., and Nelson, R., (eds) 2005. *The Oxford Handbook of Innovation*, Oxford University Press, 674 pages.

Financial Industry Business Ontology (FIBO), 2013. *http://www.omg.org/hot-topics/fibo.htm* (accessed August, 3rd 2013).

Franklin, A., McAndrews J., and Strahan, P., 2001. *E-Finance: An Introduction*, Financial Institutions Centre, The Working Paper Series, Wharton School, University of Pennsylvania, 43 pages.

Frame, W., and Lawrence, J., 2002. *Empirical Studies of Financial Innovation: Lots of Talk, Little Action*, White Working Paper 2002-12, Federal Reserve Bank of Atlanta, 38 pages.

Friedman, B., 2000. Decoupling at the Margin: The Threat to Monetary Policy from the Electronic Revolution in Banking. *International Finance* 3(2): 261-72.

Gawer, A., 2009. *Platforms, Markets and Innovation*, Cheltenham, UK and Northampton, MA, US: Edward Elgar.

Gawer, A., and Henderson, R., 2007. Platform owner entry and innovation in complementary markets: Evidence from Intel. *Journal of Economics and Management Strategy* 16(1), pp.1-34.

Gawer, A., and Cusumano, M., 2012. *Industry Platforms and Ecosystem Innovation.* DRUID 2012, CBS, Copenhagen, Denmark.

Ghosh, A., 2012. *Managing Risks in Commercial and Retail Banking.* John Wiley & Sons, 480 pages.

Gup, B., 2011. *Banking and Financial Institutions: A Guide for Directors, Investors, and Borrowers*, John Wiley & Sons, 357 pages
Greenbaum, S.I., and Thakor, A.V., 1995. Contemporary Financial Intermediation, Dryden Press, Harcourt Brace College Publishers, Fort Worth, TX.
Johnson, S. and Kwak, J., 2009. Finance: Before the Next Meltdown, DemocracyJournal.org, Fall, pp.19-24.
Greenstein, S., 2009. Open platform development and the commercial Internet, Platforms, markets and innovation, pp.219-248
Haan, J., Oosterloo, S., and Schoenmaker, D., 2009. European Financial Markets and Institutions, Cambridge University Press, 436 pages
Hagiu, A., and Wright, A., 2011. Multi-Sided Platforms, *HBS Working Paper 12-024*.
Hagiu, A., Wright, A. (2013). Marketplace or reseller?, HBS Working Paper13-092.
Hafkesbrink, J., Hoppe, H.U., and Schlichter, J., 2010. *Competence Management for Open Innovation-Tools and IT support to unlock the innovation potential beyond company boundaries*, EUL VERLAG, 336 pages
Hafkesbrink, J., and Schroll, M., 2011. Innovation 3.0: embedding into community knowledge-collaborative organizational learning beyond open innovation. *Journal of Innovation Economics* 7(1), pp.55-92.
Harianto, F. and Pennings, J., 1990. Technological innovation through interfirm linkages. In *M. Law-less and L. R. Gomez-Mejia (eds.), Strategic Management in High Technology Firms*. JAI Press, Greenwich, CT, pp. 15-41.
Hepp M., Leukel J., and Schmitz V., 2006. 'A quantitative analysis of product categorization standards: content, coverage, and maintenance of eCl@ss, UNSPSC,eOTD, and the RosettaNet Technical Dictionary', Knowledge and Information Systems (KAIS), Springer.
Hepp, M., 2006. 'Products and Services Ontologies: A Methodology for Deriving OWL Ontologies from Industrial Categorization Standards', Int'l Journal on Semantic Web & Information Systems (IJSWIS), Vol. 2, No. 1, pp. 72-99.
—. 2007. Possible Ontologies: How Reality Constrains the Development of Relevant Ontologies. *IEEE Internet Computing* 11(1), pp.90-96.
—. 2008. GoodRelations: An Ontology for Describing Products and Services Offers on the Web. In *Proceedings of the 16th International Conference on Knowledge Engineering and Knowledge Management (EKAW2008)*, Acitrezza, Italy, September 29 - October 3, 2008.

Springer Knowledge Engineering: Practice and Patterns, Lecture Notes in Computer Science 5268, pp.332-347.

Hepp, M., and de Bruijn, J., 2007. GenTax: A Generic Methodology for Deriving OWL and RDF-S Ontologies from Hierarchical Classifications, Thesauri, and Inconsistent Taxonomies. In *Proceedings of the 4th European Semantic Web Conference (ESWC 2007)*, June 3-7, 2007, Innsbruck, Austria. Springer Knowledge Engineering: Practice and Patterns, Lecture Notes in Computer Science 4519, pp.129-144.

Hepp, M., Leukel, J., and Schmitz, V., 2007. *A Quantitative Analysis of Product Categorization Standards: eCl@ss, UNSPSC, eOTD, and RNTD, in: Knowledge and Information Systems (KAIS)*. Springer 13(1), pp.77-114.

Herfurth, M., and Weib, P., 2010. Conceptual Design of Service Procurement for Collaborative Service Networks, *IFIP Advances in Information and Communication Technology*. Collaborative Networks for a Sustainable World Volume 336, pp.435-442.

Hoffmann, W.H. and Schlosser, R., 2001. Success Factors of Strategic Alliances in Small and Medium-sized Enterprises-An Empirical Survey. *Long Range Planning* 34(3), pp.357-381.

Huang, P., Ceccagnoli, M., Forman, C., and Wu, D., 2009. Participation in a platform ecosystem: Appropriability, competition, and access to the installed base. NET Institute working paper no. 09–14.

Humphrey, D., Willesson, M., Bergendahl, G. and Lindblom T. (2006). Benefits from a changing payment technology in European banking, *Journal of Banking and Finance*, 30 (6), pp.1631–1652.

IEEE Suggested Upper Merged Ontology (SUMO), 2013. *http://www.ontologyportal.org/* (accessed August, 3rd 2013).

Innovation in Retail Banking, 2009, EFMA Report.

Initiatives for Asia/Pacific Banks in 2013 (2013). *Thinking Beyond Risk Management Business Strategy*, February, Doc # FIN239561, 26 pages

IDC., 2012. *Technology Selection: Worldwide Mobile Payments 2012-2017 Forecast*, IDC Financial Insights, Doc #FIN237814.

Järvi K., Schallmo D., and Kutvonen, A., 2011. The Business of Open Innovation Intermediaries. In *Proceedings of the XXII ISPIM Conference: "Sustainability in Innovation: Innovation Management Challenges"*, 12-15 June, Hamburg, Germany.

Joshi V., 2010. E-Finance. Log in To the Future!, Sage, 2nd edition, 206 pages.

Jordan, J. 2012. *Information, Technology, and Innovation: Resources for Growth in a Connected World*, John Wiley & Sons, 396 pages

Karakostas, B., Kardaras, D., and Papathanassiou E., 2005. The state of CRM adoption by the financial services in the UK: an empirical investigation. *Information & Management* 42(6), pp.853-863.

Karippacheril, T., Nikayin, F., Reuver, M., and Bouwmanb, H., 2013. Serving the poor: Multisided mobile service platforms, openness, competition, collaboration and the struggle for leadership. *Telecommunications Policy* 37(1), pp.24-34

King, B., 2010. *Bank 2.0: How Customer Behaviour and Technology will Change the Future of Financial Services*. Cyan Communications Ltd., 399 pages

—. 2012. *Branch Today, Gone Tomorrow,* Marshall Cavendish, 53 pages

Koruna, S., 2004. External technology commercialization-policy guidelines. *International Journal of Technology Management* 27(2/3), pp. 241–254.

Kuhn, T. 1970. *The Structure of Scientific Revolutions*, 2nd ed., Chicago: University of Chicago Press.

Küster, U., König-Ries, B., Petrie, C. And Klusch, V., 2008. On the Evaluation of Semantic Web Service Frameworks. *International Journal on Semantic Web and Information Systems (IJSWIS)* 4(4), pp.31-55.

Kutvonen, A., 2011. Strategic application of outbound open innovation. *European Journal of Innovation Management* 14(4): 460-474.

Lapkin, A. 2012. *Hype Cycle for Big Data*, Gartner, 101 pages

Laursen, K., and Salter, A., 2006. Open for Innovation: The role of openness in explaining innovative performance among UK manufacturing firms. *Strategic Management Journal* 27(2), pp.131-150.

Lee, J., Cho, J., and Abdul-Rahman F., 2008. E-banking, In *Handbook of Consumer Finance Research*, Part II, pp.105-123.

Lerner, J., and Tufano, P., 2011a. *The Consequences of Financial Innovation: A Counterfactual Research Agenda*, NBER Working Paper No. 16780, 93 pages.

Lerner, J., and Tufano P., 2011b. The consequences of financial innovation: A counterfactual research agenda. *Annual Review of Financial Economics* 3, pp.41-85.

Liebena, J., and Khiaonarong, T., 2009. *Banking on Innovation. Modernisation of Payment Systems*, Physica-Verlag Heidelberg, 2009.

Liezenberg, C., and Lycklama, D., (eds). 2012. *Online payments 2012. Moving beyond the web*, Innopay BV, 96 pages.

Lichtenthaler, U., 2007. The Drivers of Technology Licensing: an industry comparison. *California Management Review*, 49(4), pp.67-89.

Meier A., and Stormer H., 2009. *eBusiness & eCommerce. Managing the Digital Value Chain*, Springer-Verlag Berlin Heidelberg.

Mellouli S., Bouslama F., and Akande A., 2010. An ontology for representing financial headline news. *Journal of Web Semantics* 8(2-3), pp.203-208.

Mention, A.-L., and Asikainen, A.-L., 2012. *Does inter-firm co-operation foster innovation in services*, IAMOT, Hsinchu, Taiwan, March 2012.

Mention, A.-L., and Torkkeli, M., 2012. Drivers, processes and effects of financial innovation: a research agenda. *International Journal of Entrepreneurship and Innovation Management* 16(½), pp.5-24.

Mention, A.-L., 2011. Innovation for Financial Services. *http://www.innovationmanagement.se/2011/09/13/innovation-for-financial-services/* (accessed August, 3rd 2013).

Minoli, D. 2008. *Enterprise Architecture A to Z: Frameworks, Business Process Modeling, SOA, and Infrastructure Technology*, Auerbach Publications, 498 pages.

Moshirian, F., 2004. Financial services: Global perspectives. *Journal of Banking & Finance* 28(2), pp.269-276.

Nsouli, S., and Schaechter, A., 2002. Challenges of the "E-Banking Revolution, Finance & Development. *IMF Quarterly* 39(3) *https://www.imf.org/external/pubs/ft/fandd/2002/09/nsouli.htm* (accessed August, 3rd 2013).

Osterwalder, A., and Pigneur, Y., 2002. An e-business model ontology for modelling e-business, Proceedings of the 15th Bled Electronic Commerce Conference, pp.1-12.

Semantic Markup for Web Services (OWL-S)., 2013. *http://www.ai.sri.com/daml/services/owl-s/1.2/overview/* (accessed August, 3rd 2013).

Park, R., and Campbell A., 2001. E-commerce in financial services: An e-agenda for the corporate parent. *European Management Journal* 19(4): 417-423.

Parker, G., and Van Alstyne, M. (2005). Two-Sided Network Effects: A Theory of Information Product Design, *Management Science*, Vol. 51, No. 10.

Peitz, M., and Waldfogel, J., (eds) 2012. *The Oxford Handbook of the Digital Economy (Oxford Handbooks)*, Oxford University Press, USA, 624 pages.

Poli, R., Healy, M., and Kameas, A., 2010. *Theory and Applications of Ontology: Computer Applications Set: Theory and Applications of Ontology*, Springer, XVIII, 576 pages.

Protege Ontology Library., 2013.

http://protegewiki.stanford.edu/wiki/Protege_Ontology_Library (accessed August, 3rd 2013).

Prahalad, C.K., and Krishnan, M.S., 2008. The New Age of Innovation: Driving Cocreated Value Through Global Networks. McGraw-Hill.

Qin, H., and Taffet, M.D., 2004. Vocabulary use in XML standards in the financial market domain. *Knowledge and Information Systems* 6(3), pp.269-289.

Rezaee, Z., 2011. *Financial Services Firms: Governance, Regulations, Valuations, Mergers, and Acquisitions*, John Wiley & Sons, 582 pages

Riedl, C., May, N., Finzen, J., Stathel, S., Kaufman, V., and Krcmar, H., 2009. An Idea Ontology for Innovation Management. *International Journal on Semantic Web and Information Systems* 5(4), pp.1-18.

Risk management principles for electronic banking., 2003. Basel Committee on Banking Supervision, *http://www.bis.org/publ/bcbs98.pdf* (accessed August, 3rd 2013)

Riivari, J., 2005. Mobile banking: a powerful new marketing and CRM tool for financial services companies all over Europe? *Journal of Financial Services Marketing* 10(1): 11–20.

Rogers E. 1962. Diffusion of Innovations, New York: Free Press.

Rochet, J, and Tirole, J., 2003. Platform Competition in Two-Sided Markets. *Journal of the European Economic Association* 1(4), pp.990-1029

Rigby, D., and Zook, C., 2002. Open-market innovation. *Harvard Business Review* 80(10), pp.80-89.

Sulaiman, A., Jaafar, N., and Mohezar, S., 2007. An overview of mobile banking adoption among the urban community. *International Journal of Mobile Communications* 5(2), pp.157-168.

Schaechter, A., 2002. *Issues in Electronic Banking: An Overview, IMF Policy Discussion Paper*, No. 02/6, International Monetary Fund.

Service Innovation Yearbook 2010-2011, 2010. European Union, 148 pages. *https://ec.europa.eu/digital-agenda/en/news/service-innovation-yearbook-2010-2011* (accessed August, 3rd 2013)

Shapiro, C., and Varian, H. (1999). *Information Rules: A Strategic Guide to the Network Economy*, Harvard Business School Publishing, 351 pages.

Shahrokhi M., 2008. E-finance: status, innovations, resources and future challenges. *Managerial Finance* 34(6), pp.365-398.

Sheth, A., 2011. *Semantic Services, Interoperability and Web Applications: Emerging Concepts, Knoesis Center*, Wright State University, USA, 420 pages.

Skarzynski, P., and Gibson, R. (2008). *Innovation to the Core: A Blueprint For Transforming the Way Your Company Innovates*, Harvard Business Press, 320 pages.

Schmookler, J.A. (1967). *Invention and Economic Growth*, Harvard University Press, Cambridge, MA.

Scholten, S., and Scholten, U., 2012. Platform-based Innovation Management: Directing External Innovational Efforts in Platform Ecosystems. *Journal of the Knowledge Economy* 3(2), pp.164-184.

Scholten, S., and Scholten, U., 2010. Platform-based Innovation Management: Directing External Innovational Efforts in Complex Self-organizing Platform Ecosystems, In *Proceedings of PICMET Int. Conference*. Portland: IEEE.

Stone, M., and Foss, B., 2002. *CRM in Financial Services: A Practical Guide to Making Customer Relationship Management Work*, Kogan Page, 2002, 720 pages.

Tiwari, R., Buse, S., and Herstatt, C., 2006. Mobile Banking as Business Strategy: Impact of Mobile Technologies on Customer Behaviour and its Implications for Banks. In *Technology Management for the Global Future,* Proceedings of PICMET, 06, July 8-13, 2006, Istanbul, pp. 1935-1946.

Tufano, P. (2003). Financial innovation, In: Constantinides, G., Harris, M. and Stulz, R. (Eds.), *Handbook of the Economics of Finance*. Elsevier, Amsterdam, Netherland, pp. 307–336.

Turban, E., and King, D., 2011. *Electronic Commerce 2012: Managerial and Social Networks Perspectives*, Prentice Hall, 792 pages.

Vanderlinden, E., 2011. Finance ontology. *http://fadyart.com/ontologies/documentation/finance/index.html* (accessed August 3, 2013).

van de Vrande, V., de Jong, P.J.J., Vanhaverbeke, W., and de Rochemont, M., 2009. Open innovation in SMEs: Trends, motives and management challenges. *Technovation* 29(6–7), pp.423-437.

Versace, M. (2012). The Case for Big Data in the Financial Services Industry, Whitepaper, *IDC Financial Insights*, 13 pages.

Ward, J., and Daniel, E., 2012. *Benefits Management: How to Increase the Business Value of Your IT Projects*, Second Edition. John Wiley & Sons.

W3C., 2004. OWL Web Ontology Language, Overview, World Wide Web Consortium (W3C) Recommendation February, 10th 2004. *http://www.w3.org/TR/owl-features/* (accessed August, 3rd 2013).

White, L.J. 2000. Technological change, financial innovation, and financial regulation in the US: the challenge for public policy. In

Performance of Financial Institutions, D. Harker and S. Zenios (eds), Cambridge University Press, Cambridge, pp. 80–91.
Worthy, J., Graham, N., and Finney R., 2003. E-commerce for financial services: working with the new UK rules. *Computer Law & Security Review* 19(2): 121-123.
Wright, J. 2004. One-sided Logic in Two-sided Markets, *Review of Network Economics*, Vol.3, Issue 1.
Yablonsky, S. 2009. 'Semantic Web Framework for Development of Very Large Ontologies', POLIBITS, Issue 39, pp.19–26.
Yablonsky, S., 2010. Cloud Service Innovation Ontology Development, In: Proceedings of The XXI ISPIM Conference 2010, Bilbao, Spain. *http://www.ispim.org/members/proceedings/ISPIM2010/commonfiles/files/25027754_Paper.pdf* (accessed August, 3rd 2013).
—. 2014. E-finance innovation services in Russia, *Int. J. Entrepreneurship and Innovation Management* (in print).
Yaron, J. 1992. *Successful rural finance institutions*, World Bank Discussion Paper 150, Washington, DC: World Bank.
Zaino, J., 2012. Financial Services Industry Sees Operational Value in FIBO. *http://semanticweb.com/financial-services-industry-sees-operational-value-in-fibo_b28395* (accessed August, 3rd 2013).
Zhang, Z., Zhang C., and Ong S.S., 2000. *Building an Ontology for Financial Investment*, Lecture Notes in Computer Science, Springer-Verlag Berlin, pp.379-395.

CHAPTER NINE

A SIMPLE BUT EFFECTIVE INNOVATION: MOBILE FINANCIAL SERVICES IN DEVELOPING COUNTRIES

JOSÉ LUIS GÓMEZ-BARROSO AND RAQUEL MARBÁN-FLORES

1. Introduction

Whilst there is some overlap between the various definitions of innovation, overall the number and diversity of definitions lead to a situation in which there is no clear and authoritative definition of innovation (Baregheh et al. 2009). With that said, it should not be forgotten that innovation is not always about the latest high technology machines and does not necessarily imply a radical departure from the past. It is not about new fashionable products, either. Simple ideas can lead to the improvement or transformation of products, services and industrial or commercial processes. Sometimes the smallest of changes can make a vast difference.

Most of the definitions given to innovation highlight that it is not a discrete act but a process. For Roberts (2007) innovation is a combination of invention and exploitation: the invention process covers all efforts aimed at creating new ideas and getting them to work; the exploitation process includes all stages of commercial development, application and transfer, including the focusing of ideas or inventions on specific objectives. From another perspective, Kalmanek (2012) posits that successful innovation requires three essential elements: a need, know-how or knowledge and favourable context.

All this is important when looking at innovation in financial services and particularly when looking at the situation of mobile banking. Innovation in the financial system has arrived thanks to the increased use, from the seventies on, of Information and Communications Technologies (ICT). It seems logical considering it is an information-intensive industry. Most of these innovations have occurred in the back-office (Boot and Marinc 2008; Berger 2003). Even when this has led to the launch of new products, such innovations have often been not visible to the client since they have been integrated into the usual distribution channels. But the use of ICT has ended up generating new ways of providing these services. Specifically, self-service technologies have enabled banks to pursue electronically mediated multi-channel strategies (Black et al. 2002). The first self-service technologies in the finance sector emerged in the 1970s when banks installed the first automated teller machines (ATMs); this was followed by telephone banking services in the 1980s and with the emergence of the Internet, by web-based banking applications in the 1990s (Hoehle et al. 2012). Internet banking has undoubtedly become the reference.

Mobile phones should also have been a reference. Mobile phones have a penetration, which has been for a long time much greater than that of the Internet and their use has been (is) considered, at least by a broad part of the population, as more direct and “friendly” (Westlund et al. 2010). But this has not been the case. In the early 2000s, mobile payment services became a hot topic and remained so even after the burst of the Internet hype. Hundreds of mobile payment services were introduced all over the world; “strikingly many of these efforts failed” (Dahlberg et al. 2008). Actually, in developed countries, next to other less noticeable exceptions, only the Japanese operator NTT Docomo’s payment system and Korean similar systems reached a significant size. The scenario has recently changed. Mobile payments still need to overcome some obstacles (Leavitt 2012) but a sophisticated type of mobile banking (Internet banking on smartphones) has already taken off. Yet, most noticeable, is the massive and thriving diffusion of a basic version of mobile banking among a growing number of emerging countries.

Would it not be more understandable that mobile money (even mobile banking) was first used in developed countries? Is it possible for an innovation in something as “developed” as the financial system to emerge within developing countries? Perhaps it is not surprising, considering that, as stated before, innovating requires addressing a series of conditions to be successful. Within this perspective, this chapter analyses the evolution of mobile financial services in developing countries. In particular, a case study is presented: M-Pesa in Kenya. The reason why M-Pesa has been selected is simple: it is the most successful mobile money initiative all over the world and, probably because of it, the most studied as well.

Underlying lessons can be extracted by identifying the significant factors behind their success.

The analysis is carried out using as a framework the previously mentioned elements identified by Kalmanek (2012): need, knowledge and favourable context. The story of planning, launching and development of M-Pesa is rewritten to be fitted into these factors. This makes up the central part of the chapter. An overview of the evolution and situation of mobile financial services precedes. A final section draws some conclusions.

2. The evolution of mobile financial services

Mobile financial applications include mobile banking and a variety of different micropayment solutions (Mallat et al. 2004). Through mobile payments systems, users pay for goods and services, either at the point of purchase or remotely. Mobile banking involves the access to, and the provision of, other financial services. Some authors (Gencer 2011) use the expression mobile money to encompass all these areas.

A number of solutions have been implemented in order to offer mobile financial services. They are based on different technology standards, namely: interactive voice response, short message service, wireless application protocol, one-time password generator and Near Field Communication. Leaving aside the technology underlying and restricting the topic to mobile banking, two are the basic options from users' point of view: advanced Internet banking running on high-end devices (smartphones-type) and simplest solutions intended to be used on devices lacking the features of last generation phones (predominantly voice and messaging phones for which there is not a single label: feature, *dumb* or basic phones are the most usual ones). The latter is what can be named as simple mobile banking or genuinely-mobile banking.

The first alternative is gaining momentum within developed countries. The diffusion of mobile broadband and the market success of smartphones have radically changed the scene of the services offered through mobile devices. Full (or tailored to the mobile platform) Internet banking services can be reached through smartphones. However, in rich countries simple payment/banking services are still in their early stages of development.

On the contrary, the situation of genuinely-mobile banking is quite different in developing countries. The first mobile money projects achieving some success were launched in the Philippines, Kenya and South Africa with the period 2003-2005. In the wake of early successes, the initiative spread among many other developing countries, slowly at first, but with a steadily growing rate within the last few years[1]. When initially launched, the projects focused basically on fund transfers (Singh 2009). The feature set has progressively grown to include (in some cases) paying bills, receiving salaries and micro-finance services such as receiving and repaying loans.

There is no single model for mobile banking successful experiences. Faced with differences in the existing regulation (or lack of) and in the range of activities allowed by the adopted business model, each experience is different (Mas and Kumar 2008). Conceptually, it is useful to think of mobile banking as consisting of two basic models (Lyman et al. 2006):

- In the bank-led model, customers have a direct contractual relationship with a licensed financial institution, even though the customer may deal exclusively with the staff of one or more retail agents hired to conduct transactions on the bank's behalf. Wizzit, a branch of the South African Bank of Athens, is one of the best-known examples of this model.
- In the nonbank-led (mobile network operators or third parties) model, customers exchange cash at a retail agent in return for an electronic record of value. This virtual account is stored on the server of the operator. Once customers have a relationship with the nonbank provider, they can order a payment of funds to anyone else participating in the system and can receive payments from them. Customers need to visit a retail agent only to add value or to convert stored value back into cash. M-Pesa in Kenya (from Vodafone-Safaricom), or GCash in the Philippines (from Globe Telecom) can be included into this category.

This distinction has not proven to be important from a commercial perspective, as successful experiences can be found under both models. Moreover, the bank-led and nonbank-led models can also function in combination, equally, in a successful manner. Banks can benefit from teaming up with third parties as the prominent example of SMART Money (which was launched in 2001, in the Philippines, as a partnership between Smart Communications, one of the country's telecommunications companies and Banco de Oroa, a commercial bank) proves. It is from a

[1] The Mobile Money deployment tracker monitors the number of live and planned mobile money services for the unbanked. At the beginning of 2013, there were 156 already ongoing initiatives and 110 planned (http://www.mobileworldlive.com/mobile-money-tracker; accessed 16 December 2012).

regulatory point of view where the real importance of this distinction lies. Under the bank-led model there stands a fully licensed and supervised financial institution. In some cases, however, the bank involved may have outsourced so much responsibility (and risk) to non-bank actors that the differences have simply faded away (Lyman et al. 2008).

M-Pesa is the landmark for mobile money/banking services in developing countries. As to the mid of 2010, after just five years of existence, the M-Pesa mobile cash transfer system was used in Kenya by more than 9 million people (23% of the total population; 40% of the adult population; 60% of the clients of the mobile telephony operator that launched the service) and the total amount of funds transferred through the system was equivalent to 10% of Kenya's GDP (The Economist 2010). A year later (mid-2011, last statistics available on its webpage) the number of clients had already reached 14 million. Moreover, Kenya has probably become the most active mobile banking market: yucash (from Essar Telecom), Zap (from Bharti Airtel) and Iko (from Telkom Kenya) are now competing with M-Pesa.

3. Elements making this innovation possible

3.1 The need

The situation of access to financial services is far from universal in developing countries. Remote locations are difficult to reach with financial services because they have low population density and the sizes of transactions are relatively small. Beyond the physical distance, it is often just a problem of income. Because the poor have little or no collateral, have no credit history, have little or no experience handling money or managing a business, there is considerable risk in serving these people (Kauffman and Riggins 2010).

In Kenya, as in many other African countries, in the absence of formal financial systems, many people were in the habit of using post offices, if available in their local area, or informal systems such as entrusting money to bus drivers or friends or acquaintances who are travelling. It is therefore with no surprise that just two years since its launch M-Pesa was already seen as the safest, cheapest, quickest and easiest to use method to transfer money (FinAccess 2009).

Moreover, Batchelor (2012) describes a spontaneous use (with no outside or external civil society influence) of airtime as a virtual currency before the launching of mobile money initiatives. People would purchase a ticket in, say, the capital city, and text the code to their upcountry relatives. The relatives could choose to, either put the code on their phone and gain airtime, or sell the airtime on to friends or merchants. That suggested a huge pent-up demand for financial services, particularly, in relation to money transferring services, within the country.

This was later confirmed during the M-Pesa planning phase. It was during the pilot project when the initiative took its real shape. In fact, although commercially launched in March 2007, M-Pesa had been founded in 2003 as a project funded by a British development agency that attempted to offer an alternative means of payment to the borrowers from a microfinance institution (Hughes and Lonie 2007). During the pilot project, initiated in autumn 2005, clients used the system in "creative" ways (making payments of all kinds and transfers), which led the mobile operator Safaricom to alter their strategy and develop a marketing strategy around the message *send money home* (Kumar et al. 2010). In this sense, M-Pesa can be considered as a genuine case of customer-driven innovation (Van de Kar and Den Hengst 2009).

The management team was flexible enough to accept that the conceptions and roles of different actors have to be rethought in those processes (Hayes and Westrup 2012). This fact links to the second element under study: the expertise to make the project feasible and to push it ahead.

3.2 The knowledge

Mas and Morawczynski (2009) suggest the keys they believe to be behind M-Pesa's success. A significant number of factors are down to the company's management: a well designed and easy-to-use service, simple, transparent tariffs, clear messages, using the strength of the Safaricom brand and the ability to build (and manage) a large network of agents.

Importantly, it can be underlined that no technological issues are mentioned. M-Pesa, as any other mobile payment/banking service, is mostly based on the application of existing and proven technology. Conceptually, the system is easy to operate. M-Pesa allows funds to be transferred through an SMS sent from a mobile telephone fitted with an activated SIM card. The service is launched from the phone's main menu and it loads quickly because the application resides on the mobile phone rather than on the network. Clients can subscribe by showing an identity document to any of the company's agents without paying any set-up fee. They can deposit money on their card by topping-up the mobile telephone being used; this money can then be transferred to the account of another handset. The receiver can then use it for payments or transfers, or if required can request the funds from an agent. Therefore, a key piece of the system has been to make 100,000 small traders who sold pre-paid Safaricom cards into M-Pesa agents. Almost 18,000 had done this by early 2010; the importance of this figure is clear when it is compared to the number of bank branches in the country at the time: 840 (The Economist 2010). By April 2011 (last statistics available) they were almost 28,000.

The advantage of using a mature technology, like SMS as the bearer for the service, is that very few assumptions are made about the specification of the mobile handset that can be used. M-Pesa is therefore accessible on as wide a range of handsets as possible. Importantly, for an emerging market service, this included the ability to access M-Pesa on even basic entry-level black-and-white display handsets (Wooder and Baker 2012). The development of the application was constrained solely by the need to adapt the operability of the user interface. Something particularly important when considering the fact that poverty for the most part also correlates with low levels of formal education. A study with mobile banking service users from four different developing countries (Medhi et al. 2011) found that a significant number of these persons did not initially understand vertical scrollbars, could not locate the symbols in the phone, had difficulty with receipts indicating multiple transactions or were not familiar with the vocabulary of banking ("view last transaction", "get balance", "change PIN", and so forth, were all alien concepts, in the absence of detailed explanations).

The work of M-Pesa's designers was exemplary in terms of service conception, anticipating many of the possible problems while making good use of the pilot phase by taking advantage of user feedback. An account of all the mishaps from the conception of the idea to the final service launch can be found in Hughes and Lonie (2007). Their description of how they solved the (not infrequent) loss of M-Pesa-specific SIM cards (introducing SIM cards without associated phone numbers) shows the importance of responding to any eventuality, as "banal" as it may seem at first sight.

3.3 The context

In 2000, there were 11 million mobile-phone users in Africa; however 8 million of those lived in South Africa. In 2005 there were 88 million in the whole continent (34 million in South Africa), 246 million in 2008, and by the end of 2011 the number of mobile telephones had reached 434 million. In terms of penetration rates, this represents 53.1 mobile phones for each 100 people compared to 32.6 per 100 people in 2008 and just 5 per 100 people in 2003. In Seychelles, Botswana, South Africa, Gabon and Namibia, penetration rates in 2011 already exceeded 100 per cent[2] (all the figures quoted in this and next paragraph are taken from ITU 2009, 2012a and 2012b).

This impressive growth that occurred in mobile subscriptions since the beginning of the twenty-first century represented a market opportunity. In Kenya, there were 4.7 mobile cellular telephone subscriptions per 100 inhabitants in 2003 (when the idea took shape); 12.9 per cent in 2005 (when the pilot project was set up) and 30.3 per cent at the end of 2007 (when the commercial operation started). Although in the first years of the decade ownership of mobile phones was low, people had rapidly embedded telephones into their communication behaviours and the potential for expansion of the use of mobile telephones was already visible (Batchelor 2012). The responsible of the project were sensitive enough to foresee the possibilities that may be ahead.

The same responsible looked after the institutional context by being in contact with the Central Bank of Kenya from the start of the pilot. The support (or at least, the non-opposition) of the regulator was also present in other mobile banking success cases such as that of the previously mentioned Wizzit, a company created in South Africa in March 2005 as a bank without branches (thus allowing it to offer any financial service). In the opinion of Hayes and Westrup (2012), it was this regulatory, or the lack of a regulatory environment that enabled M-Pesa to rapidly establish and had the consequence of restricting other competitors, either telecoms or existing commercial banks, until M-Pesa had become dominant in Kenya. Network effects are associated to this position. Lock-in strategies reinforced it: users are able to send value to non-users who can then withdraw the received amount without charge; however, the sender is charged with a significantly higher fee if the recipient is an unregistered user (Donovan 2012). Obviously, the latter is not a context factor but has to be down to managerial decisions.

On the contrary, the fact that mobile telephony has permeated, the whole population can be considered a context factor for the success of M-Pesa. Indeed, analysing the characteristics of those who only use M-Pesa, Johnson and Arnold (2012) suggest that it is able to reach a more diverse range of users than traditional bank services do and hence some of the

---

[2] As refers active mobile-broadband subscriptions, there were 27 million at the end of 2011 (3.3 per 100 inhabitants). The penetration rates of fixed telecommunication services are very much lower: 1.4% for fixed-line telephones and a paltry 0.2% for wired broadband in 2011.

barriers to financial inclusion may be overcome as the service expands further.

4. Conclusion

For Engelen et al. (2010), the present economic crisis is a crisis *of* financial innovation because securitization represents innovation whose outcomes include frozen markets, failed and bailed banks and blocked credit. At the same time, they think this is also a crisis *for* financial innovation because these events have forced media commentators, politicians and regulatory organizations to revalue the notion of financial innovation or at least question the ability of banks and other institutions to manage innovation in the general interest.

In this statement, a definition of financial innovation as an outcome of complex and even obscure processes resounds. This is in line with the usual stereotype of innovation as being an activity carried out in laboratories by enlightened scientists. However, there are many other kinds of innovation and particularly there are many other kinds of financial innovation. Besides, there are of course financial innovations that can be managed in the general interest.

This is the case for mobile financial services. Plyler et al. (2010) carried out a study on the impact of M-Pesa and found that four phenomena could be observed (with variations in terms of the location of the community and the gender): an expansion of the local economy due to a higher circulation of money; a better environment for business as transactions become easier to make; an accumulation of financial and social capital and even an improvement in physical health and more regular access to nutrition. For their part, Morawczynski and Pickens (2009) affirm that the income of users in rural areas has increased by up to 30% due to the ease of requesting and receiving funds from family members who work in the city. Apart from the above, there are also many intangible benefits that can not be measured through statistics, but can make a great difference to people's lives. These could be general benefits, such as the informal insurance system created through family networks, as money can be transferred instantly (Morawczynski and Pickens 2009), or could be very particular benefits, as the example described by Williams and Torma (2007) who referred to the savings when buying prepaid electricity[3].

---

[3] One of the most popular uses of Wizzit is to buy prepaid electricity. In order for an agricultural worker to top-up their electricity meter (the payment method used by the majority of South Africans) they have to walk half an hour to the nearest

It took, however, a surprisingly long time for the lesson to be learned. Despite having been technologically ready for years, despite their simplicity and manifest usefulness, mobile banking systems were the promise that never happened. Indeed, in the world's richest countries, leaving aside the Internet-through-mobile banking available in smartphones, mobile financial services have hardly developed. As for any other innovation, three are the factors that help to explain this situation.

The existence of a clear need is a first factor that serves to justify why some mobile banking initiatives have obtained resounding success precisely in developing countries. Among the reasons justifying their acceptance are factors that are country-specific, and to be precise, the difficulty in accessing traditional financial services. Notwithstanding this, the *simple* mobile banking can also have served (can serve indeed) niche markets in wealthier countries such as the unbanked (developed countries too have unbanked) or those technologically weakly-equipped or weakly-skilled.

Context also matters. The slowness in taking up of mobile payments and mobile banking has been a feature of the industrialized countries due to the consumers' initial lack of trust in available services (Kim et al. 2009) but also to the advantages conferred by alternative and pre-existing delivery channels (Duncombe and Boateng 2009). Behind this fact is the lack of interest of banks and payment card providers, who fear that mobile operators will eat their lunch and the approach of regulators who worry that mobile-money schemes, will be abused by fraudsters and money-launderers (The Economist 2009).

But without ignoring these circumstances, an intelligent design during the exploitation phase ("knowledge") is what has made mobile banking go from a fortunate concept to a successful innovation. Overall, the case of the development of mobile financial services in developing countries reveals the obvious: whatever the characteristics of the market in question, understanding what drives customers to use and pay for a product or service, considering customer psychology as well as the social, cultural and organizational characteristics of the communities it addresses and designing appropriate services, is essential when the goal is to introduce any kind of innovation in the market.

---

unpaved road, wait for a taxi (an unpredictable wait) to take them to the city and to wait in a queue for typically around two and a half hours. The return journey could be another two and a half hours and costs 20 rand (equivalent to half a day's pay). With a mobile telephone this can be done instantly, at a cost of less than a rand and without the risk of being robbed at some stage during the journey.

Most times there is no need to invent anything when trying to innovate. What is needed is to "exploit" the resources that are around; in a way guaranteeing consumer acceptance and economic feasibility. Or, in other words, there is a need of communicating precise customer benefits and financial incentives (or business case) for the various stakeholders.

References

Baregheh, A., Rowley, J., and Sambrook, S. "Towards a multidisciplinary definition of innovation." *Management Decision* 47, no. 8 (2009): 1323–1339.

Batchelor, S. "Changing the financial landscape of Africa: An unusual story of evidence-informed innovation, intentional policy influence and private sector engagement." *IDS Bulletin-Institute of Development Studies* 43, no. 5 (2012): 84–90.

Berger, A.N. "The economic effects of technological progress: Evidence from the banking industry." *Journal of Money Credit and Banking* 35, no. 2 (2003): 141–176.

Black, N.J., Lockett, A., Ennew, C., Winklhofer, H., and McKechnie, S. "Modelling consumer choice of distribution channels: an illustration from financial services." *International Journal of Bank Marketing* 20, no. 4 (2002): 161–173.

Boot, A.W.A., and Marinc, M. "The evolving landscape of banking." *Industrial and Corporate Change* 17, no. 6 (2008): 1173–1203.

Dahlberg, T., Mallat, N., Ondrus, J., and Zmijewska, A. "Past, present and future of mobile payments research: A literature review." *Electronic Commerce Research and Applications* 7, no. 2 (2008): 165–181.

Donovan, K.P. "Mobile money, more freedom? The impact of M-PESA's network power on development as freedom." *International Journal of Communication* 6 (2012): 2647–2669.

Duncombe, R., and Boateng, R. "Mobile phones and financial services in developing countries: a review of concepts, methods, issues, evidence and future research directions." *Third World Quarterly* 30, no. 7 (2009): 1237–1258.

Engelen, E., Erturk, I., Froud, J., Leaver, A., and Williams, K. "Reconceptualizing financial innovation: frame, conjuncture and bricolage." *Economy and Society* 39, no.1 (2010): 33–63.

FinAccess. *National Survey 2009. Dynamics of Kenya's changing financial landscape*, FSD Kenya – Central Bank of Kenya, 2009. http://www.fsdkenya.org/finaccess/documents/09–06–10_FinAccess_FA09_Report.pdf; accessed 16 December 2012.

Gencer, M. "The mobile money movement: Catalyst to jump-start emerging markets." *Innovations: Technology, Governance, Globalization* 6, no. 1 (2011): 101–117.

Hayes, N., and Westrup, C. "Context and the processes of ICT for development." *Information and Organization* 22, no. 1 (2012): 23–36.

Hoehle, H., Scornavacca, E., and Huff, S. "Three decades of research on consumer adoption and utilization of electronic banking channels: A literature analysis." *Decision Support Systems* 54, no. 1 (2012): 122–132.

Hughes, N., and Lonie, S. "M–PESA: mobile money for the 'unbanked'– Turning cellphones into 24–hour tellers in Kenya." *Innovations: Technology, Governance, Globalization* 2, no. 1–2 (2007): 63–81.

ITU. *Key global telecom indicators for the world telecommunication service sector*. International Telecommunication Union. Geneva, 2012. http://www.itu.int/ITU-D/ict/statistics/at_glance/KeyTelecom.html; accessed 16 December 2012.

—. *Measuring the Information Society – 2012*. International Telecommunication Union. Geneva, 2012. http://www.itu.int/ITU-D/ict/publications/idi/index.html; accessed 16 December 2012.

—. *Information Society statistical profiles 2009 – Africa*. International Telecommunication Union. Geneva, 2009. http://www.itu.int/dms_pub/itu-d/opb/ind/D-IND-RPM.AF-2009-PDF-E.pdf; accessed 16 December 2012.

Johnson, S., and Arnold, S. "Inclusive financial markets: Is transformation under way in Kenya?" *Development Policy Review* 30, no. 6 (2012): 719–748.

Kalmanek, C. "The essential elements of successful innovation." *Computer Communication Review* 42, no. 2 (2012): 105–109.

Kauffman, R.J., and Riggins, F.J. "Research directions on the role and impact of ICT in microfinance." In Sprague, R.H. (Ed.): *Proceedings of the 43rd Hawaii International Conference on System Sciences*: 1–10, Honolulu: CPS–IEEE, 2010.

Kim, G., Shin, B.S., and Lee, H.G. "Understanding dynamics between initial trust and usage intentions of mobile banking." *Information Systems Journal* 19, no. 3 (2009): 283–311.

Kumar, K., McKay, C., and Rotman, S. *Microfinance and mobile banking: The story so far*, CGAP Focus Note 62, Washington D.C., 2010. http://www.cgap.org/gm/document–1.9.45546/FN62_Com.pdf; accessed 16 December 2012.

Leavitt, N. "Are mobile payments ready to cash in yet?." *Computer* 45, no. 9 (2012): 15–18.

Lyman, T.R., Pickens, M., and Porteous, D. *Regulating transformational branchless banking: Mobile phones and other technology to increase access to finance*, CGAP Focus Note 43, Washington D.C., 2008. http://www.cgap.org/publications/regulating-transformational-branchless-banking-mobile-phones-and-other-technology; accessed 16 December 2012.

Lyman, T.R., Ivatury, G., and Staschen, S. *Use of agents in branchless banking for the poor: Rewards, risks, and regulation*, CGAP Focus Note 38, Washington D.C., 2006. http://www.cgap.org/publications/use-agents-branchless-banking-poor-rewards-risks-and-regulation; accessed 16 December 2012

Mallat, N., Rossi, M., and Tuunainen, V.K. "Mobile banking services." *Communications of the ACM* 47, no. 5 (2004): 42–46.

Mas, I., and Kumar, K. *Banking on mobiles: Why, how, for whom?*, CGAP Focus Note 48, Washington D.C., 2008. http://www.cgap.org/gm/document–1.9.4400/FN48.pdf; accessed 16 December 2012.

Mas, I., and Morawczynski, O. "Designing mobile transfer services: Lessons from M–PESA." *Innovations: Technology, Governance, Globalization* 4, no. 2 (2009): 77–91.

Medhi, I., Patnaik, S., Brunskill, E., Gautama, S.N.N., Thies, W., and Toyama, K. "Designing mobile interfaces for novice and low–literacy users." *ACM Transactions on Computer–Human Interaction* 18, no. 1 (2011): article number 2.

Morawczynski, O., and Pickens, M. *Poor people using mobile financial services: Observations on customer usage and impact from M-PESA*. CGAP Brief, 2009. http://www.cgap.org/gm/document-1.9.36723/BR_Poor_People_Using_Mobile_Financial_Services.pdf; accessed 16 December 2012.

Plyler, M.G., Haas, S., and Nagarajan, G. *Community-level economic effects of M-PESA in Kenya: Initial findings*. Financial Services Assessment project, 2010. http://www.fsassessment.umd.edu/publications/Community%20Effects%20Paper%20Final.pdf; accessed 16 December 2012.

Roberts, E.B. "Managing invention and innovation." *Research–Technology Management* 50, no. 1 (2007): 35–54.

Singh, S. "Mobile remittances: Design for financial inclusion." In Aykin, N. (Ed.): *Internationalization, Design and Global Development*: 515–524, Berlin Heidelberg: Springer–Verlag, 2009.

The Economist. "Out of thin air. The behind–the–scenes logistics of Kenya's mobile–money miracle." *The Economist*, no. 395 (8686; 10 June 2010), p.85.

—. "The power of mobile money." *The Economist*, no. 392 (8650; 26 September 2009), p.13.

Van de Kar, E.V., and Den Hengst, M. "Involving users early on in the design process: closing the gap between mobile information services and their users." *Electronic Markets* 19, no. 1 (2009): 31–42.

Westlund, O., Gómez-Barroso, J.L., Compañó, R., and Feijóo, C. "Exploring the logic of mobile search." *Behaviour & Information Technology* 30, no. 5 (2011): 691–703.

Williams, H., and Torma, M. "Trust and fidelity: from 'under the mattress' to the mobile phone" in *The transformational potential of M-transactions*: 10–19. The Vodafone Policy Paper Series no. 6, 2007. http://www.vodafone.com/etc/medialib/public_policy_series.Par.89230.File.dat/public_policy_series_6.pdf; accessed 16 December 2012.

Wooder, S., and Baker, S. "Extracting key lessons in service innovation." *Journal of Product Innovation Management* 29, no. 1 (2012): 13–20.

CHAPTER TEN

STRATEGIES FOR FINANCIAL SERVICE INNOVATION: INNOVATION BECOMES STRATEGY-MAKING

KATJA MARIA HYDLE, TOR HELGE AAS AND KARL JOACHIM BREUNIG

1. Introduction

This chapter explores financial service innovation in relation to strategy. Using case firms, we demonstrate how new business strategy emerges as an outcome of service innovation activities.

The traditional view on the link between strategy and innovation activities is that innovation activities exist in order to fulfil and realize strategic goals. For example, innovation may be required to achieve cost-efficient production to meet a cost-leadership strategy, or to achieve the unique services and competence required to meet a differentiation strategy. However, strategy research has been criticized for being biased towards large, US-based manufacturing firms (O'Reilly and Tushman 2008). On the other hand, innovation management research has primarily been concerned with innovations related to physical products, whereas innovation in services has not received the same attention (Droege, Hildebrand, and Forcada 2009). Hence, there is little focus on the relationship between service innovation and strategy. This chapter aims at filling this literature gap by exploring the relation between innovation and strategy in one specific subset of services: financial scale-intensive services. Scale-intensive services are standardized services produced at a large scale mainly by large firms, such as bank services, insurance services, telecommunication (telecom) services and logistics services (Pavitt 1984).

The link between strategy and financial service innovation can be informed by the innovation management literature (Froehle and Roth 2007; Kahn, Barczak, and Moss 2006) and Product Development and Management Association (PDMA) certification work (PDMA 2011). Strategy is an important dimension of innovation management. Innovation strategy refers to the articulation of the role of innovation in achieving organizational aims (Cooper, Edgett, and Kleinschmidt 2001) by aligning the overall business strategy with innovation decisions (Menor and Roth 2007). An innovation strategy should ensure that the appropriate resources and practices necessary to develop goods or services are present, and that the new goods' or services' characteristics and their delivery, match customer expectations and demands (Menor and Roth 2007).

Several authors (Johne and Storey 1998; Easingwood 1990) stress the importance of setting clear goals for the innovation program as a whole. Empirical studies suggest that leading firms are likely to have an explicit innovation strategy (Cooper, Edgett, and Kleinschmidt 2002). However, empirical literature focusing on the relation between strategy and innovation has mainly focused on product innovation. Due to differences between products and services (Zeithaml, Parasuraman, and Berry 1985) and between product innovation and service innovation (Droege, Hildebrand, and Forcada 2009), it is not clear whether findings from studies on product innovation are also valid for innovation in scale-intensive services. In particular, we question the relation between strategy and financial service innovation. Thus, we pose the first research question: *How is strategy linked to innovation in financial scale-intensive services?*

This research question reflects the traditional understanding of strategy as something that a firm *has*; in contrast, the Strategy-as-Practice (SAP) perspective focuses on strategy as something the organizational members *do*. SAP reconceptualises strategy as a social activity (Johnson, Langley, and Whittington 2007; Jarzabkowski 2005) and advocates by getting closer to the phenomenon of interest in order to gain a better understanding of the 'doing' of strategy work (Whittington 2006a). In this endeavour, SAP looks at the work that is explicitly associated with strategy, a perspective that allows us to assume a relation between innovation practices and strategy-making (Chia and Rasche 2010; Løwendahl, Revang, and Fosstenløkken 2001). However, there is little empirical research on the strategy-making that emerges from everyday activities in general (Chia and Holt 2009; Chia and Rasche 2010). In particular, to our knowledge, there is no empirical research on the relation between service innovation and strategy-making. To fill this literature gap, we pose the following second research question: *How is innovation linked to strategy-making in financial scale-intensive services?*

These two research questions go in opposite directions. The first focuses on how strategy is related to innovation, with strategy considered as a given. The second research question looks at how innovation is linked to strategy-making, where strategy is in the making.

This chapter is organized as follows. We first present the theoretical background for understanding strategy and strategy-making in relation to innovation before describing the research context and design. Then, we expose the findings, which are organized according to the two research questions. The discussion is accompanied by propositions and a framework linking strategy and strategy-making to financial service innovation. This chapter contributes to service innovation theorizing, showing how financial service innovation enables existing strategy while simultaneously enhancing strategy-making.

2. Theoretical Background

The fundamental question raised in the strategic management literature concerns how firms achieve and sustain competitive advantage (Teece, Pisano, and Shuen 1997). Several authors have emphasized different routes to maintaining competitive advantage; their contributions are often categorized into different schools of thought. Mintzberg et al. (1985) suggest 10 schools of thought in strategic management, including three prescriptive schools (e.g. planning and positioning schools) and seven descriptive schools (e.g. learning and cultural schools). Prescriptive schools focus on how strategies should be formulated. With their origins in the 1960s, these schools have the longest traditions in the field of strategic management (Mintzberg and McHugh 1985). A prominent author belonging to the prescriptive school of thought, Michael Porter (1985) suggests that firms achieve sustained competitive advantage by implementing a cost-leadership, differentiation, segmentation, or focused strategy. Thus, in the prescriptive school of strategic management, innovation is perceived as a *strategy enabler*: a tool to achieve strategic goals and sustained competitive advantage.

Despite this obvious relation between strategy and innovation, there have been relatively few attempts in the research literature to integrate the two phenomena (Tsoukas 2010). Most research has either focused on strategy or innovation and not on the two phenomena simultaneously. Empirical research trying to bridge strategy and innovation has mainly focused on product innovation. These studies typically suggest that, to succeed with innovation, it is important to have an explicit innovation strategy (Cooper, Edgett, and Kleinschmidt 2001). However, it remains unknown whether this finding is also valid for service innovation-a topic that we explore through service innovation cases (Droege, Hildebrand, and Forcada 2009).

Rather than trying to prescribe how managers should make strategies, several authors, contributing to the field of strategic management, focus on how strategies are actually made. Mintzberg et al. (1985) categorize these contributions as descriptive. One relatively new descriptive school in strategic management is SAP, which defines strategy as: ‘a situated, socially accomplished activity’ and strategizing as comprising ‘those actions, interactions, and negotiations of multiple actors and the situated practices that they draw upon in accomplishing that activity’ (Jarzabkowski, Balogun, and Seidl 2007, 7-8). Strategy-making is understood as ‘an umbrella term that describes the myriad activities that lead to the creation of organizational strategies’ (Vaara and Whittington 2012, 3).

Practice theory is used as a theoretical foundation for the SAP perspective to shed light on the enacted nature of strategizing (Feldman and Orlikowski 2011; Jarzabkowski 2005; Chia and MacKay 2007; Jarzabkowski 2004; Jarzabkowski, Balogun, and Seidl 2007; Jarzabkowski and Spee 2009; Whittington 2006a; Vaara and Whittington 2012). Schatzki explains that ‘practice theorists conceived of practices as embodied, materially mediated arrays of human activity centrally organized around shared practical understanding’ (Schatzki, Knorr Cetina, and von Savigny 2001, 2). According to Schatzki (Schatzki 2012), there are three commonalities among practice theories. First, practice theories understand ‘practice’ as ‘an organized constellation of different people’s activities’ (Schatzki 2012, 13) A practice is a social phenomenon that comprises of multiple people. Second, practice theories understand human life as being rooted in practices. Thus, the ‘social’ is not the activity of the individual and an individual’s agency or structure is not given ontological primacy. Rather, there is a social ontology wherein ‘social phenomena cannot consist simply of people’s actions, but must consist of these actions together with, or in the context of, these practices’(Schatzki 2012, 14). Third, practice theories hold that human activity relies on something that is non-propositional, such as skills (Dreyfus 1991, 2004) or habitus (Bourdieu 1977, 1990). Wittgenstein’s understanding of ‘rule following’ forms the basis of non-propositional understanding (2009). To view financial service innovation, we must focus on organized activities of different employees to uncover the practices.

Although the SAP literature uses practices to understand the relational and enacted nature of strategizing, most contributions are about explicit strategizing practices and processes (Whittington 2006a, 2006b, 2007; Chia and MacKay 2007; Rasche and Robert 2009; Jarzabkowski, Balogun, and Seidl 2007; Jarzabkowski 2008; Jarzabkowski and Spee 2009; Kornberger and Clegg 2011). According to Chia and MacKay, 'The opportunity presented by the recent turn to "practice" in philosophy and social theory is to encourage focusing on the patterned *consistency* of actions emerging from such interactions, rather than on the micro-activities of individual strategy agents' (Chia and MacKay 2007, 224). This approach focuses on daily coping actions and follows the dwelling mode of strategizing (Chia and Rasche 2010). According to Chia and Rasche (2010), there are two alternative views to researching strategizing: deliberate strategizing through the *building view* and non-deliberate strategizing through the *dwelling view*. The understanding of building and dwelling stems from Heidegger: 'Dwelling and building are related as end and means. However, as long as this is all we have in mind, we take dwelling and building as two separate activities, an idea that has something correct in it. Yet, at the same time, by the means-end schema we block our view of the essential relations. For building is not merely a means and a way towards dwelling-to build is, in itself, already to dwell' (Heidegger 1971, 144). In relation to strategy, the building mode refers to building strategy through purposeful planning by top management. The dwelling mode refers to strategizing through purposive everyday practical coping performed by any practitioner (Chia and Holt 2006, 644).

We use this understanding to bridge strategy and service innovation by exploring their relationship from two different theoretical angles. To answer the first research question, we explore strategy and innovation through the lens of the traditional prescriptive strategic theory. To this end, we perceive innovation as a tool to achieve strategic goals and sustained competitive advantage and explore how strategy influences innovation. To answer the second research question, we explore strategy and innovation through the lens of the SAP perspective. In this case, we focus on how the practices of service innovation are performed and how these practices are linked to strategy-making, following the building or dwelling view.

3. Research Design

The study is based on empirical case materials derived from 25 interviews in five large international scale-intensive service firms. We conducted interviews with partly open-ended questions in relation to their practices of service innovation (Orlikowski 2010), followed by theory-informed questions on service innovation and strategy (Eisenhardt and Graebner 2007). The units of analysis were service innovation projects. When questioning and studying service innovation projects, we aimed at investigating what the employees do, the types of problems employees solve, what kinds of tools are in use and how the actors interact.

The second aim was to turn the interviews towards theory-informed questions. The semi structured interview guide followed the framework of Froehle and Roth (2007), which consists of three levels. On the highest level of practices, Froehle and Roth (2007) distinguish resource-from process-oriented practices. On the next level, resource-oriented practices are subdivided into intellectual, organizational and physical resources, whereas process-oriented practices are subdivided into design, analysis, development, and launch stages.

To identify the service innovation practices within each dimension, multiple interviews are necessary. A theory-informed interview guide was created to reflect the dimensions of the service innovation management practices (i.e. strategy, culture, front end of innovation, portfolio management, new service development process, tools and techniques, metrics and measures, intellectual resources, and organizational resources). To obtain concrete and specific answers about these practices, informants selected two service innovation projects that had been carried out in the firm. They were asked open-ended questions about the management practices in the nine aforementioned dimensions. Then, several closed follow-up questions were asked (e.g. related to whether specific tools or measures were used) to obtain a more in-depth and complete understanding of the practices in each firm. We asked whether the management practices for these specific projects were representative of the firm's practices and whether the informant believed the practices were successful. This theory-informed top-down approach, following Froehle and Roth (2007), is relevant for viewing how service innovation is linked to strategy. In the open-ended bottom-up practice approach, the starting point is the identification of practices, which then are related to strategy.

The five selected scale-intensive service firms were all large firms that operated in both business-to-consumers (B2C) and business-to-business (B2B) markets, providing services to other firms and to consumers. To observe the relationship between strategy and innovation, we assumed that these firms have more intentional strategy and less ad hoc activities. The firms provided different types of scale-intensive services: the three main firms provided financial services within the bank and insurance industries, one firm was within the telecom industry and the last firm was in logistics.

The three financial scale-intensive service firms were contrasted with the others to compare financial versus other scale-intensive services. All firms were successful in the market, as they had expanded beyond the national border to more than three countries. To preserve anonymity, we have called the five firms Alpha (Bank), Beta (Insurance), Gamma (Insurance), Delta (Telecom) and Epsilon (Logistics).

Data were collected in 25 semi-structured interviews, each lasting between 1 and 2 hours. Interviews were recorded and transcribed. To reflect the strategy and innovation practices of the firms, we chose informants with different roles and from different firm levels (i.e. management, innovation and business development, and IT, see Table 1).

Table 1. Interviews

Firm	Key contact persons	Management	Innovation and business development	IT	Total
Alpha	1	1	3		5
Beta	1	1	1	1	4
Gamma	1	1	2		4
Delta	1	2	3	2	8
Epsilon	1	1	1	1	4
Total	5	6	10	4	25

Data was inserted into the NVivo program and coded. To understand the data, the analysis progressed in several stages. First, the material was thoroughly discussed between researchers and made into a PowerPoint presentation, which was presented to selected employees and managers in the firms so as to validate the veracity of the data and to enhance the trustworthiness of the analysis (Lincoln and Guba 1985).

Second, the data were examined in light of the research questions. For the first research question concerning strategies for service innovation, we coded the material relative to what employees specifically told us about business and innovation strategies. Following the prescriptive school, we found that all firms had general business strategies and none had innovation strategies. For the second research question emphasizing how innovation is linked to strategy-making, following SAP, we coded and compared the practices of service innovation projects across firms. Service innovation projects were coded according to whether they were B2B or B2C, both of which generally involved digitalization and automation. We also coded the projects according to whether they were incremental or radical new-to-market (N2M) service innovation, as described by the respondent. Both radical and incremental service innovations involved automation and increased customer focus.

Finally, the different firms, practices, and projects were contrasted to determine whether there were large differences between financial service innovation and service innovation in the telecom and logistic firms. One large difference was that within the telecom and logistic firms, large radical innovation projects became their own organizational entities. However, there were few differences in the relationship between innovation and strategy among the five scale-intensive firms. Innovations had an impact on all of the firms' strategic directions, as we will expose in the findings.

4. Findings

Findings are presented according to the two research questions. We first focus on strategies for service innovation (subsection 4.1) and then emphasize service innovation in relation to strategy-making (subsection 4.2). Findings are exposed with representative illustrative quotes, mainly from the financial service innovation firms.

4.1 Strategies for Service Innovation

The studied firms had defined strategic business goals and invested considerably in service innovation activities. Firms primarily perceived innovation as a tool to close the gap between the firms' current situation and their strategic ambitions.

> 'We have a strategy, but there is nothing specific about innovation. Innovation is a tool that should support the overall strategy. We have about five to six major concerns that are part of our strategy; customer experience is one of them. We have something related to coverage, something on development and then customer experience and efficiency improvements. To achieve our strategic goals, we in the organization have to operationalize those goals. Innovation is one of the pillars to reach our goals. We state, "We will excel in customer experience". [Then, we ask,] "What is the gap? How can we close that gap?" We start with different initiatives and projects, and innovation becomes part of that.' (Beta respondent)

None of the studied firms had an explicit innovation strategy; no firm articulated a strategic role of innovation in a separate strategic innovation plan. These findings may be illustrated by the following statements:

> 'Innovation has never been explicitly described in a strategy.' (Gamma respondent)

> 'We don't have an explicit innovation strategy, although we should be the best digital actor to meet these challenges and trends. The firm is product and project-oriented. Some of the current trends are global and come externally and we have to relate to them. But we are such a big actor in this country that we can think it through. We don't need to jump on every occasion.' (Alpha respondent)

> 'In our company, there are two fundamental goals: one is to increase customer satisfaction continuously and the other is to reduce costs and work more efficiently. The challenge lies in combining these two goals. What we have seen is that we do manage to combine the two by increasing self-service and customer involvement. But, we don't have an innovation strategy…In our culture, we have a quick time to market, but we don't rate the projects, or the innovations at a later stage, or have a structure to actually succeed.' (Beta respondent)

These quotes expose that the firms used innovation to fulfil strategic aims without employing an explicit innovation strategy. As Gamma respondents explained:

> 'There is a larger need to have a strategy for services than for products…it is about values and how the values lead to service innovation; radical or incremental innovation or driven by values. The question is what values are part of the innovation.'

> 'If the question is if we have a strategy to develop our services, then the answer is yes. But if the question is if we have an innovation strategy, then the answer is no!'

The following statement from a business developer in Alpha illustrates how business strategy was used in the firms:

> 'The overall strategy of this bank is that they will engage with a specific customer segment. That is the kind of strategy that we use. But the strategy says nothing about how or what to use...that is only something we do...'

Thus, financial service innovation was regarded by the firms as 'something we do'. This concept led us to ask how service innovation projects were performed and what their relation was to strategy-making.

4.2 Service Innovation in Relation to Strategy-Making

In the five scale-intensive service firms, service innovation entailed substantial digitalization and automation, both in B2C and B2B relations.

> 'Regarding new services, first and foremost, the innovation efforts are a lot larger than the services. There are fundamental structural changes in the organizing and data structure, which lead to various new customer experiences.' (Gamma respondent)

A typical service innovation in B2C was explained by an Alpha employee as: 'A service concept on Facebook where our advisors help you with your first home.' Regarding B2B service innovation, a Beta manager stated:

> 'In the last few years, the focus has been on projects aimed at process automation. This implies services that are supported technologically, so that we obtain a higher degree of self-service. The thought behind this work was inspired by airline companies that make their customers do most of the work through self-service and choices…These are B2B services because they are related to large business customers. However, during service delivery, we often talk to individuals who are receiving pensions or who are on sick leave. The focus has been to make service delivery more effective by using ICT [Information and Communications Technology] systems and customer involvement.'

Apart from automation and digitalization, we found differences between incremental and radical N2M service innovations. An example of a radical service innovation was Beta's My Consumption service. Part of a personal internal bank, My Consumption shows an individual's distributions of expenditures in different categories. There are standard categories, such as groceries, electricity, clothing, etc. and self-specified categories, such as child care, medical, etc. My Consumption allows consumers to gain an easy and quick overview of their monthly expenditures. Everything is explained in a YouTube video, with a male voice explaining to the bank customer what to do.

> 'My Consumption is the most innovative service in the bank. This is an N2M idea that shows what we are using money on. Instead of reading bank statements, now you can see it graphically…' (Beta respondent)

Digital Postal Services (DPS) is another example of an N2M service innovation in Epsilon. As a new national digital postal system, DPS allows private businesses, public authorities and individuals to send post digitally. DPS reduces distribution costs and increases the efficiency of customer processes to other businesses. This service is proposed as a solution that can manage all informal and formal documents (e.g. bank statements, insurance papers, health information, shopping receipts, information from local authorities, etc.). The DPS project is a large one, taking over several years to complete and involving 20 people. The manager of DPS from Epsilon explained:

> 'We started with the physical value chain of postal services, what the postal services offer as physical post distribution. There are a lot of similarities-the distribution of documents from A to B, things to be added-but the core is similar. The customer segment core is similar, too; customers that the Postal Services traditionally have had, such as the Bank, Energy, Telecom and public sector, have a lot of documents to be distributed. In relation to Osterwalder's business model, we differentiate ourselves with regards to how we sell and serve these customers and where we want to exploit the digital service. We have worked a lot with large-business customers regarding direct services. Middle-sized customers will be served through partner contracts as software contracts, where there are integration points to use. For the small-business customers, they have self-service... We have some advantages and one is the electronic ID. One has to be 100% sure of what one gets as a user. In our country, we have come far with the electronic ID. The Nordic has come relatively far, while the rest of Europe and the US have not come that far yet. So, that is an issue for us, how to be secure…'

An example of a more incremental service innovation is Beta's Business Portal: a B2B service in which there have been incremental service innovations to meet customer needs. A Beta manager explained:

> 'Several independent advisors had a lot of objections to the system. Then, we worked to lift the portal towards the business segment. We drove the project through 67 deliveries to improve customer value. This is untraditional; for most projects, it will take a year to have a new solution. Here, we used incremental development, continuous input, and frequent, small efforts. For instance, before, the business customer would have to be logged on and dig through a lot of information of little relevance…they

> had to call us. We wanted to solve something, not make them read about new products… Now, the system reminds business customers about unpaid bills, employees that have not received salary adjustments the last few years and so forth.'

Business Portal is a typical incremental service innovation example in, which, part of what was earlier used by business customers with certain professional expertise, such as an intricate understanding of pension systems, new legislative impact and differentiated pension schemes, is integrated into the system and automated.

In all companies, a customer focus to ensure customer retention was a large concern. As one Alpha employee explained:

> 'I started out by asking, "Ok, what do we want? Why should we put a lot of stake in the youth segment? What do we need?" …I don't want ideas; the only thing that counts is deliverables. Ideas are not a problem when you know what you want…it's about rewinding and asking "What kind of needs do we solve?"… and we have to ensure that we have customer retention.'

Customer focus, automation and self-service seemed to be the main drivers, as explained by the following statement by a Beta employee:

> 'I started in a concrete area where there would be substantial differences for customers and proved it afterwards. Then, I got responsibility for the "Simplification" project. It suited me well to start here, due to the 275 000 customers involved.'

Service innovations impacted the firms, as they were linked to the firms' futures and strategy-making. A business developer dealing with innovation in Alpha explained:

> 'We have our own Facebook page for this, where we almost had a power struggle or something of the like. We have a nice thing going on there (on Facebook). And, we have launched this service…but it is a lot more because it is political, reputational, yes, it is very important that Beta goes ahead as the largest financial corporation in this country. It has been so much fun to be part of. And, then, we have tested out such amusing digital things, and the connection between physical channels and phones with check-in deals."

Service innovation became strategy-making in these firms, as explained by an Alpha employee in charge of several service innovation projects:

> 'It's not about a top-down strategy, really. We work with those who have worked more bottom-up and tried to suggest things. We get them with us, and based on that we decide which direction we are going. How do I find that direction? That is a craft. One has to work hard, use a lot of time and get into it. Systematize, try out and think out customer scenarios. Try to think about which axes are useful that we can compete through or deliver something around. There are so many important dimensions to take into account. One dimension is profitability, of course. It is so important that I take care of profitability, as I have the responsibility for profitability in this customer segment. We have low margins for our services...although services are an investment for the Corporation. We have to make sure that we have customer retention. So, there are a lot of dimensions and you have to see me work. It is nothing I can really tell over the table. But I am very intensively involved and work a lot together with others. And, I have a lot of methods that I use on how I pose questions, involve people, and give tasks to others....'

Whereas the aim of the chosen service innovation activities might be automation or customer self-service, the organizational consequence was that customers were now doing the job that internal employees had done previously. These changes impacted the delivered services, the internal organization, the knowledge-sharing within the firms and how the firm interacted with its clients. Thus, innovation activities in scale-intensive service firms had game-changing consequences that affected several dimensions of the business model.

5. Discussion

Our first research question was: *How is strategy linked to innovation in financial scale-intensive services?* Our findings suggest that the general business strategy plays an important role in determining, which service innovation activities are selected and conducted. Financial scale-intensive service providers rarely give resources to an innovation project if it is not linked to an existing business strategy. This part of our findings is in line with the traditional prescriptive strategic theory, which comprehends innovation as a tool to achieve strategic goals and sustained competitive advantage (e.g., Porter, 1980).

Recent research on product innovation management suggests that leading manufacturing firms benefit from articulating an explicit innovation strategy, in addition to the more general business strategy. However, our findings suggest that scale-intensive service providers typically do not explicitly articulate an innovation strategy. Instead, these firms tend to judge their innovation activities in light of their general business strategy. It is difficult to explain the reason for this practice. Possible explanations may be related to the natures of scale-intensive services and the innovation projects conducted by typical scale-intensive service providers. Modern scale-intensive services, especially financial banking services, are typically very dependent on ICT (De Jong et al. 2003). Thus, innovation in scale-intensive services is partly dependent on general ICT development, which is beyond the control of scale-intensive service providers. This finding may imply that it is more important for scale-intensive service providers to evaluate new ICT service ideas against their strategic business goals than it is to formulate and implement a separate explicit innovation strategy.

On the basis of our findings, we offer the following propositions that future research should investigate further:

P1: Innovation in financial scale-intensive services is a tool to achieve strategic goals and sustained competitive advantage for scale-intensive service providers.

P2: Articulation of an explicit innovation strategy is not essential for financial scale-intensive service providers to achieve innovation success.

In the second research question, we asked: *How is innovation linked to strategy-making in financial scale-intensive services?* Listening to the informants and considering the empirical material, we found that the implications of service innovation were not directly mentioned as being strategic, although they had a strategic impact. Service innovation was related to automation, self-service, radical and incremental innovations and customer focus through involvement and retention due to services. However, the services that were launched and their innovative component were linked to the firms' customers, future customer satisfaction and customer retention. Moreover, much of the service innovation concerned automation and self-service. Consequently, the service delivery systems were radically altered as, for example, the customers began performing work that was previously performed by employees. This situation ultimately had effects on the internal organizing needs. Thus, on the one hand, service innovation dealt with future customer satisfaction and retention; on the other hand, it had large consequences for the overall organization within the firms. Service innovation can be said to be of utmost importance for both customers and employees, in terms of changing their existing relationship to the firm.

Returning to theory and the SAP perspective, we recall that the dwelling mode refers to purposive everyday practical coping, performed by any practitioner (Chia and Rasche 2010; Chia and Holt 2006). In our study, service innovations had large future consequences of the customers and employees, thus going beyond practical coping. They were performed by many different employees involved in the service innovation projects and changed the business models for customers. Following the understanding of strategy-making from SAP described in section 1 (Vaara and Whittington 2012, 3), we set forth the following proposition:

P3: Innovation activities in financial scale-intensive service providers are strategy-making.

Employees involved in service innovation projects were business developers, IT engineers, innovation captains, middle managers and others involved in the services provided by the companies. When working with service innovation, these employees become strategists. Strategy-making follows the dwelling mode. These findings extend existing research in the SAP perspective on the role of middle managers in strategy. Earlier research describes how the agency of middle managers shapes strategy, concentrating on explicit strategy processes or practitioners' own tales of how they contributed to strategy (Mantere 2008, 2005). Our findings show that employees dealing with service innovation contribute to strategy-making. Thus, we make the following proposition:

P4: Employees involved in service innovation activities in financial scale-intensive service providers are strategy-makers.

To summarize, our findings suggest that innovation in financial scale-intensive service firms enables the realization of existing strategy and enhances strategy-making. Thus, service innovation is part of both the building and the dwelling modes of strategizing (Chia and Rasche 2010; Chia and Holt 2006). Existing strategy that has been built through deliberate actions and explicit strategy processes and practices is realized through service innovation. On the other side, service innovation is part of the everyday activities of practitioners. Two major elements of these activities are the distributed learning situations experienced by employees in their interactions (e.g. with external clients) and the more directed learning process that occurs through the innovation activities themselves. Thus, service innovation activities/projects become the main facilitator for strategy changes, whereas service innovation becomes strategy-making as it leads to the creation of organizational strategies. These findings are illustrated in Figure 1.

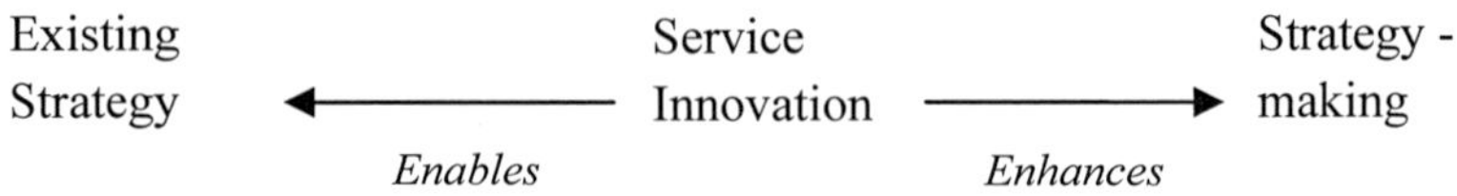

Figure 1. Relationships between strategy and innovation in financial scale-intensive service providers

6. Conclusion

This chapter focuses on strategies for service innovation and how service innovation is linked to strategy-making. Although the case service firms reported no formal innovation strategy, with their strategies emphasizing on cost reductions, segments and products, service innovation became part of realizing the business strategy. The new services launched in the market entailed important consequences for the firms. We find that strategy-making is enhanced through service innovation, making SAP an understandable framework for practitioners to use for strategizing. Our findings show that service innovation becomes strategy-making for the firm.

6.1. Managerial Implications

From our investigation on the link between strategy and innovation activities in services, managers may perceive how new business strategies emerge as outcomes of service innovation activities. The implication for managers is to understand that the relationship between service innovation and existing strategy (i.e. a way to realize it) is opposed to the relationship to strategy-making. Regardless of the aim of an innovation project in financial scale-intensive services, changes have broader game-changing effects on several dimensions of the firm's operations. For example, changes in ICT systems can produce changes in the service delivered to external clients, which, in turn, can have an impact on the internal organization, and change the opportunities to interact and share knowledge in the service production process and with the clients. These implications are important for managers to consider. The impact of service innovation on financial scale-intensive services is multifaceted in relation to strategy and to other dimensions, affecting clients.

6.2 Limitations and Future Research

A limitation of our study is that only a few very large financial service firms located in Scandinavia were investigated. Future research should empirically examine the four propositions offered in this chapter for smaller financial service firms in other parts of the world. Continued qualitative and quantitative empirical examinations, focusing on different types of financial service firms, will deepen the understanding of the relationship between strategy-making and innovation in this sector. Future studies should seek to establish more in-depth knowledge on how the learning outcome of the service innovation activities is fed back to and is integrated within the strategy process. Both positive and negative effects of innovation on strategy could be investigated. Based on our findings, it seems clear that innovation in financial services has an impact on strategy, but the effects on strategy need a more systematic focus. The effect of financial service innovation on internal organizational changes and external customer relations could also be further researched.

References

Bourdieu, Pierre. 1977. *Outline of a theory of practice*. Cambridge: Cambridge University Press.

—. 1990. *The logic of practice*. Stanford, CA: Stanford University Press.

Chia, Robert, and Robin Holt. 2006. "Strategy as practical coping: A Heideggerian perspective." *Organization Studies* no. 27 (5):635-655. doi: 10.1177/0170840606064102.

—. 2009. *Strategy without design: The silent efficacy of indirect action.* Cambridge: Cambridge University Press.

Chia, Robert, and Brad MacKay. 2007. "Post-processual challenges for the emerging strategy-as-practice perspective: Discovering strategy in the logic of practice." *Human Relations* no. 60 (1):217-242.

Chia, Robert, and Andreas Rasche. 2010. "Building and dwelling world-views—Two alternatives for researching strategy as practice." In *Cambridge handbook of strategy as practice*, edited by Damon Golsorkhi, Seidl. David, Linda Rouleau and Eero Vaara, 34–46. Cambridge: Cambridge University Press.

Cooper, R.G, S.J Edgett, and E.J Kleinschmidt. 2001. *Portfolio Management for New Products*. 2nd ed. New York:: Basic Books.

Cooper, R.G., S.J. Edgett, and E.J. Kleinschmidt. 2002. "Optimizing the stage-gate process: What best-practice companies doing." *Research Technology Management* no. 45:21-27.

De Jong, J.P., J.A Bruins, W. Dolfsma, and J. Meijgaard. 2003. Innovation in service firms explored: what, how and why? . Zoetermeer, Holland: EIM Business & Policy Research.
Dreyfus, Hubert L. 1991. *Being-in-the-world: A commentary on Heidegger's being and time, division I.* Cambridge, Mass.: MIT Press.
—. 2004. "Could anything be more Intelligible than Everyday Intelligibility? : Reinterpreting Division I of Being and Time in the light of Division II." *Bulletin of Science Technology Society* no. 24 (3):265-274.
Droege, Henning, Dagmar Hildebrand, and Miguel A. Heras Forcada. 2009. "Innovation in services: Present findings, and future pathways." *Journal of Service Management* no. 20 (2):131-155.
Easingwood, C.J. 1990. Service design and service strategies. Paper read at 1st International Research Seminar in Service Management, at Institute d'Administration des Enterprises, Aix-en-Provence, France.
Eisenhardt, Kathleen M., and Melissa E. Graebner. 2007. "Theory building from cases: Opportunities and challenges." *Academy of Management Journal* no. 50 (1):25-32. doi: 10.5465/amj.2007.24160888.
Feldman, Martha S. , and Wanda J. Orlikowski. 2011. "Theorizing practice and practicing theory." *Organization Science*:1-14.
Froehle, C.M, and A.V Roth. 2007. "A resource-process framework of new service development." *Production and Operations Management* no. 16 (2):169-188.
Heidegger, Martin. 1971. *Poetry, language, thought.* Translated by A. Hofstader. Vol. Harper and Row. New York.
Jarzabkowski, Paula. 2004. "Strategy as practice: Recursiveness, adaptation, and practices-in-use." *Organization Studies* no. 25 (4):529-560.
—. 2005. *Strategy as practice: An activity based approach.* London: Sage.
Jarzabkowski, Paula 2008. "Shaping strategy as a structuration process." *Academy of Management Journal* no. 51 (4):621-650.
Jarzabkowski, Paula, Julia Balogun, and David Seidl. 2007. "Strategizing: The challenges of a practice perspective." *Human Relations* no. 60 (1):5-27.
Jarzabkowski, Paula, and A. Paul Spee. 2009. "Strategy-as-practice: A review and future directions for the field." *International Journal of Management Reviews* no. 11 (1):69-95.
Johne, Axel, and Chris Storey. 1998. "New service development: a review of the literature and annotated bibliography." *European Journal of Marketing* no. 32 (3/4):184.

Johnson, Gerry, Ann L. M. Langley, and Richard Whittington. 2007. *Strategy as practice: Research directions and resources*. Cambridge, UK: Cambridge University Press.

Kahn, K.B, G Barczak, and R Moss. 2006. "Dialogue on best practices in new product development perspective: Establishing an NPD best practices framework." *Journal of Product Innovation Management* no. 23:106-116.

Kornberger, Martin, and Stewart Clegg. 2011. "Strategy as performative practice: The case of Sydney 2030." *Strategic Organization* no. 9 (2):136-162. doi: 10.1177/1476127011407758.

Lincoln, Yvonne S. , and Egon G. Guba. 1985. *Naturalistic inquiry*. Beverly Hills, CA: Sage.

Løwendahl, Bente R., Øivind Revang, and Siw M. Fosstenløkken. 2001. "Knowledge and value creation in professional service firms: A framework for analysis." *Human Relations* no. 54 (7):911-931.

Mantere, Saku. 2005. "Strategic practices as enablers and disablers of championing activity." *Strategic Organization* no. 3 (2):157-184. doi: 10.1177/1476127005052208.

—. 2008. "Role expectations and middle manager strategic agency." *Journal of Management Studies* no. 45 (2):294-316. doi: 10.1111/j.1467-6486.2007.00744.x.

Menor, L.J, and A.V Roth. 2007. "New service development in retail banking: construct development and measurement validation." *Journal of Operations Management* no. 25:825-846.

Mintzberg, Henry, and Alexandra McHugh. 1985. "Strategy Formation in an Adhocracy." *Administrative Science Quarterly* no. 30 (2):160-197.

O'Reilly, Charles A., and Michael Tushman. 2008. "Ambidexterity as a Dynamic Capability: Resolving the Innovator's Dilemma." *Research in Organizational Behavior* no. 28 (2):185-206.

Orlikowski, Wanda J. 2010. "Practice in research: phenomenon, perspective and philosophy " In *Cambridge handbook of strategy as practice*, edited by Damon Golsorkhi, Linda Rouleau, David Seidl and Eero Vaara, 23-33. Cambridge: Cambridge University Press.

Pavitt, Keith. 1984. "Sectoral patterns of technical change: Towards a taxonomy and a theory." *Research Policy* no. 13 (6):343-373.

PDMA. *NPDP Certification Study Guide* 2011. Available from http://www.pdma.org/p/cm/ld/fid=26.

Porter, M.E. 1985. *Competitive Advantage: Creating and sustaining superior performance*. New York: The Free Press.

Rasche, Andreas, and Chia Robert. 2009. "Researching Strategy Practices: A Genealogical Social Theory Perspective." *Organization Studies (01708406)* no. 30 (7):713-734.
Schatzki, Theodore, Karin D. Knorr Cetina, and Eike von Savigny. 2001. *The practice turn in contemporary theory*. London: Routledge.
Schatzki, Theodore R. 2012. "A primer on practices: Theory and research." In *Practice-Based Education: Perspectives and Strategies*, edited by Joy Higgs, Ron Barnett, Stephen Billett, Maggie Hutchings and Franziska Trede. Rotterdam: Sense Publishers.
Teece, D.J, G Pisano, and A Shuen. 1997. "Dynamic capabilities and strategic management." *Strategic Management Journal* no. 18 (7):509-533.
Tsoukas, Haridimos. 2010. "Practice, strategy making and intentionality: A Heideggerian onto-epistemology for strategy-as-practice." In *The Cambridge Handbook of Strategy as Practice*, edited by Damon Golsorkhi, Linda Rouleau, David Seidl and Eero Vaara, 47-62. Cambridge: Cambridge University Press.
Vaara, Eero, and Richard Whittington. 2012. "Strategy-as-practice: Taking social practices seriously." *The Academy of Management Annals*. doi: 10.1080/19416520.2012.672039.
Whittington, Richard. 2006a. "Completing the practice turn in strategy research." *Organization Studies* no. 27 (5):613-634. doi: 10.1177/0170840606064101.
—. 2006b. "Learning more from failure: Practice and process." *Organization Studies* no. 27 (12):1903-1906. doi: 10.1177/0170840606071945.
—. 2007. "Strategy practice and strategy process: Family differences and the sociological eye." *Organization Studies* no. 28:1575-1586.
Wittgenstein, Ludwig. 2009. *Philosophical investigations*. Translated by G. E. M. Anscombe, P. M. S. Hacker and Joachim Schulte. Revised fourth edition ed: Wiley-Blackwell. Original edition, 1953.
Zeithaml, Valarie A, A Parasuraman, and Leonard L Berry. 1985. "Problems and Strategies in Services Marketing " *Journal of Marketing* no. 48 (2):33-46.

CHAPTER ELEVEN

ADVANTAGES AND DISADVANTAGES OF OPEN INNOVATION: EVIDENCE FROM FINANCIAL SERVICES[1]

ANDREY MARTOVOY

1. Introduction

Over the last decade, open innovation, as a conceptual and practical approach to the development of new and improvement of existing products (goods and services) or processes, has attracted considerable attention by both practitioners and scholars. In simple words, it refers to the ability of the firm to capture tangible and intangible benefits by sourcing knowledge from the external environment and/or by exploiting the knowledge developed internally outside the organisational boundaries.

Financial services, being a considerable sector of the economy (5.9% of the gross value added in 2010; Eurostat, 2011), have been traditionally attributed with conservatism with refer to innovation. However, over the last several decades, market deregulation and international economic integration in Europe and North America forced financial institutions to reconsider the way they do business in a response to increased competition. A review of the existing literature has shown the importance of open innovation in the banking sector (Auh et al., 2007; Fasnacht, 2009; Oliveira and von Hippel, 2011). Innovation in financial services takes various forms and shapes; however, it is increasingly being driven by automation and thus information and communication technologies play an accrued role into shaping financial innovations (Barras, 1986, 1990;

[1] This chapter is a revised and expanded version of a paper entitled 'Open innovation in banking services: advantages and disadvantages' (Martovoy et al., 2012) presented at the XXIII ISPIM Conference Action for Innovation: Innovating from Experience, Spain, 17-20 June, 2012.

Pennings and Harianto, 1992; Uchupalanan, 2000). Meanwhile, decision of a financial institution and its partner to cooperate with each other in the open innovation framework is based on anticipation and evaluation of the expected benefits and costs of the joint innovation effort. Not much is known about perceived advantages and disadvantages of open innovation in general and within financial services in particular. Understanding these issues is important for all parties involved in the cooperation, because this will have an eventual positive or negative impact on their commercial outcomes. As compared to advantages of open innovation, disadvantages are significantly less explored in the extant literature. This constitutes a novel frontier in the open innovation research domain (Dahlander and Gann, 2010; Huizingh, 2010; West and Gallagher, 2006). Our exploratory chapter addresses this gap precisely by developing a conceptual approach and shedding light on both advantages and disadvantages of open innovation drawing upon the qualitative data from joint innovation projects between financial institutions and ICT providers.

Based on a thorough literature review, we have developed a conceptual approach to classify modes of knowledge flows, taking into account involved parties, direction of knowledge flow, its mode and degree of formalisation. It helped us provide a logical overview of the complex nature of open innovation. Analysis of existing studies allowed us to develop a classification of advantages and disadvantages of inbound and outbound open innovation following the pecuniary and non-pecuniary logic coined by Dahlander and Gann (2010).

The conducted literature review revealed a lack of research on open innovation in financial services, especially in the case of financial institutions cooperating with IT firms to develop new products or processes. Similar to the extant studies, our research findings suggest that both banks and IT companies can benefit from the cooperation because of the following reasons: leveraging complementarities, cost reduction, time-to-market, gaining stronger credibility and access to partners' networks. Besides, we have found two novel arguments for this: (1) improvement of performance and flexibility of backstage operations and (2) diversity among the involved innovation partners.

Apart from this, bureaucracy, costs associated with cooperation, risk of selecting partners who do not meet expectations and/or deadlines, and conflict in objectives alignment among the partners, refer to the encountered disadvantages of cooperation between banks and IT firms. An additional argument about the risk of imbalance of bargaining power due to different stock of resources and competences possessed by partners seems to be novel as compared to the existing studies.

Our chapter is structured in the following way: theoretical underpinnings of the research questions are given in section 2. Methods of data collection are explained in section 3. Research findings and discussion are given in section 4, while the conclusions are summed up in section 5.

2. Literature Review

In this section we review the concept of open innovation (sub-section 2.1) as well as the advantages and disadvantages of this approach (2.2). Each sub-section is followed by the review of literature on how these topics have been tackled by scholars in the context of financial services.

2.1 Open Innovation

2.1.1 Concept of Open Innovation

Open innovation is a concept that nowadays has become increasingly popular among both scholars and practitioners. Extant literature suggests that its core idea is not really novel (Huizingh, 2011; Linstone, 2010) and rooted into the several preceding notions such as "not-invented-here" syndrome (Katz and Allen, 1982); complementary assets (Teece, 1986); lead users (von Hippel, 1986); absorptive capacity (Cohen and Levinthal, 1990); exploitation and exploration (March, 1991); "buy-in" syndrome (Boyens, 1998 as cited by Lichtenthaler and Ernst, 2006); and innovation with customers (co-creation) (Prahalad and Ramaswamy, 2004; Vargo and Lusch, 2004). Nevertheless, the open innovation concept provides a fresh insight into the multifaceted nature of innovation practices and integrates all formerly independent streams of research into a comprehensive conceptual framework.

Open innovation stands for "the use of purposive inflows and outflows of knowledge to accelerate internal innovation and to expand the markets for external use of innovation, respectively" (Chesbrough, Vanhaverbeke and West, 2006, p. 1). As seen from this definition, open innovation can be inbound when external knowledge is used internally and outbound when the knowledge originally developed within organisational boundaries is exploited externally. A firm can practise either one of the approaches or the both ones in parallel. The latter case is denoted by the "coupled" open innovation process (Gassmann and Enkel, 2004). Another notable aspect, of the definition of open innovation, concerns the purposive nature of knowledge flows. It leads to the argument that, for instance, an *unintentional* outflow of knowledge, as in the case of "knowledge spillover" (Arrow, 1962; Marshall, 1890; Romer, 1986), is not considered open innovation *per se*. Depending on the logic of exchange (pecuniary or non-pecuniary), the inbound innovation can take two forms, namely, "acquiring" or "sourcing", while the outbound innovation can be categorised into the "selling" or "revealing", respectively (Dahlander and Gann, 2010).

2.1.2 Open Innovation: Knowledge Flow Attributes

Taking into account the fact that open innovation is about inter-organisational purposive knowledge flows, the following main attributes can be considered for further analysis: (1) parties (between which knowledge is transferred), (2) direction (where knowledge is transferred to), (3) mode (through which means/channels knowledge is transferred), and (4) degree of formalisation of knowledge flow (Fig. 1).

The chart suggests that at least two parties are involved in a knowledge flow: an innovating firm (given on the left side) and external entity (on the right side). The latter may encompass various actors such as other entities belonging to an enterprise's group, customers, suppliers, competitors, government or public authorities, and so on (Fig. 1). In the case of financial services, a central/national bank can also be an example. As can be seen from the list on the right side of Fig. 1, an external actor can be a legal entity or an individual.

From an innovating firm's point of view, the direction of knowledge flow can be inbound and outbound (marked with respective arrows on the top of Fig. 1). The chart does not restrict from describing an innovating firm that uses both of these approaches in parallel (coupled open innovation).

Various modes of knowledge flow are available to an innovating firm (Fig. 1). Some of them can be predominately inbound (e.g. dedicated market research), outbound (e.g. spin-outs), or both inbound and outbound (e.g. transfer of rights to use intellectual property in a form of licensing-in and licensing-out). Such modes as events, publications in academic journals and professional magazines, specialised databases, other informational products and informal personal interactions can be used by an innovating firm in both directions: to source knowledge needed for innovation (i.e. screening of external business environment, collection of secondary information) or to make knowledge available to other actors.

The presence of a merger as a mode of knowledge flow is conditional; however, it is based upon the assumption that, at least, at the beginning of the fusion process two independent entities exist with their respective knowledge stocks enabling *inter-organisational* flows.

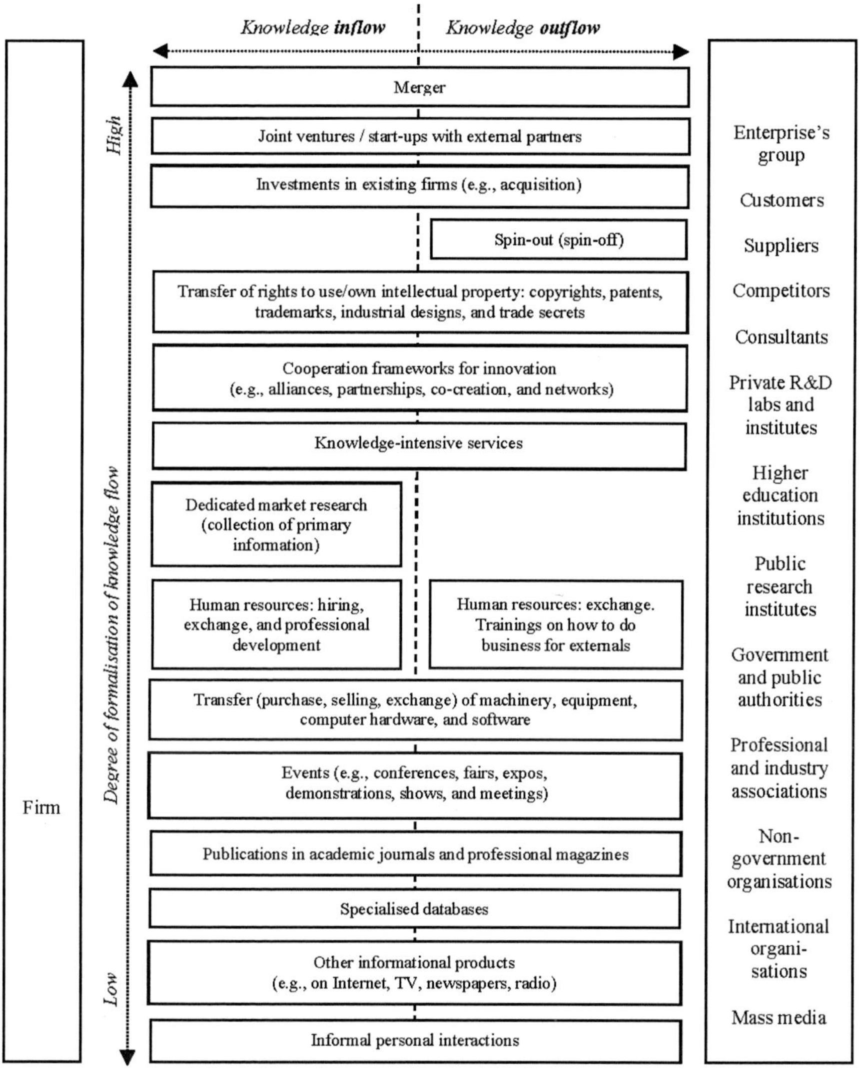

Figure 1. Knowledge flows: involved parties, direction, modes, and the degree of formalisation.

Source: Developed by authors based on the following studies: Bianchi et al. (2011); Chesbrough, Vanhaverbeke and West (2006); Cohen, Nelson and Walsh (2002); Eurostat (2012); Perkmann and Walsh (2007); Schartinger et al. (2002); van de Vrande et al. (2009).

The modes can be ranged, yet arbitrarily, according to the degree of formalisation. Higher degree of complexity of knowledge flow requires higher degree of formalisation and coordination of its process, and vice versa. Such modes are given at the top of Fig. 1, while less formalised ones are presented at the bottom.

Following this logic, an acquisition of a firm, with an aim to access its knowledge base, can be considered a more formalised mode of knowledge inflow that requires a relatively higher degree of coordination than, for instance, access to a database in order to collect secondary information about a market. Higher degree of complexity, formalisation and coordination, entails higher costs associated with a knowledge flow. Usually, usage of more formalised modes (e.g. joint ventures/start-ups with external partners, investments in existing firms, and spin-out) is not limited solely by the knowledge management logic (Stewart and Ruckdeschel, 1998). Innovating firms may resort to them because of other strategic goals, such as access to market, control over suppliers, and so on. Meanwhile, in the cases where the primary purpose of the modes is represented by the knowledge-flow rationale, we denote them by the *modes of knowledge flow*.

2.1.3 Open Innovation in Financial Services

Open innovation in financial services has been recently addressed in a few studies. However, earlier references to the importance of external and internal sources of innovation in this sector can be found in the marketing related literature on new service development as well as in several dedicated studies.

Extant literature suggests that financial institutions resort to different modes of knowledge inflow to develop new or improve existing financial offerings: thorough market research and screening of external environment (Edgett, 1994; Edgett and Jones, 1991; Edgett and Parkinson, 1994; Scheuing and Johnson, 1989); listening to and engaging customers (Athanassopoulou and Johne, 2004; Cooper and Edgett, 1996; Martovoy and Dos Santos, 2012; Storey and Easingwood, 1993; Oliveira and von Hippel, 2011); involvement of employees (Lievens and Moenaert, 2001; Thomke, 2003; Vermeulen, 2004); cooperation with suppliers (Pennings and Harianto, 1992), consultants (Vence and Trigo, 2009), competitors (Fasnacht, 2009) and other entities belonging to a bank's group (Vence and Trigo, 2009).

In the existing literature, product innovation in financial services is usually attributed with the dependency on external sources of knowledge. In this vein, Barras (1986, 1990) refers to the so called "reverse cycle of service innovation". To him, taking an example of the banking sector, a service life-cycle depends on the consequent stages of adoption of information and communication technologies (ICT): (1) incremental process innovation, followed by (2) radical process innovation and (3) product innovation. This means that financial institutions tend to be adopters of technologies developed in other sectors (i.e., knowledge inflow), particularly in the ICT sector. Empirical findings of another study, reaching 152 banks located in the United States, showed that accumulation of experience in information technology and networking within banking sector and across sectors (i.e. hardware and software suppliers) favours adoption of video-banking services (Pennings and Harianto, 1992). Recent cross-country empirical study has revealed that over the period 2006-2008, innovation activity and technological and non-technological innovation in financial services seem to be both positively correlated with the number of mobile cellular subscribers (Mention, Martovoy and Torkkeli, 2014, forthcoming).

Besides the importance of knowledge inflow, a few empirical studies suggest that financial institutions can benefit from knowledge outflow in a form of licensing-out. Recently, in some jurisdictions (e.g. U.S.A.), financial institutions have been given with a non-conventional tool for the sector to control knowledge transfer, namely, protection of intellectual property. Scholars argue that financial innovations are quickly imitated; however, original innovators do benefit from larger market shares (Tufano, 1989). Findings of another empirical study, drawing upon 29-year dataset (years 1971-2000) from the U.S. Patent and Trademark Office, suggest that the number of patent filings and awards for financial formulas and methods has been growing (Lerner, 2002). This means that more room for licensing and litigation strategies can be expected and even witnessed in financial services, especially in the U.S. markets (Lerner, 2008). Meanwhile, the history of the sector development preceding the financial crisis of the year 2008, suggests that market players have enough stimuli to be innovative even without patent protection (Miller, 1986). Hence, introduction of patenting can be a weak trigger of financial innovation, yet imposing higher costs on society in terms of litigations and market distortions due to monopoly power (Lerner, 2002).

Existing studies show that, contrary to the traditional wisdom, financial institutions may sometimes engage into the outbound open innovation practices. To that respect, Drew (1995) refers to the case of a U.S. bank that developed specialised software, deployed it successfully in-house and succeeded into gaining additional benefits by licencing it out to other foreign banks, afterwards.

2.2 Advantages and Disadvantages of Open Innovation

As any other activity or strategic approach, open innovation has its benefits and costs, which can be pecuniary and non-pecuniary, immediate or long-term, tactical or strategic (Dahlander and Gann, 2010; Huizingh, 2011). In the scholarly literature, advantages and disadvantages[2] of open innovation are approached from several perspectives: transaction-cost theory (e.g., Coase, 1937; Williamson, 1987), resource-based view (e.g., Barney, 1991; Penrose, 1959; Wernerfelt, 1984) and knowledge-based theory (e.g., Grant, 1996; Nonaka, 1994). In this section we provide an overview of studies, which addressed costs and benefits of both inbound and outbound open innovation. In doing this, we adopt the approach based on the delineation between pecuniary and non-pecuniary advantages and disadvantages of open innovation (Dahlander and Gann, 2010). Pecuniary logic refers to direct monetary benefits or losses, while non-pecuniary logic stands for indirect monetary benefits or losses. Due to the multi-faceted nature of non-pecuniary advantages and disadvantages of open innovation, we grouped them into several distinct categories based on a criterion of what area of firm's operations is a primary bearer of benefits or losses (refer to Table 1 in section 4).

2.2.1 Advantages of Inbound Open Innovation

Advantages of knowledge inflow appear to be among the most explored aspects in the literature on open innovation. Earlier references to the importance of knowledge available outside organisational boundaries can be traced in the studies on inter-organisational cooperation and strategic alliances. Overall, scholars refer to the following pecuniary advantages of inbound open innovation: decreasing of costs, improvement of margins (e.g., Baum and Oliver, 1991; Chesbrough and Crowther, 2006) and attaining profitable growth (e.g., Chesbrough and Crowther, 2006).

Extant literature suggests that non-pecuniary advantages of inbound open innovation can influence the following areas: innovation output, process of production/service delivery, risk and process; markets; competition; resources; employees; management; organisational resilience and culture (refer to Table 1). In this vein, scholars argue that inbound open innovation can be beneficial as it may lead to improvements of innovation quality (Rigby and Zook, 2002) and to finding a radically new

---

[2] Hereinafter within this chapter we make no difference between benefits and advantages, as well as between costs and disadvantages, unless stated specifically.

approach to solve customer problems (Lakhani et al., 2006), what we refer here to as innovation output. Besides, being open to external knowledge can positively influence the development of new technologies (Harianto and Pennings, 1990) that will improve process of production and/or service delivery. Some scholars point out that inbound open innovation can be useful to diversify risk of innovation and to share it with external partners (Hoffman and Schlosser, 2001). It seems that inflow of knowledge can also lead to improvement of firm's innovation pipeline: shortening time-to-market (Rigby and Zook, 2002), improvement of the innovation process *per se* (van de Vrande et al., 2009) and accelerating internal innovation Chesbrough, Vanhaverbeke and West, 2006). Besides, advocates of the inbound open innovation highlight that it can influence market position of a firm by market expansion (e.g., Chesbrough, Vanhaverbeke and West, 2006; Hoffman and Schlosser, 2001) or by keeping up with current market developments and customers (van de Vrande et al., 2009). Competitive position is another reason of why firms engage in inbound open innovation: to follow competitors (Garcia-Pont and Nohria, 2002) or to monitor potentially disruptive technologies capable of threatening incumbent firms (Chesbrough and Crowther, 2006).

Another approach, that explains benefits of the inflow of knowledge, refers to the resource-based view (Penrose, 1959; Wernerfelt, 1984), namely, management of dependence on other firms (Pfeffer and Salancik, 1978); access to external ideas, knowledge, expertise and technologies (e.g., Hoffman and Schlosser, 2001; Laursen and Salter, 2006b); leveraging complementarities (Cassiman and Veugelers 2006; Dyer and Singh, 1998; van de Vrande et al., 2009) and accessing partners' networks (Mention and Asikainen, 2012). Finally, firm's employees, management, organisational resilience and culture, can indirectly benefit from inbound open innovation through the following: learning new skills (Baum, Calabrese and Silverman, 2000); flexibility and redistribution of tasks (Mention and Asikainen, 2012), bouncing back from environmental shocks (Miner, Amburgey and Stearns, 1990) and surmounting internal rigidities caused by impediments to innovation (Keupp and Gassmann, 2009).

2.2.2. Disadvantages of Inbound Open Innovation

Following a similar approach, as taken above, disadvantages of inbound open innovation can be either pecuniary or non-pecuniary.

Extant literature suggests that the pecuniary logic is explained by the transaction costs theory (Coase, 1937; Williamson, 1985), meaning that an inflow of external knowledge, for instance, through the modes attributed with a higher degree of formalisation (Fig. 1), may lead to higher transactions costs (e.g., Keupp and Gassmann, 2009; Rotering, 1990 as cited by Brockhoff, 1992; van de Vrande et al., 2009).

Apart from the pecuniary perspective, the following aspects of firm's operations may be negatively affected by the inbound open innovation: innovation output, intellectual property management, competitive position, resources and competences, innovation process, governance of cooperation, and organisational culture (Table 1). Bátiz-Lazo and Woldesenbet (2006) argue that cooperation with external partners may undermine commercial potential of existing products. Within the intellectual property management issues, scholars argue that the inbound open innovation may lead to secrecy concerns (e.g. Rotering, 1990; Thomas and Trevino, 1993) and problems in division of outcomes of cooperation (Keupp and Gassmann, 2009; Rotering, 1990). Dahlander and Gann (2010) point out that an emphasis on the inflow of knowledge may weaken an innovating firm as there is a risk of outsourcing critical dimensions of business that can result in the deterioration of a firm's competitive position. One of the earlier studies on inter-organisational cooperation suggests that a firm relying on external sources may undermine internal resources and competences by developing dependency on partners, loosing technological competence, e.g. by substituting internal R&D (Pisano, 1990) and slowing down self-development of innovation (Rotering, 1990 as cited by Brockhoff, 1992). Other scholars refer to the issues in innovation process, namely, to the fact that dealing with many sources and ideas at any given moment of time can lead to the attention allocation problem (Laursen and Salter, 2006b; Ocasio, 1997) or to the difficulty in choosing and combining between numerous alternatives (Laursen and Salter, 2006b; Sapienza, Parhankangas and Autio, 2004). In the cases where an inflow of knowledge is achieved by means of inter-firm cooperation, its governance may be another issue: risk of poor governance of joint learning processes (Larsson et al., 1998); difficulties in keeping many partnerships with various actors (Ahuja, 2000); risk of selecting wrong partners (van de Vrande et al., 2009); difficulty in balancing innovation with daily tasks, communication, aligning of partners (van de Vrande et al., 2009); and bureaucracy and conflicting rules (van de Vrande et al., 2009). Finally, adoption of inbound open innovation can be difficult due to the several issues rooted into organisational culture of an innovating firm: "not invented here" syndrome (Katz and Allen, 1982); problem in maintaining internal commitment over a period of time (Chesbrough and Crowther, 2006); organisational resistance and fear of losing control over proprietary technologies (Keupp and Gassmann, 2009) and trust issues (Salampasis et al., 2014).

2.2.3 Advantages of Outbound Open Innovation

Being in line with the pointed out approach, we delineate between pecuniary and non-pecuniary advantages of outbound open innovation. Advocates of the knowledge outflow argue that an innovating firm can directly (on a monetary basis) benefit from it because of the following reasons: generation of revenues from out-licensing (e.g. Rigby and Zook, 2002), infringements (Koruna, 2001), selling products and/or services in addition to licensed technology (Lichtenthaler, 2007); lowering transaction costs of future technology transfers (Chesbrough and Schwartz, 2007); reduction of costs and improvement of efficiency (Nidumolu, Coimbatore and Rangaswami, 2009; van de Vrande et al., 2009) and increasing growth (van de Vrande et al., 2009).

The review of the extant literature allowed the grouping of non-pecuniary advantages of open innovation into the following categories: innovation output, innovation process, markets, competitive position, resource management, external environment, employees and reputation (Table 1). Scholars argue that purposive outflows of knowledge can be useful for innovation output: to measure real value of invention (Rigby and Zook, 2002) and to benefit from incremental innovations thanks to ideas coming from licensees (Lichtenthaler, 2007; Murray and O'Mahony, 2007). Moreover, outbound open innovation seems to improve innovation processes (van de Vrande et al., 2009) because of the following: shortened firm's learning curve (Koruna, 2001; Lichtenthaler, 2007); flexibility to innovate and manufacture or "freedom to operate" (Grindley and Teece, 1997) by avoiding potential patent infringement through cross-licenses (Koruna, 2001); and acceleration of internal innovation (Chesbrough, Vanhaverbeke and West, 2006) and building dynamic capabilities for open innovation through learning from knowledge transfer (Kutvonen et al., 2010; Lichtenthaler, 2011). Besides, several scholars argue that the purposive outflow of knowledge can influence firm's market position: expansion of markets both in terms of geography and product markets (e.g. Chesbrough, Vanhaverbeke and West, 2006; Koruna, 2001; Lichtenthaler, 2007); reaching network externality (Koruna, 2001); setting industry standards (Conner, 1995; Ehrhardt, 2004; Lichtenthaler, 2007); and keeping up with current market developments and customers (van de Vrande et al., 2009), even on markets where the company is not yet active, by using outbound open innovation to set up listening posts (Kutvonen, 2011). Similar to this, arguments supporting outbound innovation appear to be linked to firm's competitive position: clarification of core business of a firm (Rigby and Zook, 2002), securing technological leadership by focusing on solely a firm's core competences (Lichtenthaler, 2007) or relying on technological and outbound open innovation proficiency as the primary business model, i.e., becoming an "aggressive open innovator" (Kutvonen, 2011). Advocates of the resource-based view argue that firms can benefit from outbound open innovation because of the following: external partners may have more relevant resources to commercialise invention (Chesbrough and Rosenbloom, 2002); usage of out-licencing as a tool to access technology of external partners (Koruna, 2001; Lichtenthaler, 2007); entry into technological markets and networks where technology trading is more efficient and frequent (Bidault and Fischer, 1994); allocation of resources and support (Henkel, 2006) and additional flexibility allowing heightened control over technological path dependency (Kutvonen, 2011). Outflow of knowledge can positively influence links with external business environment by achieving legitimacy from external environment (Nuvolari, 2004), strengthening inter-organisational network (Lichtenthaler, 2007) and creating supportive market ecosystems (Kutvonen, 2011). Practising the outbound open innovation may improve human resources management at an innovating firm by the optimal usage of employees' knowledge and expertise (van de Vrande et al., 2009) and strengthening their commitment (Rigby and Zook, 2002). Finally, reliance on knowledge outflow may enhance firm's reputation by licencing out to well-known firms (Lichtenthaler, 2007).

2.2.4. Disadvantages of Outbound Open Innovation

Those scholars who warn firms to adopt outbound open innovation practices with caution base their arguments on the following pecuniary rationale: transaction costs (van de Vrande et al., 2009); licensees can commercially outperform the original innovation developer (Rigby and Zook, 2002) and difficulties to capture benefits in the case revealed knowledge (Dahlander and Gann, 2010).

Apart from this, extant literature suggests that the purposeful outflow of knowledge can be indirectly (non-pecuniary) harmful for an innovating firm due to the negative impact on the following areas: markets, competitive position, employees, governance of cooperation and organisational culture. In the first instance, scholars argue that outbound open innovation can be problematic due to the specific nature of innovation, tailored for a limited number of customers who may not represent the whole market (van de Vrande et al., 2009). Besides, it can deteriorate current customer base (Huizingh, 2011). Outflows of knowledge, in a form of revealing, can be detrimental to the firm's competitive position as there can be a risk of leaking internal resources to competitors (Laursen and Salter, 2006a). Moreover, employees may lack commitment and need knowledge to exploit knowledge externally (van de Vrande et al., 2009), for instance, in a case of a spin-out established by an innovating firm. Finally, outbound open innovation may trigger issues related to balancing innovation with daily tasks, conflicting rules within inter-organisational cooperation (van de Vrande et al., 2009), uncovering the "only-used-here" syndrome (Boyens, 1998 as cited by Lichtenthaler and Ernst, 2006) or related to the trust issues (Salampasis et al., 2014).

2.2.5 Advantages and Disadvantages of Open Innovation in Financial Services

To the best of our knowledge, benefits and costs of open innovation in financial services have been discussed only in a few studies.

Drawing upon a qualitative study and not being focused on open innovation *per se*, Vermeulen (2004) highlights four main barriers to product innovation at banks and insurance companies: (1.) considerable degree of functional departmentalisation results in tensions between departments, conflicts with daily activities and over resources; (2.) limited adoption of new service development tools such as project-based approach and product champions; (3.) conservative organisational culture residing mainly in the "traditional" rather than marketing departments that a favours risk avoiding behaviour and (4.) constraining information technology being apparent in the shortage of informational technology (IT) personnel, problems in administrative systems integration and complexity of information systems.

Advantages and challenges of "open architecture" in financial services have been pointed out by Fasnacht (2009) in the context of banks selling third party products. For him, benefits of such an "open architecture" include: possibility to run business offshore; increase of revenues and value of different stakeholders; reduction of risks; facilitation of growth strategy and acceleration of economies of scale. However, the following aspects can be considered as the disadvantages of this approach: loosing strategic flexibility when external collaboration is overemphasised; undermining market potential of proprietary products due to the presence of external products in a bundle and data protection (i.e. client data available to third-party distribution channel might be used for their internal marketing purposes).

Overall, the conducted literature review has revealed a wealth of studies on the advantages and disadvantages of open innovation; however, they have been mainly addressed in the context of the manufacturing sector (specifically, high-tech). Meanwhile, little is known about the extent to which these findings can be applicable to financial services characterised with such distinctive features as higher degree of regulation and difficulty with the appropriability of innovation outcomes (Mention and Torkkeli, 2012). Since the literature review has shown that financial institutions in their innovation activity tend to rely on external sources of knowledge, especially of technological nature (i.e. inbound, rather than outbound open innovation), the main research question of this study is the following: what are the advantages and disadvantages of open innovation in financial services in the case of cooperation between financial institutions and IT providers?

3. Research Context and Design

Taking into account the explorative nature of the formulated research question, we opted to collect empirical data through semi-structured face-to-face interviews. We pre-defined and selected cases of cooperation between financial institutions (mainly banks) and IT companies involved in the joint development of new and/or improvement of existing services. We asked interviewees to select any case of cooperation they had over the last three years for further discussion. We aimed at exploring both advantages and disadvantages faced by financial institutions and IT companies in cooperation with each other. Questions for each interview were open-ended and addressed both perspectives of the dyadic cooperation between IT firms (supplier of technologies) and retail banking institutions (qualified as primary users and diffusion vectors of these technologies to end users):

1. Could you briefly describe the major idea of the product/process your organisation develops in cooperation with external partners?
2. What are the partners with whom your company cooperates to develop product/process?
3. On what stage is this project at the moment?
4. In overall, do you consider this cooperation successful or not?
5. Who initiated this cooperation: your company or partners? In case your company initiated this cooperation, why did it decide to cooperate with external partners? Please, give main reasons.

6. What are the benefits (advantages) for your company to cooperate with external partners to develop new product/process?
7. What are the costs, problems or disadvantages your company encounters in the cooperation with external partners to develop new product/process?

The cases have been drawn from the publicly available information on the Internet and from the Accenture BeLux Financial Services Innovation Awards nominee list (Accenture BeLux, 2011). Presence of Luxembourg is justified by the role the financial sector plays in its economy. In 2010 the entire financial sector in Luxembourg accounted for 38% GDP with the major contribution coming from banking services - 19% GDP (Luxembourg for Finance, 2012). According to the recent Global Financial Centres Index, Luxembourg has been ranked 18th in the World (year 2013), improving its position from 24th rank in year 2012 (Z/Yen Group, 2013). Within Europe, it occupies the 5th rank after London, Zurich, Geneva, and Frankfurt.

Seven in-depth interviews have been conducted to collect data on cooperation between suppliers (IT companies) and banks in Luxembourg. These examples of cooperation include the development of new services focused on innovative mobile and Internet-based payment solutions, as well as interactive media tools and have currently reached a stage where new offerings are close to market entry or have recently entered the market. Interviewees have been represented by chief executive officers, their deputies, and managers responsible for the development of new services.

After the establishment of the initial contact by phone or email the interviews were conducted at the Public Research Centre Henri Tudor (Luxembourg) or at the interviewees' respective organisations. Each interview lasted about one hour; it was recorded and transcribed afterwards. Data collection was carried out between February and April in 2012.

4. Findings and Discussion

Taking into account the dichotomic approach to open innovation, the findings of our study are presented in line with both advantages (sub-section 4.1) and disadvantages (sub-section 4.2) of open innovation in banking services in cases when banks and IT companies cooperate with each other to develop new services (Table 1).

4.1 Advantages of Open Innovation in Financial Services

In-depth interviews showed that financial institutions resort to cooperation with IT companies because of several reasons.

First, they may lack necessary expertise and consider partnering with IT suppliers as a means of leveraging complementarities. One interviewee from a novel payment solution provider pointed out that they selected only those partners who could contribute to the overall strength and scale of the solution. These findings seem to be in line with the one of the conventional schools of thought, namely, the resource-based theory (Barney, 1991; Penrose, 1959; Wernerfelt, 1984), highlighting the importance of access to unique resources in order to leverage internal innovation.

Second, one of our interviewees explicitly stated that the cost reduction was the ultimate goal for cooperation with the IT provider so as to develop new a financial service solution. This cost-driven logic influences tactical and strategic decisions of many organisations, including financial institutions, especially nowadays amid the economic recession in the European Union. Obviously, we have not been surprised to encounter these findings as it was largely discussed in the extant literature (e.g., Baum and Oliver, 1991; Chesbrough and Crowther, 2006; Hoffman and Schlosser, 2001; Mention and Asikainen, 2012; Rigby and Zook, 2002; van de Vrande et al., 2009). Another interviewee pointed out that their IT firm developed a cooperation framework with banks in which the latter could benefit from lower prices in exchange of the banks' contribution (in monetary and non-monetary terms) to the development of IT solution for financial operations.

Table 1. Advantages and disadvantages of the inbound and outbound open innovation*

Inbound open innovation		Outbound open innovation	
Advantages	**Disadvantages**	**Advantages**	**Disadvantages**
Pecuniary	**Pecuniary**	**Pecuniary**	**Pecuniary**
– Decreasing of costs, improvement of margins (Baum and Oliver, 1991; Chesbrough and Crowther, 2006; Hoffman and Schlosser, 2001; Mention and Asikainen, 2012; Rigby and Zook, 2002; van de Vrande et al., 2009)* – Profitable growth (Chesbrough and Crowther, 2006; van de Vrande et al., 2009)	– Transaction costs (Keupp and Gassmann, 2009; Mention and Asikainen, 2012; Rotering, 1990, as cited by Brockhoff, 1992; van de Vrande et al., 2009)*	– Generate revenues from out-licensing (Dahlander and Gann, 2010; Koruna, 2001; Lichtenthaler, 2007; Rigby and Zook, 2002) – Generate revenues from infringements (Koruna, 2001) – Generate revenues from selling products and/or services in addition to licensed technology (Lichtenthaler, 2007) – Lowering transaction costs of future technology transfers (Chesbrough and Schwartz, 2007) – Reduction of costs and improvement of efficiency (van de Vrande et al., 2009); also by licencing-out to increase competition among suppliers (Nidumolu, Coimbatore and Rangaswami, 2009) – Increase of growth (van de Vrande et al., 2009)	– Transaction costs (van de Vrande et al., 2009) – Licensees can commercially outperform the original innovation developer (Rigby and Zook, 2002) – In the case of revealing: difficulty to capture benefits (Dahlander and Gann, 2010)

		–	
Non-pecuniary *Innovation output* – Improvement of quality of products and services (Rigby and Zook, 2002) – Finding radically new approach to solve a problem (Lakhani et al., 2006) *Process of production / service delivery* – Development of new technologies (Harianto and Pennings, 1990) – Improvement of performance and flexibility of backstage operations* (this study) *Innovation risk* – Innovation risk diversification (Hoffman and Schlosser, 2001; Mention and Asikainen, 2012) *Innovation process*	**Non-pecuniary** *Innovation output* – "Cannibalisation" of existing products (Bátiz-Lazo and Woldesenbet, 2006) *Intellectual property management* – Secrecy concerns, protection of intellectual assets (Mention and Asikainen, 2012; Rotering, 1990, as cited by Brockhoff, 1992; Thomas and Trevino, 1993) – Issues in division of contributions and outcomes of cooperation (Keupp and Gassmann, 2009; Rotering, 1990, as cited by Brockhoff, 1992) *Competitive position* – Risk of outsourcing critical dimension of	**Non-pecuniary** *Innovation output* – Tool to measure real value of invention (Rigby and Zook, 2002) – Incremental innovations thanks to ideas coming from licensees (Lichtenthaler, 2007; Murray and O'Mahony, 2007) *Innovation process* – Shortening of firm's learning curve because of improvement (Koruna, 2001; Lichtenthaler, 2007) – Flexibility to innovate and manufacture by avoiding potential patent infringement through cross-licenses (Grindley and Teece, 1997; Koruna, 2001) – Accelerating internal innovation (Chesbrough, Vanhaverbeke and West, 2006). – Improvement of innovation process (van de Vrande et al., 2009) – Building dynamic capabilities for open innovation (Kutvonen, Torkkeli and Lin, 2010;	**Non-pecuniary** *Markets* – Customer demand is too specific and innovation does not match needs of a whole market (van de Vrande et al., 2009) – Can deteriorate current customer base, hence short term gains can be followed by long term losses (Huizingh, 2011). *Competitive position* – Risk of leaking internal resources to competitors in case of revealing (Laursen and Salter, 2006a) *Employees* – Employees may lack commitment (van de Vrande et al., 2009) – Employees may lack knowledge and

– Shortening time-to-market (Rigby and Zook, 2002)* – Accelerating internal innovation (Chesbrough, Vanhaverbeke and West, 2006). – Improvement of innovation process (van de Vrande et al., 2009) – Reasonable degree of diversity among the involved innovation partners can be beneficial for innovation process and its output* (this study) *Markets* – Expanding markets (Chesbrough, Vanhaverbeke and West, 2006; Hoffman and Schlosser, 2001; Mention and Asikainen, 2012; van de Vrande et al., 2009) – Keep up with current market developments and customers (van de Vrande et al., 2009)	business (Dahlander and Gann, 2010) *Resources and competences* – Development of dependency on partners (Rotering, 1990, as cited by Brockhoff, 1992) – Loss of own technological competence (Pisano, 1990; Rotering, 1990, as cited by Brockhoff, 1992) – Slowdown of self-development of innovation (Rotering, 1990, as cited by Brockhoff, 1992) – Lack of absorptive capacity as a barrier to inbound innovation (Cohen and Levinthal, 1990) – Risk of imbalanced bargaining power due to different stock of resources and competences possessed by partners* (this study) *Innovation process* – Dealing with many	Lichtenthaler, 2011) *Markets* – Geographical or product market expansion (Koruna, 2001; Chesbrough, Vanhaverbeke and West, 2006; Lichtenthaler, 2007; van de Vrande et al., 2009) – To reach network externality (i.e. critical number of users where value of a product depends on number of customers) (Ehrhardt, 2004; Koruna, 2001) – Setting industry standards (Conner, 1995; Ehrhardt, 2004; Lichtenthaler, 2007) – Keeping up with current market developments and customers (van de Vrande et al., 2009) and setting up listening posts for weak signals (Kutvonen, 2011) *Competitive position* – Clarify core business of a firm (Rigby and Zook, 2002) – Guarantee of technological leadership by focusing solely on a firm's core competences (Koruna,	competences needed to exploit knowledge externally (van de Vrande et al., 2009) *Governance of cooperation* – Balancing innovation with daily tasks, communication, aligning of partners, organisation of innovation (van de Vrande et al., 2009) – Bureaucracy and conflicting rules (van de Vrande et al., 2009) *Organisational culture* – "Only-used-here" syndrome as a barrier for outbound innovation (Boyens, 1998, as cited by Lichtenthaler and Ernst, 2006) – Too much emphasis on own product and technologies can be detrimental to license-out

Competitive position – To follow competitors (Garcia-Pont and Nohria, 2002) – – Way to monitor potentially disruptive technologies capable to threaten incumbent firms (Chesbrough and Crowther, 2006) *Resources* – Management of dependence on other firms (Salancik and Pfeffer, 1978) – Access to external ideas, knowledge, expertise and technologies (Hagedoor and Schakenraad, 1990; Harianto and Pennings, 1990; Hoffman and Schlosser, 2001; Laursen and Salter, 2006b; Mention and Asikainen, 2012; Powell et al. 1996; van de Vrande et al., 2009) – Leveraging complementarities (Cassiman and Veugelers 2006; Dyer and	sources and ideas at any given moment of time can lead to the attention allocation problem (Laursen and Salter, 2006b; Ocasio, 1997) – Difficulty to choose and combine between numerous alternatives (Laursen and Salter, 2006b; Sapienza, Parhankangas and Autio, 2004). *Governance of cooperation* – Risk of poor governance of joint learning processes (Larsson et al., 1998) – Difficulties in keeping many partnerships with various actors (Ahuja, 2000) – Risk of selecting partners who do not meet expectations and deadlines (van de Vrande et al., 2009)* – Difficulty in balancing innovation with daily tasks, communication, aligning of partners (van de Vrande et	2001; Lichtenthaler, 2007) – – Enabling outbound open innovation as a core business model (Kutvonen, 2011) *Resource management* – External partners may have more relevant resources to commercialise invention (Chesbrough and Rosenbloom, 2002) – To use licence out as a tool to access technology of external partner (Koruna, 2001; Lichtenthaler, 2007) – Entry into technological markets and networks (Harrison and Sullivan, 2011; Kutvonen, 2011) – Allocating resources and support (Henkel, 2006) – Control over technological path dependency (Kutvonen, 2011) *External business environment* – Achieving legitimacy from external environment (Nuvolari, 2004) – Strengthening inter-organisational	inventions (Lichtenthaler and Ernst, 2007) – – Trust issues (Salampasis et al., 2014)

Singh, 1998; van de Vrande et al., 2009)* – Access to partners' networks (Mention and Asikainen, 2012)* *Employees* – Learning new skills (Baum, Calabrese, and Silverman, 2000) *Management* – Flexibility and redistribution of tasks (Mention and Asikainen, 2012) *Organisational resilience* – Bouncing back from environmental shocks (Miner, Amburgey and Stearns, 1990) *Organisational culture* – To overcome internal rigidities caused by impediments to innovation (Keupp and Gassmann, 2009)	al., 2009)* – Bureaucracy and conflicting rules (van de Vrande et al., 2009)* *Organisational culture* – "Not invented here" syndrome (Katz and Allen, 1982) – Problem with maintaining internal commitment over period of time (Chesbrough and Crowther, 2006) – Organisational resistance and fear of losing control over proprietary technologies (Keupp and Gassmann, 2009) – Trust issues (Salampasis et al., 2014)	network (Lichtenthaler, 2007) – Defensive out-licensing by feeding entry barriers or diverting competitive innovation (Chesbrough and Rosenbloom, 2002; Kutvonen, 2011) – Creation of supportive market ecosystems (Kutvonen, 2011) *Employees* – Usage of employees' knowledge and expertise optimally (van de Vrande et al., 2009) – Motivation and retention of employees and strengthening their commitment (Rigby and Zook, 2002; van de Vrande et al., 2009) *Reputation* – Enhancement of firm's reputation by licencing out to well-known firms (Stuart, 1998; Lichtenthaler, 2007)*	

Note: Unveiled advantages and disadvantages of open innovation in financial services are marked with (*).

Third, an interviewee, from a mobile payment solution start-up, pointed out that by cooperating with external partners for development and deployment of novel financial solutions, they benefited from a shorter time-to-market advantage. Due the fact that the technology they developed is not patentable in the EU (though, partially it can be protected in USA), the crucial point was to develop and introduce the solution shortly to override emerging competitors. This finding does not seem to be novel since the extant literature suggested a similar conclusion, yet in another context (e.g., Rigby and Zook, 2002).

Fourth, it seems that relatively small providers of technology-based financial solutions may seek cooperation with larger banks in order to develop and introduce new financial offerings. One of the interviewees admitted that by cooperating with large, well-known and respectful partners, they expected to benefit from stronger credibility and trust that might positively influence both provider and the financial solution itself. This was crucial for this small provider especially at the stage when the company decided to enter into new foreign markets. This kind of advantage is not listed in the column for inbound open innovation (Table 1); however, it appears to be similar to the argument that refers to the reputation rationale of outbound open innovation (Lichtenthaler, 2007; Stuart, 1998).

Fifth, financial service providers seem to benefit from accessing the networks of their partners. One interviewee from a payment solution company emphasised that, on a market-introduction stage of their new financial solution, it was important to find partners, who had large and relevant networks in order to reach larger customer segment in the short run. These findings seem to be corresponding to the one already pointed out in the existing literature, namely "access to partners" networks' (Mention and Asikainen, 2012).

Sixth, a senior manager of an IT firm pointed out that their in-depth cooperation with banks in the development of internal technological solutions for portfolio management helped to bring value to their clients (banks) by boosting performance and improvement of flexibility of financial operations. This firm succeeded in establishing well-designed continuing relationship with their clients by setting up a community concept where banks are considered as a unique network of excellence from which innovation needs and ideas can be drawn for further development. Reliance on this community is an important pillar of innovation for this IT firm because banks, directly facing needs of their clients, are the primary source of innovation ideas. Because both the pointed out advantages of cooperation in innovation refer to the quality aspects of internal operations, a separate category called "improvement of performance and flexibility of backstage operations" has to be added under the section "process of production / service delivery" of the non-pecuniary advantages of inbound open innovation (Table 1). This is especially relevant for firms operating in the sector of services.

Seventh, one interviewee from an IT firm emphasised that by active cooperation with various banks in development and usage of a software solution, the innovation process and the way the final product was used at banks benefited from diverse inputs and backgrounds of various banks. It leads us to the argument that nurturing a "reasonable degree of diversity among the involved innovation partners can be beneficial for innovation process and its output". Hence, appropriate advantage has to be added under the section "innovation process" of the non-pecuniary advantages of inbound open innovation (Table 1).

4.2 Disadvantages of Open Innovation in Financial Services

Results of the data collection suggest that both banks and IT companies encounter problems in cooperation with each other. These issues may undermine the potential for outcome-oriented open innovation practices.

First, one of our interviewees complained that banks were inert and rigid in terms of organisational culture that made cooperation with them difficult, while not allowing for prompt and flexible interaction. Once annual budget is approved in the beginning of fiscal year, it is extremely difficult to approach banks with an innovative idea at a later stage. This insight echoes findings available in the existing studies, which pointed out possible problems with bureaucracy and conflicting rules in the cooperation for innovation (e.g., van de Vrande et al., 2009).

Second, several interviewees admitted that cooperation with external partners might entail considerable time costs, especially when the novel idea was still underdeveloped. In such a situation an idea needs to be properly discussed with prospect partners. Existing studies of open innovation explain this issue from the premises of transaction costs theory (Coase, 1937; Williamson, 1985).

Third, a director of a start-up company, that provides technological solutions for financial institutions, pointed out that one of the barriers in negotiating with banks in deployment of a new product was to pass a point of credibility, meaning that financial institutions were somewhat concerned with the risk of placing high value order (in monetary terms) to the start-up firm made of several employees. This issue seems to be in line with the earlier references to the risk of selecting partners who do not meet expectations and deadlines (van de Vrande et al., 2009).

Fourth, a senior manager of a start-up that develops and introduces a novel technological payment solution implicitly admitted that in the cases where the deployment of new financial solution was dependent on banks and their good will it was hard for the start-up to convince different retail banks to launch the new service. For the interviewee, the bargaining power in that case was on the side of banks. It means that in the cooperation frameworks, characterised with the imbalance of bargaining power because of different sets of resources possessed by partners, both process and results of cooperation in innovation can be to some extent problematic. Therefore, an extra argument called "risk of imbalance of bargaining power due to a different stock of resources and competences" has to be added under the "resources and competences" section of the non-pecuniary disadvantage of the inbound open innovation.

Fifth, an interviewee from an IT firm pointed out that, while cooperating with banks for the improvement of an existing IT solution for financial operations, his firm was not able to follow requests for innovation originating from banks due to lack of resources (e.g., knowledge, skills and time) and limited development capacities available internally. This argument refers to the point emphasised earlier in the existing literature; namely, the risk of selecting partners who do not meet expectations and deadlines (van de Vrande et al., 2009).

Sixth, the same interviewee from the IT firm argued that the most important issue of their cooperation with clients (banks) was the alignment of objectives. In the cases where strategic alignment of objectives is reached among all partners, cooperation appears to be more productive. This point refers to the part of argument already available in the existing literature, namely, partners' alignment (van de Vrande et al., 2009).

5. Conclusions

In this explorative study, we have attempted to shed light on the advantages and disadvantages of open innovation and to collect empirical evidence of these phenomena in the context of cross-sectional open innovation practices between banks and IT firms. A thorough analysis of the existing literature on open innovation allowed us to develop the conceptual framework of knowledge flows (Fig. 1), which takes place between at least two involved parties: an innovating firm and an external entity. These flows can be attributed with the direction (i.e. inflow and outflow of knowledge); mode (i.e. merger, joint ventures, investment in existing firms, spin-out, transfer of rights to use/own intellectual property, cooperation frameworks with external entities, knowledge-intensive services, dedicated market research, human resources management, transfer of machinery, events, publications, databases, informational products and informal personal interactions) and degree of formalisation (higher or lower formalised modes of knowledge transfer). Being far from an exhaustive one, the conceptual approach presented in this chapter is a step forward into the discussion on what modes of knowledge flow are relevant in relation to the open innovation paradigm.

Meanwhile, we proceeded further with the analysis of existing studies, which addressed the issues of advantages and disadvantages of open innovation. In this way we have followed the delineation between the inbound and outbound open innovation crossed with the pecuniary and non-pecuniary rationale (Dahlander and Gann, 2010).

Extant studies suggest that pecuniary advantages of the inbound open innovation may influence the following areas: decrease of costs and improvement of margins; attaining profitable growth. Non-pecuniary advantages of the inbound open innovation can positively affect the following: innovation output, process of production/service delivery, innovation risk, innovation process; markets; competitive position; resources; employees; management; organisational resilience and culture.

Pecuniary disadvantages of the inbound open innovation seem to be mainly conditioned by transaction costs, while the non-pecuniary disadvantages are related to innovation output, intellectual property management, competitive position, resources and competences, innovation process, governance of cooperation and organisational culture.

In the same vein, an analysis of the extant literature suggests that pecuniary advantages of outbound open innovation refer to the following: generation of revenues from out-licensing, infringements, selling products and/or services in addition to licensed technology; reduction of costs and improvement of efficiency; lowering costs of future technology transactions and growth increase.

In the non-pecuniary perspective, benefits of outbound open innovation may have a positive impact on innovation output, innovation process, markets, competitive position, resource management, external business environment, employees and reputation.

Finally, pecuniary disadvantages of the outbound open innovation can be caused due to the following reasons: transaction costs; licensees can commercially outperform the original innovation developer; difficulty in capturing benefits in the case of revealed knowledge.

Non-pecuniary disadvantages of the outbound open innovation seem to have negative impact on the following: markets, competitive position, employees, governance of cooperation and organisational culture.

The conducted literature review showed a paucity of research on open innovation in financial services, especially in the case of banks cooperating with IT firms in order to develop new services or processes. Having carried out face-to-face interviews with chief executive officers, their deputies and managers, responsible for the development of new services at both banks and IT firms showed that, similar to some existing studies (Barney, 1991; Baum and Oliver, 1991; Mention and Asikainen, 2012; Rigby and Zook, 2002; Stuart, 1998), both parties might benefit from cooperation because of the following reasons: leveraging complementarities, cost reduction, time-to-market, gaining stronger credibility and access to partners' networks. Meanwhile, we have encountered at least two reasons, not addressed in existing studies, to explain why inbound open innovation can be beneficial for banks and IT firms: (1) improvement of performance and flexibility of backstage operations (falls under the category "process of production/service delivery"); and (2) a reasonable degree of diversity among the involved innovation partners can be beneficial for innovation process and its output (falls under the category "innovation process"). These findings extend our current understanding of the advantages of open innovation, in general, and in financial services in particular (Table 1).

In relation to the disadvantages of inbound open innovation, our research findings suggest that almost all of them are supported by existing studies (Coase, 1937; van de Vrande et al., 2009): bureaucracy; costs associated with cooperation; risk of selecting partners who do not meet expectations/deadlines and conflict in objectives alignment among the partners. Meanwhile, we have found one more disadvantage of cooperation in innovation not addressed in the existing studies to the best of our knowledge: it refers to the risk of imbalance of the bargaining power due to the different stock of resources and competences possessed by partners (falls under the category "resources and competences") (Table 1).

5.1. Managerial Implications

In our opinion, practitioners will benefit from this study by having a comprehensive overview of all possible advantages and disadvantages of inbound and outbound open innovation, taking into consideration both pecuniary and non-pecuniary logics.

Financial service providers, as well as their innovation partners, opting for a higher degree of openness in innovation management, should be aware of various drawbacks of this choice. On the other hand, those financial institutions that are characterised by a significant degree of conservatism (higher degree of closeness), with regards to the innovation process, may miss out on the benefits gained by open innovation. This would be a noticeable strategic mistake for the innovators amid the vibrant and competitive environment they operate in nowadays. Finding the proper balance between being closed or being open in innovation activity is critical not only for financial institutions but also for firms, which operate in other sectors of the economy. For financial services, the balance at project or organisational level should be addressed by taking into consideration inherent peculiarities of the sector, which have been thoroughly discussed in the extant literature (e.g., Mention and Torkkeli, 2012).

Besides, the developed concept of knowledge flows together with its attributes will be helpful for financial service providers and their partners in comprehension of the rather complex picture of open innovation.

5.2 Limitations and Future Research

Overall, the carried out study can serve as a basis for the consequent quantitative stage of research aimed at the quantification of the phenomena on a representative sample of financial institutions. As it was an explorative study we interviewed only a limited number of financial service providers. A larger and diversified sample would allow us to proceed further with the exploration of advantages and disadvantages of open innovation in financial services.

Since the empirical part of this chapter originates from Luxembourg, other cross-national studies would be helpful to explore the research phenomena. Empirical findings of this study have been obtained in the context of cooperation for innovation between banks and ICT firms (inbound open innovation). Therefore, exploring this topic in other cross-sectional contexts will improve our understanding of open innovation in financial services.

5.3 Acknowledgements

We would like to thank all our interviewees in Luxembourg who were so kind in sharing with us their positive and negative experiences of cooperation in innovation. The usual disclaimer applies.

References

Accenture BeLux. *Financial Services Innovation Awards: One-pagers Subscribed Concepts*, 2011.

Ahuja, Gautam. "The Duality of Collaboration: Inducements and Opportunities in the Formation of Interfirm Linkages." *Strategic Management Journal* 21, no. 3 (2000): 317–343.

Arrow, Kenneth J. "The Economic Learning Implications of by Doing." *The Review of Economic Studies* 29, no. 3 (1962): 155–173.

Athanassopoulou, Peggy and Axel Johne. "Effective Communication with Lead Customers in Developing New Banking Products." *International Journal of Bank Marketing* 22, no. 2 (2004): 100–125.

Auh, Seigyoung, Simon J. Bell, Colin S. McLeod and Eric Shih. "Co-production and Customer Loyalty in Financial Services." *Journal of Retailing* 83, no. 3 (2007): 359–370.

Barney, Jay. "Firm resources and sustained competitive advantage." *Journal of Management* 17, no. 1 (1991): 99-120.

Barras, R. "Towards a Theory of Innovation in Services". *Research Policy* 15, no. 4 (1986): 161-173.

Barras, R. "Interactive Innovation in Financial and Business Services: The Vanguard of the Service Revolution". *Research Policy* 19, no. 3 (1990): 215-237.

Bátiz-Lazo, Bernardo and Kassa Woldesenbet. "The Dynamics of Product and Process Innovations in UK Banking". *International Journal of Financial Services Management* 1, no. 4 (2006): 400-421.

Baum, Joel A C, and Christine Oliver. "Institutional Linkages and Organizational Mortality". *Administrative Science Quarterly* 36, no. 2 (1991): 187-218.

Baum, Joel A. C., Tony Calabrese and Brian S. Silverman. "Don't Go it Alone: Alliance Network Composition and Startups' Performance in Canadian Biotechnology". *Strategic Management Journal* 21, no. 3 (2000): 267-294.

Bianchi, Mattia, Alberto Cavaliere, Davide Chiaroni, Federico Frattini, and Vittorio Chiesa. "Organisational Modes for Open Innovation in the Bio-pharmaceutical Industry: An Exploratory Analysis." *Technovation* 31, no. 1 (2011): 22–33.

Bidault, Francis and William A. Fischer. "Technology Transactions: Networks Over Markets." *R&D Management* 24, no. 4 (1994): 373-386

Boyens, Karsten. *Externe Verwertung von technologischem Wissen*. DUV, Dt. Univ.-Verlag, 1998.

Brockhoff, Klaus. "R&D Cooperation Between Firms-A Perceived Transaction Cost Perspective." *Management Science* 38, no. 4 (1992): 514–524.

Cassiman, Bruno and Reinhilde Veugelers. "In Search of Complementarity in Innovation Strategy : Internal R & D and External Knowledge Acquisition." *Management Science* 52, no. 1 (2006): 68–82.

Chesbrough, Henry and Adrienne Kardon Crowther. "Beyond High Tech: Early Adopters of Open Innovation in Other Industries." *R and D Management* 36, no. 3 (2006): 229–236.

Chesbrough, Henry and Kevin Schwartz. "Innovating Business Models with Co-development Partnerships." *Research-Technology Management* 50, no.1 (2007): 55-59.

Chesbrough, Henry and Richard S. Rosenbloom. "The Role of the Business Model in Capturing Value from Innovation: Evidence from Xerox Corporation's Technology Spin-off Companies." *Industrial and Corporate Change* 11, no. 3 (2002): 529–555.

Chesbrough, Henry, Wim Vanhaverbeke and Joel West. 2006. *Open Innovation: Researching a New Paradigm*. Ed. HW Chesbrough, Wim Vanhaverbeke, and Joel West, Oxford University Press.

Coase, Ronald H. "The Nature of the Firm." *Economica* 4, no. 16 (1937): 386-405.

Cohen, Wesley M., Richard R. Nelson and John P. Walsh. "Links and Impacts: The Influence of Public Research on Industrial R&D." *Management Science* 48, no. 1 (2002): 1–23.

Cohen, Wesley M. and Daniel A Levinthal. 1990. "Absorptive Capacity: A New Perspective on Learning and Innovation." *Administrative Science Quarterly* 35, no. 1: 128-152.

Conner, Kathleen R. "Obtaining Strategic Advantage from Being Imitated: when can encouraging "clones" pay?." *Management Science* 41, no. 2 (1995): 209-225.

Cooper, Robert G. and Scott J. Edgett. "Critical Success Factors for New Financial Services." *Marketing Management* no. 5 (1996): 26–38.

Dahlander, Linus and David M. Gann. "How Open Is Innovation?" *Research Policy* 39, no. 6 (2010): 699–709.

Drew, Stephen A. W. "Accelerating Innovation in Financial Services." *Long Range Planning* 28, no. 4 (1995): 1–10.

Dyer, Jeffrey H. and Harbir Singh. "The Relational View: Cooperative Strategy and Sources of Interorganizational Competitive Advantage". *Academy of Management Review* 23, no. 4 (1998): 660-679.

Edgett, Scott and Steve Jones. "New Product Development in the Financial Service Industry: a Case Study." *Journal of Marketing Management* no. 7 (1991): 271–284.

Edgett, Scott and Steven Parkinson. "The Development of New Financial Services: Identifying Determinants of Success and Failure." *International Journal of Service Industry Management* 5, no. 4 (1994): 24–38.

Edgett, Scott. "The Traits of Successful New Service Development." *Journal of Services Marketing* 8, no. 3 (1994): 40–49.

Ehrhardt, Marcus. "Network Effects, Standardisation and Competitive Strategy: How Companies Influence the Emergence of Dominant Designs." *International Journal of Technology Management* 27, no. 2 (2004): 272-294.

"Eurostat." *Science and technology: Results of the community innovation survey 2008 (CIS2008).* http://epp.eurostat.ec.europa.eu/portal/page/portal/science_technology_innovation/data/database (accessed Feb. 17, 2012.

"Eurostat." *Statistics*. http://epp.eurostat.ec.europa.eu/portal/page/portal/statistics/search_database (accessed Nov. 15, 2011).

Fasnacht, Daniel. *Open Innovation in the Financial Services*. Berlin: Springer-Verlag, 2009.

Garcia-Pont, Carlos and Nitin Nohria. "Local Versus Global Mimetism: The Dynamics of Alliance Formation in the Automobile Industry." *Strategic Management Journal* 23, no. 4 (2002): 307–321.

Gassmann, Oliver and Ellen Enkel. "Towards a Theory of Open Innovation : Three Core Process Archetypes." In *R&D Management Conference*, 2004.

Grant, Robert M. "Toward a Knowledge-based Theory of the firm." *Strategic Management Journal* 17 (1996): 109-122.

Grindley, Peter C. and David J Teece. "Managing Intellectual Capital: Licensing and Cross-Licensing in Semiconductors and Electronics." *California Management Review* 39, no. 2 (1997): 8-41.

Hagedoorn, John and Jos Schakenraad. "The effect of strategic technology alliances on company performance." *Strategic Management Journal* 15, no. 4 (1994): 291-309.

Harianto, F. and J. Pennings. "Technological Innovation Through Interfirm Linkages". In M. Law-less and L. R. Gomez-Mejia (eds.), *Strategic Management in High Technology Firms*. JAI Press, Greenwich, CT, 1990.

Harrison, Suzanne S. and Patrick H. Sullivan. *Edison in the Boardroom Revisited: How Leading Companies Realize Value from Their Intellectual Property*. New Jersey: John Wiley & Sons, 2011.

Henkel, Joachim. "Selective Revealing in Open Innovation Processes: The Case of Embedded Linux." *Research Policy* 35, no. 7 (2006): 953–969.

Hoffmann, Werner H. and Roman Schlosser. "Success Factors of Strategic Alliances in Small and Medium-sized Enterprises—An Empirical Survey". *Long Range Planning* 34, no. 3 (2001): 357-381.

Huizingh, Eelko K.R.E. "Open Innovation: State of the Art and Future Perspectives." *Technovation* 31, no. 1 (January 2011): 2–9.

Katz, Ralph and Thomas J. Allen. "Investigating the Not Invented Here (NIH) syndrome: A look at the performance, tenure, and communication patterns of 50 R&D Project Groups". *R&D Management* 12, no. 1 (1982): 7-20.

Keupp, Marcus Matthias and Oliver Gassmann. "Determinants and Archetype Users of Open Innovation." *R&D Management* 39, no. 4 (2009): 331–341.

Koruna, Stefan. "External technology commercialization: policy guidelines". Proceedings of the 4th PICMET Conference, Portland, Oregon, 2001. http://citeseerx.ist.psu.edu/viewdoc/download?doi= 10.1.1.199.9100&rep=rep1&type=pdf (accessed Apr. 5, 2013)

Kutvonen, Antero, Marko T. Torkkeli, and Binshan Lin. "Pre-commercialisation Activities in External Exploitation of Technology." *International Journal of Innovation and Learning* 8 no. 2 (2010): 208-230.

Kutvonen, Antero. "Strategic Application of Outbound Open Innovation", *European Journal of Innovation Management* 14, no. 4 (2011): 460-474.

Lakhani, Karim R., Peter A. Lohse, Jill A. Panetta, and Lars Bo Jeppesen. 2007. "The Value of Openness in Scientific Problem Solving". *Working paper*. *Harvard Business School*, 2007.

Larsson, Rikard, Lars Bengtsson, Kristina Henriksson, and Judith Sparks. "The Interorganizational Learning Dilemma: Collective Knowledge Development in Strategic Alliances". *Organization Science* 9, no. 3 (1998): 285-305.

Laursen, Keld and Ammon Salter (a). "My precious: The role of appropriability strategies in shaping innovation performance", 2005. http://www2.druid.dk/conferences/viewpaper.php?id=2583&cf=17 (accessed Apr. 4, 2013).

Laursen, Keld and Ammon Salter (b). "Open for Innovation: The Role of Openness in Explaining Innovation Performance Among U.K.

Manufacturing Firms." *Strategic Management Journal* 27, no. 2 (February 2006): 131–150.

Lerner, Josh. "Where Does State Street Lead? A First Look at Finance Patents, 1971 to 2000." *The Journal of Finance* LVII, no. 2 (2002): 901–930.

—. 2008. "The Litigation of Financial Innovations". *National Bureau of Economic Research Working Paper Series* No. 14324, no. 4: 807-831.

Lichtenthaler, Ulrich and Holger Ernst. "Attitudes to Externally Organising Knowledge Management Tasks: a Review, Reconsideration and Extension of the NIH Syndrome." *R and D Management* 36, no. 4 (September 2006): 367–386.

Lichtenthaler, Ulrich and Holger Ernst. "External Technology Commercialization in Large Firms: Results of a Quantitative Benchmarking Study." *R&D Management* 37, no. 5 (2007): 383–397.

Lichtenthaler, Ulrich. "Open Innovation: Past Research, Current Debates, and Future Directions." *Academy of Management Perspectives* 25, no. 1 (2011): 75–93.

—. "The Drivers of Technology Licensing: An Industry Comparison". *California Management Review* 49, no. 4 (2007): 67-89.

Lievens, A. and R.K. Moenaert. "Communication Flows During Financial Service Innovation." *International Journal of Bank Marketing* 19, no. 2 (2001): 68–88.

Linstone, Harold A. "Comment on 'Is Open Innovation a Field of Study or a Communication Barrier to Theory Development?'" *Technovation* 30, no. 11–12 (2010): 556.

"Luxembourg for Finance." *Etude d'impact de l'industrie financière sur l'économie luxembourgeoise: Version chiffres de 2010.* http://www.luxembourgforfinance.lu/sites/luxembourgforfinance/files/etude-impact-2010.pdf (accessed Apr. 5, 2013).

March, James G. "Exploration and Exploitation in Organizational Learning." *Organization Science* 2 no .1 (1991): 71-87.

Martovoy, Andrey and Jennifer Dos Santos "Co–creation and Co–profiting in Financial Services." *International Journal of Entrepreneurship and Innovation Management* 16, no. 1/2 (2012): 114-135.

Martovoy, Andrey, Antero Kutvonen, Anne-Laure Mention and Marko Torkkeli "Open Innovation in Banking Services: Advantages and Disadvantages." In *Proceedings of the XXIII ISPIM Conference Action for Innovation: Innovating from Experience*, ISPIM, Barcelona, Spain, 2012.

Marshall, Alfred *Principles of Economics*. London: Macmillan, 1890.

Mention, Anne-Laure and Anna-Leena Asikainen "Does Inter-firm Co-operation Foster Innovation in Services", in *IAMOT*, Hsinchu, Taiwan, March 2012.

Mention, Anne-Laure and Marko Torkkeli. "Drivers, Processes and Consequences of Financial Innovation: A Research Agenda." *International Journal of Entrepreneurship and Innovation Management* 16, no. 1/2 (2012): 5-29.

Mention, Anne-Laure, Andrey Martovoy and Marko Torkkeli "Open Innovation in Financial Services: What are the External Drivers?" *International Journal of Business Excellence* (2014) (forthcoming).

Miller, Merton H. "Financial Innovation: The Last Twenty Years and the Next." *The Journal of Financial and Quantitative Analysis* 21, no. 4 (1986): 459–471.

Miner, Anne S., Terry L. Amburgey and Timothy M. Stearns. "Interorganizational Linkages and Population Dynamics: Buffering and Transformational Shields". *Administrative Science Quarterly* 35, no. 4 (1990): 689-713.

Murray, Fiona and Siobhán O'Mahony. "Exploring the Foundations of Cumulative Innovation: Implications for Organization Science." *Organization Science* 18 no. 6 (2007): 1006-1021.

Nidumolu, Ram, Coimbatore K. Prahalad and M. R. Rangaswami. "Why Sustainability is Now the Key Driver of Innovation." *Harvard business review* 87 no. 9 (2009): 56-64.

Nonaka, Ikujiro. "A Dynamic Theory of Organizational Knowledge Creation."*Organization Science* 5, no. 1 (1994): 14-37.

Nuvolari, Alessandro. "Collective Invention During the British Industrial Revolution: The Case of the Cornish Pumping Engine." *Cambridge Journal of Economics* 28 no. 3 (2004): 347-363.

Ocasio, William. "Towards an Attention Based View of the Firm." *Strategic Management Journal* 18, Summer Special Issue (1997): 187–206.

Oliveira, Pedro and Eric von Hippel. "Users as Service Innovators: The Case of Banking Services." *Research Policy* 40, no. 6 (2011): 806–818.

Penrose, Edith. 1959. *The Theory of the Growth of the Firm*, John Wiley, New York.

Pennings, Johannes M. and Farid Harianto. "The Diffusion of Technological Innovation in the Commercial Banking Industry." *Strategic Management Journal* 13, no. 1 (1992): 29–46.

Penrose, E. T. (1959) The Theory of the Growth of the Firm, John Wiley, New York

Perkmann, Markus and Kathryn Walsh. "University–industry Relationships and Open Innovation: Towards a Research Agenda." *International Journal of Management Reviews* 9, no. 4 (2007): 259–280.

Pisano, Gary P. "The R&D Boundaries of the Firm: An Empirical Analysis." *Administrative Science Quarterly* 35, no. 1 (1990): 153–176.

Powell, Walter W., Kenneth W. Koput and Laurel Smith-Doerr. "Interorganizational Collaboration and the Locus of Innovation: Networks of Learning in Biotechnology." *Administrative Science Quarterly* (1996): 116-145.

Prahalad, Coimbatore Krishnarao, and Venkatram Ramaswamy. "Co-opting Customer Competence." *Harvard Business Review* 78.1 (2000): 79-90.

Rigby, Darrell and Chris Zook. "Open-market Innovation." *Harvard Business Review* 80, no. 10 (2002): 80–93.

Romer, Paul M. "Increasing Returns and Long-Run Growth." *Journal of Political Economy* 94, no. 5 (1986): 1002–1037.

Rotering, C.H., 1990. *Forschungs- und Entwicklungs-Kooperationen zvischen Unternehinen*, Poeschel-Verlag, Stuttgart.

Salampasis, Dimitrios, Mention, Anne-Laure, Torkkeli Marko. "Open Innovation and Collaboration in the Financial Services Sector: Exploring the role of trust". Special Issue on "Innovation for Financial Services", *International Journal of Business Innovation and Research* 8, no: 5 (2014): 466-484.

Salancik, Gerald R. and Jeffrey Pfeffer. *The external control of organizations: a resource dependence perspective*. Harper and Row, 1978.

Sapienza, Harry J., Annaleena Parhankangas and Erkko Autio. "Knowledge relaTedness and Post-spin-off Growth". *Journal of Business Venturing* 19, no. 6 (2004): 809-829.

Schartinger, Doris, Christian Rammer, Manfred M. Fischer and Josef Fröhlich. "Knowledge Interactions Between Universities and Industry in Austria : Sectoral Patterns and Determinants." *Research Policy* 31, no. 3 (2002): 303–328.

Scheuing, Eberhard E. and Eugene M. Johnson. "A Proposed Model for New Service Development". *Journal of Services Marketing* 3, no. 2 (1989): 25-34.

Stewart, Thomas and Clare Ruckdeschel. "Intellectual capital: The new Wealth of Organizations." *Performance Improvement* 37, no. 7 (1998): 56-59.

Storey, Christopher and Christopher Easingwood. "The Impact of the New Product Development Project on the Success of Financial Services." *The Service Industries Journal* 13, no. 3 (1993): 40–54.

Stuart, Toby E. "Network Positions and Propensities to Collaborate: An Investigation of Strategic Alliance Formation in a High-technology Industry." *Administrative Science Quarterly* (1998): 668-698.

Teece, David J. "Profiting from Technological Innovation: Implications for Integration, Collaboration, Licensing and Public Policy". *Research Policy* 15, no. 6 (1986): 285-305.

Thomas, James B. and Linda Klebe Trevino. "Information Processing in Strategic Alliance Building: A Multiple-Case Approach." *Journal of Management Studies* 30, no.5 (1993): 779-814.

Thomke, Stefan. "R&D Comes to Services: Bank of America's Pathbreaking Experiments." *Harvard Business Review* 81, no. 4 (2003): 70–79.

Tufano, Peter. "Financial Innovation and First-mover Advantages". *Journal of Financial Economics* 25, no. 2 (1989): 213-240.

Uchupalanan, Kittiwat. "Competition and IT-based Innovation in Banking Services." *International Journal of Innovation Management* 4, no. 4 (December 2000): 455–489.

van de Vrande, Vareska, Jeroen P.J. de Jong, Wim Vanhaverbeke, and Maurice de Rochemont. "Open Innovation in SMEs: Trends, Motives and Management Challenges." *Technovation* 29, no. 6–7 (2009): 423–437.

Vargo, Stephen L. and Robert F. Lusch. "Evolving to a New Dominant Logic for Marketing." *Journal of Marketing* 68, no. 1 (2004): 1–17.

Vence, Xavier and Alexandre Trigo. "Diversity of Innovation Patterns in Services." *The Service Industries Journal* 29, no. 12 (2009): 1635–1657.

Vermeulen, P. "Managing Product Innovation in Financial Services Firms." *European Management Journal* 22, no. 1 (2004): 43–50.

von Hippel, E. "Lead Users: A Source of Novel Product Concepts." *Management Science* 32, no. 7 (July 1, 1986): 791–805.

Wernerfelt, Birger. "A Resource-Based View of the Firm." *Strategic Management Journal* 5, no. 2 (1984): 171-180.

West, Joel and Scott Gallagher. "Challenges of Open Innovation: The Paradox of Firm Investment in Open-source Software." *R and D Management* 36, no. 3 (June 2006): 319–331.

Williamson, Oliver E. "Transaction Cost Economics: The Comparative Contracting Perspective." *Journal of Economic Behavior & Organization* 8, no. 4 (1987): 617-625.

"Z/Yen Group." *The Global Financial Centres Index 13: March 2013.* http://www.zyen.com/images/GFCI_25March2013.pdf (accessed Apr. 5, 2013).

CHAPTER TWELVE

ORGANIZATIONAL READINESS FOR OPEN INNOVATION IN THE FINANCIAL SERVICES SECTOR: THE MISSING ELEMENT OF TRUST

DIMITRIOS SALAMPASIS

1. Introduction

This chapter aims at exploring the role of trust as a core element towards the development of organizational readiness mechanisms for open innovation within the financial services sector. Open innovation as a concept is perceived as an organizational mindset and its adoption and actual implementation require prior substantial changes within the organizational setting. Managing change is a highly challenging task, which requires important and prompt readiness on an organizational level, as a whole.

Organizational readiness has been explored within different research fields and contexts, however, little is known regarding the open innovation organizational readiness in the financial services sector especially under the multi-dimensional functionality of organizational trust.

Open innovation has received wide acceptance but also criticism. The interrelation between inbound, outbound and coupled processes creates important implications in terms of the academic, organizational and managerial perspective. Heim (2011, p.4) while pointing out that there is a continuous development and progress towards the adoption of open innovation both *"within consumer and industrial manufacturing companies, as well as the service industry"*, explicitly underlines that the holistic full adoption of open innovation is meant to create a true competitive advantage.

Financial services are considered as the backbone of the global market and the economic environment since their main function lies within the management of personal and corporate assets and the exclusive management of financial and banking transactions. Needless to say that the current debt and subprime crises have created a new set of rules in the global business and financial market and have a substantial impact within the financial services sector undergoing a tremendous loss of trust from financial, marketing and organizational perspectives.

The 2013 Edelman Trust Barometer endorses this direction by reporting that the financial services sector is the least trusted industry globally. Under this perspective, I believe that it becomes imperative for the financial services industry leaders to reinforce new behaviors within their organizations in order to re-build trust.

The structure and the culture prevailing within the typical financial institution are primarily responsible for the existence and perpetuation of fragmented and heterogeneous environments found in financial services organizations (Wesemann, 2006). In order to overcome this situation it is important to see the advantage of breaking down the walls between businesses in the organization and in order to succeed, new organizational process models and governance policies are necessary.

The financial crisis has created a new realization of our financial world and has led to the destruction of institutionalized practices empowering the motivation for change. Regaining trust will be successful only through change, within a creative destruction process. The financial services sector needs to change and start thinking differently in terms of product, process and service innovation. Apparently this is not easy; financial innovation tools remain in the box and *"it is like playing with a toolbox, or lots of little Lego bricks, that you already have [...] this is what financial innovation looks like. We are not redefining the world right now"* (Hughes, 2010, p.1).

Salampasis *et al.* (2014a) argue that open innovation is the vehicle to regain trust and at the same time trust plays a paramount role in open innovation as an organizational mindset. The financial services sector needs to regain trust and this will come alongside existing leadership styles in order to re-enforce credibility, leverage and impact and top management should facilitate high performance teams, motivated workforce, respect and effective and socially responsible strategies. This is consistent with the argument of Heffernan *et al.*, (2008, p.192) that *"the concept of trust is particularly salient in the context of the financial services sector because customers are not in a strong position to make objective assessments of service quality"*.

The financial services sector is in the process of understanding and realizing the fact that the tools of knowledge production and dissemination have been democratised and this grants access to actors functioning outside the traditional boundaries of the firm who can co-create value and work upon existing knowledge platforms and practices, which can be applicable in different formations and levels both for the financial firm (organizational level) and other agents and stakeholders in the peripherals (Jeppesen and Lakhani, 2010). Quick adaptation to change means better penetration into the marketplace. This is translated into a need for solutions, which *"encompass new business models, operating models, customer demands and legislative constraints"* (KPMG, 2012, p.1).

The organizational readiness of a financial services organization towards the adoption and implementation of open innovation strategies is still obscure. Various models have been suggested perceiving open innovation in different organizational levels and from a micro, meso and macro prisms but to my knowledge no model exists so far that could be fully applicable in the context and peculiarities of a financial services organization.

Organizational readiness as a concept has been vastly explored in different areas and contexts and the development of this conceptual framework regarding the elements that constitute an organization *"ready"* from an institutional perspective towards the adoption of open innovation brings new insights in the establishment of an internal structure, discipline and culture as a proprietary process towards the development of an open innovation organizational readiness framework (Evan, 2011). I also share the focus *"on the organizational level on the adoption, routinization and decommissioning pathway stages"* as suggested by Williams (2011, p.213).

The argument emerging from this chapter lies within the realization that in order for the financial services sector to regain trust, the adoption of open innovation practices seems to be the key facilitator in this process and its adoption is possible only through the establishment of internal organizational trust at all levels of the organization. This is in line with Hsieh and Tidd (2012, p.606) who state that open innovation is not a *"universal prescription but may be more relevant to more novel development projects"* and, I would add, at least within the financial services sector. I do not share the views of Blois on the fact that the creation of trust is impossible because of the fact that constant demonstration of trustworthiness can imply a manipulative intent embedded behavior (Blois, 1999), either on a relational, organizational or inter-organizational level. Perceiving and appreciating trustworthiness is a matter of environmental context and framework and not a panacea (Halliday, 2003).

This book chapter is structured as follow: the analysis begins by an extensive review of the open innovation and organizational readiness literature (section 2). A brief presentation of the methodological approach follows (section 3). Section 4 is dedicated to a detailed analysis of the relationship between organizational readiness, open innovation and trust. In the next section (section 5) a conceptual framework in the realms of a financial services organization is proposed. Section 6 explores an overall overview of the chapter. The final section (section 7) is dedicated to a number of concluding remarks, limitations, academic and managerial implications and pathways for future research.

2. Literature Review

2.1 Open Innovation

2.1.1 Concept of Open Innovation

By definition, open innovation is a *"paradigm that assumes firms can and should use external ideas as well as internal ideas, and internal and external paths to market, as the firms look to advance their technology"* (Chesbrough, 2003, p. xxiv). As a concept, it has received wide acceptance (Huizingh, 2011) and criticism (Linstone, 2010; Trott and Hartmann, 2009). From a managerial and strategy perspective, open innovation *"has become the latest management buzzword"* (Hagel and Brown, 2008, p.27), a "*strategic business imperative for non-linear growth; the Holy Grail for executives today"* (Soni, 2008, p.172), or *"...it is most powerful as a mechanism to access sources of inspiration and innovation and create new sources of value from outside the organization"* (Tuff and Jonash, 2009, p.2) since it summarises "a *set of socio-political and economic changes"* (Schroll, 2009a).

The core element of the concept derives from the interrelation among inbound (outside-in), outbound (inside-out) and coupled (bidirectional) open innovation processes (Chesbrough and Crowther, 2006; Enkel et al., 2009; Gassmann and Enkel, 2004); referring to the mutual competence that companies should possess and nurture in order to be able to receive and operationalize know-how from the outer part and layer of the organization *per se*, the ability to avoid disclosure of information, competences and R&D in terms of sharing and openness (Spithoven *et al.*, 2011) and the co-creation with complementary partners through alliances, joint ventures and cooperation of jointly developed and commercialized innovation (Zhang *et al.*, 2010).

A brief overview of the three open innovation processes shows that the inbound process refers to the in-sourcing of external knowledge by means of licensing in, spinning in, acquisition and collaboration alongside the value chain (Gassmann and Enkel, 2004; Savitskaya *et al.*, 2010). On the other hand, the outbound process refers to the external utilization of internal knowledge and more specifically the performance of potential value creation from the *"surplus of research"*, which would remain unused (based on the closed innovation model) but now it can be utilized by fitting itself within other business models (Savitskaya *et al.*, 2010, p.11). The coupled process, which is perceived via the existence of porous boundaries, depicts a simultaneous cumulative formation of the inbound and outbound open innovation processes and is defined as *"linking outside-in and inside-out by working in alliances with complementary companies during which give and take are crucial for success*" (Enkel and Gassmann, 2004, p.1).

Open innovation is characterized as a porous business model and is aligned to the notion of transparency, openness and sharing (Chesbrough, 2003), or the fact that the boundaries of the firm become permeable leading to the formulation of a delicate balance between the creation of value and the need for capturing value (Livieratos *et al.*, 2012). Open innovation leads to an open culture, an open business model and an operational absorptive capacity (Spithoven *et al.*, 2011) which is elaborated through the correspondence and interrelation of a substantial number of factors such as sincerity, long lasting relationships, long term cooperation and common/mutual value creation. The absorptive capacity is related to the exploration of external knowledge (Cohen and Levinthal, 1990) and the ability of the firm to generalize "*commercializable outputs"* after having passed the procedure of value recognition, validity, implementation and internal knowledge conceptualization (Kostopoulos *et al.*, 2011, p.1336).

The functionality of open innovation lies upon the shift from a closed to an open paradigm. This propensity to the open paradigm is clearly illustrated within the fact that "c*losed innovation springs entirely from internal company innovation activity, largely in the form of organized R&D"* (Helfat and Quinn, 2006, p.86). On the other hand, the open innovation model advances its emergence from "*sources external to the company in combination with supplementary internal company innovation activity"* (Helfat and Quinn, 2006, p.86). A trade-off between benefits of discovery and costs of divergence is clearly depicted in the simulation model by Almirall and Casadesus-Masanell (2010 p.44) who argue that discovery *"might arise not from the exercise of full strategic freedom but from restricting the available choices and learning from those made by others"*. This is summarized to the understanding of the actual *"shifting from the question how do we create and protect innovation to the question how can we find a way to generate value and capture the greatest possible amount of that value, regardless of whether others take part in the value chain"* (Livieratos *et al.*, 2012, p.2).

Open innovation, as a concept, has developed throughout the years and has been associated with several other concepts such as open source (West and Gallagher, 2006), user co-creation (Franke and Piller, 2004), user centred innovation and customer integration by von Hippel and distributed innovation (Sawhney and Prandelli, 2000). Schweisfurth *et al.* (2011) propose another classification identifying five concepts and research streams of open innovation; collective invention, user-innovation networks, common based peer production, crowdsourcing and open-source innovation.

2.1.2 Open Innovation in Financial Services

Open innovation in financial services is a research field of study, which has received recent attention. The adoption of open innovation strategies is still quite obscure (Fasnacht, 2009; Martovoy and Dos Santos, 2012; Mention and Torkkeli, 2012; Mention *et al.*, 2014; Salampasis *et al.*, 2014a). Existing contributions in the field perceive the topic from different angles. Furthermore, there is very limited empirical evidence regarding the development of specific measurable constructs that establish a concrete framework of open innovation strategies adoption and measurable open innovation performance indicators. It is important, however, to acknowledge earlier studies regarding the importance of external and internal sources of innovation in this sector especially from the scope of marketing on new service development,

Financial services form a vital sector in business. 5.77 million people are employed which is equal to around 6% of total non-farm employment in the US explicitly underlining the fact that *"the wealth generated by the financial services industry contributed nearly 6 percent, or more than $828 billion, to 2009 US GDP"* (SIFMA, 2010, p.4). Haldane and Mandouros (2011) state that in 2009 financial intermediaries accounted for 8% of total GDP and 10% in the US and in the UK respectively. However, based upon the 2013 McKinsey Global Institute Analysis, despite the fact that the world's financial assets have reached a value of §225 trillion during the second quarter of 2012 a very weak 1.9% of annual growth rate since 2007 is depicted compared to the annual 7.9% growth in the period between 1990-2007.

The unprecedented challenges that financial services institutions are facing globally are remarkable since a great number of banking and investment institutions continue to experience major disruptions in their business, mainly due to mergers and acquisitions and governmental interventions. Today's uncertain regulatory environment leads upon the realization of new operational and organizational challenges requiring continuous adaptation, external knowledge, resources, substantial changes and new market insights in order to sustain competitiveness, while exploring new opportunities for growth. It is becoming apparent that all the necessary tools, so as to comply with all the abovementioned changes, cannot be developed and formulated in-house and in solitude.

Current examples of innovations in financial services, especially within ICT (e.g. the development of applications, visualization and cloud client computing platforms) depict a shift towards a more open and collaborative paradigm, aiming at advancing and leveraging the role and applicability of the provided services. These services result in operational benefits for financial services organizations, enabling efficient, effective and confident adoption of technological advances, processes and knowledge that will ensure a greater operational reliability so as to meet the highly demanding requirements of the financial sector worldwide.

Cloudera (2012) in line with this open mindset adoption identifies four interrelated pillars towards the contemporary challenges of financial services; commoditization and digitization of financial products and services, increased activity, new data sources and increased regulation. This means that the scale of challenges financial services companies need to manage is overwhelming. Contrary to traditional systems, the adoption of open innovation can create competitive advantage. This is crystalized within the understanding of the shift from a closed to an open model and also the simultaneous co-existence of the innovation locus both within organizational boundaries and outside.

Salampasis *et al.* (2014a) underline the managerial implications of open innovation adoption in relation to financial services and the fact that effective collaboration and financial innovation have an impact in the financial services in terms of marketing and the profile of the financial services user. It is a matter of realization from the top management regarding the social and economic factors affecting the demand for financial services and the implications that they have on the needs and profile of the user behaviour. This is also applied to the building of sustainable user relationships, the process of this relationship development and the impact that the technology has in the delivery of the financial services. This means that financial services companies will have the ability to tackle increasingly complex problems by unlocking the power of collaboration, which requires an open mindset. It is apparent that the developed capability to understand and act upon shared knowledge and best practices *"opens the door to a richer and more robust financial ecosystem"* (Cloudera, 2012, p.6).

2.1.3 Open Innovation Organizational Adoption

Open innovation being realized within an organization *"naturally requires some time to mature and work effectively"* (Enkel *et al.*, 2011, p.1161). This is interpreted twofold: from the one side open innovation means introduction of a new way to organize the innovation process which requires substantial and multi-level changes and on the other side the development of a maturity framework so as to benchmark excellence in open innovation.

Enkel *et al.*, (2011, p.1166) identify three major managerial challenges regarding the open innovation adoption "*in relation to the transformation of business models and R&D organizations, the internal change in culture and the process distinction of open innovation*", elaborating further, though on these challenges by bringing forward the establishment and the development of other parameters and constructs required in the open innovation process. Regarding the enabling of open innovation initiatives, they are looking upon the presence of partnership capacity, the creation of a climate for innovation and the placement of right systems and tools in relation to five identified maturity levels (initial/arbitrary, repeatable, defined, managed and optimizing). All these elements require substantial prior changes and the development of the right antecedents within an organization. These organizational antecedents are explored in the following pages.

The adoption of open innovation strategies requires prior substantial changes in a company's innovation paradigm mainly in terms of transformation of *"a company's solid boundaries into a more semi-permeable membrane to enable innovation to move more easily between the external environment and the company's international innovation process"* or to *"fully integrate those external knowledge sources that are a prerequisite for enriching the internal knowledge base"* (Bevanda and Turk, 2009, p.2).

In order to be able to implement those changes, prior substantial developments need to take place, which are reflected within the readiness of the organization to adopt and execute. This view is endorsed by Wagner and Piller (2013, p.31) who claim that *"open innovation calls for a shift in strategic orientation, the organization and the companies' culture. These requirements are not dissimilar to those of traditional innovation management. Open innovation also needs to be planned, managed, monitored and formalized"*.

A highly interesting parameter to be briefly discussed in relation to the organizational open innovation perspective is the innovation quotient and its relationship to open innovation. During the 2012 European Open Innovation Summit in Brussels, Dr. Linda Beltz, Director Technology Partnerships in Weyerhaeuser, discussed the maximization of open innovation effectiveness, which derives from the understanding of the company's innovation quotient that helps the company understand how to achieve its vision. This is related to the development of the right organizational structures in order to adopt an open innovation mindset.

Following the practices of Weyerhaeuser, Dr. Beltz described the framework for open innovation in the evaluation of the innovation quotient elaborated calculatively and non-calculatively in the pillars of strategy (strategic intent), the role of open innovation (expectation of open innovation) and the organizational culture (cultural acceptance).

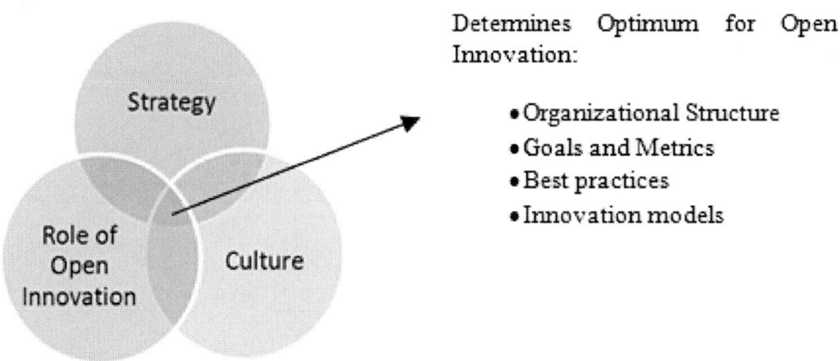

Figure 1. Optimum for Open Innovation

Dr. Beltz proposed three attributes of different open innovation organization structures: centralized, hybrid and decentralized. These three different attributes are depicted into the following figure.

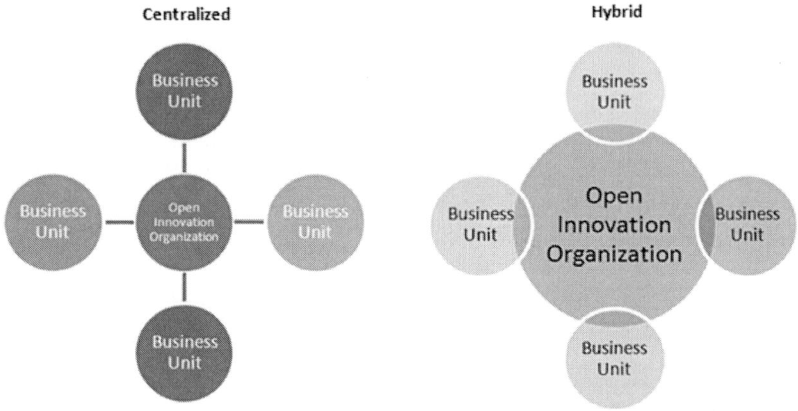

Figure 2. Open Innovation Organization Structures[1]

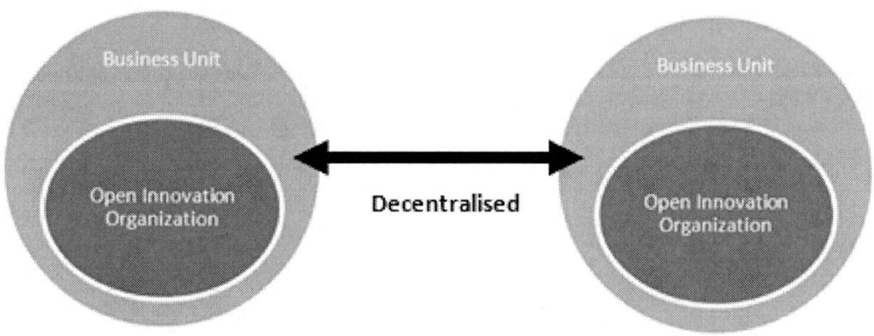

Figure 3. Open Innovation Organization Structures

These three types of organizational structures, that support and promote open innovation, have different characteristics and functionalities and are used in relation to the *ad hoc* strategic plan and orientation of the organization, but at the same time, are primarily related to the organizational readiness mechanisms an organization has established in order to adopt open innovation strategies.

[1] All the above-mentioned figures have been used under the written permission and IP ownership of Weyerhaeuser after full consultation with Dr. Linda Beltz. I wish to thank Weyerhaeuser and Dr. Beltz for their permission to use the material.

2.2 Organizational Readiness

2.2.1 Understanding t*he concept*

Organizational readiness as a concept, being associated with change, has been vastly explored in different sectors including the public sector (Nor Shahriza *et al.*, 2011; Cinite *et al.*, 2009; Maheshwari and Singhthe, 2010), the private sector focusing on the corporate level (Helm *et al.*, 2003), the information systems (Cui and Liu, 2010; Mouzakitis and Askounis, 2010), the educational sector (Nordin, 2012), the health care sector (Fuller *et al.*, 2007; Gagnon *et al.*, 2010; Snyder-Halpern, 2002; Hagedorn and Heideman, 2010; Stamatakis *et al.*, 2012; Williams, 2011) and the health services sector (Helfrich *et al.*, 2009; Rütten *et al.*, 2009).

By definition, readiness is "*a mindset that exists among employees during the implementation of organizational changes. It comprises the beliefs, attitudes, and intentions of change target members regarding the need for and capability of implementing organizational change. Readiness for organizational change is important to any change effort because the state of readiness for change may influence the strategy followed throughout the change effort*" (Armenakis and Fredenberger, 1997, p.144) or *"an individual's beliefs, attitudes and intentions regarding the extent to which changes are needed and the organization's capacity to successfully undertake those changes"* (Armenakis *et al.*, 1993, p.681). This means that readiness for change is a combination of organizational (Armenakis *et al.*, 1993) and individual models (Prochaska *et al.*, 2001).

Weiner (2009) discusses organizational readiness for change both in psychological and structural terms giving emphasis on the organization's resources in relation to finance, infrastructure, people and information. However, Weiner leads a sceptical pathway regarding the concrete conceptualization of organizational readiness for change by wondering whether readiness is a structural construct or a psychological one and brings forward a theory trying to *"reconcile the structural view and the psychological view by specifying a relationship between them"* (Weiner, 2009, p. 7). This leads towards a clear distinction between the institutional perspective in relation to the organization as a construction (in terms of infrastructure and processes) and the organization as a cumulative formation in relation to organizational culture, people's psychological readiness, organizational behaviour, values and principles requiring *"collective, coordinated behaviour change [...] in order to effectively implement the change"* (Weiner, 2009, p.6).

Armenakis and Fredenberger (1997) discuss the components forming the notion of readiness related to the faith the employees have towards the change agent and his competences regarding the management of change, the realization and understanding of the necessity proposed by the change, the balanced reflection upon the urgency regarding the change i.e. that the need for change is understood by all parties and is not simply imposed by top-level management and finally the willingness of the employees to be actively involved in the change and contribute to the creation of an effective and efficient organization.

In relation to the abovementioned multi-level managerial challenges and prior changes, Rafferty *et al.* (2013, p.112), while identifying a gap in the literature regarding the reflection of the multi-level processes in relation to organizational readiness, develop a multi-level review of change readiness *"outlining the antecedents and consequences of individual, work group and organizational change readiness"* [...] suggesting that *" the processes that contribute to the emergence of change readiness at the individual and collective levels differ at the individual, group and organizational levels"*.

Penland (1997) presents an interesting relationship between organizational readiness and the implementation of Quality Management Systems by developing a model of organizational readiness strategies focusing on three environmental factors; strategic leadership, vision perspective and positive culture. Strategic leadership is *"the process of identifying, crystallizing and communicating changes that will assure integration and harmony within current and future environments"* (Penland, 1997, p.70). The vision perspective includes the crystallization on the specific focus of the organization, the identification of barriers hindering improvement, development and change and the goals and expectations on performance measurement and evaluation. In addition, the nurturing of a positive culture embraces *"a strong value for team participation and shared leadership as basic management practices to enhance probabilities for success"* since it is *"comprised of beliefs, values, attitudes, norms and philosophies that significantly influence its ultimate success or failure"* (Penland, 1997, p.71).

Weiner (2009, p. 2) argues that *"organizational readiness for change is not only a multi-level construct, but a multi-faceted one"*. This leads to the understanding that readiness requires preparation both on a psychological and behavioural level so as to be efficiently and effectively implemented. It endorses the readiness for individual change regarding the staff perceptions, which is realised through a variety of stages; the precontemplative, the contemplative, the preparatory, the action and the maintenance stage. Cunningham *et al.*, (2002, p.378) suggest that *"the movement through these stages is governed by decisional balance, the anticipated risks of change vs the potential benefits of change"*.

2.2.2 Organizational Readiness for Open Innovation

Tuff and Jonash (2009) state that open innovation is hard, since it requires a delicate balance of skills and the effective ability and openness to overcome challenges expected or unexpected. Open innovation as an organizational paradigm requires substantial changes prior to its adoption and implementation. *"Organizational readiness for change is considered a critical precursor to the successful implementation of complex changes"* (Weiner, 2009, p.2).

Hafkesbrink and Schroll (2009) identify and cluster the organizational competences for open innovation in SMEs of the Digital Economy. They identify three organizational competences for open innovation within three dimensions; organizational readiness, collaborative capabilities and absorptive capacities. *"As a backbone of each of these dimensions appear the technological enhancement and existing of adequate collaboration and communication tools"* (Bevanda and Turk, 2011, p.1). It is important to underline the fact that a clear distinction between individual and organizational competences must be made and for this distinction Hafkesbrink and Schroll (2009, p.10) argue that *"every organizational competence involves one or more individual competences"*. The proposed model puts organizational readiness along with collaborative capability, absorptive capacity and effectiveness of knowledge valorisation under the functional umbrella of organizational competences for open innovation. In detail, regarding the organizational readiness for open innovation, Hafkesbrink and Schroll (2009, p.12) identify four organizational antecedents; *"... the cultural openness of an organization, dynamic capabilities for organizational change and renewal, designing specific organizational structures and processes and technological enhancement..."*

Bevis and Cole (2010) present a tool for open innovation readiness directly focusing on assisting the supporting SMEs that may fear the adoption and implementation of open innovation. The proposed open innovation readiness tool is outlined into five stages; learning about open innovation and how to innovate (the first stage where a learning environment regarding open innovation is developed), preparing for open innovation (the second stage brings upfront a self-assessment procedure and period regarding the existing internal competences of the company, the business, the size and governance and the potential approaches to innovation), initiating an open innovation project with confidence (this third stage is related to the presentation of an *"Innovation Map"* in order to visualize the form of innovation, the place and the role of each existing partner within the process), managing an open innovation project (the fourth stage is about project management) and maturing as an open innovator (the fifth and last stage that *"looks towards succeeding projects which might lack the initial seed idea"* (Bevis and Cole, 2010, p.10)).

Tuff and Jonash (2009) regarding the assessment of organizational readiness for open innovation and the identification of the key barriers, which must be foreseen and surpassed, propose a number of questions to be addressed under an organizational level. These questions are related to the existing protocols that enable the connection with the outside expertise, the identification of all the relevant structural barriers, the way the management of the organization perceives intellectual property protection, how this might have a positive or a negative effect towards collaborative attitude and how risk is related to ambition, strategic planning and incentives for cross-cultural and cross-boundary ventures.

Wagner and Piller (2013), while making an important distinction between need-driven and solution-driven methods to acquire information, present an auditing tool regarding the evaluation of open innovation readiness that *"enables companies to assess their readiness for open innovation as a basis for defining targeted internal measures aimed at promoting the benefits of open innovation*" (Wagner and Piller, 2013, p.31). They describe three dimensions of open innovation readiness: organization/methods, culture and absorptive capacity. These three dimensions are interrelated and interconnected to the organizational strategic orientation. This is the formulation of an innovation strategy which should be in line with the strategic goals of the search for external knowledge. They also underline the importance of the distinction between exploration and exploitation within the corporate strategy since *"this distinction matters for the use and design of search and integration processes"* (Wagner and Piller, 2013, p.28).

2.2.3 Open innovation adoption and trust

Tuff and Jonash state that the adoption and implementation of open innovation, besides the realization of the changes and the difficulties of implementing all the relevant and necessary changes, require two vital elements: discipline and commitment.

This chapter endorses this direction by taking a step backwards and arguing that in order to have discipline and commitment, a critical ingredient in the process of building up an *"open innovation ready"* organization is the establishment of internal organizational trust. Ruyter *et al.* (2001, p.272) define commitment as *"an enduring desire to maintain a valued relationship"*, distinguishing between affective and calculative commitment. The basis of an affective commitment lies within the development and existence of a general positive feeling towards the exchange partner. On the other hand, the calculative commitment is characterized by a negative nature since it is related to *"a firm's motivation to continue the relationship because it cannot easily replace its current partner and because it cannot obtain the same resources and outcomes outside its current relationship"* (Ruyter *et al.*, 2001, pp.272-273).

Morgan and Hunt (1994) underline the embeddedness of vulnerability within the core of commitment, as a concept, encouraging the realization that *"trust leads to a high level of affective commitment or, in other words, a strong desire to maintain a relationship"* (Ruyter, 2001, p.273). In the same study, while elaborating upon the commitment-trust theory, the authors clearly state that the simultaneous co-existence and interrelation between trust and commitment leads to outcomes that promote efficiency, productivity and effectiveness; leading to cooperative behaviours. Furthermore, it is necessary at this point to determine the role that this commitment is playing within the organizational level towards the forging of higher motivation and organizational citizenship behaviours (Morgan and Hunt, 1994).

This chapter perceives discipline as the way to be able to stick to the values and strategic priorities set in order to realise the strategic goals in order to adopt open innovation. This derives from the understanding of change management, communication to the organizational status and ability to justify. This is in line with the views of Perkinson (2005, p.31), who defines discipline as *"orderly or prescribed conduct or pattern of behaviour"* directly linked to trust which is built within a behavioural safety process. *"Greatness is not a function of circumstances. Greatness is largely a matter of conscious choice and discipline"* (Collins, 2005, p.31).

Open innovation requires a strategic innovation mindset, discipline and relevance towards the organizational behaviour, culture and norms. Becoming ready for open innovation is a highly challenging and strenuous process developed towards a multi-level organizational environment which requires strategic focus and passion and *"which enables clarity about producing long-term results and discipline to decline opportunities that distract from the mission"* (Mazyck, 2012, p.210). The role of trust towards this perceived discipline is highly critical since it shapes their incentives towards their focus and strategic orientation which in return has a substantial influence towards their attitudes and behaviour (Hansen *et al.*, 2011). This means that by the time strategic discipline is in place and the trustworthy environment has a positive influence towards the realization of the strategic goals towards the adoption of open innovation employees are *"likely to develop an increased motivation to give back to their organization as manifest through increased organizational citizenship behaviour"* (Hansen *et al.*, 2011, p.32)

3. Research context and design

This conceptual chapter is based upon a thorough review of the literature, fostering the contribution to theory development and the conceptualization of the research area (Knafl and Howard, 1984).

This approach has been chosen so as to justify and endorse my willingness to deepen the understanding of the abstract notion of trust and conceptualize it in relation to open innovation and organizational readiness.

My aim, regarding this chapter, has always been to understand and present what is required to exist prior to the adoption of open innovation strategies in a financial services organization. Financial crisis requires change, open innovation requires change and regaining external trust requires change; however, the core problem lies within the understanding of the antecedents of change i.e. the development of an organizational framework encouraging change.

The following research questions have been considered:

1. How organizational readiness is perceived in financial services organizations?
2. What is the relationship between the challenges faced by financial services organizations and open innovation adoption?
3. What is the functional role of organizational trust in the process?
4. How is the realization of the need for change in the financial services sector effectively enabled?

The literature review is conducted building upon the following literature streams: open innovation, organizational readiness, trust and organizational behaviour in the financial services sector serving as an empirical setting.

The development of the conceptual framework has eased the precise and accurate definition and comprehension of the research problem. The purpose of conceptualization is to initially get a basic insight into the topic and also valuable hints concerning the design, research strategy and focus of the main study leading to the development of the proposed conceptual framework (Lösch, 2006).

The chapter follows the cognitive processes proposed by Morse, which involve comprehending, synthesizing, theorising and recontextualizing or putting new knowledge back into the context of how the other researchers have articulated the evolving knowledge (Walker, Cooke and McAlister, 2008). Trust is investigated in relation to organizational readiness and organizational readiness in relation to trust embedded open innovation as an organizational mindset.

Due to the fact that I have already conducted prior research in the field, the conceptual framework has been presented as such, however, having reflected upon the dynamic character of the model, changes are proposed and additional elements are added, elements, which are examined in relation to trust, enabling a better and more concise formulation of the proposed conceptual framework.

4. A trust embedded organizational readiness model for open innovation

4.1 Definition of Trust

The 1972 Nobel Laureate on Economics Professor Kenneth J. Arrow in his well-known paper *"Gifts and Exchanges"*, states that *"virtually every commercial transaction has within itself an element of trust, certainly any transaction conducted over a period of time. It can be plausibly argued that much of the economic backwardness in the world can be explained by the lack of mutual confidence"* (Arrow, 1972, p.357). Gibb argues that, *"trust is instinctive, unstrategized and, as a feeling, is close to love"* (Blomqvist, 1997, p.272). However, Furlong (1996, p. 1) states that *"despite the plethora of material emerging on the subject [...] trust remains an elusive notion [...] resulting in a confusing potpourri of definitions applied to a host of units and levels of analysis [...] led to a proliferation of definitions each used in a different context"*.

In terms of conceptualization, the chapter adopts the definition proposed by Mayer *et al.*, (1995, p.712) that trust is "*the willingness of a party to be vulnerable to the actions of another party based on the expectation that the other will perform a particular action important to the trustor, irrespective of the ability to monitor or control that other party"*. This refers to the *"extent that people can trust others, they can work together to create benefits that each individually cannot generate alone"* (Dunning *et al.*, 2012, p.687). The basis of this abovementioned analysis lies within the notion of expectation which is reflected in the definition by Simpson (2007, p.589) that trust is *"a specific set of socially learned expectations that people hold about various social systems, ranging from other people to social organizations to the larger moral social order"*.

Trust is *"one of the basic variables in any human interaction"* (Blomqvist, 1997, p.271) since it shares a major influence on every human aspect. Based upon the trust level theory initially developed by Gibb, trust is the core element regarding the determination of the interaction of processes having an effective impact on the system. Dunning *et al.* (2012) discuss trust not only as an economic act but as a social and emotional act. Emotions do definitely play a vital part in the cognitive and psychological elaboration of trust in two ways: in terms of anticipated emotions and in terms of immediate emotions.

Dunning *et al.* (2012, p.690) define anticipated emotions as *"the forecasts people make about their emotional reactions to the outcomes of their actions"* and immediate emotions as the *"emotions people feel about the decision options in front of them at the moment they consider whether or not to trust"*. The social perspective of trust is related to the altruism and morality people wish to develop and the signal exchange that is taking place within the relationships, achieving a potential recognition by means of cooperation and reliability (Andreoni and Bernheim, 2009; Lotz *et al.*, 2011, both cited by Dunning *et al.*, 2012). In addition, Henrich *et al.* (2010 cited by Dunning *et al.*, 2012) open up the field to the cultural level discussing the use of pro-social norms that facilitate the maintenance of a stable social structure allowing its members to develop and make progress.

Beugelsdijk (2006) considers trust as a multi-level phenomenon, which can be studied in two levels: the micro and the macro. This definite multi-dimensionality (Brattström *et al.*, 2012) incorporates a number of elements and functions that exist individually, but neither necessarily interdependently nor constantly. Especially in the financial services sector this multi-dimensionality is comprised of three constructs: dependability, knowledge and exceeding expectations (Heffernan *et al.*, 2008). On a macro level *"trust is regarded as a property of individuals or a characteristic of interpersonal relationships. Through on-going transactions, firms develop trust around norms of equity of knowledge-based trust, which has also been labelled process-based trust"* (Beugelsdijk, 2006, p.374). Regarding the micro level of trust, a great number of typologies emerge from the extensive literature leading to the realization of a multi-disciplinary approach to the concept and at the same time a lack of concrete conceptualization.

Lewicki and Bunker (1996) while discussing the development and maintenance of trust in relation to work relationships identify three commonly accepted typologies of trust under the micro level; calculus-based trust, knowledge-based trust and identification based trust. All these typologies share different antecedents, characteristics and interpretation based on the specific context and a further more detailed elaboration would be out of the goals and expectations of this present study.

The abovementioned multi-dimensionality of trust is perceived in three different levels. Based on the extensive existing literature (Fawcett *et al.*, 2012; Johnson and Grayson, 2005; Gulati and Sytch, 2008a; Gulati and Sytch, 2008b; Mayer *et al.*, 1995; McAllister, 1995;; Ring and Van De Ven, 1994; Schoorman, *et al*, 2007), in the first dimension, trust can be perceived at an individual level, interpersonal level, between individuals and organizations, between organizations (interorganizational perspective) and between individuals and information systems. Trust is depicted solely as a relational entity and cannot be perceived in isolation.

In the second dimension, highly related to the development of organizational readiness strategies, McAllister brings forward the cognition-based trust and the affect-based trust in relation to interpersonal trust, which is characterised as *"a pervasive phenomenon in organizational life"* (McAllister, 1995, p.25). Interpersonal trust is perceived under the extent that a person shows confidence and willingness for action based upon the words, actions and decisions depicted by the other person, enabling the realisation of the existence of both cognitive and affective foundations. The cognition-based trust is *"grounded in individual beliefs about peer reliability and dependability"* and the affect-based trust is *"grounded in reciprocated interpersonal care and concern"* (McAllister, 1995, p.25). It is important here to underline that despite the fact that these two dimensions of trust share a causality-based relationship; their functionality is unique in terms of sharing different and distinct association patterns.

A third dimension is related to competence and goodwill trust. By definition, competence trust refers to *"the confidence in the abilities of the other party to perform its share of workload in an exchange. When competence trust is high, one is more willing to be vulnerable to the other party in risky situations"* (Lui, 2009, p.334). On the other hand, goodwill trust *"emphasizes faith in the moral integrity, which is produced through interpersonal interactions that lead to social-psychological bonds of mutual norms, sentiments, and friendships in dealing with uncertainty"* (Ring and van de Ven, 1994, p.93).

4.2 Organizational readiness and trust

As it has been already discussed, organizational readiness and trust as concepts have been thoroughly and separately investigated in numerous research and diverse contexts. It is important at this stage to explore what is the relation between organizational readiness and trust *"by translating the abstract notion of predictable behaviour into the tangible notion of systematized processes and structures"* (Brattström *et al.*, 2012, p.750).

Trust along with partnership building and commitment is established via effective and efficient participation. These three elements, being considered highly important regarding the long-term organizational performance improvement, are part of the normative-reeducative strategies included in the proposed change strategies typology by Choi and Ruona (2011), in relation to the change strategies and individual readiness for organizational change. Similarly, trust belongs to the elements explicitly contributing to the possible antecedents of organizational readiness for change (Cinite *et al.*, 2009). In addition, by means of the organizational readiness for changes scales, Fuller *et al.*, (2007) consider trust and cooperation among the staff as an important assessment parameter regarding the organizational climate, which they consider as a dimension influencing organizational change. Furthermore, it is argued that *"firms which have a history of trust and collaboration across hierarchical levels are likely to experience a smoother implementation experience that firms which have a tradition of adversarial relationships between managers/professionals and other employees"* (Helm *et al.*, 2003, p.271).

Berber *et al.* (2012) present an interesting conceptual model regarding the role of trust in organizations and readiness to change as predictors of successful organizational innovations. Readiness for change is perceived in the following three pillars; emotional, cognitive and intentional. While exploring the relationships among trust in organization, readiness to change and perceived success of organizational level innovation, the authors argue that *"when employees trust in their organization, they will not see change as threat and hence they will fully commit themselves to the change process"* (Barber *et al.*, 2012, p.10).

In the endeavour to develop a concrete and comprehensive framework regarding the assessment of organizational readiness for change, Lehman *et al.* (2002) identify four major areas: motivation of change, institutional resources of the program, personality attributes of the staff and organizational climate of the program. Within the organizational climate, they identify six scales. Two of them, staff cohesiveness and staff autonomy, consider trust as their core and vital element since trust is interpreted as a moderator regarding group work enabling effective collaboration and also a means of efficiency and trustworthiness deriving from leadership and management. This is related to the abovementioned analysis on competence-based and affect-based trust where we see that the employee is appreciated both in terms of competences and attitude towards the rest of the staff regardless hierarchical zones and levels.

Madsen *et al.* (2005) identify the relevant factors individual organizational readiness affecting on a second level the readiness for organizational change. Among the many potential factors, which could affect this influence, the authors have decided to examine the organizational commitment and the social relationships in the workplace. Trust and perceived organizational support in peers are related to readiness for change. Organizational readiness is the threshold to the establishment of an organizational culture of performance since *"all the employees must be able to understand the expectations of management from them. There must be a climate of openness, information sharing, and trust"* (Maheshwari and Singh, 2010, p.72).

"Work group psychological safety describes a group climate characterized by interpersonal trust and mutual respect in which people are comfortable being themselves" (Rafferty *et al.*, 2013, p.123). This is interpreted in the fact that a work-group psychological safety shares a positive effect towards group-change readiness, leading to openness towards change, flexibility and sharing attitude; facilitating smoothly not only the expectations, needs and competences required but also creating a positive emotional atmosphere towards change.

The creation of a positive culture becomes a vital part of an organizational readiness strategy. The creation of an environmental culture is important since it influences the way the organization will be able to embrace change in a successful or an unsuccessful way. Penland (1997, p.71) believes that an environmental culture is *"comprised of beliefs, values, attitudes, norms and philosophies"*. Trust creates a significant feeling within this so-called *"cultural climate"* since it empowers cooperation, appreciation and comprehension towards the mission the organization needs to lead, making the cognitive acceptance of change adaptable.

5. A trust embedded model for open innovation organizational readiness in financial services organizations

Campbell (in KPMG, 2011, p.1) argues that *"change and innovation are endemic within the financial services arena [...] however; the financial crisis of the last few years has forced a scope and pace of change which would challenge even the most adaptable of professionals".*

I also argue that the financial crisis must be seen as an opportunity and a catalyst towards change, also enabled by globalization. Institutionalized and traditional practices are being constantly challenged due to an increasingly intangible and digitalized world.

Wesemann (2006) and Dell Wyse (2011) discuss the main challenges and outside influences that financial services organizations are facing today, requiring quick and effective response and thus fuelling the demand for change:

	Challenges
1	Regulation
2	Close collaboration with other organizations
3	Faster market penetration in terms of new products and services
4	Effective and efficient risk management
5	Data quality, protection and information security
6	Operational challenges in terms of compliance
7	Increase in the efficiencies for a better competitive position
8	Mergers and acquisitions
9	Governmental intervention

Figure 4. Challenges faced by financial services organizations

In these challenges I would also like to add the positioning in a constantly changing globalized environment, the multicultural and cross border cooperation and the management of the increased mobility of highly skilled human capital. Needless to say that, all these challenges exist within a turbulent, unstable global economic environment, characterized by a loss of trust from the customers and the users side, towards both the sector and the institutions themselves. As it has already been discussed, open innovation can be the core facilitator of this change; however, its adoption requires effective and efficient organizational readiness.

Organizational readiness for the adoption of open innovation in financial services institutions requires changes and reform, however, this *"reform will be more difficult in an environment where global financial markets remain fragile, where governments struggle to meet budgetary requirements and where jobs are under pressure"* (Loughman in KPMG, 2011, p.3). Furthermore, it is important to underline the fact that the current economic environment has unveiled processes and practices within the financial services sector, which are far from appropriate to overcome these challenges, constituting a dangerous barrier towards this reform. So this means that, the way a financial services firm would organize itself, has an influence regarding its likelihood of being open (Freel and Aslesen, 2013).

Open innovation as a concept can be interpreted within multiple and various ways. This does not mean of course that as a concept it does not entail established variables and practices. Salampasis *et al.* (2014b) argue that despite the fact that it is widely acknowledged that open innovation can be the key for future business success, it is not yet vastly adopted in terms of company structure and approach. For this reason and in these terms of reference, open innovation is perceived from a different angle, since it is more than a paradigm, a process, a framework or a business model.

I believe that open innovation is an organizational mindset, which is perceived under a collaborative aspect requiring the core element of trust. This is grounded on the fact that open innovation is not only related to knowledge inflows and outflow, as prior literature depicts, but it is driven upon an entire ecosystem of values, motivations, skills and competences, characteristics, attributes and attitudes; all these realized by the human element. Knowledge exchange and sharing is the mean but not the aim.

I believe that open innovation is perceived under the simultaneous co-existence of four core elements considered as the organizational antecedents of open innovation: knowledge sharing attitude, collaborative culture, ambidextrous thinking, and diversity management. (Salampasis *et al.*, 2014b). This understanding is in line with the argumentation of Tuff and Jonash (2009, p.3) that *"implemented well, open innovation should include a process-a set of activities whose purpose is to find or generate good ideas, technologies and the infrastructure needed to adapt and support those activities. In this way, open innovation becomes an organizational mindset"*.

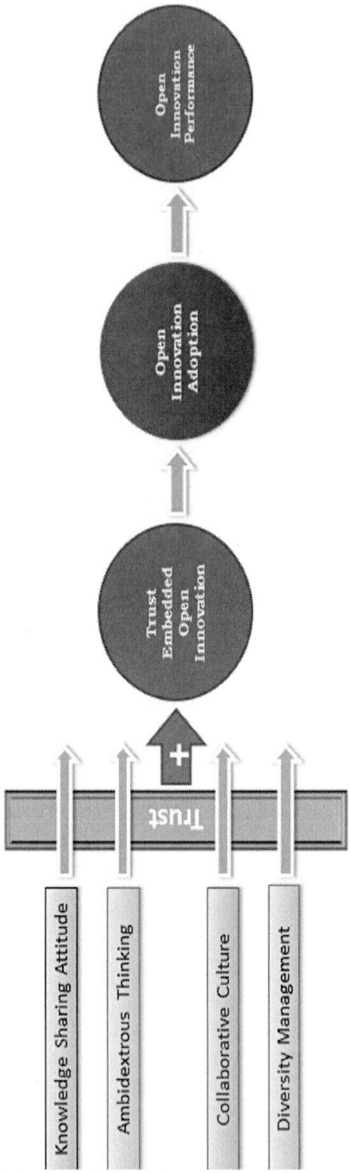

Figure 5. Trust embedded organizational readiness for open innovation adoption in the financial services sector

The above mentioned four antecedents of open innovation are *"filtered"* as *one cumulative formation* through a layer of trust depicting the actual embeddedness of trust within the core of the concept of open innovation, formulating a cumulative conception.

It is important to acknowledge the fact that trust shares different functions within the cumulative and/or non-cumulative relationships among the antecedents of open innovation and the open innovation adoption. Furthermore, the adoption of open innovation is expected to have a positive effect on open innovation performance, since it *"puts forward the non-linear, dynamic and interactive nature of the innovation process"* (Mention, 2011, p.44) characterised by interaction, cooperation on innovation and effective collaboration, ensuring a continuous committement to innovation (Mention and Torkkeli, 2012).

The various conceptual relationships between each construct and the organizational antecedents of open innovation have already been described in detail in my previous work on the subject (Salampasis *et al*, 2014a+b; Salampasis *et al.*, 2015). However, two more newly identified constructs related to the collaborative culture are introduced in the chapter; global dexterity (Molinksy, 2012) and emotional intelligence and transparency (Harvey *et al.*, 2012).

In his recently published book *Global Dexterity: How to adapt your behaviour across cultures without losing yourself in the process*, Molinsky presents a tool which is needed so as to achieve a simultaneous behavioural adaptation to new cultural contexts while staying authentic and grounded in your own natural style. This is a matter of developing the capability to switch behaviours and overcome the emotional and psychological challenges of doing so.

Global dexterity functions as an antecedent to/predictor of organizational trust in the sense that the more global dexterity people have in the organization, the more open they will likely be to these innovative practices. I believe that in order to be able to foster a collaborative culture, especially within globalized environments the psychological cross-cultural behavioural adaptation is a paramount driving force crystalized within a trustworthy environment (Molinsky, 2013). This *"code-switching"* capability fosters *"positive impression management outcomes such as fitting in, being well-liked, and winning the respect, trust, and friendship of clients, colleagues, and subordinates while also sparking a positive spiral of interpersonal communication within a given professional relationship"* (Molinsky, 2007, p.623).

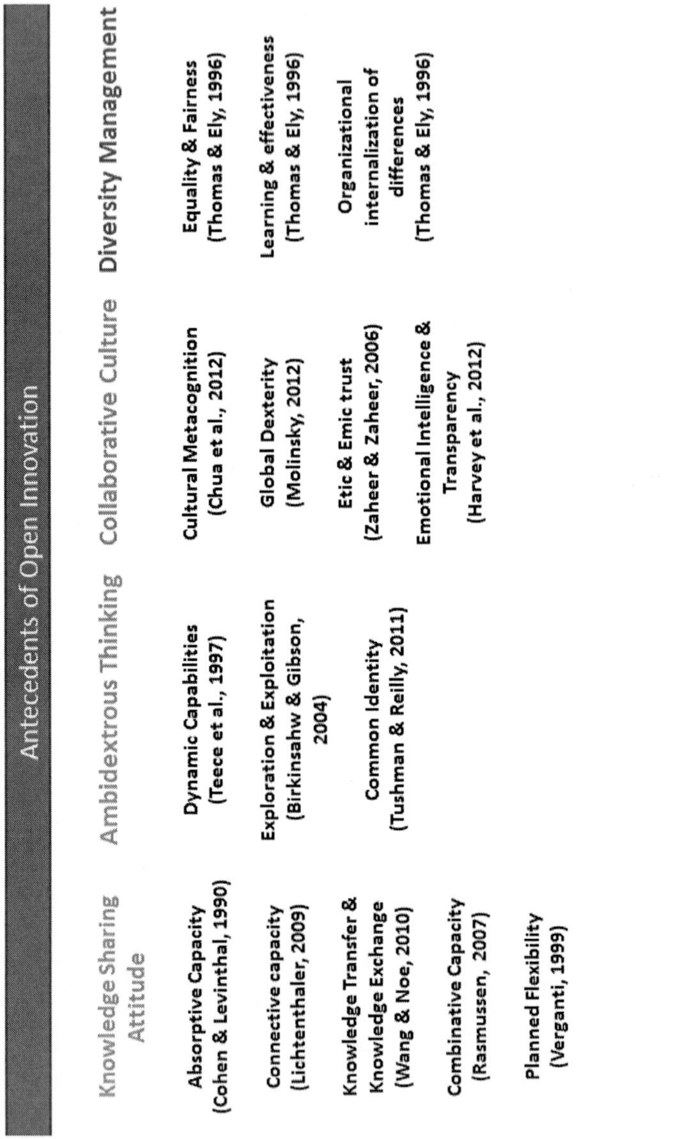

Figure 6. Variables of the organizational antecedents of open innovation[2]

[2] For a detailed analysis kindly refer to the previous work conducted by the author.

As a concept, emotional intelligence has vastly been examined in various contexts and levels (Dulewicz and Higgs, 1999, 2000; Goleman, 1995, 1998; Salovey and Mayer, 1990). The reason why I have chosen emotional intelligence and emotional transparency as a construct of collaborative culture is the fact that they belong to the core elements of a sustainable-relationship development and team building. Teams are considered as the foundation of the organization and in order to work effectively they require the establishment of mutual trust, focus and commitment to the strategically set goals. Harvey *et al.* (2012, p.629) argue that emotions *"encapsulate interactional contexts and is a universal phenomenon"*. They bring forward a number of elements constituting the core of emotions, emotional relationship, emotional acceptance, emotional availability, emotional philosophy, emotion coaching, emotional attitude, emotional boundaries, emotional self-acceptance and emotion regulation.

All these elements are crystalized within the way emotions are understood, managed and within their influential power towards a person, a team and organization and in relation to inclusion, creativity and performance. Emotional intelligence needs to be perceived on a team context and not in solitude and this realization from a managerial standpoint is imperative (Druskat and Wolff, 2001). Under an organizational perspective, trust among members, a sense of group identity and a sense of group efficacy constitute the essential elements of group effectiveness, elements empowered by the creation of *"emotionally intelligent norms the attitudes and behaviours that become habits that support behaviours for building trust, group identity and group efficacy"* (Druskat and Wolff, 2001, p.82). Heffernan *et al.* (2008, p.192) discuss the impact of emotional intelligence and trust on bank performance and clearly state that *"now trust and emotional intelligence have been highlighted as components in development of successful relationships in a business-banking context"* while a strategic shift towards relationship marketing strategies is observed in the financial services sector.

Finally, it is also important to underline that the proposed conceptual framework is in line with the contingency theory. Hsieh and Tidd (2012, p.601) underline the locus of the theory that *"no single organizational structure is effective in all circumstances. Instead there is an optimal organizational structure that best fits a given contingency, such as size, strategy, task uncertainty or technology"*. This is the reason why the proposed model does not refer to institutional and structural processes but gives only the elements which an organizational readiness for open innovation should consist of on an ad-hoc basis.

6. Discussion

In this chapter I tried to depict the necessity of trust via the formation of a proposed conceptual framework regarding the organizational readiness towards the adoption of open innovation strategies in the financial services sector. I introduced the element of trust by arguing that trust is embedded within the process of creating an open innovation *"ready"* financial services organisation. I also argued that in order for the financial services sector to regain trust, the establishment of internal organizational trust is the one and foremost antecedent.

Following upon the abovementioned analysis, some very important and relevant comments regarding the organizational readiness towards the adoption of open innovation in the financial services organizations need to be addressed.

The organizational environment has a lot to do with helping or hindering trust. I propose four principles which, if adhered to in an organization's culture, will increase trust. Those are a) the focus on the other party for the other party's sake, b) an inclination to transparency, c) a habit of collaboration and d) an insistence on viewing things in the longer term not shorter, and in terms of relationships not transactions. Most financial institutions do poorly on all four of these items. And also it is important to underline the fact that the drivers of inter-organizational trust are the same as the drivers of intra-organizational trust-they are beliefs and attitudes that create an environment conducive to trustors taking risks, and trustees being trustworthy.

In the upcoming book, *Getting to We: Negotiating Agreements for Highly Collaborative Relationships,* Kate Vitasek outlines three things that are essential to establishing a *"what's-in-it-for-we"* mindset: trust, transparency and compatibility. Trust is the most important of these guiding principles, because it is the core quality of any collaborative partnership. Trust enables everything else that follows in getting to *"we"*.

Trust lowers transaction costs, fosters innovation and provides the necessary space for the flexibility and agility needed in today's markets. Trust requires a high level of transparency because without it parties are less likely to share information openly, financial or otherwise. In addition, a trusting and collaborative relationship should have a certain level of compatibility between the parties they don't have to love each other but they do have to be somewhat aligned in both their behaviors, values and their cultures. It's very difficult to visualize long-term alignment and success in the absence of a shared vision based on trust, transparency and compatibility. Trust should never be taken for granted because it's a given that *"business happens"*: events and challenges will occur that shake and test a relationship's core values, including trust. It is also hard to establish a culture of trust without buy-in and commitment from the top down that goes beyond a focus on the quarterly bottom line.

Regarding other works and approaches of formulating an open innovation organizational readiness, I would like to partly differentiate myself by saying that I perceive organizational readiness as a whole and not solely on a procedural and structural level. I define organization as a holistic and multidimensional formation including everything that functions under its umbrella. It is apparent that institutional or structural readiness is the vital element in the process but I believe that the definition of why we need the change will define the "*what*" and the *"how"*.

Regarding the adoption of open innovation in the financial services sector, I strongly believe that it can contribute towards the required changes to be done in order to set up more sustainable business models. I also argue that the complexity and the global reach of the financial services sector and the way this is managed on a multi-level perspective and in various ways, in terms of management, tradition and regulatory framework, consist a major challenge, which needs an incremental, long-term process that will reveal the advantages open innovation strategies bring and minimize the potential vulnerabilities open business models can entail. This is why I focus on the trust embeddedness of open innovation as an organizational mindset, setting the principles and stable elements of this shift.

The financial services sector will recover but I strongly believe that in order to gain external trust, the starting point is the cultivation and establishment of internal trust. You cannot expect to be trusted by partners, customers, etc., if the organizational trust within the organization has not been established. And this is where I believe that the proposed framework can help towards both the realization of the importance of trust and its organizational establishment within a financial organization.

7. Conclusion

7.1 Implications

7.1.1 Academic Implications

This study contributes to the literature of open innovation in relation to organizational behaviour following the argumentation of Tushman *et al.* (2012, p.25) that *"the impact of open innovation on the organization theory and strategic management literatures has been minimal"*. It draws attention to the development of a conceptual framework regarding the organizational readiness of financial services organizations towards the adoption of open innovation. *"Fundamentally, open innovation is all about capitalizing not only the ideas of others, but deriving benefit from ideas that your organization does not currently have a use for that others might. [...] open innovation is all about putting the right ideas into the hands of the right people in order to develop a commercially viable new product or service"* (Rowell, 2008, p.3). Furthermore, it brings new insights regarding the relationship between the understanding of the boundaries of innovation and the actual locus of innovation, meaning that organizational readiness for open innovation depicts the innovation developments both within the firm and on a community level redefining the complexity of organizational boundaries. In addition, it encourages a more multi-disciplinary research in the field, by driving a mindset away from static models leading to a more dynamic relationships perceived within organizational and innovation management.

7.1.2 Managerial Implications

In terms of managerial perspective, it is important to realize that the primary determinant of the adoption of open innovation in terms of organizational readiness is to fit within the organization's strategic goals, structure and climate. It is important for top management to understand that the organization is the people; that the adoption of open innovation is a difficult and incremental process and that the establishment of an organizational trustworthy environment is the starting point for making any kind of change. This means that the adoption of open innovation requires the establishment of non-linear thinking and this shift in the mindset will come by fostering innovation and creativity.

Especially for the human resource management departments of the financial services organizations, it is important to put the people in the core of the organizational readiness process and make sure that the need for change is communicated, since its awareness should be better able to generate an effective adoption of open innovation strategies.

Moreover, regarding the financial services sector, the main outcome of this chapter lies upon the realization of a new approach towards the inside and outside environment since *"the era of centralization and single-platform strategies is drawing to and end"* (KPMG, 2012, p.4). So this means that we are looking upon dyadic changes both in terms of organizational and industrial operation. Transformation is of top priority giving a breathing space for quick adaptation, seeing the challenges and opportunities and abandoning the *"business as usual"* existing mindset.

Finally, this chapter endorses Hansen's proposition regarding the encouragement of *"public policy makers, financial authorities and financial services providers to continue, improve and/or develop consumer financial education programmes"* (Hansen, 2012, p.291)

7.2 Limitations

It is important to underline the fact that there are some limitations deriving from this study, which deserve to be acknowledged. One important limitation is the fact that this chapter is looking on open innovation organizational adoption as a whole without differentiating among inbound, outbound and coupled open innovation processes. A second limitation derives from the fact that the conceptual framework is applied within the financial services sector using a holistic approach. Within financial services, there may be specific forms of innovation, let aside services in general. These forms are normally referred to as tailored or customized meaning that despite the fact that they might exist in many sectors of business to business services, it does not necessarily mean that they can apply to the financial services sector as a whole (Micudâ, 2011). Finally, another limitation lies within the fact that trust under an organizational level is examined as a whole and not explicitly on a micro, meso and macro level.

7.3 Future research pathways

As it can be seen by the literature review, open innovation as a concept, despite the fact that it has been vastly explored, shares a very limited research impact on services and especially financial services. Even in terms of conceptualization what open innovation is and what it is not, the concept is still being debated (Hossain, 2013).

Particularly, in the research area of financial services the adoption and implementation of open innovation are still quite obscure, especially when it comes to the conceptualization of organizational readiness.

It is crucial to explore the managerial challenges particularly in the global open innovation context and it is essential to investigate how open innovation can be implemented for sustainable development within the financial services sector both holistically and per industry.

Furthermore, further qualitative and quantitative research is needed in relation to the role of organizational trust as an enabler towards the open innovation adoption and implementation in the financial services sector and auditing tools to measure the effective and efficient impact of trust embedded open innovation organizational readiness in the financial services sector.

Acknowledgements

The writing of this chapter would have been almost impossible without the valuable help of the following people who devoted their time, energy, skills and knowledge to answer my questions, to exchange e-mails and to share with me their insights giving me incentive for a more focused research in the development of my conceptual model.

So I would like to take this opportunity and thank:

1. Kate Vitasek, Faculty for the center for Executive Education at the University of Tennessee
2. Andy Molinsky, Associate Professor of Organizational Behaviour, Brandeis University's International Business School
3. Charles Green, renowned author, consultant-advisor and business founder

References

Abdinnour-Helm, Sue, Lengnick-Hall, Mark and Lengnick-Hall, Cynthia. “Pre-implementation Attitudes and Organizational Readiness for Implementing an Enterprise Resource Planning System.” *European Journal of Operational Research* 146.2 (2003): 258-273.

Almirall, Esteve, and Casadesus-Masanell, Ramon. “Open versus Closed Innovation: A model of discovery and divergence”. *Academy of Management Review*, 35.1 (2010): 27-47.

Armenakis, Achilles and Fredenberger, William. “Organizational Change Readiness Practices of Business Turnaround Change Agents.” *Knowledge and Process Management* 4.3 (1997):143-152.

Armenakis, Achilles, Harris, Stanley and Mossholder, Kevin. "Creating Readiness for Organizational Change." *Human Relations* 46.6 (1993): 681-704.

Arrow, Kenneth J. “Gifts and Exchanges.” *Philosophy & Public Affairs* 1.4 (1972): 343-362

Berber A., Rofcanin Y., Kırçova O., “Trust in Organization and Readiness to Change as Predictors of Successful Organizational Innovations: Conceptual Model with Preliminary Support”, *Yönetim* (İstanbul Üniversitesi İşletme İktisadı Enstitüsü), 23.73 (2012): 7-18

Bevanda, Vanja and Turk, Marko. "Exploring semantic infrastructure development for open innovation", *in the 5th International Scientific Conference "Entrepreneurship and Macroeconomic Management: Reflections on the World in Turmoil"* ((2011)

Bevis, I. Keith, and Cole, Adrian. "Open Innovation Readiness: a Tool" in *The Dynamics of Innovation: proceedings of ISPIM XXI International Conference*. International Society for Professional Innovation Management Ltd, ISPIM XXI International Conference, Bilbao, Spain, 6-9 June 2010

Beugelsdijk, Sjoerd. "A Note on the Theory and Measurement of Trust in Explaining Differences in Economic Growth." *Cambridge Journal of Economics* 30.3 (2006): 371-387.

Blois, Keith J. "Trust in Business to Business Relationships: an evaluation of its status" *Journal of Management Studies* 36.2 (1999): 197-215.

Blomqvist, Kirsimarja. "The Many Faces of Trust." *Scandinavian Journal of Management* 13.3 (1997): 271-286.

Brattström, Anna, Löfsten, Hans and Richtnér, Anders. "Creativity, Trust and Systematic Processes in Product Development." *Research Policy* 41.4 (2012): 743-755.

Chesbrough, Henry. "Open Innovation: The New Imperative for Creating and Profiting from Technology" *Harvard Business School Press*, (2003)

—. "The Era of Open Innovation". *MIT Sloan Management Review*, 44.3 (2003): 35-41.

Choi, Myungweon and Ruona, Wendy E A. "Individual Readiness for Organizational Change and Its Implications for Human Resource and Organization Development." *Human Resource Development Review* 10.1 (2011): 46-73.

Cinite, Inta, Duxbury, Linda and Higgins, Chris. "Measurement of Perceived Organizational Readiness for Change in the Public Sector." *British Journal of Management* 20.2 (2009): 265-277.

Cloudera. "*White Paper: Why Are Financial Services Firms Adopting Cloudera's Big Data Solutions?*" Palo Alto (2012): 1-6

Cohen, M. Wesley, and Levinthal, A. Daniel. "Absorptive Capacity: A New Perspective on Learning and Innovation". *Administrative Science Quarterly*, 35.1 (1990): 128-152.

Collins, Jim. *Good to great and the social sectors: A monograph to accompany* Good to Great. New York, NY: Harper Collins (2005).

Cui, Guoxi, and Liu, Kecheng. "Organizational Readiness Analysis for Enterprise Information Systems Implementation." *Journal of Software* 5.5 (2010): 554-561.

Cunningham, Charles, Woodward, Christel, Shannon, Harry, Macintosh, John, Lendrum, Bonnie, Rosenbloom, David and Brown, Judy. "Readiness for Organizational Change: A Longitudinal Study of Workplace, Psychological and Behavioural Correlates." *Journal of Occupational & Organizational Psychology* 75.4 (2002): 377-392.

Dell Wyse. "Enabling Financial Services Organizations to Innovate and Prosper under tighter scrutiny- The role of visualization and cloud client computing in advancing financial services" *White Paper* (2011): 1-12 http://www.wyse.com/sites/default/files/documents/whitepapers/Dell-Wyse-in-Financial-and-Banking-white-paper-2012-10-28.pdf

de Ruyter, Ko, Moorman, Luci and Lemmink, Jos. "Antecedents of Commitment and Trust in Customer-Supplier Relationships in High Technology Markets." *Industrial Marketing Management* 30.3 (2001):271-286.

Druskat, Vanessa Urch, and Wolff, Steven B. "Building the Emotional Intelligence of Groups." *Harvard Business Review* 79.3 (2001): 80-90.

Dulewicz, Victor, and Higgs, Malcolm. "Can emotional intelligence be measured and developed?" *Leadership & Organization Development Journal*, 20.5 (1999): 242-252.

Dulewicz, Victor, and Higgs, Malcolm. "Emotional intelligence: a review and evaluation study", *Journal of Managerial Psychology*, 15.4 (2000): 341-372.

Dunning, David, Fetchenhauer, Detlef and Schlösser, Thomas M. "Trust as a Social and Emotional Act: Noneconomic Considerations in Trust Behaviour." *Journal of Economic Psychology* 33.3 (2012): 686-694.

Enkel, Ellen, Gassmann, O. and Chesbrough, H. "Open R&D and open innovation: exploring the phenomenon." *R&D Management*, 39.4 (2009): 311-316.

Enkel, Ellen, Bell, John and Hogenkamp, Hannah. "Open Innovation Maturity Framework" *International Journal of Innovation Management* 15.6 (2011): 1161-1189.

Evan, Frank. "Defining Success in Open Innovation". NineSigma White Paper (2011): 1-8

Fawcett, Stanley, Jones, Stephen and Fawcett, Amydee. "Supply Chain Trust: The Catalyst for Collaborative Innovation." *Business Horizons* 55.2 (2012): 163-178.

Franke, Nikolaus, and Piller, Frank. "Value Creation by Toolkits for User Innovation and Design: The Case of the Watch Market." *Journal of Product Innovation Management* 21.6 (2004): 401-415.

Freel, Mark and Aslesen, Wiig, Heidi. "The organizational antecendents of openness in small firms" paper to be presented at the 35th DRUID Celebration Conference 2013, Barcelona, Spain, June 17-19 http://druid8.sit.aau.dk/acc_papers/d3pm8srctgbd42fchfrb99q4v0ir.pdf

Fuller, Bret, Rieckmann, Tracy, Nunes, Edward, Miller, Michael, Arfken, Cynthia, Edmundson, Eldon and McCarty, Dennis. "Organizational Readiness for Change and Opinions toward Treatment Innovations." *Journal of Substance Abuse Treatment* 33.2 (2007): 183-192.

Furlong, Dominic. "Conceptualization of Trust in Economic Thought". Institute of Development Studies, University of Sussex. (1996), http://books.google.lu/books?id=rTqwAAAAIAAJ

Gagnon, Marie-Pierre, Labarthe, Jenni, Legare, France, Ouimet, Mathieu, Estabrooks, Carole, Roch, Genevieve, Ghandour, El Kebir and Grimshaw, Jeremy. "Measuring Organizational Readiness for Knowledge Translation in Chronic Care." *Implementation Science* 6.1 (2011): 72.

Gassmann, Oliver and Enkel, Ellen. "Towards a theory of open innovation: three core processes archetypes". Paper presented at the R&D Management Conference, Lisbon, July 6-9 (2004).

Goleman, D. *Emotional Intelligence: Why It Can Matter More than IQ*, Bantam Books, (1995), New York, NY.

Goleman, Daniel. *Working with Emotional Intelligence*, Bloomsbury Publishing, (1998), London.

Gulati, Ranjay and Sytch, Maxim. "Does Familiarity Breed Trust? Revisiting the Antecedents of Trust." *Managerial and Decision Economics* 29.2-3 (2008a): 165–190.

Gulati, Ranjay and Sytch, Maxim. "The Dynamics of Trust." *Academy of Management Review* 33.1 (2008b): 276-278.

Hafkesbrink, Joachim, and Schroll, Markus. "Organizational Competencies for Open Innovation in Small and Medium Sized Enterprises of the Digital Economy" *Proceedings of the R&D Management Conference 2009* Butler, J. (Ed.) Vienna, Austria, 21-24 June 2009.

Hagedorn, Hildi, and Heideman, Paul. "The Relationship between Baseline Organizational Readiness to Change Assessment Subscale Scores and Implementation of Hepatitis Prevention Services in Substance Use Disorders Treatment Clinics: a Case Study." *Implementation Science* 5.1 (2010): 46.

Hagel, John and Brown Seely. "Creation Nets: Harnessing the Potential of Open Innovation." *Journal of Service Science* 1.2 (2008): 27-40.

Haldane Andrew G and Madouros Vasileios. *What is the contribution of the financial sector? VOX* Research-based policy analysis and commentary from leading economists, 22 November 2011 [online] http://www.voxeu.org/article/what-contribution-financial-sector (accessed November 2012)

Halliday, Vaux, Sue. "Which trust and when? Conceptualizing trust in business relationships based on context and contingency", *International Review of Retail, Distribution and Consumer Research* 13.4 (2003): 1.

Hansen, Duane, Dunford, Benjamin, Boss, Alan, Boss, Wayne and Angermeier, Ingo. "Corporate Social Responsibility and the Benefits of Employee Trust: A Cross-Disciplinary Perspective." *Journal of Business Ethics* 102.1 (2011): 29-45.

Hansen, Torben. "Understanding Trust in Financial Services: The Influence of Financial Healthiness, Knowledge, and Satisfaction." *Journal of Service Research* 15.3 (2012): 280-295.

Harvey, Shane, Bimler, David, Evans, Ian, Kirkland, John and Pechtel, Pia. "Mapping the Classroom Emotional Environment." *Teaching and Teacher Education* 28.4 (2012): 628-640.

Heim, C. Matthew. *2011 Open Innovation Scorecard Survey Report: Best Practices, Challenges and New Opportunities*. NineSigma, Cleveland, Ohio, (2011): 1-24.

Heffernan, Troy, O'Neill, Grant, Travaglione, Tony and Droulers, Marcelle. "Relationship marketing: The impact of emotional intelligence and trust on bank performance", *International Journal of Bank Marketing* 26.3 (2008): 183-199.

Helfat, E. Constance and Quinn, J. Brian. "Open Innovation: The New Imperative for Creating and Profiting from Technology". *Academy of Management Perspectives*, 20.2 (2006):86-88.

Helfrich, Christian, Li, Yu-Fang, Sharp, Nancy and Sales, Anne. "Organizational Readiness to Change Assessment (ORCA): Development of an Instrument Based on the Promoting Action on Research in Health Services (PARIHS) Framework." *Implementation Science* 4.1 (2009): 38.

Hossain, Mokter. (2013) "Open innovation: so far and a way forward", *World Journal of Science, Technology and Sustainable Development*, 10 (1), pp.30-41.

Hsieh, Kuo-Nan, and Joe Tidd. "Open Versus Closed New Service Development: The Influences of Project Novelty." *Technovation* 32.11 (2012): 600-608.

Huizingh, K.R.E. Eelko. Open innovation: State of the art and future perspectives. *Technovation*, 31.1 (2011): 2-9.

Hughes, Jennifer. "Financial Innovation Tools Remain in the Box." *Financial Times*, (2010) September 24 in http://www.ft.com/cms/s/2/bfaf5a48-c7b8-11df-8683-00144feab49a.html#axzz2QVoUKxmR.

Jeppesen Lars, Bo, and Lakhani, R. Karim. "Marginality and problem-solving effectiveness in broadcast search". *Organization Science* 21.5 (2010): 1016-1033

Johnson, Devon and Grayson, Kent. "Cognitive and Affective Trust in Service Relationships." *Journal of Business Research* 58.4 (2005): 500-507.

Kostopoulos, Konstantinos, Papalexandris, Alexandros, Papachroni, Margarita and Ioannou, George. "Absorptive Capacity, Innovation, and Financial Performance." *Journal of Business Research* 64.12 (2011): 1335-1343.

KPMG International. "Financial Services: Optimizing Banking Operating Models-from Strategy to Implementation" (2012): 1-14 http://www.kpmg.com/BE/en/IssuesAndInsights/ArticlesPublications/Documents/optimizing-banking-operating-models.pdf.

—. "A roundup of developments in VAT, GST, Trade and Customs and other indirect taxes: Special feature: the financial services sector". *Global Indirect Tax Brief* 23 (2011): 1-40 http://www.kpmg.com/Global/en/IssuesAndInsights/ArticlesPublications/Global-indirect-tax-brief/Pages/global-indirect-tax-brief-special-feature.aspx

Lehman, Wayne, Greener, Jack and Simpson, Dwayne. "Assessing Organizational Readiness for Change." *Journal of Substance Abuse Treatment* 22.4 (2002): 197-209.

Lewicki, J. Roy, and Bunker, Benedict, Barbara. "Developing and maintaining trust in work relationships." in Kramer, M. Roderick, and Tyler, R. Tom (Eds.), *Trust in organizations; Frontiers of theory and research:* (1996): 114-139. Thousand Oaks, CA: Sage.

Linstone, Harold A. "Comment on 'Is Open Innovation a Field of Study or a Communication Barrier to Theory Development?'" *Technovation* 30.11-12 (2010): 556.

Livieratos, Antonis, Papoulias, Demetrios and Petit, Sandra. "Open Innovation as an Alternative to Support Growth: The Coupled Processes Emphasized." *Proceedings of the 2012 18th International Conference on Engineering, Technology and Innovation* (2012): 1-8.

Lui, Steven. “The Roles of Competence Trust, Formal Contract, and Time Horizon in Interorganizational Learning.” *Organization Studies* 30.4 (2009): 333-353.

Madsen, Susan R, Miller, Duane and Cameron, John. “Readiness for Organizational Change: Do Organizational Commitment and Social Relationships in the Workplace Make a Difference?” *Human Resource Development Quarterly* 16.2 (2005): 213-234.

Maheshwari, Mridul, and Manjari Singh. “Organizational Readiness for Performance-Related Pay: Focus on Government of India Employees.” *Vikalpa: The Journal for Decision Makers* 35.1 (2010): 63-73.

Martovoy, Andrey, and Dos Santos, Jennifer. “Co-creation and co-profiting in Financial Services.” *International Journal of Entrepreneurship and Innovation Management* 16.1-2 (2012): 114-135.

Mayer, Roger, Davis, James and Schoorman, David. “An integrative model of organizational trust.” *Academy of Management Review* 20.3 (1995): 709-734.

Mazyck, Donna. “Moving Forward: NASN in 2012 and Beyond.” *NASN School Nurse* 27.4 (2012): 208-211.

McAllister, Daniel. “Affect-and-cognition-based trust as foundations for international cooperation in organizations.” *Academy of Management Journal* 38.1 (1995): 24-59.

McKinsey Global Institute. “Financial globalization: retreat of reset? Global capital markets 2013”. McKinsey & Company (2013): 1-80

Mention, Anne-Laure, and Torkkeli, Marko. “Drivers, Processes and Consequences of Financial Innovation: A Research Agenda.” *International Journal of Entrepreneurship and Innovation Management* 16.1 (2012): 5-29.

Mention, Anne-Laure. “Co-operation and Co-opetition as Open Innovation Practices in the Service Sector: Which Influence on Innovation Novelty?” *Technovation* 31.1 (2011): 44-53.

Mention, Anne-Laure, Martovoy, Andrey, and Torkkeli, Marko. (2014) ‘Open innovation in financial services: what are the external drivers?’, *International Journal of Business Excellence* (accepted)

Micuda, ID. “Typologies of Innovation in the Financial Services Sector: Limits and Implications.” *Recent Advances in Business Administration* (2011): 27-31.

Molinsky, Andrew. “Cross-cultural code-switching: the psychological challenges of adapting behaviour in foreign cultural interactions.” *Academy of Management Review* 32.2 (2007): 622-640.

Molinsky, Andy. *Global Dexterity: How to Adapt Your Behaviour Across Cultures without Losing Yourself in the Process*, Harvard Business Review Press (2013): 240.

—. "The psychological processes of cultural retooling", *Academy of Management Journal* 56.3 (2013): 682-710

Morgan, Robert and Hunt, Shelby. "The Commitment-Trust Theory of Relationship Marketing." *Journal of Marketing* 58.3 (1994): 20-38.

Mouzakitis, Spyros, and Askounis, Dimitris. "A Knowledge-Based Framework for Measuring Organizational Readiness for the Adoption of B2B Integration Systems." *Information Systems Management* 27.3 (2010): 253-266.

Nordin, Norshidah. "The Influence of Leadership Behaviour and Organizational Commitment on Organizational Readiness for Change in a Higher Learning Institution." *Asia Pacific Education Review* 13.2 (2012): 239-249.

Nor Shahriza, Abdul Karim, Norshidah, Mohammad, Lili, Marziana Abdullah and Mohamed Jalaldeen Mohamed Razi. "Understanding Organizational Readiness for Knowledge Management in the Malaysian Public Sector Organization: A Proposed Framework." *Research and Innovation in Information Systems (ICRIIS), 2011 International Conference*

Penland, Teck. "A Model to Create 'Organizational Readiness' for the Successful Implementation of Quality Management Systems." *International Journal for Quality in Health Care* 9.1 (1997): 69-72.

Perkinson, Larry. "Discipline in the Extremes-Potentially damaging to behavioural safety processes" Professional Safety April (2005): 31-35

Prochaska, Janice, Prochaska, James and Levesque, Deborah. "A Transtheoretical Approach to Changing Organizations." *Administration and Policy in Mental Health and Mental Health Services Research* 28.4 (2001): 247-261.

Public Affairs Division, P. A. and, and Directorate, C., 2008. OECD Annual Report (p.116).

Rafferty, Alannah, Jimmieson, Nerina and Armenakis, Achilles. "Change Readiness: A Multilevel Review." *Journal of Management* 39.1 (2013): 110-135.

Ring, Peter Smith and Van De Ven, Andrew. "Developmental processes of cooperative interorganizational relationships." *Academy of Management Review* 19.1 (1994): 90-118.

Rowell, Amy, "Open innovation: The New R&D Paradigm Driving Profitable Product Development," Aberdeen Group, September 2008, pp.1-6 http://www.i-n-w.org/whats_new/open_innovation/aberdeen_group.pdf

Rütten, A, Röger, U, Abu-Omar, K and Frahsa, A. "Assessment of Organizational Readiness for Health Promotion Policy Implementation: Test of a Theoretical Model." *Health Promotion International* 24.3 (2009): 243-251.

Salampasis, Dimitrios, Mention, Anne-Laure, Torkkeli Marko. "Open Innovation and Collaboration in the Financial Services Sector: Exploring the role of trust". Special Issue on "Innovation for Financial Services", *International Journal of Business Innovation and Research*, 8.5 (2014a): 466-484

Salampasis, Dimitrios, Mention, Anne-Laure, Torkkeli Marko. "Trust embedded open innovation: Literature review, synthesis and research propositions", in *Proceedings of the 2014 Academy of Management Meeting*, Philadelphia, USA (2014b)

Salampasis, Dimitrios, Mention, Anne-Laure, Torkkeli Marko. "Trust embeddedness within an open innovation mindset". Special Issue on "The Value of Trust in Entrepreneurship", *International Journal of Business and Globalization*, 14 (2015)[3]

Salovey, P., and Mayer, J.D. "Emotional intelligence. Imagination, Cognition, and Personality", 9, 185-211. (1990) in *Emotional Intelligence: Key readings on the Mayer and Salovey model* (edited by Salovey, Peter, Brackett, Marc and Mayer, John), Dude Publishing, New York, 2004.

Savitskaya, Irina, Salmi, Pekka, and Torkkeli, Marko. "Barriers to Open Innovation: Case China". *Journal of Technology Management and Innovation*, 5.4 (2010): 10-21.

Sawhney, Mohanbir, and Prandelli, Emanuela. "Communities of Creation: Managing Distributed Innovation in Turbulent Markets" *California Management Review* 42.4 (2000): 24-54.

Schoorman, David, Mayer, Roger and Davis, James. "An integrative model of organizational trust: past, present and future." *Academy of Management Review* 32.2 (2007): 344-354.

Schroll, Alexander. "Is it really Open Innovation?" (2009) weblog, accessed 3rd June 2012, http://www.open-innovation.net/

Schweisfurth, Tim, Raasch, Christina and Herstatt, Cornelius. "Free Revealing in Open Innovation: a Comparison of Different Models and Their Benefits for Companies." *Int. J. of Product Development* 13.2 (2011): 95-118.

[3] Issue number and page range not yet available

SIFMA. U.S. Financial Services Industry-Contributing to a More Competitive US Economy (2010): 1-8.

Simpson, A. Jeffrey. "Foundations of interpersonal trust." in Kruglanski, W. Arie, and Higgins, T. Edward (Eds.), *Social psychology: Handbook of basic principles*, (2007, 2nd ed., pp. 587-607). New York: Guilford.

Snyder-Halpern, Rita. "Indicators of Organizational Readiness for Clinical Information Technology/systems Innovation: a Delphi Study" *International Journal of Medical Informatics* 63 (2001): 179-204.

Soni, Pavan. "Open Innovation: A Strategic Imperative for Non-linear Growth." *Management of Innovation and Technology*, Proceedings of the 2008 IEEE ICMIT (2008): 172-177

Spithoven, André, Clarysse, Bart, and Knockaert, Mirjam. "Building absorptive capacity to organise inbound open innovation in traditional industries". *Technovation* 31.1 (2011): 10-21.

Stamatakis, Katherine, McQueen, Amy, Filler, Carl, Boland, Elizabeth, Dreisinger, Mariah, Brownson, Ross and Luke, Douglas. "Measurement Properties of a Novel Survey to Assess Stages of Organizational Readiness for Evidence-based Interventions in Community Chronic Disease Prevention Settings." *Implementation Science* 71 (2012): 65.

Trott, Paul, and Hartmann, Dap. "Why "Open Innovation" is old wine in new bottles". *International Journal of Innovation Management* 13.4 (2009): 715-736.

Tuff, Geoff and Jonash, Ben. "*Open Innovation: No Longer an Option. Principles and Actions for Getting It Right*. Monitor Company Group Limited Partnership (2009): 1-11

Tushman, Michael, Lakhani, Karim and Lifshitz-assaf, Hila. "Open Innovation and Organizational Design." Journal of Organization Design 1.1 (2012): 24-27.

Vitasek, Kate, Nyden, Jeanette and Frydlinger, David. *Getting to We: Negotiating Agreements for Highly Collaborative Relationships*, Palgrave Macmillan (forthcoming, August 13, 2013): 256

Wagner, Philipp and Piller, Frank. "Increasing innovative capacity: is your company ready to benefit from open innovation processes?" *Performance* 4.2 (2013): 22-31

Weiner, Bryan. "A Theory of Organizational Readiness for Change." *Implementation Science* 4.1 (2009): 67.

Wesemann, Darren. "How Financial Services Organizations Can Help Ensure Success with SOA-7 Lessons Learned Based on SunGard's Adoption of SOA". *Sungard Common Services Architecture White Paper Series*. New York, NY, USA. (2006):1-14 http://www.cio.com/documents/whitepapers/sungardcsa062207.pdf

West, Joel, and Gallagher, Scott. "Challenges of open innovation: the paradox of firm investment in open-source software". *R&D Management*, 36.3 (2006): 319-331

Williams, Iestyn. "Organizational Readiness for Innovation in Health Care: Some Lessons from the Recent Literature." *Health Services Management Research: An Official Journal of the Association of University Programs In Health Administration/HSMC, AUPHA* 24.4 (2011): 213-218.

Zhang, Yongcheng, Meixiang Huang, and Dongdong Hao. "Knowledge Capacity and the Process Types of Open Innovation." *Proceedings of the 2010 International Conference on Information, Networking and Automation (ICINA)* (2010):196-199

CHAPTER THIRTEEN

HOW "STRUCTURAL COLLABORATION" LEADS TO VALUE PROPOSITIONS IN THE FINANCIAL SECTOR

DELPHINE VANTOMME AND TOM DE RUYCK

1. Time to innovate is now!

In the (post-) crisis area, challenging the status quo through innovation will be critical to restore profitability in the financial sector. The commoditization of products within the industry is making it very difficult to compete on price. Moreover, a whole array of non-banking entities is entering the market to close the gap between the offerings of banks and the needs of the customers. Suddenly, banks face competition from telcos, supermarkets, tech firms and innovative start-ups; all experienced in building online relationships, developing and marketing transparent products. "Customers judge across their entire set of experiences rather than just comparing your organization to others like it. We want our technology to be as intuitive and user-friendly as Apple products, the service we receive to be as thoughtful as we might get from Nordstrom, and personalization and ease of payment as good as Amazon's" (McGrath, 2012). So from a bank's point of view, the competitive frame of reference has expanded considerably and at a frightening pace. As a result, only financial institutions that invest in service innovations, taking advantage of a profound understanding of consumer needs and demands, will be able to outperform competition (de Rooij and Marchall, 2010).

However, impediments to innovate are probably more persistent in the financial sector than in any other industry. Strict regulations, low margins, legacy, long-time to market, focus on short term financial success, commoditization of services and products, IT driven NPD, lack of organizational structures and funds fostering innovation and so on most often, result in banks embracing the opposite of an open innovation minded culture (Accenture Research, 2011).

We argue that with the rise of web 2.0 and social media, new tools are available for organizations to facilitate open innovation and structural collaboration processes (Chesbrough, 2003; De Wulf and De Ruyck, 2013). In the next pages, we explain the why and how of installing structural collaboration with internal and external stakeholders (consumers, employees, management, advertising agency …) and elaborate on the success criteria and the implications for the organization. We end with the DVV Insurance (brand of Belfius Insurance, former Dexia group) case study-or how a financial player absorbed its surroundings to inspire breakthrough innovations. Find out how DVV Insurance immersed in the daily life of Millennials and learned not only that most of their products were too complicated, too expensive and not relevant for the daily frustrations of youngsters, but also became the first insurance company in Belgium to co-create a new insurance package and accompanying go-to-market strategy tailored to the needs of this specific target group. Following the campaign, the insurer saw a 50% increase in Top of Mind awareness for the target group, + 200% website visits and + 30% new business. Today, the collaboration is still ongoing and together with Gen Y the roadmap for the 2013 campaign is being shaped and fine-tuned.

2. Power to the people: how to install structural collaboration

When we talk about open innovation or structural collaboration, we mean the integration of the voice of the customer in all decision-making flows of your company. In most companies, customers are only allowed to give feedback at the very end of a decision-making flow, through traditional market research. This paper gives insights on how to involve the customer in every single phase of the decision making flow on an ongoing basis.

In 2012, only 3% of all companies have experience in developing new products and services with their consumers. In most cases this collaboration starts with a pilot project (Van Belleghem and De Ruyck, 2012). If the test is successful, the collaboration can gradually be built up in a more structural manner. Less than one out of ten companies that co-create with their customers also uses this collaboration for the launching of new products or services. We may say that the focus of co-creation is mainly on the initiation of new ideas (Frost and Sullivan, 2011). But even if consumers are more or less continually involved in the process of dreaming up new ideas, this is still not enough to be able to speak of 'structural collaboration'. Structural collaboration means that the customer is involved in all aspects of your company's life (Fig.1). This includes:

1. Getting new insights: exploration of the target group. Listen directly on how they perceive the product and service quality to optimize the commercial portfolio. This also implies discovering new market trends and unmet needs from your most relevant customers.
2. The development of new ideas and fine-tuning of existing ideas. Create new commercial value together with the customer.
3. Key role during implementation. Include customers during the implementation phase to make sure that your interpretation of their ideas is done in a correct way.
4. Continuous evaluation and optimization. Use the voice of the customer as a continuous flow of information to improve loads of smaller, tactical issues and to re-shape the future of your company with your customer as your primary consultant.

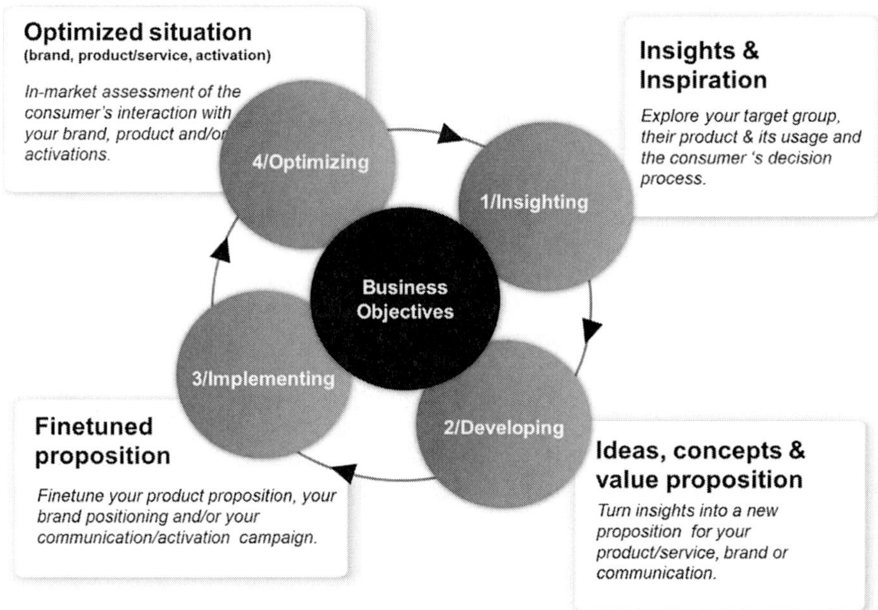

Figure 1. Overview of structural collaboration & business issues

An article by Cook (2008) in the '*Harvard Business Review*' claims that companies are better at solving all their main business problems if they closely collaborate with their consumers. The good news is that consumers are also willing to help companies out with this: more than half of them (Van Belleghem, 2012) want to collaborate with one of their favourite brands around one or more of these issues. The goal of this chapter is to look into the necessary ingredients for a company to structurally get the consumer on board.

2.1 The objectives of structural collaboration

Based on 15 one-hour in-depth telephone interviews (open questions) with senior executives of global brands from different industries (Fig 2) we came to the conclusion that companies, which are working on structural collaboration with their customers have four clear objectives in mind with this approach:

1. **Create better products, improve customer service and communicate in a more impactful way**. This is by far the most important objective for large brands to collaborate with consumers. By succeeding in this objective, the overall performance of the organization will increase.
2. **Become more agile**. By involving customers in every phase of a decision making chain, things move faster. Companies can take better decisions faster and have a better feeling of what will be needed to be as successful in the future. A big plus in today's fast moving world.
3. **Add consumer-feeling to the gut-feeling**. A lot of managers rely on their gut-feeling, which is wonderful. Structural collaboration should add 'consumer-feeling' to it. By collaborating so often, managers create the ability to put on the consumers' hat during a meeting and think as the customer; allowing them to make more consumer relevant choices.
4. **Marketing & PR**. Companies that are listening and involving consumers in decision making are popular nowadays. Tell all your customers that you take decisions based on consulting with other customers and they will like you more. Leveraging the internal collaboration platforms towards the external communication has an impact on the overall perception. This is not the main goal, but a very welcomed indirect effect.

Caroline Van Hoff	Concept Development Manager	Heineken International
Charles Hageman	Research Manager	KLM
Erkinheimo Pia	Global Collaboration Manager	Nokia
Graham Kahr	Social Commerce Product Manager	Zappos
Hans Similon	Evangelist	Mobile Vikings
Joella Marsman	Marketing Researcher	HJ Heinz
Marc Fouconnier	CEO	Famous
Marjan Rintel	VP Marketing & Brand	KLM
MartijnVan Kesteren	Yunomi Leader Benelux	Unilever
Pascale Mignolet	International Market Research Director Coffee & Tea	Sara Lee
Philip Rogge	CEO	Microsoft BE
Piet Decuypere	CEO	Danone
Pol Van Biervliet	CEO	Cisco BE
Stan Knoops	Head of Consumer Insights Europe	Unilever R&D
Tormod Askildsen	Senior Director Community Engagement & Events	Lego

Figure 2. Overview of interviewees

2.2 An evolution, not a revolution

It's clear that structural collaboration with consumers is not about having the right technology to make it happen. It is about a mentality shift for most organizations. A shift from a 'we know best'-attitude towards an open mentality. The most beautiful result of collaborating companies is the creation of what we just called the 'consumer feeling'. Adding the consumer feeling to the gut feeling of companies is the biggest change one can achieve through structural collaboration.

To reach this situation, there are a number of steps to be taken. Based on our research, we have learned that all companies started small and evolved towards bigger and bigger collaboration projects. In the end, collaboration was really embedded into their organization. It was a process of change, not a revolution.

The evolution towards structural collaboration happens in three steps:

1. Collaboration always starts with a first time try-out. Companies organize a co-creation project in which they allow the customer to participate in one specific project. Most occurring examples are co-creation of a new product, a new package or new marketing communication.
2. If this try-out is experienced as a success, the second step is to apply collaboration on a project-based level in the organization. At this stage, companies have the habit to involve customers in every important new project they work on.
3. After a while, it becomes hard for them to take decisions without the voice of the customer during the process and they decide to structurally collaborate.

2.3 Three pillars for structural collaboration with your customers

Based our interviews, we concluded that there are three crucial pillars if you want to be successful in the evolution towards structural collaboration.

2.3.1. Select the right participants

In our opinion there are two possible types of-meaningful-structural customer collaboration: an open online platform where everyone can participate and a closed online community where you select the people to join in.

In the large open communities you have little direct control over who joins in and who doesn't. The members come together in a very spontaneous way to discuss particular subjects that are of their interest. Your role with regards to these people is simply to listen. This will allow you to discover a series of unfulfilled market needs, which may eventually lead to new products and services. Of course, you are also free to ask them questions, but you must always remember that these are open communities-anyone else might be listening to their answers!

Companies that want to involve the customer in more strategic decisions and which have a need for an in-depth feedback, tend to work with a closed online community with a limited number of relevant customers. If you want to solve a specific management problem, it is better to discuss possible solutions with a smaller, closed group of between 50 and 150 people with a keen interest into your category. It could also be a group of your most ardent fans, fans whom you have carefully vetted and selected yourself. The major advantage of this approach is that you have everything in your own hands-and this is advisable when you don't want the whole world to know what decisions are being taken.

Having said so, it is important to acknowledge the fact that not every customer can either be able or suitable for helping you solve any management problems. To give your company access to the right advice on a daily basis, you need to listen to the right (and relevant) people. For your communities, seek to attract people who can offer an added value. The minimum condition is that they must have a clear commitment to the company and what this stands for. They might be an expert in the sector, a knowledgeable and enthusiastic amateur in the sector or just a big fan of your brand. Research has shown that, without this kind of emotional commitment, people seldom have enough interest in contributing effectively to an online community (De Ruyck, et al., 2010). In other words, you need to talk to people who are interesting and interested. If they don't have an opinion or the natural motivation to take part is missing, your community will not achieve what you want it to achieve. But, natural engagement is not enough. In order to make your community a real success you need to manage it well. A number of things are important: be open and transparent about the goals of each project, listen in an active way (allow participants to put their issues on your agenda too), make it a fun experience (after all people are doing this in their spare time) and give enough feedback on what you did with their answers.

2.3.2. Internal communication is not enough. Internal = External

Managers show more interest in a project or approach that gets external credits, than in a project with a sole internal focus. In other words: make sure your structural collaboration is not completely taking place behind the scenes of your organization.

Sharing your collaboration work with the whole organization and the rest of the world has a number of advantages. Next to an increase in motivation of your management, it will also increase the motivation of the participants within your communities. Furthermore, research has shown that consumers have a higher level of trust and a better perception of brands that co-create. So, there is also a commercial benefit by leveraging your efforts externally.

There are a few communication tactics you can apply to increase the internal and external impact of your collaboration process:

- Meet-up with participants: Collaboration occurs within a digital platform but it is an interaction among people. To increase the interaction and the emotional bondage, make sure your employees meet-up with these people in the real world as well. Show them around your company, tell them your challenges and treat them like part-time employees.
- Go for tangible results: If you work together with your consumers on a structural level, make sure you have concrete deliverables. These results (e.g. new products, insights, advertising, packaging…) should be shared with the world to make the collaboration aspirational both for the market and for the involved manager.
- Bite size and creative reporting: share the results of your collaboration with your employees in a short, compelling and creative way. Make sure it is easy to digest and to share.
- Apply content marketing techniques (Van Bellegem, 2012): don't communicate 1 or 2 times about your collaboration, but talk about it on a more frequent basis. Use three levels of content: big content campaigns (e.g. when you have BIG news: launch of an initiative or showing the end result), content projects (e.g. a theme that you talk about for a few days/weeks) and content updates (small, daily updates with relevant information).

2.3.3 Measure impact

To keep the collaboration flow on-going, there is need for evidence that the approach indeed works. Therefore we advise you to use a number of clear success indicators that you can measure during the implementation of structural collaboration in your organization. There is no standard list of KPIs to use; they differ from company to company, as they are closely linked to the company's culture and (long-term) objectives. There are a few KPIs that apply to all companies to follow up on the impact of structural collaboration:

- Success of innovation, impact of communication and improvement of customer service: by involving customers early in the process, your company will take better decisions. Product launches, new advertising campaigns and so on, should have a higher success rate than before the collaboration was implemented.
- Cost reduction: by integrating the voice of the customer in the entire decision-making flow, the cost of ad hoc market research could be reduced. Next to that, by creating better products and services based on the input of the market, the impact of word-of-mouth will increase, which may lead to lower media budgets.
- Consumer feeling of the organization: you can measure to what extent your management has a better feeling of the attitude and behavior of your target market. The goal is that managers can think as consumers and improve their performance through this new required skill.
- Brand perception: listening actively will humanize your brand and make it more popular.
- Define your KPIs, measure them and celebrate success!

3. Change of internal implementation process needed

Collaboration should lead to decisions that are taken through cooperation between the market and your company. The proof of structural collaboration is in the implementation of the ideas. In order to succeed in this crucial step, there is a need to change the internal decision streams. The challenge is to integrate consumer feedback and input into every phase of the decision cycle.

Remember that structural collaboration does not come overnight. It starts with a try-out that fits within the existing culture. Make sure that, as from the start, you know what your next step will be. In other words: it is important to start with a try-out, but it is as important to start with a long-term view. Make sure you know where you're going. After the try-out, it is a matter of including collaboration into projects where the fit feels right. People (internal and external) get bored fast. Make sure you have a flow ready in your collaboration process to keep the conversations going and plan with room for flexibility. Once you have completed a number of successful collaboration projects, the possibility to move forward to structural collaboration arrives.

Make sure that along the way, you take into account these last tactical tips to make collaboration work:

- Have clear objectives for each collaboration project. Make sure that you don't collaborate just for the sake of it. To get the feedback of consumers in the decision flow, it has to be very clear what the objectives are; objectives that are in line with the business goals.
- Involve all stakeholders early in the process. The more departments are involved during the beginning of the process the better. In order to integrate the collaboration flow in the decision flow, it is crucial to have a buy-in from the relevant teams.
- Manage expectations. Collaboration won't bring in the next big idea for your company. Customers are great sparring partners, but don't set the expectations too high. Make sure that during the integration of their feedback in the decision flows, everybody is aware of what to expect from the collaboration.
- Have a community manager appointed. Make sure you have somebody assigned to manage the community. This person is responsible for managing the conversation with participants of the collaboration process and sharing the insights internally. He or she brings the consumer's voice to life within the company.
- Create internal and external credibility. By delivering results and integrating the voice of the customer in your decision flows, you will gain credibility among the participants of the collaboration platform. Credibility among employees will also grow as they will see that collaboration adds value. Marketing your collaboration efforts is not a bad thing, but it should not be the only thing.

4. How DVV Insurance co-created the new Gen Y strategy through structural collaboration

In 2004, DVV Insurance (brand of Belfius Insurance, former Dexia group) was facing an aging client portfolio. This was not only a threat from a demographical, but also from a revenue point of view. For an insurance company, this older age group had become less and less profitable for several reasons: investment in second property, less savings and so on. On the other hand, when attracting new clients in the age group 20-30, this was mainly accomplished through the DVV car insurance offering. At that time, the DVV car insurance had a very competitive pricing model, especially for young drivers (with a high bonus malus) as compared to other players in the market. However, attracting mainly unexperienced young drivers, involved in car accidents, the most of all age groups is not the most profitable situation to be in as an insurer.

With the outbreak of the financial crisis in 2008, financial revenues dropped further and DVV Insurance was forced to re-orient and invest in a new strategy to attract Millennials through profitable products. With a limited marketing budget, the marketing team realized that they could not target Millenials as a whole. Therefore, it was decided to work with different key moments targeting different sub-segments of the Millennials.

With no experience and feeling of the target group at all, DVV Insurance wanted, as a first step, a thorough understanding of 'Nestleavers', i.e. youngster aged 18-30 that are about to leave the parental home (or have just left), to live on their own for the first time, financially independent of their parents. The purpose of this exercise was a thorough understanding of the living environment, values, lifestyle, challenges and frustrations of the target group taking this important step and to learn how they are related to insurances and insurance products when it comes to living on your own for the first time.

From the very beginning DVV Insurance was willing to collaborate with the Nestleavers in a very open way based on mutual respect and true dialogue. Next to that, they considered collaboration as an important touchpoint within the company. So, it was important to find a way to collaborate that resonated within the target group and that at the same time would help DVV Insurance re-juvenate the brand image of DVV. Thirdly, the approach needed to bring the target group to life, internally, through connecting all stakeholders involved. In other words, the goal was not only to collaborate with the target group, but also to foster cross-departmental collaborations and to connect both internal (marketing, sales, IT, management) and external stakeholders (ad agency, media planners, …) with the Nestleavers to maximize the learning curve, internal impact, knowledge sharing, consecutive learning and co-creation. Finally, DVV wanted to be able to leverage the collaboration externally in communication, PR, press releases, on the website, etc.

Although at first a bit doubtful about whether the target group would be interested in participating in an intense collaboration about insurances, it was clear that, if this initiative was a success, the collaboration would be taken into the next level and evolve further towards a structural collaboration (Fig 3).

As a first step, at the end of 2011, a large-scale online survey was conducted. With the purpose of being the first insurance company in Belgium to claim the moment of 'leaving the nest', the recruitment of the participants was set-up through a large media campaign on two popular radio stations among youngsters (one in Flanders and one in Wallonia). To resonate with the target group, the survey was fully gamified, providing instant feedback and benchmarking with peers after each chapter in the survey. With more than 3000 youngsters participating, the survey was a big success and the results were shared and discussed on the two radio stations involved and picked up by different other media.

For DVV Insurance, the survey revealed three important findings that needed better and deeper understanding: insurance products are too complicated, too expensive and not relevant to the daily frustrations of youngsters.

Therefore, in February 2012 a more engaging, intense collaboration was installed through an online community, in which 150 'Nestleavers', discussed for three weeks, 24/7 on three major topics:

- Week 1: Knowledge and experience with insurances, insurance companies and DVV Insurance.
- Week 2: The search for information, channel usage and expected communication from an insurer.
- Week 3: Evaluation and fine-tuning of new insurance products/concepts.

The immersion showed DVV Insurance the need for (1) a unique selling proposition (USP) to differentiate from competition, (2) demonstrating thorough understanding of the target group in product offering, communication and price setting and (3) bringing 'simplicity' and 'direction' in this complex world of insurances. Combining these major consumer insights with internal risk analysis and business knowledge, this has resulted in a new and unique insurance package within the Belgian market: Cocoon Start.

Figure 3. The trajectory DVV Insurances and the Nestleavers engaged in and still are

Figure 4. Starting page of 'The Big Nestleavers Survey'

Cocoon Start is aimed at tenants aged 30 at the most, who are renting a house (200m² maximum) or an apartment (125m² maximum). The package consists of all the insurances a young tenant is supposed to have: a fire and theft insurance, to which a family insurance is added, as well as, some extras, which are adapted to the life of 'Nest leavers' (insurance for PC, laptop, tablet, smartphone, insuring friends who help out during the move…). For a mere €25 a month they get the entire package and nest leavers even get the first 6 months for free!

With Cocoon Start, DVV Insurance had developed an insurance package that is 'Millennial proof' thanks to its simplicity (transparent, one price …), relevance (adjusted to the needs of Nestleavers) and price-setting (affordable). However, with a 'direct line' to the target group in the community, DVV insurance was determined to hear the voice of the target group when taking important decisions related to the go-to- market.

With the advertising agency actively involved at all stages of the immersion, three campaigns were developed appealing to the Nestleavers. At least, that is what the DVV team thought. During the re-activation of the community for another week, it became rapidly very clear that two of the three campaigns could be 'parked' as not relevant of too demeaning. Only the Shit! Campaign evoked an AHA Erlebnis, made them smile and demonstrated a clear link to insurances. While 'Shit!' was not perceived offensive in Flanders, 'Merde!' needed to be weakened to 'M****!' in the French community.

Figure 5. the SHIT! campaign

Because external leverage of the close collaboration within the constraints of a limited marketing budget was one of the initial objectives, a playful small survey outside the community on the cursing behavior of Gen Y was set up to enforce the go-to-market and the SHIT! Campaign. The press conference on the launch of Cocoon Start did not miss its' effect thanks to striking quotes on youngster's cursing behavior. Community members were invited to the press conference, gave testimonials on the national TV about their experience with cursing, insurances and-indirectly-the structural collaboration.

On September 13th 2012, Cocoon Start was launched above and below the line through radio, cinema and online bannering. Business impact was measured internally and externally. Following the campaign, the quarterly brand tracker showed a 50% increase in TOM for the target group and significant increase in brand associations with image statements as 'enthusiastic', 'creative', 'innovative', 'forward thinking'; all statements pointing towards the direction of rejuvenation of the brand. Online bannering generated more than 150K of new leads and DVV Insurance reported + 200% website visits and + 30% new business. Also participants in both the surveys and the community considered participating in the co-creation trajectory as a very positive experience and were turned into real brand ambassadors.

Nowadays, DVV Insurance has set-up structural collaborations through online communities with different target groups and committed not to take any important business decision without hearing the voice of its most important stakeholder: the consumer.

5. Conclusions

The DVV Insurance case demonstrates that the financial sector can also break down walls and put consumers where they belong: at the heart of the business. It shows that companies investing in structural consumer connections, come-up with more consumer-relevant products/services and marketing actions and eventually become more 'human' as a brand. And that is exactly what the financial sector needs: become 'open' to the outside world and do what consumers expect from them in difficult and insecure times, such as the downturn of the financial crisis. This would make banks more 'contemporary' and 'genuine' and allow them to re-store consumer trust from the inside out. Through positive (brand) experience, banks would create positive conversations around the brand. Next to the external impact, DVV Insurance experiences some internal leverage from the consumer connection by gaining the ability to move fast. Actually, the Nestleavers determined next steps, rather than the hidden agenda of departments, which made things, move quicker internally. The end result is that DVV became a more 'agile' company; and that is the type of company that will be successful tomorrow.

The way to becoming a truly 'open' and 'agile' company is a journey that asks for a step-by-step approach. Some companies will immediately make a start with 'Structural Collaboration'. Others need to do a pilot project first before they move on. Some companies start to use it for a specific product category or within a specific department of the company and extend towards other categories over time. No matter how a company starts, it will always be an evolution rather than a revolution. Change never comes overnight and definitely not in the financial sector.

References

Accenture. "Innovation Excellence: What Banks Can Learn from Top Innovators in Other Industries". Accenture Research. (2011): 1-8 http://www.accenture.com/SiteCollectionDocuments/PDF/Accenture-APAC-BNK-BrightIdeas.pdf

Chesbrough, Henry W. "The Era of Open Innovation". *Sloan Management Review*, 44.3 (2003): 35-41.

Cook, Scott. "The contribution revolution" (cover story). *Harvard Business Review* 86.10 (2008): 60-69.

de Rooij, Mieke and Marshall, Anthony. "Insatiable Innovation: From sporadic to systemic". *IBM Institute for Business Value study* (2010) http://www-935.ibm.com/services/us/gbs/thoughtleadership/insatiable innovation/

De Ruyck, Tom, Schillewaert, Niels, Ludwig, Stephan and Van Kesteren, Martijn. "How fans became future shapers of ice-cream brand Ben & Jerry's", *Esomar Qualitative Research Conference*. (2010). http://www.slideshare.net/TomDeRuyck/how-fans-became-future-shapers-of-an-ice-cream-brand-ben-jerrys-community

De Wulf, Kristof and De Ruyck, Tom. "The Consumer Consulting Board: Consumers shaping your business", InSites Consulting (2013):1-196

Frost and Sullivan. "Growth Team Membership™ 2011 Global R&D/Innovation and Product Development Priorities Survey: Revitalizing Product Development". *GIL Community* (2011): 1-29 http://www.gilcommunity.com/files/3113/6379/7156/Global_RD_Innovation_Survey_Report_2011.pdf

McGrath, Rita. "Five Big Trends in Business Innovation in 2012". *Forbes* (2012) http://www.forbes.com/sites/forbesleadershipforum/2011/12/19/five-big-trends-in-business-innovation-in-2012/

Van Belleghem, Steven and De Ruyck, "To. From co-creation to collaboration". InSites Consulting, Slideshare (2012) http://www.slideshare.net/stevenvanbelleghem/from-cocreation-to-collaboration

Van Belleghem, Steven, Eenhuizen, Marloes and Veris, Elias. "Social Media around the world study", InSites Consulting, S*lideshare* (2011) http://www.slideshare.net/stevenvanbelleghem/social-media-around-the-world-2011

Van Belleghem, Steven. "A six step content marketing model". InSites Consulting, S*lideshare* (2012) http://www.slideshare.net/stevenvanbelleghem/a-six-step-content-marketing-model

CONTRIBUTORS

Tor Helge Aas is a postdoctoral researcher at Norwegian School of Economics' Center for Service Innovation and a senior researcher at Agder Research's Department of Innovation. He has a PhD in strategy and management from Norwegian School of Economics, and a MSc in information and communication technology from University of Agder. Dr. Aas has a broad interest in innovation management, as well as management control and strategic management research, particularly related to the service sector. His research concentrates on topics like innovation strategy, management of innovation processes, management control of innovation activities (including innovation metrics and portfolio management) and innovation collaboration (including open innovation, high involvement in innovation and innovation systems). Dr. Aas has published on these topics in several international peer-reviewed journals, conferences and books.

Frederic Adam is a Professor and the Director Master of Business Studies in Innovation in European Business and the Head of the Graduate School of the College of Business and Law at University College Cork in Ireland. Other positions he holds include: Principal Investigator in the Financial Services Innovation Centre (FSIC), Editor-in-Chief of the Journal of Decision Systems and the Chair of the Working Group 8.3 on DSS of the International Federation for Information processing (IFIP). He holds Doctorates from the National University of Ireland and Université Paris VI (France). His research interests are in decision-making and decision support and in ERP. He has over 25 journal papers published in international journals including Information and Management, the Journal of Strategic Information Systems, Decision Support Systems, and the Journal of Information Technology. He held visiting Research fellow positions at the London School of Economics (2005-2007) and at Lund University, Sweden (2009-2011) and has successfully supervised eight PhD students to completion.

Francesca Arnaboldi is an Associate professor in banking and finance at University of Milan (Italy). She gained her BSc and MSc in Finance from Bocconi University (Italy), her MSc in Financial Management from the University of London, CeFiMS (UK), and her PhD in Finance from the University of Bologna (Italy). Francesca has been working as a visiting Researcher in the Centre for Banking Research at Cass Business School, City University, London (UK) since 2009 and she is a member of the Research Center on Financial Studies at University of Modena and Reggio Emilia (Italy). Francesca's research interests focus on the areas of financial innovation; international banking; bank competition and performance; bank corporate governance, regulation and supervision. Her research has been presented at international conferences and published in books and journals.

Karl Joachim Breunig is an Associate Professor at the business school of Oslo and Akershus University College of Applied Science, Norway. Karl Joachim Breunig is currently receiving his PhD in Strategic Management from BI Norwegian Business School and holds an MSc from London School of Economics. His research concentrates on knowledge work and innovation, in particular in relation to services. He pioneered the knowledge management profession in Norway as Knowledge Manager in an international telecommunications consultancy, and was Co-founder of the Knowledge Management Forum in Norway, serving as its first President. He has been engaged in research projects on knowledge management, innovation, and internationally distributed knowledge work in a number of both public-sector organizations and private organizations - in several different industries.

Fergal Carton is a senior researcher in the FSIC at University College Cork in Ireland. Fergal's research domain is the integration of information technologies in financial services, with a specific focus on the interface between transactional data and decision support. With 15 years' experience as a management consultant, starting with the Boston Consulting Group in London, he has worked on over 30 projects involving the definition of IT strategy, enterprise systems integration and business model development. With a primary degree in Computer Science (University College Dublin), and an MSc in Management from the European School of Management Studies (ESCP-EAP) in Paris, Fergal's doctoral research focused on the value of enterprise-wide systems in supporting management decision making. Fergal spearheads FSIC research activities relating to payments and specifically the integration of mobile payment into mainstream financial services.

Peter Claeys is an Assistant Professor at the Vrije Universiteit Brussel, in the research group APEC. He obtained his Ph.D. at the European University Institute, and after a Marie Curie Fellowship at AQR, became an Assistant Professor at the Universitat de Barcelona. His work focuses on the econometric modelling of various aspects of fiscal policy, including the macroeconomic effects of government spending, fiscal consolidation, spillover of budget decisions and fiscal federalism. He has worked on various projects on fiscal policy for the European Commission, the ECB, the OECD and the Spanish and Swedish government.

Marisalvo da Silva holds a Ph.D. in Industrial Engineering from the University of São Paulo in 2005 with a dissertation "A Contribution to the Study of Innovative Companies in Brazil". In 1999 he earned his Master's in Administration from the University of Brasilia, where he did additional graduate work in the area of Education. He graduated in 1990 with a Bachelor's in Accounting Sciences from the Federal University of Bahia. Mr. Silva has extensive experience in the areas of Financial Institution Strategic Management and Higher Education Management, with an emphasis in Business Management, Organizational Architecture, Project Management and Process Management. He currently is a Consultant, and Master's and graduate level professor in the areas of Internationalization, Services Innovation, Competitive Intelligence, Business Strategies, Corporate Governance and Operational Management. He has more than 25 papers published in journals and international conferences in the fields of innovation management, competitive intelligence, quality management and business strategy.

Tom de Ruyck is the Head of Consumer Consulting Boards at InSites Consulting and in charge of InSites' global activities in terms of community research: thought leadership, steering innovation and business development. InSites is one of the world's leaders in this field: it has moderation teams in more than 30 countries worldwide and builds over 150 private online research communities a year for global clients like Heinz, Unilever, Danone, Red Bull, Heineken, IKEA, Microsoft & many more. He has given +200 speeches all around the world at major international marketing, research and technology conferences. Leading in-depth workshops and chairing research events is among his favorite activities. He is co-author of 'The Consumer Consulting Board' and published over 50 white papers (ESOMAR), articles in academic journals (a.o. IJMR), business books and trade magazines. Besides that, he is an influential blogger/tweeter (@tomderuyck). His work was awarded on several occasions (e.g. “Fernanda Monti Award”, 'Tweeter of the Year' 2011, MOAward for the “Innovation of 2012” and the “Leadership Award for Contribution to Market Research”).

Denis Dennehy is a PhD candidate and researcher with the Business Information Systems department at University College Cork in Ireland. His research adopts a design science research approach which led to the development of a visualization tool in the form of a Partnership Management Canvas. He won the Marion McAneney Graduate Research Award in 2012; a national award that acknowledges excellence in reviewing academic literature on any aspect of innovation and identifying gaps in our understanding. Most recently he won the Best Academic Paper Award at the 2013 Innovation for Financial Services Conference in Singapore. Prior to this he completed a research masters which explored the gap between policy and practice in international development and was motivated by his work in a developing country. He has worked on a number of industry focused research projects and lectures on postgraduate and undergraduate programs. His published topics include mobile payments, design science, knowledge management and international development.

José Luis Gómez-Barroso is an Associate Professor at Universidad Nacional de Educación a Distancia (UNED) where he gained his PhD and a MSc in Economics. He also holds a MSc in Telecommunication Engineering from the Universidad Politécnica de Madrid as well as another MSc in Law from the Universidad Complutense. Dr. Gómez-Barroso has participated in different research projects on ICT-based innovation, some of them commissioned by the European Commission.

Olli-Pekka Hilmola is working as a Professor in Lappeenranta University of Technology (LUT), in Kouvola, Finland. He is affiliated with numerous international journals through editorial boards, including the Baltic Journal of Management, Industrial Management and Data Systems, Decision Support Systems, and International Journal of Shipping and Transport Logistics. Dr. Hilmola has published more than 110 refereed journal manuscripts.

Katja Maria Hydle is a senior research scientist at IRIS Social Science. She earned her political science education in Switzerland and Belgium and is completing her PhD in Strategy from BI Norwegian Business School. She has extensive research experience with service providers both nationally and internationally. Hydle has a broad interest in service work, strategy and innovation and have worked in large research projects on transnational service provision, collaboration practices and service innovation. She has published in these topics in international peer-review journals, conferences and books.

Rahul Kapoor received his Bachelor's degree in Mechanical Engineering from MNNIT Allahabad, India, followed by Master's degree in Industrial Management from Lappeenranta University of Technology, Finland. He works as a Research Assistant in Technology Business Research Center with the team of patent researchers in Lappeenranta University of Technology. His research interests are in patent data mining, patent analytics, licensing and technology management. Rahul's current research work deals with the appropriability potential of intellectual property in different industries. He has past experience in the field of manufacturing, production, ERP and web programming.

Raquel Marbán-Flores is an Associate Professor at Universidad Complutense de Madrid where she previously gained her PhD and MSc in Economics. Dr. Marbán-Flores is an active researcher in the field of microfinance. Lately, her research interests focus on the new routes of access to the finance sector opened by ICT. For some time, she was able to combine research activities with a professional career in an institution devoted to those topics.

Andrey Martovoy holds a position of R&D Engineer at the Public Research Centre - Henri Tudor. He joined the centre in April 2011 after more than ten-year period of teaching, research, and consulting experience in marketing, market research, management, and innovation. He earned the honours Specialist's Degree in Services Management; the 'summa cum laude' Master's Degree in Development, Innovation and Change from the University of Bologna (Italy) along with a research internship at the Manchester Institute of Innovation Research (United Kingdom); and Ph.D. degree in marketing. Andrey successfully contributed to a range of EU-funded educational and research projects and visited several universities in Belgium, Finland, France, Germany, Italy, Portugal, United Kingdom, and USA as an exchange faculty member/scholar. He is a Scientific Panel Member of the International Society for Professional Innovation Management (ISPIM). His recent publications address managerial and economic aspects of open innovation in financial services.

Anne-Laure Mention is leading a research unit focusing on innovation economics and management within the Public Research Centre Henri Tudor, Luxembourg. She is actively involved in research projects, mainly focusing on innovation and performance measurement and management in the financial and business to business services industries. Her research interests mainly concentrate on open and collaborative innovation, intellectual capital measurement and management, innovation and technology management. She has been a Visiting Researcher at McGill University, Canada, at Ferrara University, Italy and at Singapore Management University. She received an IBM Faculty Award for the project entitled 'Towards accrued transparency of operations in the fund industry' in 2011 focusing on organisational innovation and an award for the project entitled "Measuring the impact of Open Innovation" in 2013. She is also a founding member of WICI, LUXIC, and the Deputy Head of the ISPIM Advisory Board. She is also a member of several scientific committees and editorial boards and a member of the New Club of Paris. She is one of the founding editors of the Journal of Innovation Management.

Dimitrios Salampasis is a Doctoral Researcher at the Public Research Centre Henri Tudor in Luxembourg conducting research in the area of business innovation management and more specifically in the field of open innovation in financial services. At the same time he is pursuing his PhD on Industrial Engineering and Management at the Lappeenranta University of Technology in Finland. He holds a Bachelor Degree on Public and Business Administration and two Master Degrees in European Studies and Educational Psychology. He is also a recent graduate of the Master in Entrepreneurship and Innovation by the University of Luxembourg (First Class Honors). He has extensive working experience in the public and private sector in Greece and abroad and international NGO experience in the field of education and training. He has participated in numerous conferences around the world as a facilitator, trainer and rapporteur and he received the ISPIM Best Paper Award in September 2012.

Teemu Santonen received his Ph.D. (Econ.) degree in Information Systems Science from Aalto University in Finland in 2005. Currently he is acting as a principal lecturer at the Laurea University of Applied Sciences and doing international research and pedagogical collaboration with Austrian, Canadian, Danish, French, German and Indian partners. Santonen has published several articles in international peer-refereed journals and conferences relating to innovation management while receiving 1.7 MEUR funding for his projects. In 2008 his project was rewarded as the best school related innovation in Finland by the Finnish inventor association. In Laurea, Santonen has filed several invention disclosures, which have resulted a start-up company and patent. Santonen is also a scientific panel member of The International Society of Professional Innovation Management (ISPIM) and has been a board member of The Finnish Strategic Management Society. Besides academic experience, Santonen has more than a decade of practical development and consulting experience in leading Finnish financial, media and ICT sector organization relating to competitive intelligence, new business and technology development.

Stuart Smith is an innovation and technology entrepreneur and educator with more than 20 years of experience working on innovation projects. Since 2012 he has been Chief of Service Innovation at the National University of Singapore (NUS), Institute of Systems Science (ISS). Originally trained as an environmental technologist at Imperial College of Science Technology & Medicine, he advised organizations on urban environmental monitoring systems. In the 1990's he joined a major global telecoms firm working in an "Internet Centric" innovation team. This team delivered some of the most ambitious internet projects of the time. In 2003 he acquired market research agency Wood Holmes and transformed the organization into a leading global innovation company. In 2012 he stepped down from the CEO role at Wood Holmes and sold the company to larger agency. His current work includes lecturing and teaching on Service Innovation, Design Thinking, User Experience Design (UXD) and well as running research and consulting projects in various areas (e.g. financial innovation or the new digital economy). He teaches for the e-Government leadership center in Singapore and is an investor in digital startups, acting as a mentor for 2 seed accelerator funds Searchcamp (UK) and JFDI (Singapore).

Marko Torkkeli is a Professor of Technology and Business Innovations at the Lappeenranta University of Technology in Kouvola, Finland. His research interests focus on technology and innovation management, strategic entrepreneurship, growth venturing, and decision support systems. He has published in journals such as the Int. J. Production Economics, Int. J. Foresight and Innovation Policy, Int. J. Business Excellence, Int. J. Technology Management and Int. J. Technology Intelligence and Planning. He is a member of the editorial boards of the Int. J. of Services Sciences and the Int. J. of Innovation Management. He is a Visiting Researcher at INESC Porto, Portugal, a Docent of Technology-based Business at University of Jyväskylä, Finland, a Docent of Technology and Innovation Management at Helsinki University of Technology, Finland and Affiliated Faculty at Singapore Management University. He serves as the Director of Publications of the International Society for Professional Innovation Management (ISPIM) and is one of the founding editors of the Journal of Innovation Management.

Delphine Vantomme is the head of research and consulting services for the financial industry at InSites Consulting. Delphine's relevant sector accounts are ING, Deutsche Bank, KBC, Rabobank, and AXA. Content wise her focus is on Innovation research, guiding companies from the fuzzy front end through all stages of the innovation funnel, based on consumer centric approaches and methods.

Sergey Yablonsky is a skilled professor with a proven track record in scientific research (text book, papers, conference proceedings) and corporate collaboration (development of IT services, knowledge management consulting, digital business and digital marketing, intersection of IT and business, joint research projects, supervising master's theses and PhDs). He is also the founder and CEO of Russicon Company, where his main focus has been on creating computer linguistics and ontology-support tools and resources. Russicon's language processor and linguistic resources were licensed by Adobe Systems Incorporated, InSo International (USA), Accent Software International Ltd. (USA), Phoenix Int. (USA), Franklin Electronic Publishers (USA), Lernout & Hauspie (Belgium) et al.